PERFORMANCE AND TRANSLATION IN A GLOBAL AGE

This global overview of how translation is understood as a performative practice across genres, media and disciplines illuminates the broad impact of the 'performance turn' in the arts and humanities. Combining key concepts in comparative literature, performance studies and translation theory, the volume provides readers with a dynamic account of the ways in which these fields fruitfully interact. The chapters display interdisciplinary thinking in action across a wide spectrum of performance practices and media from around the world, from poetry and manuscripts to theatre surtitles, audio description, archives, installations, dialects, movement and dance. Paying close attention to questions of race, gender, sexuality, embodiment and accessibility, the collection's rich array of methodological approaches and experiments with scholarly writing demonstrate how translation as a performative practice can enrich our understanding of language and politics.

AVISHEK GANGULY is Associate Professor and Chair of the Department of Literary Arts and Studies at Rhode Island School of Design. He is an interdisciplinary scholar working on the ethics and politics of translation, theatre and performance, contemporary literatures in English, sound studies and public humanities. He is co-editor with Emily Apter, Mauro Pala and Surya Parekh of *Gayatri Chakravorty Spivak: Living Translation* (2022). He is currently working on a monograph on the cultural politics of 'Global Englishes' and a research project at the intersection of humanities and design.

KÉLINA GOTMAN is Professor of Performance and the Humanities at King's College London. She writes widely on the history and philosophy of disciplines and institutions, language, performance writing and translation. She is author of *Choreomania: Dance and Disorder* (2018, David Bradby Award for outstanding research) and *Essays on Theatre and Change: Towards a Poetics Of* (2018); co-editor of *Foucault's Theatres* (2020); editor of *Theories of Performance: Critical and Primary Sources*, 4 vols. (2022); and translator of Félix Guattari's *The Anti-Oedipus Papers* (2006) and playwright Marie NDiaye's *The Snakes* (2016). She collaborates internationally in the arts.

THEATRE AND PERFORMANCE THEORY

Series Editor
Tracy C. Davis *Northwestern University*

Each volume in the Theatre and Performance Theory series introduces a key issue about theatre's role in culture. Specially written for students and a wide readership, each book uses case studies to guide readers into today's pressing debates in theatre and performance studies. Topics include contemporary theatrical practices; historiography; interdisciplinary approaches to making theatre; and the choices and consequences of how theatre is studied; among other areas of investigation.

Books in the Series

Jacky Bratton, *New Readings in Theatre History*
Tracy C. Davis and Thomas Postlewait (eds.), *Theatricality*
Shannon Jackson, *Professing Performance: Theatre in the Academy from Philology to Performativity*
Ric Knowles, *Reading the Material Theatre*
Nicholas Ridout, *Stage Fright, Animals, and Other Theatrical Problems*
D. Soyini Madison, *Acts of Activism: Human Rights as Radical Performance*
Derek Miller, *Copyright and the Value of Performance, 1770–1911*
Paul Rae, *Real Theatre: Essays in Experience*
Michael McKinnie, *Theatre in Market Economies*
Ric Knowles, *International Theatre Festivals and 21st-Century Interculturalism*
Avishek Ganguly and Kélina Gotman (eds.), *Performance and Translation in a Global Age*

PERFORMANCE AND TRANSLATION IN A GLOBAL AGE

EDITED BY

AVISHEK GANGULY

Rhode Island School of Design

KÉLINA GOTMAN

King's College London

Shaftesbury Road, Cambridge CB2 8EA, United Kingdom

One Liberty Plaza, 20th Floor, New York, NY 10006, USA

477 Williamstown Road, Port Melbourne, VIC 3207, Australia

314–321, 3rd Floor, Plot 3, Splendor Forum, Jasola District Centre, New Delhi – 110025, India

103 Penang Road, #05–06/07, Visioncrest Commercial, Singapore 238467

Cambridge University Press is part of Cambridge University Press & Assessment, a department of the University of Cambridge.

We share the University's mission to contribute to society through the pursuit of education, learning and research at the highest international levels of excellence.

www.cambridge.org
Information on this title: www.cambridge.org/9781009296816

DOI: 10.1017/9781009296786

© Cambridge University Press & Assessment 2023

This publication is in copyright. Subject to statutory exception and to the provisions of relevant collective licensing agreements, no reproduction of any part may take place without the written permission of Cambridge University Press & Assessment.

First published 2023

A catalogue record for this publication is available from the British Library.

Library of Congress Cataloging-in-Publication Data
NAMES: Ganguly, Avishek, editor. | Gotman, Kélina, editor.
TITLE: Performance and translation in a global age / edited by Avishek Ganguly, Rhode Island School of Design ; Kélina Gotman, King's College London.
DESCRIPTION: Cambridge ; New York, NY : Cambridge University Press, 2023. | Series: Theatre and performance theory | Includes bibliographical references and index.
IDENTIFIERS: LCCN 2022043137 | ISBN 9781009296816 (hardback) | ISBN 9781009296786 (ebook)
SUBJECTS: LCSH: Drama – 21st century – Translating. | Translating and interpreting. | Theater. | Literature and society. | LCGFT: Essays.
CLASSIFICATION: LCC PN886 .P47 2023 | DDC 418.02–dc23/eng/20221201
LC record available at https://lccn.loc.gov/2022043137

ISBN 978-1-009-29681-6 Hardback

Cambridge University Press & Assessment has no responsibility for the persistence or accuracy of URLs for external or third-party internet websites referred to in this publication and does not guarantee that any content on such websites is, or will remain, accurate or appropriate.

Contents

List of Figures	*page* vii
List of Contributors	ix
Acknowledgements	xi

Introduction: Translation in Motion   1
Avishek Ganguly and Kélina Gotman

PART I   TRANSLATION AS MEDIUM AND METHOD

1   Medieval Soundings, Modern Movements: Histories and Futures
of Translation and Performance in Caroline Bergvall's *Drift*   31
Joshua Davies

2   Transcolonial Performance: Mohamed Rouabhi
and the Translation of Race on the French Stage   48
Olivia C. Harrison

3   Experiments in Surtitling: Performing Multilingual
Translation Live and Onscreen in the Contemporary Theatres
of Singapore, Taiwan and Berlin   64
Alvin Eng Hui Lim

4   Translating an Embodied Gaze: Theatre Audio Description,
Bodies and Burlesque Performance at the Young Vic
Theatre, London   87
Eleanor Margolies and Kirstin Smith

5   Performative Accents: Bilingualism, Postcolonialism
and Francophonie in Michèle Lalonde's Poster-poem
'Speak White'   104
Kélina Gotman

v

vi *Contents*

PART II   TRANSLATION, NATION-STATE AND
          POST-NATIONALISM

6   Transembodiment as Translation: Staging the
    Włast/Komornicka Archive   137
    Bryce Lease

7   Translating Triumph: The Power of Print and the
    Performance of Empire in Early Modern Europe   154
    Daniel J. Ruppel

8   From Novella to Theatre and Opera: Translating 'Otherness'
    in *Cavalleria rusticana*   186
    Enza De Francisci

9   Gestural Archives: Transmission and Embodiment as
    Translation in Occupied Palestine   201
    Farah Saleh

PART III   'TRANSLATION AT LARGE':
           DIALOGUES ON ETHICS AND POLITICS

10 'Translation Is Always Not Enough …'   229
    Gayatri Chakravorty Spivak in conversation with Avishek Ganguly

11 Afterword: Can Translation Do Justice?   244
    Sruti Bala

Works Cited   248
Index   269

Figures

2.1 'Soon Ah Will Be Done'. Scene from *Vive la France*. Photograph by Eric Legrand. Courtesy of Mohamed Rouabhi. — *page* 55

2.2 'Fight the Power'. Scene from *All Power to the People!* Photograph by Pascal Gély. Courtesy of Mohamed Rouabhi. — 58

2.3 'Die Nigga!' Screen capture of video recording of *All Power to the People!* Courtesy of Mohamed Rouabhi. — 60

3.1 Lady Macbeth's death scene, *Macbeth* (dir. Lu Po-Shen), Tainaner Ensemble (2007). Courtesy of the Asian Shakespeare Intercultural Archive (A|S|I|A, http://a-s-i-a-web.org). — 74

3.2 Viewing *Li Er Zai Ci* (dir. Wu Hsing-Kuo), Contemporary Legend Theatre (2001), in English, Mandarin and Japanese. Courtesy of the Asian Shakespeare Intercultural Archive (A|S|I|A, http://a-s-i-a-web.org). — 80

7.1 *Ehrenpforte* ('Arch of Honour') of Maximilian I. Courtesy of the National Gallery of Art, Washington, DC, Accession No. 1991.200.1. — 160

7.2 Title Page of *Ordine Pompe, Apparati, et Ceremonie Della Solenne Intrata Di Carlo V., Imp[erator] Sempre Aug[ustus] Nella Citta Di Roma* (1536), and verso. — 167

7.3 Ceffino, *La triumphante entree de lempereur nostre sire* … (f°2r). — 170

7.4 Epigraph to *Le triumphe d'Anvers* (1550) (sig. A2v). — 179

7.5 Arch on the Pont de la Vigne from Le triumphe d'Anvers (sig. I1r). — 183

9.1 History classroom in Suspended Accounts exhibition in London (January 2016), © Andy Stagg, courtesy of the Mosaic Rooms. — 204

9.2 History class in A Fidayee Son in Moscow live performance at Dance Base, Edinburgh (February 2017), © Brian Hartely. — 204

viii   *List of Figures*

9.3 The third section of the video 'A historical moment',
     © Salem Thawaba.   208
9.4 The kitchen setting of the installation in Granoff Center
     at Brown University in Providence (March 2016),
     © Farah Saleh.   210
9.5 Experimenting with archiving gestures with other artists over
     Skype at Dance Base in Edinburgh (May 2017),
     © Maciej Czajka.   212
9.6 A filled-in Landing Card completed by a member
     of the audience, © Farah Saleh.   213
9.7 The audience watching the video documentation at the
     beginning of the performance, Fruitmarket in Edinburgh
     (February 2019). Courtesy of the Fruitmarket, © Chris Scott.   217
9.8 What My Body Can/t Remember, Fruitmarket in Edinburgh
     (February 2019). Courtesy of the Fruitmarket, © Chris Scott.   219

Contributors

SRUTI BALA is Associate Professor in the Department of Theatre Studies at the University of Amsterdam.

JOSHUA DAVIES is Senior Lecturer in Medieval Literature at King's College London.

ENZA DE FRANCISCI is Senior Lecturer in Translation Studies in the School of Modern Languages and Cultures at the University of Glasgow.

AVISHEK GANGULY is Associate Professor in the Department of Literary Arts and Studies at the Rhode Island School of Design.

KÉLINA GOTMAN is Professor of Performance and the Humanities at King's College London.

OLIVIA C. HARRISON is Associate Professor of French and Italian, Comparative Literature, Middle East Studies and American Studies & Ethnicity at the University of Southern California.

BRYCE LEASE is Professor of Theatre and Performance Studies at the Royal Central School of Speech and Drama, University of London.

ALVIN ENG HUI LIM is Assistant Professor in the Department of English, Linguistics and Theatre Studies at the National University of Singapore.

ELEANOR MARGOLIES is a UK-based writer and theatre maker.

DANIEL J. RUPPEL is a performer, theatre-maker, and Visiting Assistant Professor in Theatre History at Susquehanna University, Pennsylvania.

FARAH SALEH is a dancer and choreographer and PhD candidate at Edinburgh College of Art.

List of Contributors

KIRSTIN SMITH is Associate Professor in Drama in the School of Literature, Drama and Creative Writing at the University of East Anglia.

GAYATRI CHAKRAVORTY SPIVAK is University Professor in the Humanities at Columbia University.

Acknowledgements

This book has been many years in coming; although in some ways it started in the context of the symposium 'Theater & Performance + Translation & Multilingualism' at the Rhode Island School of Design (RISD), in Providence, RI, in 2015, organized by Avishek Ganguly with talks by Olivia C. Harrison and Kélina Gotman, many conversations and debates, twists and turns, have transpired along the way. In certain respects, the conversations long antedate even this, during our years at Columbia University where questions of language and the 'global', performance and theatre, were formative to intellectual trajectories that continue to move today. Working across continents and time zones has not been easy, but perhaps this was essential to the task at hand, keeping us always aware of the disjunctions and disorientations as well as the alignments that carry us through and that thwart communication and co-labour every day. In so many ways, the challenges we have faced with writing and thinking together across distances have forced consideration of how embodied our everyday lives are: we know this well, and yet the false promise of electronic co-presence signals an ever-more urgent need to reinscribe at least our thinking into the lived ecologies of our current places and times; this does not mean one is less 'global', but local with the full and fierce awareness of just how far other places can be. This is exacerbated by restrictions on travel – themselves critical not only on account of human health, but more broadly to the health of the entire planet. Writing during a time of increasing crises – yet within the particular academic mode that is nearly of necessity always 'slow' – we dig deeper into the problems of translation, explored here with regard to theatre and performance, to poetry, to archives, to history and to violence, to racism and xenophobia, to inequality and justice, and so much more.

We would like in particular to thank our contributors, for their extraordinary patience as this has taken shape through the ongoing global pandemic and emergence of new European war, the rise of violent

xii *Acknowledgements*

majoritarianisms in South Asia and elsewhere, continued violence directed against Black, Indigenous, Asian and other minority communities in North America and the ensuing protests, not to mention the steadily unfolding climate crisis and so many further world events rendering the question and problem of 'performance' and 'translation' – as well as the 'global' – ever more pressing. Thanks also to our reviewers, for their thoughtful and rigorous readings; to John Doddy, for expert support with copy editing, as we were preparing the manuscript for submission; thank you to King's College London and the Rhode Island School of Design for financial support with manuscript preparation; thank you in particular to Anna Snaith, Head of the Department of English at King's, and at RISD: RISD Research, and the Turner Theatrical and Performance Design Fund for supporting the initial symposium. Thank you also to the Interweaving Performance Cultures 'International Research Center' at the Freie Universität-Berlin where a visiting fellowship for Avishek Ganguly enabled the completion of some of the work on this volume. Kélina Gotman was able further to develop thinking around comparativism, theatre and language in the context of a Friedrich Hölderlin Guest Professorship in Comparative Dramaturgy at the Institute for Theatre, Film and Media Studies, Goethe University of Frankfurt; with thanks to colleagues and students for conversation. At Cambridge University Press, Kate Brett and Emily Hockley have offered key support and interest in this project from its inception; thanks also to George Laver and Natasha Burton, as well as to Narmadha Nedounsejiane and Santosh Laxmi Kota for expert support with production. Sivan Rubinstein kindly offered use of a still from her choreographic project *Active Maps*, part of the *Migration through Dance* series, for the cover image; thank you also to dancer Harriet Parker-Beldeau. This is, as with any book, a partial project. So many other avenues might be taken. We hope it contributes in a very small way towards some debate and discussion, and that much more will continue.

Introduction
Translation in Motion
Avishek Ganguly and Kélina Gotman

As we write this introduction, the world is still reeling from a pandemic that is far from over even as we hear disturbing drumbeats of a purported global military conflict, a 'World War III' spilling over from the current Russian invasion of Ukraine. Images of yet another refugee crisis sparked by acts of death and destruction are all over our newsfeeds and timelines again, this time perhaps more visible because it is happening on the fringes of Europe and not in some far away 'Third World country', bringing to the fore a set of issues that only exacerbate what the past decades have announced: intensely interlocking financial and cultural inter-dependence, as well as widespread and systemic vulnerability, information war, surveillance and fear. While we do not treat all these issues directly in this volume, we attempt to articulate a theoretical approach that understands languages, bodies, movements and nations as acts and events that are crosshatched by performance and translation; shaping how individuals and groups relate to one another, move between fields of experience or analysis, and negotiate shared histories and imagined futurities in distinctive ways. A song, an accent, a gesture or an image performatively enact solidarity or relation, just as they reinforce axes of power and resistance. It is these micro-acts of translation that performatively 'do' the global – and the local, as well as the inter- or trans-national – that we explore in *Translation and Performance in a Global Age*.

A few scenes capture this well: in December 2019 the Narendra Modi-led Hindu-nationalist Bhartiya Janata Party (BJP) government in India passed the Citizenship Amendment Act (CAA), which promised to offer fast-track citizenship to immigrants from neighbouring Afghanistan, Bangladesh and Pakistan but pointedly excluded Muslims from the list of eligible groups. Together with the proposed National Register of Citizens (NRC) that could call into question the citizenship status of many Indian Muslims, this was widely construed as an unprecedented attempt to make religion a criterion for Indian citizenship and directly challenge the secular founding principles laid down in the country's constitution. The new law was met with massive protests that were marked, among other things, by the collective singing of anti-authoritarian songs by huge crowds assembled on the streets and university campuses, parks and meeting grounds.[1] However, in a remarkable instance of solidarity fostered in translation, among the two most popular songs sung by the protesting citizens were the Urdu nazm *'Hum Dekhenge'* [We Shall See] written by renowned leftist poet Faiz Ahmed Faiz as a protest against the military dictatorship of General Zia ul Haq in Pakistan in the 1980s, and the Italian anti-fascist anthem *'Bella Ciao'* [Goodbye, Beautiful] whose origins can be traced back to nineteenth-century folk songs from the northern part of that country.[2] While *'Bella Ciao'* mostly circulated in its newly produced Hindi translation, the collective singing of *'Hum Dekhenge'*, in a language that while not as widely spoken as Hindi still retains a substantial number of Indian speakers, sometimes involved an individual singer taking an impromptu lead in annotating or translating the words for the rest of the group.[3]

At the other end of the world, at the Super Bowl pre-game ceremony in February 2020, inter-disciplinary artist Christine Sun Kim performed her American Sign Language (ASL) translation of the US National Anthem to a televised audience of nearly 100 million people. The National Association for the Deaf (NAD) and the National Football League (NFL) have collaborated on featuring ASL interpreters in the past but the selection of Kim, a critically acclaimed Deaf artist whose work employs sound, text and performance, was a major attempt at centring the Deaf community as well as the prevalence of ASL in contemporary US society.[4]

There is, also, the curious case of *Parasite*, the Korean feature film that made history by becoming the first 'foreign language' film to win 'Best Picture' at the Academy Awards a few weeks later, prompting commentators to declare that this might signal a decisive shift in the film viewing

---

[1] 'Editorial: The Protests Are Not Just Anti-CAA, but Pro-Constitution', *The Wire*, 31 December 2019, https://thewire.in/rights/india-citizenship-protests-democracy-constitution-caa

[2] 'Songs, Poems and Films: A Playlist for Protest', *Film Companion*, 11 January 2020, www.filmcompanion.in/features/bollywood-features/songs-poems-and-films-a-playlist-for-protest/

[3] Mukal Kesavan, 'Power of Anthems: Plurality of Languages Threatens the Coherence Majoritarians Want', *The Telegraph India*, 25 January 2020, www.telegraphindia.com/opinion/power-of-anthems/cid/1739593

[4] Kim appreciated the gesture but still thought it was a missed opportunity because of the manner in which the television cameras covered the event. See Christine Sun Kim, 'I Performed at the Superbowl. You Might have Missed Me', *The New York Times*, 3 February 2020, www.nytimes.com/2020/02/03/opinion/national-anthem-sign-language.html

Introduction

habits of a mostly monolingual US audience. As Bong Joon Ho, the film's celebrated director, had said earlier at the Golden Globes awards: 'Once you overcome the one-inch tall barrier of subtitles you will be introduced to so many more amazing films.'[5] These are but only a few instances of the vast and vibrant lives of translation in song, poetry, gesture, speech, subtitle, closed caption, bodies and objects, not to mention on theatrical stages, which we describe in terms of 'translation at large'.[6] Translation in a global world, we argue, is not only literary, but profoundly performative, embedded in how ideas and gestures transform and move. As Kélina Gotman argues in 'Translatio', published in a special issue of *Performance Research*, edited by Amelia Jones and dedicated to 'Trans/Performance', performance studies as a discipline is itself radically translational, engaged at its core in thinking how discourses, concepts and figures travel across sites of knowledge and geopolitical power. Designating at once passages between epistemic regimes and global empires, the medieval Latin concept of *translatio* suggests far more than the 'translation' of distinct national languages but a complex form of movement, a way of affiliating and reaffiliating bodies and places, extending or narrowing gazes and rerouting modes of attention.[7] This approach furthers an important body of work in Performance Studies as well as in studies of Theatre and Drama that acknowledges the embodied ways cultural discourse and practice is lived and shared – relationally – first of all; and this approach recognises that with this expansive remit, understanding 'translation' as concept as well as praxis, come further opportunities for thinking myriad ways 'translation' itself as an operative term is translated into and passes through adjacent disciplinary fields. Thus, *Translation and Performance in a Global Age* draws from dominant theorisations about translation as literary work while addressing itself also importantly to the challenge of thinking translation performatively, within a theatrical setting and beyond. This acknowledges the concept of linguistic performativity articulated by J. L. Austin, who

---

[5] Quoted in Andrew R. Chow, '*Parasite*'s Best Picture Oscar Is Historic. Is This the Beginning of a New Era in Film?', *Time*, 9 February 2020, https://time.com/5779940/parasite-best-picture-oscars/

[6] In employing the 'at large' formulation we echo anthropologist Arjun Appadurai's landmark theorisation of 'modernity at large' from the early 1990s and seek to draw further attention to the centrality of translation in processes of cultural globalisation. See Arjun Appadurai, *Modernity At Large: Cultural Dimensions of Globalization* (Minneapolis: University of Minnesota Press, 1996).

[7] Kélina Gotman, '*Translatio*', *Performance Research* 21, no. 5 (2016): 17–20. On epistemic violence and the travels of language through colonial management and administration, particularly Spanish and English, see also Mary Louise Pratt, 'Language and the Afterlives of Empire', *PMLA* 130, no. 2 (2015): 348–357.

suggests that certain forms of language can act upon the world, while furthering such a notion of performativity to include gestural and other non-linguistic 'acts'.[8]

Such sutures, as we have been attempting to argue, help take stock better of global transformations. To take another contemporary example, for translators and cultural theorists Catherine Boyle and Renata Brandao, attending to ways language moves around the world helps illuminate the power politics and 'worldmaking' potential of 'language acts': their project, *Worldmaking in the Time of Covid-19*, launched in March 2020, draws a team of twenty researchers reading across Arabic, English, French, German, Hebrew, Italian, Japanese, Korean, Mandarin, Russian, Portuguese and Spanish to trace how words like 'war, conflict, contagion, invasion, fear, sanity and cleansing inhabit the ways in which we articulate our responses – collective and subjective – to moments of crisis'; and ways narratives and figures circulate, shaping how we see the world around us.[9] 'Travelling concepts' and 'Travelling acts' are two further strands of the Language Acts project, thinking how worlds are made and remade globally through scenographies of crisis and imagination, on and off stage. Another compelling example of such thinking can be found in the recent essay 'Translating Poetry, Translating Blackness' by John Keene where the writer and translator argues for more translations of non-Anglophone Black voices into English as way of expanding the corpus of Afro-Diasporic narratives beyond current, largely US-centric conversations;[10] Kaiama L. Glover, in her translations of and work on Haitian literature, raises the same question in a slightly different way by asking, 'what is the task of the translator within [the] racially hierarchized transatlantic space?' and offers the example of the continued mistranslation of Vodou in English language publications as a case in point.[11] Many more examples of such thinking around how language moves and how translation serves as a cipher for thinking global and local motion could be described. What we aim to do with this volume is to collect a rich handful of approaches to thinking

---

[8] John L. Austin, *How To Do Things with Words*, 2nd ed. (Cambridge: Cambridge University Press, 1975).

[9] 'Worldmaking in the Time of Covid-19', Language Acts and Worldmaking, accessed 19 May 2021, https://languageacts.org/worldmaking-time-covid-19/

[10] John Keene, 'Translating Poetry, Translating Blackness', 2016, accessed 2 June 2022, https://www.poetryfoundation.org/harriet-books/2016/04/translating-poetry-translating-blackness.

[11] Kaiama L. Glover, '"Blackness" in French: On Translation, Haiti, and the Matter of Race', in *L'Esprit Créateur*, 59, no. 2 (Summer 2019): 25–41, and 'Haiti in Translation: Dance on the Volcano by Marie Vieux-Chauvet, An Interview with Kaiama L. Glover', accessed 2 June 2022, https://networks.h-net.org/node/116721/discussions/158058/haiti-translation-dance-volcano-marie-vieux-chauvet-interview.

Introduction

theatre, performance and performativity within geopolitical frameworks involving complex acts of negotiation, friction, community and companionship, to define some of the ways we performatively constitute and reconstitute ourselves through shifting modes of expression in the twenty-first century.

Genealogical Re/formations: Translation and Performance in a Comparative Mode

The argument we offer is in part a disciplinary, and in part an inter-disciplinary one: we have noticed, as we detail here, how much 'translation' has become theorised in literary arenas, particularly Comparative Literature, as a trope for understanding comparativism otherwise; and at the same time, how much 'performance' has gained ground as a theoretical lens for capturing notions of embodiment, orality and gesture, to cite but a few elements of discourse and practice that exceed the literary frame. At the same time, we have been galvanised by the immense body of work in Theatre and Performance Studies that draws attention to ways translation plays out far beyond dramaturgical practice, as questions of textual translation, and issues of worldmaking, dialect and gesture continue to bear critical fruit theoretically and within theatre practice work.

Translation and Performance in a Global Age thus recognises that not only is translation a matter for linguists and literary critics to think, or drama scholars to theorise, but that given its near constant presence in everyone's lives, there is a pressing need further to situate discussions of translation in and as performance. We aim to suggest that translation serves here as a trans-medial concept, one that – alongside performance – articulates something of the discursively and gesturally relational nodes of expression and interchange that make up our worlds. This is true not least at a time when the English language continues to hold a dominant position on the world stage, and when micro acts of languaging renegotiate 'English' and other moments of hegemonic language-making everywhere. We suggest therefore that complex and sometimes unclassifiable gestures, accents and inflections make up our lived experiences, and that these can be understood not only in translational but also in performance terms; and, that the double lens helps illuminate ways translation is performative, as well as ways our performances in the everyday *do* translation. For the vast majority of moving, migrant bodies, for instance – refugees, asylum seekers and white-collar workers alike – the first port of call for their perhaps unwitting revelations of 'unpermitted' or 'permitted' selves (those that tend literally to require permits for mobility) is not just the fingerprint or retina scan but also the voice. And, these vocal as well as non-verbal interjections into the public sphere often take place – and are received – in and as translation, between languages and performative codes. Whether one is translating from one version or dialect of Swahili, French or English to another, or between 'national' languages (like 'Spanish' or 'Bengali'), the sound of a speaker enacting inflections can render her body and personhood vulnerable or, conversely, empowered.

The supplementation of the visual (written/read) with the sonic (spoken/heard), we argue, invites long overdue critical intervention into the discussion of translation as an ethical act. In thinking about the aesthetics of the Black radical tradition, Fred Moten draws our attention to 'a historical movement from the priority of the sonic gesture to the hegemony of the visual (which is to say theoretical) formulation'.[12] Perhaps the 'grid of visibility' for otherness, so often placed on problems of recognition and legibility, needs to be complemented with at least a parallel and imbricated track, which we might call the 'grid of audibility', for the oral/aural ways in which languaging outs 'difference'? Indeed Part I of our volume, as detailed later, examines a number of oral/aural translation acts in performance terms.[13] Hence, the contention of our volume is that acts of speaking as well as non-verbal language, micro-accentuations and inter-medial passages within and between languages need to receive further critical attention, through a performance frame, on a global scale. Although translation has been understood as a literary act or a diplomatic exercise – as well as a matter of pragmatics (as Gayatri Chakravorty Spivak notes in her interview, 'Translation is Always Not Enough…', published at the end of this volume, the vast majority of paid translations in the world are for technical manuals) – a sustained study of its expression in and as 'performance' offers further opportunity to think translation at large.

By imbricating translation and performance here, we acknowledge the by-now commonplace binaries of writing/speaking or text/performance, and their reversals, instead attempting to displace the conversation onto translation as a medium and mode, or critical method, which works with

---

[12] Fred Moten, *In the Break: The Aesthetics of the Black Radical Tradition* (Minneapolis: University of Minnesota Press, 2003), 59.

[13] Rey Chow proposes a similar approach in Rey Chow, *Not Like a Native Speaker: On Languaging as Postcolonial Experience* (New York: Columbia University Press, 2014).

Introduction

and in excess of these agonisms.[14] Translation becomes a vector; and theories of translation become performative inasmuch as they are engaged in acts of speech and of repetition. This further draws on the work of Austin, previously alluded to, and the foundational role his concept of 'speech acts' has played in performance theory, all while it has bracketed stage worlds from the notion of language *doing* (as he famously put it, saying 'I do' on stage, for instance, cannot possibly involve an actual marriage act, although performance art has long since derided these arbitrary distinctions).[15] For philologist and philosopher Barbara Cassin, Austin's approach to the 'performative', articulated in 1962, adopted by Émile Benveniste from 1966, near contemporaneously with Noam Chomsky's notion of competence and performance, can also be read in relation to far earlier Sophist acts of performative languaging; the genealogies themselves proliferate, as one acknowledges further terms.[16] Acts of literature, theatre and art attest to such multi-purposive sites and modes of performance, ways our being in and with language aim to reach towards or to show, or indicate, or bring together, prove or enjoin; tilt us this way or that, shift points of allegiance on geocultural, affective and political grids. Thus, as hard as one may try to learn accents or expressions, and as transformed as our accents may become – or as hybrid as they may remain – for many, perhaps for all of us, we carry around manners of speaking, pronouncing, languaging and gesturing, equally as burdens and as treasures, markers of other places and people we may never have directly known. This is not only the case for 'foreigners' but, as the chapters in this volume attest, saturates acts of speech that demarcate histories, geographies and genealogies at every street corner. We are not just – to use the old phrase – lost in translation – but constituted by it performatively every day.

Translation and Performance in a Global Age therefore offers a set of inter-related arguments generated by but also situated at the intersection of three disciplinary (or interdisciplinary) formations: Comparative Literature, Translation Studies, and Theatre and Performance Studies. The scope of this conversation perhaps corroborates the ambitious nature of our project: an attempt to move with performance towards a trans-medial and trans-discursive understanding of translation. Over the past three decades,

---

[14] See, for instance, Carlos Rojas, 'Translation as Method', *Prism: Theory and Modern Chinese* 16, no. 2 (2019): 221–235. For an important argument about translation as queer methodology, see Evren Savci, *Queer in Translation: Sexual Politics under Neoliberal Islam* (Durham: Duke University Press, 2021).

[15] See Austin *How To Do Things with Words*.

[16] Barbara Cassin, 'Sophistics, Rhetorics, and Performance: Or, How to Really Do Things with Words', translated by Andrew Goffey, *Philosophy and Rhetoric* 42, no. 4 (2009), 349–372.

8   AVISHEK GANGULY AND KÉLINA GOTMAN

scholars of Comparative Literature, Cultural Studies and Postcolonial Studies including Jacques Derrida, Spivak, Édouard Glissant, Tejaswini Niranjana, Emily Apter, Naoki Sakai, Lawrence Venuti, Homi Bhabha, Abdelkebir Khatibi, Sandra Bermann and others have been arguing for an understanding of translation as an ethical and political act. In the field of Translation Studies, Susan Bassnett, André Lefevere, Mona Baker, Maria Tymoczko, Michael Cronin and others, while remaining focused on translation as primarily a transfer of meaning between languages, have similarly been trying to move towards a growing inter-disciplinary arena for thinking complex practices of cultural negotiation.[17] And in Theatre and Performance Studies, as Susan Bassnett and David Johnston have argued in a recent state-of-the-field article, questions of translation have mostly been articulated as a matter of translating play texts from one language into another, or as a metaphor for the transfer from page to stage, while remaining largely focused on navigating binaries of translation practice like 'foreignizing/domesticating' first expounded by Venuti in the 1990s.[18] An early salutary attempt to draw attention to these questions was the special issue of *Theatre Journal* on the topic of theatre and translation edited

---

[17] See for instance, Jacques Derrida, 'Des Tours de Babel', in *Difference in Translation*, edited and translated by Joseph F. Graham (Ithaca: Cornell University Press, 1985), 165–207 and Jacques Derrida, *Monolingualism of the Other; or, The Prosthesis of Origin*, translated by Patrick Mensah (Stanford: Stanford University Press, 1998); Gayatri Chakravorty Spivak, 'The Politics of Translation', in *Outside in the Teaching Machine* (London: Routledge, 1993), 179–200, republished in *The Translation Studies Reader*, edited by Lawrence Venuti (London: Routledge, 2012), 312–330, and Gayatri Chakravorty Spivak, 'Translation as Culture'. *Parallax* 6, no. 1 (2000): 13–24; Emily Apter, *Against World Literature: On the Politics of Untranslatability* (London: Verso, 2013) and Emily Apter, *The Translation Zone: A New Comparative Literature* (Princeton: Princeton University Press, 2006); Lawrence Venuti, *The Translator's Invisibility: A History of Translation*, 2nd ed. (London: Routledge, 2008) and Lawrence Venuti, *The Scandals of Translation: Towards An Ethics of Difference* (London: Routledge, 1998); Édouard Glissant, *Caribbean Discourse: Selected Essays*, translated by Michael Dash (Charlottesville: University Press of Virginia, 1989) and Édouard Glissant, *Poetics of Relation*, translated by Betsy Wing (Ann Arbor: University of Michigan Press, 1997); Homi Bhabha, *The Location of Culture* (London: Routledge, 1994); Naoki Sakai, *Translation and Subjectivity: On Japan and Cultural Nationalism* (Minneapolis: University of Minnesota Press, 1997); Tejaswini Niranjana, *Siting Translation: History, Post-structuralism and the Colonial Context* (Berkeley: University of California Press, 1992); Abdelkebir Khatibi, *Love in Two Languages*, translated by Richard Howard (Minneapolis: University of Minnesota Press, 1990); Sandra Bermann and Michael Wood, *Nation, Language, and the Ethics of Translation* (Princeton: Princeton University Press, 2005); Susan Bassnett, *Translation Studies* (London: Routledge, 2013); Susan Bassnett and André Lefevere, *Constructing Cultures: Essays on Literary Translation* (Clevedon, UK and Philadelphia: Multilingual Matters, 1998); Mona Baker, *Translation and Conflict: A Narrative Account* (London: Routledge, 2018); Maria Tymoczko, *Enlarging Translation, Empowering Translators* (London: Routledge, 2014); and Michael Cronin, *Translation and Identity* (London: Routledge, 2006).

[18] See Susan Bassnett and David Johnston, 'The Outward Turn in Translation Studies', *The Translator* 25, no. 3 (2019): 181–188, 185; and Venuti, *The Scandals* of Translation.

Introduction 9

by Jean Graham-Jones in 2007.[19] However, most of those discussions were still engaged in questions of translation vis-à-vis theatre practice, with an occasional detour into matters of editing and publishing; we aim to draw from these precedents further to articulate an expanded concept of translation, placing the concerns of theatre practitioners and theorists in conversation with approaches to translation being discussed in Comparative Literature and in the performance humanities more broadly. This rapprochement between Theatre and Performance Studies, performed in part via Comparative Literature and Translation Studies, may appear counterintuitive at first or else over-evident, yet while Theatre and Performance Studies are frequently very close institutionally (with shared departments and journals), they remain typically often also very much apparently at odds, due to still lingering paradigms of anti-theatricality characterising the emergence of Performance Studies in contrast to drama. Perhaps translation as operative concept may become another means of reconciliation?

Thus within Theatre Studies, a range of recently published books address myriad ways dramatic works are translated and staged, including notably Geraldine Brodie's *The Translator on Stage* (Bloomsbury, 2017), Geraldine Brodie and Emma Cole's edited *Adapting Translation for the Stage* (Routledge, 2017), Silvia Bigliazzi, Peter Kofler and Paola Ambrosi's edited *Theatre Translation in Performance* (Routledge, 2013), Roger Baines, Cristina Marinetti and Manuella Perteghella's edited *Staging and Performing Translation: Text and Theatre Practice* (Palgrave Macmillan, 2010), Phyllis Zatlin's *Theatrical Translation and Film Adaptation: A Practitioner's View* (Multilingual Matters, 2005), and Maria M. Delgado, Bryce Lease and Dan Rebellato's edited *Contemporary European Playwrights* (Routledge, 2020), which further acknowledges complex ways the 'European' world of recent drama continues to be translated culturally and critically into multilingual settings. In Performance Studies, the important work of Diana Taylor situates the problem of translation at the heart of performance theory: in 'Translating Performance', Taylor suggests that the term itself is an imperial holdover from the dominance of English; colleagues in the hispanophone world, she notes, alternately use the anglicised *performance* (sometimes as *el performance*, sometimes *la performance*), translating from the English while alternating genders in a 'linguistic cross-dressing that invites English speakers to think about the sex or gender of *performance*'; or else they playfully deploy *lo performático*, among other myriad hispanicisations. *Performance*, she adds, 'includes but is not reducible to any

[19] See *Theatre Journal* 59, no. 3 (2007).

10 AVISHEK GANGULY AND KÉLINA GOTMAN

of these words usually used to replace it: *teatralidad, espectáculo, acción, representación*'. It tends to denote performance art, where the notion of 'performance' elsewhere signals everything from business management to linguistic performativity.[20] Importantly, 'performance' appears to be an untranslatable concept, something that gives pause as to the arguably Anglo-Saxon, distinctly neoliberal character or quality of 'performance' as a way of theorising doing and accomplishing, in a manner that is non-mimetic and non-theatrical.[21] For Paul Rae, Performance Studies might be called 'Wayang Studies', after the Indonesian and Malaysian practice of *wayang*, alternately denoting street opera or puppet theatre and, more recently, something slightly invisible pulling strings behind the scenes, or something designated (with some design) as theatrical; a further meaning he notes is along the lines of 'saving face' in a social situation, putting on a show of another sort. All of these and more align notions of performance with the complex cultural translations taking place in political life and in the everyday; 'performance' alone (in English) does not quite capture the entangled dramatic and dramaturgical, theatrical and performative notions of shadow, imagining or giving shape.[22] For Lada Čale Feldman and Marin Blažević, performance research stimulates 'glocal troubles' in Croatia, where with the global expansion of Performance Studies, issues of translation sit at the heart of what to call the field. The long-established German *Theaterwissenschaft* (as well as *Literaturwissenschaft* and *Volkskunde*, or folklore studies), together with Russian formalism, Prague structuralism, Anglo-American New Criticism, French post-structuralism, Italian semiotics (not to mention the older discourses of performance study like the *Natyasastra* in India or theories of theatre and performance in China), produce a '*mélange*' that any department would recognise as baffling, to say the least; 'performance' (like 'performative' and 'performativity') adds a dimension of integration and dissensus, a shifting ground for theorisation that queries at once institutional and discursive alliance and geopolitical affiliation, as well as a host of pragmatic issues with regard to

---

[20] Diana Taylor, 'Translating Performance', *Profession* (2002): 44–50, 44–47.

[21] Marcos Steuernagel further muses on the possible 'untranslatability' of Performance Studies in 'The (Un)translatability of Performance Studies', in the trilingual online publication edited by Diana Taylor and Marcos Steuernagel, *What Is / ¿Qué son los estudios de / O que são os estudos da Performance Studies?*, accessed 19 May 2021, https://scalar.usc.edu/nehvectors/wips/the-untranslatability-of-performance-studies

[22] Paul Rae, 'Wayang Studies?', in *The Rise of Performance Studies: Rethinking Richard Schechner's Broad Spectrum Approach*, edited by James Harding and Cindy Sherman (Basingstoke: Palgrave Macmillan, 2011): 67–84, 73–76.

Introduction

what language one performs in or speaks, on stage or off, in the classroom or at a conference. Thankfully, they conclude, Croatian inflections resist the 'hegemonic economy of the global intercultural market, whether of postdramatic theatre or performance art. Performance research including'.[23] 'Performance' theorisation continues to move and to fail fully to translate: Dariusz Kosiński somewhat playfully reminisces on the ill-fated, short-lived use of the term 'performatics', theorised in a special issue of *Performance Research* in 2008, following the Polish translation of Richard Schechner's *Performance Studies: An Introduction*, a volume which in Polish maintained the English title, while appending the Polish *Performatyka: wstęp* (literally, *Performatics: An Introduction*), a double play of translation and untranslatability.[24] It seems 'performance' as a concept emerged with force in the last quarter of the twentieth century and the first decades of the twenty-first just as academic disciplines and departments were becoming all the more translational, engaged in a global trade of translations, exchanges, and 'international' or 'global' conferences that were themselves wary of grand claims to internationalism.[25] With current borders firming again, in the wake of right-wing, ethnonationalist movements and the Covid-19 pandemic, far more networked (and re-networked) acts of performative translation will continue to shape performance thinking and acts of languaging and gesturing, as well as the social choreography of belonging and displacement worldwide.

This, then, is the situation we face: a prolific body of critical literature that has been variously thinking language, (un)translatability and performance within the field of performance and theatre studies, problems of translation in theatre practice – an art form always engaged in language offered presently and live, and the increasing purchase of performance thinking on disciplines far outside theatre and performance studies, but all the while this thinking has not fully taken stock of embodied and performative ways of thinking, writing or producing 'theory'. The latter is especially true in

---

[23] Lada Čale Feldman and Marin Blažević, 'Translate, or Else: Marking the Glocal Troubles of Performance Research in Croatia', in *Contesting Performance: Global Sites of Research*, edited by Jon McKenzie and Heike Roms (Basingstoke: Palgrave Macmillan, 2009): 168–187, 168–184.

[24] Dariusz Kosiński, 'After Performatics', *Performance Research* 23, nos. 4–5 (2018): 262–265, 262.

[25] Famously, Performance Studies international (PSi) opted for the lowercase 'i' for the inaugural conference in 1997, and numerous iterations since have continued to play with and to query ethics and politics of (translingual) global circulation, from the oceanic, transnational 'Fluid States' in 2015, held across more than two dozen locations, to the 2021 edition, 'Constellate'. The organisation's online journal since 2017, *GPS (Global Performance Studies)* plays with the notion of geolocation as a way further continually to displace any sense of centrality or priority, all while operating in the global lingua franca, English, at least for now (as we write, a trilingual Arabic/English/Spanish issue is being prepared).

disciplines such as Comparative Literature and Translation Studies, where far more theorisation remains to be done fully to integrate performance thinking and theoretical research on textuality and political culture. For instance, in the recent 600-page *A Companion to Translation Studies* (2014) edited by Sandra Bermann and Catherine Porter, only one essay addresses performance: 'What does it mean to perform translation?' Bermann asks in her essay in that collection.[26] Yet while she recognises that translation does not only take place either in language or in writing, her response does not fully address the material and affective registers of performance as such: the speaking, listening, touching, moving, hearing and even the silence that transport languages across (to invoke just the Latin roots of 'translation') and between bodies, or across and between objects and machines, archives and records, digits and ciphers, sites and lived spaces. Other recent books on translation and critical theory including Emily Apter's *Against World Literature: On the Politics of Untranslatability* (Verso, 2013), Esther Allen and Susan Bernofsky edited *In Translation* (Columbia University Press, 2013), Lawrence Venuti's *Translation Changes Everything* (Routledge, 2013), Vicente Rafael's *Motherless Tongues: The Insurgency of Language amid Wars of Translation* (Duke University Press, 2016), and Rosemary Arrojo's *Fictional Translations: Rethinking Translation through Literature* (Routledge, 2018) that powerfully highlight the ethics of translation also dedicate insufficient attention to ways performance operates in and through these political sites. An emerging and exciting new affinity towards translation in works of poetry is perhaps one notable exception to the continuing prevalence of fiction as the dominant mode for reflection on translation in literary and critical and cultural theories.[27]

Our volume thus addresses these communities of scholars, translators and readers and stages a conversation we believe productively responds

---

[26] Sandra Bermann, 'Performing Translation', in *A Companion to Translation Studies* edited by Sandra Bermann and Catherine Porter (Oxford: Wiley-Blackwell, 2014), 285–297.

[27] Two recent instances that engage with the possibilities of a performative reconstitution of translation beyond the literary along the lines of what we are arguing here can be found in the award-winning work of poets Don Mee Choi (*DMZ Colony*, Seattle: Wave Books, 2020) and Sawako Nakayasu (*Say Translation Is Art*, Brooklyn: Ugly Duckling Presse, 2020). Among scholarly works two prominent examples would be Karen Emmerich's *Literary Translation and the Making of Originals* (New York and London: Bloomsbury, 2017) which not only consolidates poststructuralist approaches towards rethinking translation beyond the original/copy binary but also includes extended discussions of translations of forms beyond the dominant genres of prose writing like poetry; and Lawrence Venuti's polemical *Contra Instrumentalism* that asserts, 'STOP treating translation as a metaphor. START considering it a material practice that is indivisibly linguistic and cultural', and dedicates an entire chapter to the discussion of film subtitles, in Lawrence Venuti, *Contra Instrumentalism: A Translation Polemic* (Lincoln: University of Nebraska Press, 2019), ix.

Introduction 13

to and further articulates an emerging critical landscape moving across Translation Studies, Comparative Literature, and Theatre and Performance Studies. This conversation can also be thought of as a response to the recent call for an 'outward turn in Translation Studies'.[28] In their 2019 editorial alluded to earlier, Bassnett, one of the founders of the field of Translation Studies, and Johnston advocate for this turn by suggesting that 'the field needs to expand outwards, to improve communication with other disciplines, to move beyond binaries....'[29] *Performance and Translation in a Global Age* offers performance as a generative and indispensable frame and method for thinking translation, attending to ways translation plays out across disciplinary arenas and modes of cultural production in and through performance. And the present volume attempts further to bridge another set of enduring divides, between theoretical and practical approaches to translation. The scholars and critics collected here indeed are all translators and theorists, practicing artists, interpreters and dramaturgs; many of us wear a number of hats, translating between our own translation practices and theorising some of the work of translation as being itself a performative critical act.[30]

Indeed, as the contributions in this volume attest, the question of 'performance' has always been translational, and the language with which performance theory has been written has by and large been engaged in thinking the workings of (performative) prose. From the experiments in 'performance writing' at Dartington College in the 1990s, exemplified by the work of Caroline Bergvall, discussed in depth in Chapter 1, with regard to her recent project *Drift*, to the proliferating artists' pages in *Performance Research*, performance theory, it seems, has always been caught, or else made, in the work of translation between artistic method and scholarship. This is not only because performance is a 'global' (or 'international') discipline and anti-discipline, but also because the fact of working multi-modally across continents has meant that ways of constructing discourse and authority have always been at stake. Taylor, discussed previously, writing of her work with the Hemispheric Institute and collaborators across the hispanophone and lusophone worlds, heralds a 'collaborative, multilingual, and interdisciplinary consortium of

---

[28] Bassnett and Johnston, 'The Outward Turn'.
[29] Bassnett and Johnston, 'The Outward Turn', 187.
[30] On the work of translating translation practice into translation theory, see especially Kélina Gotman, 'On the Difficult Work of Translating Translation; Or, the Monolingualism of Translation Theory. Languaging Acts In (and After) Marie NDiaye's *Les serpents*', *Studies in Theatre and Performance* 40, no. 2 (2019): 162–189.

institutions, artists, scholars, and activists throughout the Americas'. For Taylor, the trilingual context – compounded with the ephemerality of performance 'documents' and materials themselves – compels participants to invent modes of thinking performativity across linguistic and geocultural ecologies. *Escrachar* (Argentina) or *funar* (Chile) are among a few of the many terms and concepts that suggest the alignment of 'performance' with specifically collective action.[31] Translation, as we have been arguing, is how performance operates as a theoretical mode, and as method; and it matters *how* 'performance' is written. Thus, it is crucial that some of the interventions in this volume are themselves engaged in writing performatively, querying the structures and systems of discourse with which translation, performance and geopolitics are thought – the habit formations of authority or tone that characterise scholarly discourse and which performance writing has aimed, along with collective actions, to unsettle.

This methodological heterodoxy comes at a time when notions of 'trans' method are critically vital. In the special issue of *Performance Research* dedicated to 'Trans/Performance' mentioned earlier, Jones sets translation and transitivity, transfer and gendered (trans) ambivalence at the heart of performance research: in 'Trans-ing performance', she writes '[t]he prefix trans- mobilizes a series of concepts that [...] offer rich possibilities to the understanding of performativity or performance as process – linking, mediating and interrelating qualities in ongoing ways, connecting the trans- (implying exceeding, moving towards, changing; going across, over or beyond) to the performative (saying as doing, or that which performs something while articulating it).'[32] In this view, performance and 'trans-' are inter-penetrating concepts, hovering in a fluid set of interchanges grounded in inter-mediality and linguistic as well as critical and cultural passage. This position resonates with that taken by David Gramlin and Aniruddha Dutta in their 'Introduction' to 'Translating Transgender', a recent special issue of *TSQ: Transgender Studies Quarterly*.[33] Gramlin and Dutta argue that '[t]ranslations are often obligated to serve primarily as pragmatic substitutions for one another, while the tactile, mutable, precarious

---

[31] See Diana Taylor, 'The Many Lives of Performance: The Hemispheric Institute of Performance and Politics', in *Contesting Performance: Global Sites of Research*, edited by Jon McKenzie et al. (Basingstoke, UK: Palgrave Macmillan, 2010), 25–36, 25–31. Taylor first outlines the problem of translating the notion of 'performance' in 'Translating Performance'; see also Diana Taylor, *The Archive and the Repertoire*. See further Jon McKenzie, *Perform or Else: From Discipline to Performance* (London: Routledge, 2001); Austin, *How To Do Things with Words*.

[32] Amelia Jones, 'Introduction: Trans-ing Performance', *Performance Research* 21, no. 5 (2016): 1–11, 1.

[33] David Gramlin and Aniruddha Dutta, 'Translating Transgender', *TSQ: Transgender Studies Quarterly* 3, nos. 3–4 (November 2016): 333–356.

Introduction 15

relation between the translation and the translated is made to recede into secondary relevance, into its "production history"'.[34] Our contributors address these tactile, mutable and precarious relations: thus for Bryce Lease, trans-gendering provokes the question of what he calls 'transembodiment as translation'. As he suggests, transembodiment is not so much a methodology as 'a *structure* and a *consequence* of the process of transmission in the theatre'. The neologism he offers, 'transembodiment', theorises embodiment as an always already translational and theatrical as well as performative act, one that queries (and queers) processes of subjectivation. Building on the insights of feminist and post-colonial translation studies, Olivia C. Harrison, in this volume, also argues that translation is gendered and trans-gendering as well as what she calls 'transcolonial'.[35] Translation is made up of all the nuanced ways voice and gesture are biopolitically inscribed and geopolitically prescribed through performative acts.

Translation is performative, and performance is translational; caught in the act of translating, theorists as well as translators find themselves in the fruitful and complex position of capturing in language something that always eludes direct reference, always escapes the critical, the linguistic or the stage frame (perhaps this is where Rae's *wayang* studies helpfully circumscribes the notion of shadow work). As Bigliazzi, Kofler and Ambrosi rightly note in their introduction to *Theatre Translation in Performance* (2013), the dearth of translation studies of theatre lamented in the 1980s gave way to a fresh and productive new range of critical approaches to theatre translation for performance, engaging with questions of 'authority, authenticity, multilingualism, interpretation, cultural relocation, and resistance to domestication and/or foreignization in a culturally oriented age'.[36] The translation of a dramatic text to a performance text does not only involve language (word choice), or attention to the community of audience-goers receiving the work[37]; more fundamentally, as they suggest and as we maintain here, 'translation' operates in theatrical practice as a process of cultural, aesthetic and political negotiation within which the translator is always a co-author but often also a local informant and mediator.

---

[34] Gramlin and Dutta, 'Translating Transgender', 334.
[35] For feminist theories of translation as trans-gendering see for example Samia Mehrez, 'Translating Gender', *Journal of Middle East Women's Studies* 3, no. 1 (2007): 106–127.
[36] Silvia Bigliazzi, Peter Kofler and Paola Ambrosi, 'Introduction', in *Theatre Translation in Performance*, edited by Silvia Bigliazzi, Peter Kofler and Paola Ambrosi (New York: Routledge, 2013), 1–26, 4.
[37] See on this for example, Rafael Spregelburd, 'Life, Of Course', translated by Jean Graham-Jones, *Theatre Journal* 59, no. 3 (2007): 373–377, 377.

16   AVISHEK GANGULY AND KÉLINA GOTMAN

'Translational collaboration' – frequently enabled by the rehearsal process characteristic of theatrical productions – intensifies questions of authorial intent, singularity, double-entendre, voice or timbre and context also present in literary translation studies. With theatre, further negotiated through the work of acting, directing, producing – and the myriad negotiations of accent and location brought up therein – the issue of translation's work as a tool, medium and occasion for cultural negotiation becomes paramount. Indeed, if there is one genre ideally situated to thinking location and dislocation, spatiality and embodiment, it is theatre.[38] And if there is one critical paradigm that can further help think ways location and dislocation move through gesture, subjectivation, and more, it is performance.

Thus, this volume treats the proliferation of trans-genres germane to theatre and theatricality as well as to performance taken in a capacious sense to include song, dance, theatrical surtitling, performance poetry, audio description, political procession and much more; in this sense, what *Translation and Performance in a Global Age* aims to do with the question of the 'performative' is not only further to think the performance of (or, following W. B. Worthen, the performativity of) dramatic texts or performativity inherent in 'global' speech and literature, but also the concepts and practices of 'trans-' as an approach to movement that passes between two (or more) sites or modalities, and grates at multiple instantiations of speech and gesture within acts of languaging every day.[39] In other words, performance signals a proliferation of sites of negotiation – ethical encounters enacted inter-corporeally and inter-medially. With this, we conceptualise 'performance' as a term that is not so much merely 'untranslatable' as one that invites just the sorts of constant translations such as language and gesture are subjected to all the time: acts perpetually displaced, dislocated, never quite located in the first place, atopic just as they are hyper-topic. 'Performance' signals *parfournir*, the old French for 'completing' or 'carrying out', and at the same time very much the opposite – hesitation, a failure fully to carry forth, to arrive at or to complete; a dance of gesturing-toward, just as one hurries back in one's

---

[38] Bigliazzi, Kofler and Ambrosi, 'Introduction', 13. See also Cristina Marinetti, 'Transnational, Multilingual, and Post-dramatic: Rethinking the Location of Translation in Contemporary Theatre', in *Theatre Translation in Performance*, edited by S. Bigliazzi, P. Kofler and P. Ambrosi, 27–37.

[39] On the performativity inherent in the dramatic play script, see W. B. Worthen, 'The Imprint of Performance', In *Theorizing Practice: Redefining Theatre History*, eds. W. B. Worthen and Peter Holland (Basingstoke, UK: Palgrave Macmillan, 2003), 213–234; Sarah Bay-Cheng reprises this in her analysis of the problem of 'translating' experimental typography in 'Translation, Typography, and the Avant-Garde's Impossible Text', *Theatre Journal* 59, no. 3 (2007): 467–483.

Introduction 17

speech to a previous inflection, where one 'came from', where one might no longer be a 'stranger'. If theatre is a game of masking and unmasking (or of 'saving face'), performance may be understood as an eddying motion: as an agent or act or process of transformation and change. This does not mean theatre is always a doubling, but that between acts of doubling and acts of transformation lie an infinite number of translational moments and performative gestures to theorise.

The language with which we speak of translation matters. As noted, the contributions in this volume reflect on the languages with which they write. Emily Apter has recently alerted us to the ways 'border crossing' has become 'an all-purpose, ubiquitous way of talking about translation [such] that its purchase on the politics of actual borders – whether linguistic or territorial – [has] become attenuated'.[40] We believe something similar has been happening with the increasing use of expressions such as 'staging translation' or 'performing translation' in overwhelmingly written contexts; this often renders translation as metaphorically performative.[41] Instead, our volume argues that translation is simultaneously a specific medium of work and a craft – a *techne* – and it encompasses the intimate as well as the public acts of conciliation and obstruction, equivalence and incompletion that make, unmake and remake the discourses within which languaging bodies move. *Translation and Performance in a Global Age,* therefore, departs from literary conventions and proposes to rearticulate translation in terms that honour what is specific to performance as medium, epistemology and ontology. Our emphasis on corporeality and speech draws from theories in theatre and performance engaged in liveness and material bodily being, while shifting the locus of thought on translation to the myriad ways language operates not only in written (primarily literary) works but also importantly in and through the bodies – and tongues – that carry them. Hence, even as we argue for a 'performative turn' in translation studies, we respond to a similar impulse in literary and cultural studies with a set of chapters that addresses the material instances within which translation performatively takes time and takes place. This contributes to acts of epistemic de-colonisation taking hold worldwide: de-colonisation is not only a

---

[40] Emily Apter, 'Translation at the Checkpoint', *Journal of Postcolonial Writing* 50, no. 1 (2014): 56.

[41] As scholars of literature and performance/interdisciplinary humanities, we have deep appreciation for the work of metaphor; but as recent scholarship in other fields has shown, there is also a danger in overemphasising the metaphoricity or the metaphorical nature of ethical and political and cultural actions or processes. See for example Eve Tuck and K. Wayne Yang, 'Decolonization is not a Metaphor', *Decolonization: Indigeneity, Education and Society* 1, no. 1 (2012): 1–40.

diversification of subjects or bodies but the undoing of orders of priority within which and with which authority, as discourse as well as practice, takes shape.

Following Spivak, we acknowledge that the act of translation presents itself as a 'double bind', something 'necessary but impossible'; yet in this impossible necessity, it is also a moment of negotiation. Translation is necessary, in so far as it is 'relating to the other as the source of one's utterance' – apparent, as Spivak also points out, in the term *anu-vada* in most North Indian languages, 'speaking after, *translatio* as *imitatio*' – but it is also impossible since the idiom, 'singular to the tongue', fails to go over in translation.[42] Judith Butler, attending to the ethics of the translational act, argues in *Parting Ways: Jewishness and the Critique of Zionism* that 'translation ... stages an encounter with the epistemic limits of any given discourse'. If this encounter appears as a crisis, Butler asserts that it is one from which translation 'cannot emerge through any strategy that seeks to assimilate and contain difference'.[43] Thinking at the edges of the literary, the performative and the translational, we propose a measure of difference in which difference itself is never entirely assimilated or contained; we argue for a performative reconstitution of translation as an act that would not only be trans-disciplinary but also necessarily trans-medial. Taken together, the contributions in this volume offer an approach towards imagining translation that engages with the expansive ecology of (frequently gestural) languaging within which the translational act unfolds.[44] Even as we locate the imperative to translate in what Spivak identifies as 'hearing to respond', we want to prepare for a form of 'translation-as-response' that goes beyond language in the textual and sometimes verbal senses and engages with sounds and voices, motions and movements, accents and accentuations, materiality and archives, script and code.[45] In sum, the performative potential of audience constituencies receiving, using and deflecting acts of language produces, we believe, an ethics and politics that can redraw the map of comparative translation

---

[42] Spivak, 'Translation as Culture', 21.

[43] Judith Butler, *Parting Ways: Jewishness and the Critique of Zionism* (New York: Columbia University Press, 2012), 13.

[44] For a recent example of how translation has been approached by practitioners and scholars of visual art for instance, see the volume of essays edited by Leeza Ahmady, Iftikhar Dadi and Reem Fadda, *Tarjama/Translation: Contemporary Art from the Middle East, Central Asia, and its Diasporas* (New York: Arte East, 2009).

[45] On translation as social relation borne transhistorically, see Sakai, *Translation and Subjectivity*; also Sonia Massai, *Shakespeare's Accents: Voicing Identity in Performance* (Cambridge: Cambridge University Press, 2020).

Introduction 19

theory vis-à-vis theatre, as well as the role of performative practices in literary cultures today. Translation is not only an ethical relation between translator and reader or translator and text but also an embodied and material practice that takes place mundanely, everywhere, and in many respects for everyone. We contend that thinking translation in and as performance therefore cannot simply be a matter of extending the terms of its literary provenance to new modes of cultural production: it requires us to examine how our concept of translation is fundamentally changed and expanded in that process. Paying close attention to the inflections and relations embodied in acts of translation moves what Apter has called the 'translation zone' towards a site of multimodal, trans-medial and performative encounters.[46] Thus, translation no longer remains only a way of doing comparative literature under (or with or against) globalisation; as Avishek Ganguly has recently argued, in gesturing towards 'the planetary', translation becomes far more than a strategy for enabling theatrical or literary texts to 'pass' across imagined borders.[47] Translation emerges here as the vital way in which we all come to enact relations to others' languages, bodies, things and places. Drawing again on Butler, we therefore submit: translation performs assembly, it imagines collectivities.[48]

In the technophilic space of global capital, Apter notes, translation allows markets to flow and bodies to move. Yet it also confounds movement; arrests articulation. A case in point is the continued hegemony of 'Global English', a fantasy of (primarily written) monolingualism that contravenes the realities of the spoken: always thought to be 'broken', 'rotten', in the terms first put forward by Dohra Ahmad in *Rotten English: A Literary Anthology*, it is reimagined as creole pluralities by Ganguly in 'Global Englishes, Rough Futures'.[49] It is therefore necessary to note that the ways of translation can be deeply ambivalent: translation has worked to facilitate conquest and genocide in the past and it continues to generate 'moments of maximal translatability – violence, arrest, deportation,

---

[46] Emily Apter, *The Translation Zone* (Princeton: Princeton University Press, 2006). For a recent survey of the intersections of performance and inter-/trans-media see Sarah Bay-Cheng, Jennifer Parker-Starbuck and David Z. Saltz, eds., *Performance and Media: Taxonomies for a Changing Field* (Ann Arbor: University of Michigan Press, 2015).

[47] See Avishek Ganguly, 'Border Ethics: Translation and Planetarity in Spivak', *Intermédialités/Intermediality* 34 (2019), https://doi.org/10.7202/1070871ar

[48] See Judith Butler, *Notes toward a Performative Theory of Assembly* (Cambridge, MA: Harvard University Press, 2015).

[49] Dohra Ahmad, *Rotten English: A Literary Anthology* (New York: W. W. Norton, 2007); Avishek Ganguly, 'Global Englishes, Rough Futures', in *My Name Is Language*, edited by Nicoline van Harskamp (Berlin: Archive Books, 2020), 21–40.

linguistic profiling – that occur at borders'.[50] The ambivalence that attends the event of translation is not just of modern vintage either; drawing upon recent scholarship, it may not be an exaggeration to say that the entire process of European colonisation of the Americas beginning in the fifteenth century and the inception of settler-colonial regimes was mediated by large-scale acts of translation where it was put in service of empire building and mass religious conversion.[51] With the recent global financial meltdown, soaring crises of displaced and stateless peoples, pressing issues of climate justice, the resurgence of far-right nationalist-populist discourse in democratic polities and in violence against Black, Indigenous, Dalit and other minority communities, as well as a devastating pandemic, it has therefore never been more urgent to open up a space of thinking about the ways in which translation, never perfect but often enabling, literally takes its place – gets targeted or becomes weaponised, endangers intangible heritage in its lack but inaugurates new audiences when supported, imperils as well as saves lives at borders and war zones, in hastily put up field hospitals, and almost regularly, at sea. Translation, we are moved to claim, generates divergent and contradictory effects and affects, and not just as writing or on stage. If we are able to think of the regime of contemporary crises – economic, ecological, political, technological – as massive failures of imagination, then translation, imperfect but necessary, might well be one of our best antidotes.

This is not least because translation is 'a field of power'[52] – it is neither entirely past nor present, nor is it merely a moment of 'becoming'; it is traversed by genealogies, constituted performatively across ecologies, homes and environments we make and manage; homes that are temporary, broken, reconstituted or disappeared; undone and redone through bodies that are refused homes or shelter; that stick or migrate. Indeed, translation is, as Spivak highlights, 'a peculiar act of reparation – toward the language of the inside, a language in which we are "responsible"', suffering 'the guilt of seeing it as one language among many'.[53] Language,

---

[50] Apter, 'Translation at the Checkpoint', 72.

[51] See for instance Walter Mignolo and Freya Schiwy, 'Double Translation: Translation/Transculturation and the Colonial Difference', in *Translation and Ethnography: The Anthropological Challenge of Intercultural Understanding*, edited by Bernhard Streck and Tulio Maranhão (Tucson: University of Arizona Press, 2003), 3–30.

[52] Gayatri Chakravorty Spivak, 'More Thoughts on Cultural Translation', *transversal – eipcp multilingual webjournal*, April, 2008, http://eipcp.net/transversal/0608/spivak/en

[53] Spivak, 'Translation as Culture', 14. For a different take on translation as reparation, see Paul F. Bandia, *Translation as Reparation: Writing and Translation in Postcolonial Africa* (Manchester, UK; Kinderhook, NY: St. Jerome Publishing, 2008).

Introduction

like the feeling of a 'native tongue', is temporally and geoculturally entangled; it is an inalienably and ineffably relational practice, for Glissant, who suggests its 'loss' is never assured any more than its acquisition was given.[54] Translation remains a crossing, a form of *mestizaje*: a complex imbrication of belongings and differentials, states of rift and risk.[55] It is the stuff of everyday life – an act of repair – inscribed in embodied histories and practices.[56] We argue that translation, perhaps 'a *petit métier*', a form of perpetual cobbling, inhabits a performative zone that foregrounds fractured embodiments and fraught materialities.

Another Look at Internationalism: Translation, Performance and the World in the Twenty-first Century

Talking about how 'the question of 'diaspora'' in relation to peoples of African descent cannot be broached within the framework of monolingual English, Brent Edwards had powerfully argued that 'the cultures of black internationalism can be seen only *in translation*' (emphasis in original).[57] And more recently, in their 'Introduction' to a special issue of the interdisciplinary journal *translation* dedicated to the idea that 'translation is not a matter confined solely to the domain of linguistics', Naoki Sakai and Sandro Mezzadra argue, '[a] new theory and practice of translation can help us to imagine new spatial and political constellations that emerge out of the current spatial turmoil, and also test and challenge the stability of the "international world", and the Eurocentricity upon which the internationality of the modern world was initially erected.'[58] It is in the spirit of this wide-ranging journal issue, which invites the reader to imagine the heterogeneity that inheres in every medium, that we argue for an accent on the performative dimension of intersecting languages – something akin to Joseph Roach's notion of surrogation, as that which nearly replaces while simultaneously displacing what came before.[59] In the past

[54] See Édouard Glissant, 'Beyond Babel', *World Literature Today* 63, no. 4 (1989): 561–564, and generally his *Poetics of Relation*.

[55] See Gloria Anzaldúa, *Borderlands/La Frontera: The New Mestiza* (San Francisco: Aunt Lute, 1987).

[56] On translation as/and repair, see Avishek Ganguly, 'Five Theses on Repair in Most of the World', in *Repair: Sustainable Design Futures*, edited by Markus Berger and Kate Irvin (London and New York: Routledge, 2022), 15-17.

[57] Brent Hayes Edwards, *The Practice of Diaspora: Literature, Translation and the Rise of Black Internationalism* (Cambridge, MA and London, England, 2003), 7.

[58] Naoki Sakai and Sandro Mezzadra, 'Introduction', in *Translation: A Transdisciplinary Journal* 4 (2014): 9–29.

[59] Joseph Roach, *Cities of the Dead: Circum-Atlantic Performance* (New York: Columbia University Press, 1996).

few years it has been heartening to see new academic initiatives and journal issues take up this notion of translation in and as performance, a small but growing community of scholars and translators and performers with whom we align our work. Two prominent institutional endeavours that have increasingly engaged with the question of translation vis-à-vis performance are the annual Nida School of Translation Studies in Italy, and the 'Translation Acts' research initiative as part of the new Language Acts and Worldmaking project at King's College London discussed earlier.[60] Drawing upon Spivak's notion that the idiom does not go over in translation, Mark Fleishman and Sruti Bala have put together a set of articles in 'Translation and Performance in an era of Global Asymmetries', a recent issue of the *South African Theatre Journal* that focuses on the 'notion of the idiomatic, understood both linguistically and extra-linguistically – particularly in the form of bodies and voices'.[61] Bala argues that 'performance demands something different from the "standard" act of translation; it requires it to become something else', a theoretical position we are in full agreement with, in order to 'foreground an understanding of translation that is performative, where the act of performance serves to translate, and the act of translation lends itself to performance'.[62] In her Afterword to this volume, Bala further reflects on the notion of translation and justice, a way to respond to Spivak's question 'What is it to translate?' and to displace this question away from the habitual problem of 'doing justice' to an original work and thinking translationality instead as a perpetual carrying over. Asymmetry and incommensurability then give way to thinking something far more constantly horizontal, 'inter-subjective' and reparative; translation has too long done the work of colonisation, of injustice.[63]

Even as all of the following chapters thus offer performance as a medium and critical discourse particularly suited to the task of rethinking translation and geopolitics in the contemporary moment, we remain aware that this might well be a contingent and ephemeral framework, not only because translation (like performance) does not let us sit secure in any single discourse (or indeed language), but also because 'translation is always

---

[60] See 'Nida School of Translation Studies', Nida Research Centre for Translation, accessed 26 May 2021, www.nidaschool.org/nsts-home and 'Translation Acts', Language Acts and Worldmaking, accessed 26 May 2021, https://languageacts.org/translation-acts/

[61] Mark Fleishman and Sruti Bala, 'Translation and Performance in an Era of Global Asymmetries', *South African Theatre Journal* 32, no. 1 (2019): 1–5, 2.

[62] Sara Matchett and Mark Fleishman, 'Editorial: Translation and Performance in an Era of Global Asymmetries, Part 2', *South African Theatre Journal* 33, no. 1 (2020): 1–4, 1.

[63] Drawing upon Western philosophies of justice and rights, Apter has proposed another rethinking of this conjuncture in 'What Is Just Translation?', *Public Culture* 33 (1) (2021): 89–111.

Introduction 23

an imperfect solution to a problem'.[64] Like performance, which hovers between certain accomplishment (performative command) and uncertain retreat, translation tarries, it frustrates closure – keeps the problem of passage open, the journey and return. It is this space of vacillation that we seek to occupy, 'doing justice' by knowing translation will always fail to recuperate or claim, capture or circumscribe.

As the following chapters make clear, attempts to theorise the specificities of embodiment and the materiality of translation on the one hand, and its ethical and political work on the other, confirm the timeliness and importance of thinking translation performatively. The chapters are grouped into two sections that share a methodological and thematic focus. Where one approach to a volume on performance and translation in a global age might seek global coverage – a sort of 'world literature' fiction of completion (or its attempt), we have deliberately sought oscillations, eddies. The chapters in Part I present an approach to the interface between performance and translation that emphasises medium and method, including through orality, aurality and their entanglements within performative visuality: the way translation is not only a written code or enacted on the page but something that takes place in speech, sound and image, as a way of doing. Spanning a wide range including sound poetry, intermedial theatrical production and live audio description as well as theatrical surtitling and everyday accentuation – audible for instance in the sound of an 'r' – these chapters argue that translation is a performative act that takes place in situ. As such, translation emerges as a site-specific medium and way of being in the world. Translation mediates and as such articulates encounter as form.

We begin this section with 'Medieval Soundings, Modern Movements: Histories and Futures of Translation and Performance in Caroline Bergvall's *Drift*' by Joshua Davies, which engages with the work of performance poet and pioneer performance writer Bergvall, long an interlingual and translational writer working across histories of language and speech. Davies argues that Bergvall's highly visual and multilingually sounded poetry, in particular her recent book of poems *Drift*, a product of a long creative engagement with the Old English poem known as 'The Seafarer', operates at the intersections of translation and performance. Highlighting Bergvall's counterintuitive use of 'the medieval cultural record' to think through modern cultures of movement and migration, Davies shows how her work and its interlocutors 'excavate[s] the difference

---

[64] Donna Laundry and Gerald MacLean, eds., *The Spivak Reader* (London and New York: Routledge, 1995), 304.

between what is seen and what is sounded'. This work refuses chronology to find within language traces and remains of other times and tones. In 'Transcolonial Performance: Mohamed Rouabhi and the Translation of Race on the French Stage', Olivia C. Harrison reads two contemporary plays that stage 'the catachrestic translation of Blackness in France'. While *Vive la France!* stages a trenchant critique of structural racism in the French context, *All Power to the People!* performs a genealogy of 'the Black condition' in the United States. Emphasising the performance of race in translation, Harrison shows that it is precisely the multi-media presentation of Rouabhi's works, requiring, for instance, a simultaneous reading of projected text and listening to audio tracks while watching co-imbricated scenes of French and US racism that makes possible 'the co-appearance of both terms of translation, in the source and target language, in a way that a literal, textual translation does not'.

The third chapter in this section, 'Experiments in Surtitling: Performing Multilingual Translation Live and Onscreen in the Contemporary Theatres of Singapore, Taiwan and Berlin' by Alvin Eng Hui Lim, treats live surtitling in the theatre as an occasion for studying the performance of translation on the screen. Focusing on a range of multilingual performances – a live performance of *Exit* (2018) by Drama Box (Singapore); a recorded video of *Macbeth* (2007) by Tainaner Ensemble and *Li Er Zai Ci* (2001) by Contemporary Legend Theatre; and a live and livestreamed performance of *Beware of Pity* (2017) by Complicité at the Schaubühne Berlin – where textual display and spoken language come together to determine the audiences' toggling acts of engagement – Lim builds on Jean-Luc Nancy's concept of a 'visual sound'. The chapter draws our attention to how performed speech and surtitles play out a constant tension between what the audience sees and hears, and consequently between what they listen to and comprehend, or perhaps more significantly, don't. In 'Translating an Embodied Gaze: Theatre Audio Description, Bodies and Burlesque Performance at the Young Vic Theatre, London', Eleanor Margolies and Kirstin Smith further this interrogation of relationships between oral–aural modes and translation by tackling the confounding status of theatre audio description as only a textual translational operation rather than a simultaneously performative practice that is intermedial, embodied and situated. Examining two performances – Julie Atlas Muz and Mat Fraser's *Beauty and the Beast*, which they jointly audio-described, and Amelia Cavallo's self-audio-described cabaret act 'Scarf Dance', they draw attention to the ethics and politics of the theatrical gaze, identifying the need for a new 'critical audio description' consistent with what

Introduction 25

they recognise as 'a wide range of radical translation practices'. We conclude Part I with Kélina Gotman's 'Performative Accents: Bilingualism, Translation, Francophonie in Michèle Lalonde's Poster-Poem, "Speak White"'; here the author opens with the idea that lived speech takes place as a set of perpetual displacements, and that this takes place through an under-theorised, often contradictory double move: trying to erase one's accent in order to approach nearer to the pure, 'authentic' spoken version of one's language while de-stabilising normative speech where it works as a remnant of local colonial relations. Gotman routes her argument through Rey Chow and Khatibi among other thinkers of language to read Québécois poet Michèle Lalonde's landmark 'Speak White', offering ways of thinking what she calls after Chow affective and performative 'xenophony'. She concludes by highlighting the modulations that make everyday speech in translation a political act: a vibrant set of affiliations with other languages and genealogies. The text is itself reflexive, engaged in rethinking *francophonie* and the postcolonial movements of language that reorganise granular, phonemic power.

If the chapters in Part I explored translation as medium and method, then Part II of the volume turns to translation as a situated act most prominently vis-à-vis the nation-state and post-nationalism. While all the chapters in this volume consider questions of nationalism, settler/colonialism and post-colonialism through some combination of the linguistic, performative, archival and gestural play of alterities, the contributions in this part specifically think about national and trans-national sites of translation in performance. All four chapters highlight ways in which translation can be understood not only to capture (to render) moments or 'characters' in national and transnational history, but also to move these at times playfully, even roguishly, along. The ambiguities of national performances routed via archival 'text' and unarchived, or unarchivable bodies thus come more fully into view, as relational acts. Toggling between present archives and embodied moments of reading, as well as between the erasures and marks of bodily life in politically charged contexts including post-coloniality and de-colonisation, and trans-gender/queer trans-forms, this section rethinks what it means to read and to work with the temporality of the 'living' archive and the bodies captured – always only partially – within it.

We begin with 'Transembodiment as Translation: Staging the Włast/Komornicka Archive' by Bryce Lease, which examines how translation is performed when a contested archive is staged. Lease explores the life and times of Maria Komornicka, the Polish poet who in 1907 decided to transform herself physically and become known as Piotr Włast. While there is new artistic and scholarly interest in this act of transformation in contemporary writing on Polish poetry today, Lease focuses on a recent staging of the Włast/Komornicka archives by Weronika Szczawińska and Bartek Frąckowiak, *Komornicka. Biografia pozorna* [Komornicka. Ostensible biography] (2011), a production that attempts to 'translate this body from archival remains to stage presences'. This act of translating a transgressive figure, Lease argues, evidences what he calls (trans)embodiment. Daniel J. Ruppel's 'Translating Triumph: The Power of Print and the Performance of Empire in Early Modern Europe' comes next and revisits another archive-in-translation – the records of performances of imperial conquests in early modern print cultures in Europe. On the one hand, Ruppel reads the multi-modal translation strategies of the Hapsburg 'triumphs' in terms of what performance historian Roach, talking about 'performance genealogies', has called 'surrogation'; on the other hand, he argues that these multilingual documentations of performances, texts as well as objects, move beyond the now familiar 'domesticating/foreignizing' binary of translation and offer the possibility of being read as hetero- and trans-lingual address pace Naoki Sakai, rather than just as textual effects. Along the way, Ruppel's work also challenges positivistic nationalist histories that tend to see early modern western Europe as 'an inexorable coalescing of nations'.

In 'From Novella to Theatre and Opera: Translating "Otherness" in *Cavalleria Rusticana*', Enza De Francisci focuses on the multiple translations and varied careers of that late nineteenth-century novella, initially written in Sicilianised Italian dialect. Translated first into a play in Italian, and later into an opera, this complex of works, De Francisci argues, within the larger context of Risorgimento Italy, shows various performances of inter-lingual, inter-semiotic and inter-genre translations intimately tied to the creation of 'a particular "brand" of italianità and sicilianità' necessary for forging the newly unified country's artistic identity for internal and international circulation. The last chapter in this part, 'Gestural Archives: Transmission and Embodiment as Translation in Occupied Palestine' by UK-based choreographer Farah Saleh, documents Saleh's attempt to reconstruct a new archive of gestures, which she claims has either been left out or obscured in the Israeli and Palestinian nationalist narratives. Saleh's work on archiving, re-enacting and deconstructing a gestural collective identity furthers Lease's thinking about the translation of a body from the archive to the stage in terms of (trans)embodiment. Inspired by Vilém Flusser's writings, Saleh employs interactive video dance installation and participatory performance to put forward a way of thinking translation as and in choreographic gesture.

Introduction 27

Our penultimate contribution is an extended conversation on the topic of translation and performance between Gayatri Chakravorty Spivak and Avishek Ganguly: 'Translation is Always Not Enough...'. When asked about her speculations on any possible relationship between translation and performance in her own work, going back to her influential essay 'The Politics of Translation' published twenty-five years ago, Spivak begins by saying that the question might be more complex than simply positing a relationship. Instead, she refers the reader/listener first to Derrida's notion of 'spacing' as the place to begin thinking about non-languaged aspects of meaning-making (approaching, in this sense, the spatiality of theatre and performance) and as such as 'the work of death'; and second, to the idea that translation takes place after the death of the sonic/phonic body of language. We close with the aforementioned 'Can Translation do Justice?' by performance studies and decolonial critic Sruti Bala, who responds to Spivak's work on the politics of translation and reflects on the volume's contributions to theorising translation in and as performance as a whole; Bala's emphasis on justice yet again swerves the work of translation towards the ethical, a powerful mark of the relational possibilities and risks translation continues to afford every day. Collectively, the contributions and the interview in this volume explore the openings and limits of dominant thinking about translation as a global genre while attempting to move the discourse towards thinking translation in more capacious and expansive even if still imperfect ways – as an act that is granular, and performative: embodied, spoken, sited, archived, gestured, trans-medial, always in motion, holding and carrying through.

PART I

Translation as Medium and Method

CHAPTER I

Medieval Soundings, Modern Movements
Histories and Futures of Translation and Performance in Caroline Bergvall's Drift

Joshua Davies

Caroline Bergvall's poetry operates at the intersections of translation and performance. Multilingual and multimodal, her work pursues questions of subjectivity and power across time, space and discipline. This chapter follows the tracks of *Drift*, a work that was published as a book of poetry in 2014 but was also produced as a performance that toured Europe from 2013 and artwork first displayed in New York in 2015.

Drift is the product of a long-term creative engagement with the Old English poem known as 'The Seafarer'. It is not a translation, or not just a translation, and Bergvall uses the poem and its history as what she calls a 'template for writing' that brings other texts and histories into the orbit of her project and opens up a broader and deeper meditation on the poetics and cultural politics of migration.[1] The project operates in a performative now that brings disparate voices and events into contact, moving across national and linguistic boundaries and what Magreta de Grazia describes as that 'secular divide' between medieval and modern.[2] In the book, the reader encounters visual and verbal poems; words drawn from a variety of medieval and modern languages and none; stories of tourists, refugees and saints; and a reflection on the process of composition.

Bergvall's use of the medieval cultural record to think through modern cultures of movement is counterintuitive. According to Thomas Nail, for instance, writing in his 2015 book *The Figure of the Migrant*, 'the migrant is the political figure of *our time*.'[3] Bergvall, as a multilingual and mobile artist, has been concerned with questions of movement and cultural belonging throughout her career. But in *Drift* she gives particular focus to the question

---

[1] Caroline Bergvall, *Drift* (New York: Nightboat Books, 2014), 151.
[2] Margreta de Grazia, 'The Modern Divide: From Either Side'. *Journal of Medieval and Early Modern Studies* 37 (2007): 453.
[3] Thomas Nail, *The Figure of the Migrant* (Stanford: Stanford University Press, 2015), 235. Emphasis my own.

of the capaciousness of the concept of 'our time'. How are the boundaries of that collective, possessive identity formed, in the past and present? And how open are the borders of the present temporal moment? In what circumstances and under what pressures are peoples and cultures said to belong, or not, within 'our time'? *Drift* attempts to expand the boundaries of the historical present as Bergvall writes a history of the seen and not-seen, the present and the absent, the medieval and the modern, within the now.

'Drift' is a word with capacious meanings. Leisurely, peaceful bathing. Uncontrolled, dangerous accumulation. Driving. Driven. It is a word shared between English, Old Frisian, Dutch, Old Norse, Swedish and Danish.[4] As translation, it contains an allusion to the Situationist movement and Guy Debord's theorisation and practice of the 'derive',[5] often translated as 'drift'. It is a word that speaks eloquently of Bergvall's interests and practice. As Linda A. Kinnahan observes, Bergvall's poetry produces encounters with language as an 'infinitely flexible, layered, and multidimensional medium, in terms of time, space, and form'.[6] Or, as Bergvall put it in her essay on the poetic possibilities of Middle English, it is a word 'that reaches for the irritated, excitable uncertainties of our embodied spoken lives by working with, taking apart, seeing through the imposed complicities of linguistic networks and cultural scaffolds'.[7] This chapter will trace some of the networks and scaffolds *Drift* relies on and deconstructs, taking a direct route through the published book and using it to frame a discussion of the work's other sources, interests and iterations.[8] It will pursue the poem's performances and translations of scholarly and poetic practice to engage the histories the text reveals and the futures it imagines.[9]

---

[4] See Oxford English Dictionary, 'drift', in *Oxford English Dictionary* (Oxford: Oxford University Press, 2021), www.oed.com/view/Entry/57712?rskey=lnYglH&result=1&isAdvanced=false#eid.

[5] See Tom McDonagh, 'Situationist Space', in *Guy Debord and the Situationist International*, edited by Tom McDonagh (London: The MIT Press, 2002), 241–265.

[6] Linda A. Kinnahan, 'Interview with Caroline Bergvall'. *Contemporary Women's Writing* 5 (2011): 233.

[7] Linda A. Kinnahan, 'Interview with Caroline Bergvall', in *Meddle English: New and Selected Texts* (New York: Nightboat Books, 2011), 18. On Bergvall's medieval interests see, for instance, Robert Sheppard, *The Meaning of Form in Contemporary Innovative Poetry* (Basingstoke: Palgrave Macmillan, 2016), 85–91 and Richard Owens, 'Caroline Bergvall her Shorter Chaucer Tales'. *Postmedieval: A Journal of Medieval Cultural Studies* 6 (2015): 146–153.

[8] On Bergvall's 'iterative poetics', see Jacob Edmond, '"Let's Do a Gertrude Stein on It": Caroline Bergvall and Iterative Poetics'. *Journal of British and Irish Innovative Poetry* 3 (2011): 37–50.

[9] My thinking in this chapter has been formed to a large degree by my own collaborative work with Bergvall. Since 2015, alongside my colleague Professor Clare A. Lees, I have worked on a number of projects with her, including public performances, student-focused teaching sessions, research-led workshops and publications. Over the course of this chapter I acknowledge how some of the events on which we have worked together have shaped my ideas. See also the discussion of Bergvall's work in Clare Lees and Gillian Overing, *The Contemporary Medieval in Practice* (London: University College London Press, 2019), 49–72.

Medieval Soundings, Modern Movements

'Anon am I'

The published volume *Drift* begins with sixteen line drawings. Simultaneously markers of lines of yet-unwritten or already-erased poetry and a series of visual poems, the images prompt the reader to put their expectations aside and attend to the complexity and ambiguity of Bergvall's representations. Following the images, a section called 'Seafarer' begins with a poem entitled 'Song 1', the opening lines of which are intimately related to an Old English poem known as 'The Seafarer'. But Bergvall's text moves in and around the Old English 'Seafarer', sometimes translating, sometimes re-writing:

> Let me speak my true journeys own true songs
> I can make my sorry tale right soggy truth
> sothgied sodsgate some serious wrecan my ship
> sailing rekkies tell Hu ic how ache wracked from
> travel gedayswindled oft thrownabout bitterly
> tested gebanging head keeling at every beating
> waves What cursed fool grimly beshipped
> couldnt get signs during many a nightwacko
> caught between whats gone ok whats coming
> on crossing too close to the cliffs Blow wind
> blow, anon am I[10]

The opening line of this poem is a workable translation of the first line of the Old English poem: 'Mæg ic be me sylfum soðgied wrecan' (I can make a true song about myself).[11] From the second line onwards, however, Bergvall re-works some of the sounds and thoughts of the Old English to produce a language that is harder to place or parse. The second line ends with 'soggy truth', which puns on the sound and sense of 'soðgied' (true tales) but resists singular, transparent meaning, a transformation which is confirmed and qualified by the next words in line three: 'sothgied sodsgate some serious wrecan my ship'. Again, sounds are repeated and re-worked. The Old English 'wrecan', the semantic range of which incorporates vengeance, anger and misery, appears here to mean something akin to the Modern English words 'wreck' or 'wrecking'.[12] In the midst of the line it simultaneously means more and less

---

[10] Bergvall, *Drift*, 25.
[11] 'The Seafarer', in *The Exeter Anthology of Old English Poetry*, edited by Bernard J. Muir (Exeter: Exeter University Press, 1994), 232, line 1. All translations my own unless otherwise noted.
[12] See Joseph Bosworth, 'wrecan', in *An Anglo-Saxon Dictionary Online*, edited by Thomas Northcote Toller, Christ Sean, and Ondřej Tichy (Prague: Faculty of Arts, Charles University, 2014), https://bosworthtoller.com/36617

34 JOSHUA DAVIES

than this. Other allusions to Old English words are present too, including 'wrecca' (an exile)[13] and 'wreccan' (raise up).[14] Similar sounds emerge again in the fourth line as 'rekkies,' which puns on the Modern English 'recce', derived from 'reconnaissance',[15] as well as 'wrecan.' Tracking the similarities and differences of this word and its sounds reveals Bergvall's interest in how language gives form to, and conceals, histories, events and identities.[16]

While Bergvall creates 'wrecan' and 'rekkies' by bringing Modern English into contact with Old English, three words in lines five, six and eight – 'gedayswindled', 'gebanging' and 'nightwacko' – function by merging Old English and Modern English elements. The first, 'gedayswindled,' is a re-working of the Old English word 'geswincdagum', which means something like 'days of struggle'.[17] The meaning of 'gedayswindled' is not transparent but it conveys a sense of remembered dissatisfaction through the presence of 'swindled' and the use of the Old English prefix 'ge', which retains – just, possibly, for some speakers – a sense of past tense in Modern English due to its survival in German. A similar effect is achieved in 'gebanging', which conveys not just the sense of an aching head, but the idea that this discomfort has been caused by something in the recent past. The Old English word 'gebiden' (bide) occupies a place in the background of the word's workings, lending form to Bergvall's inventions.[18] Similarly, 'nightwacko' preserves the sound of the Old English 'nihtwaco' (nightwatch),[19] but offers a different and slightly obscure meaning.[20] What emerges from this process is an untimely language that refuses to reveal a singular source or meaning as Bergvall leaves the ambiguities of the poem and its text unresolved.

---

[13] See Bosworth, 'wrecca', in *An Anglo-Saxon Dictionary Online*, https://bosworthtoller.com/36618
[14] See Bosworth, 'wreccan', in *An Anglo-Saxon Dictionary Online*, https://bosworthtoller.com/36619
[15] See Oxford English Dictionary, 'recce', in *Oxford English Dictionary*, www.oed.com/view/Entry/159389?rskey=63wEgz&result=1&isAdvanced=false#eid
[16] Some of these questions were addressed in 'Adventures in the Illuminated Sphere', an event at Whitechapel Gallery, 26 February 2015, which I co-organised with Bergvall and Lees and featured contributions from Margreta Kern, Gillian Overing, Imogen Stidworthy, undergraduate and postgraduate students from the Department of English at King's College London, and others. See further: www.whitechapelgallery.org/events/adventures-in-the-illuminated-sphere/
[17] See Bosworth, 'ge-swinc-dæg', in *An Anglo-Saxon Dictionary Online*, https://bosworthtoller.com/16285
[18] See Bosworth, 'ge-bidan', in *An Anglo-Saxon Dictionary Online*, https://bosworthtoller.com/13666
[19] See Bosworth, 'niht-wacu', in *An Anglo-Saxon Dictionary Online*, https://bosworthtoller.com/23750
[20] My thinking regarding Bergvall's translation practice was developed during a project entitled 'Sonic illumination: Performance, play and the language of Old English poetry' that took place at King's College London in April 2015. Participants included Bergvall, Lees, Tom Chivers, Ewan Forster and Christopher Heighes, Jennifer Neville and students from the English Departments at King's College London and Royal Holloway, University of London.

Medieval Soundings, Modern Movements

The final line, 'Anon am I', which becomes the refrain of this group of poems, merges the speakers of the Old English poem and Bergvall's own texts by punning on contemporary and antiquated meanings of 'anon'. The phrase creates a collective 'I'. To use Richard Schechner's words, it is an 'I' in which 'multiple selves co-exist in an unresolved dialectical tension.'[21] The *Oxford English Dictionary* (*OED*) gives the primary contemporary meaning of 'anon' as an abbreviation of 'anonymous', but it also supplies a range of supplementary meanings, some of which are antiquated but remain present in Modern English. The most immediate of these alternative meanings is, as the *OED* describes, an expression of 'soon, in a short time, in a little while'. In Bergvall's use, then, this transforms the meaning of her refrain from, 'I am anonymous', to something like, 'soon I will become'. Another, more obscure, meaning of 'anon' is derived from Old English and described by the *OED* as 'in (or into) one body, company, or mass; in one; together; in one accord; in unity'.[22] The *OED* cites the Old English poem known as *Christ III* as evidence: 'teonleg somod þryþum bærneð þreo eal on an grimme togædre'[23] (the flame will burn the three together all at once, fiercely and forcefully). These meanings speak of the formation and disintegration of the self, across space and time. This interest is confirmed by the manner in which Bergvall brings other names, narratives and events into the trajectory of her poems, as the second sequence of poems in the book, entitled 'North', re-works elements of the *Vinland Sagas*, the stories of the Norse settlements in Greenland and North America, before weaving in the story of Ohthere of Hålogaland.[24] This is a narrative of northern exploration given by a visitor to King Alfred's court in ninth-century Wessex and interpolated into the so-called Alfredian translation of Orosius's *History against the Pagans*.[25] Bergvall uses his Norwegian name, Ottar, but draws on the Old English text, offering a micro-history of early medieval movement and encounter.

Bergvall's method in 'The Seafarer' poems fits what Marjorie Perloff identified, in an analysis of Bergvall's earlier performance, 'About Face' as a 'desire

---

[21] Richard Schechner, *Between Theatre and Anthropology* (Philadelphia: University of Pennsylvania Press, 1985), 6.

[22] See Oxford English Dictionary, 'anon', in *Oxford English Dictionary*, www.oed.com/view/Entry/8053?rskey=8RhJgU&result=2&isAdvanced=false#eid

[23] 'Christ in Judgment', in Muir, *Exeter Anthology*, 85, lines 102–104,

[24] See Gísli Sigurþsson, ed., *The Vinland Sagas: The Icelandic Sagas about the First Documented Voyages across the North Atlantic*, trans. Keneva Kunz (London: Penguin, 2008).

[25] See Malcolm Godden, ed. and trans., *An Old English History of the World: An Anglo-Saxon Rewriting of Orosius* (Cambridge, MA: Harvard University Press, 2016).

36   JOSHUA DAVIES

to decompose words so that their phonemic, morphemic and paragrammatic properties emerge'.[26] As the section progresses, the decomposition becomes more explicit. Here is the thirteenth poem in the sequence, titled 'Hafville 2':

> Then the wind ddrope and they were beset by w inds from then
> orth and fog for manyd ays they did not know where they were
> sailing Thef air wind f ailed and they wholly l ost their reck their
> reckoning did not not know from what direction D riven here and
> there The f og was sodense that they l ost all ss ense of dirrrtion and
> l ost thr course at sea There was much fog and the w inds were light
> and unf and unfavourable They driftedf ar and wide on the high sea
> Mo stof those onboard completely l ost l ost l ost their reckoning Th
> ec rew had no idea in which direction they were ststeering A thick
> fo g which d i d n o t l ift for days The sh ip was driven offf course tol
> and They were ossted about astea for a longt time and f iled tor each
> their destination We mbarkt and sailed but a fog so th but a fog so
> th but a fog so th th th th thik k overed us that we could scarcely see
> the poop or the prow of the boa t[27]

In these lines Bergvall's language fragments and re-forms. She excavates the difference between what is seen and what is sounded. As the opening line unfolds, the reader is forced to perform the diminishing drive of the wind as they are slowed down by the extra 'd' in 'ddrop' but then the wind picks up again and cleaves the word 'w inds' in two. The 'sodense' 'f og', which causes the seafarers to lose 'all ss ense of dirrrtion' causes the reader to struggle, too. In this poem the travellers are a group – a 'they' – whereas in others they are an 'I' or 'we'.

   Lyn Hejinian suggests that 'in writing that is propelled by sonic associations […] or what one might call musicality, the result may, paradoxically, be a form of realism, giving the poem's language material reality, palpability, presence, and worldliness'.[28] Throughout *Drift*, Bergvall's language work produces a sense of construction and deconstruction that is both physical and linguistic, internal and performed. One of the effects of this is a partial dissolution of the boundaries of the historical subject. De-centred subjectivity is even more pronounced in *Drift*'s performance and installation than in the published text. In performance, Bergvall stands in front of a screen of graphics by Thomas Köppel. Words and symbols, medieval and modern, float and surge, streaming in currents, in patterns the viewer can't

---

[26] Marjorie Perloff, 'The Oulipo Factor: The Procedural Poetics of Christian Bök and Caroline Bergvall'. *Textual Practice* 18 (2004): 41.
[27] Bergvall, *Drift*, 37.
[28] Lyn Hejinian, *The Language of Inquiry* (Berkeley: University of California Press, 2000), 330.

Medieval Soundings, Modern Movements 37

understand.[29] Bergvall's voice modulates between song and speech, whisper and call. Ingar Zach's percussion provides punctuation, otherworldly echoes and repetitions, and a non-human sense of scale.

In the installation of *Drift* at Callicoon Fine Arts, New York, a performance entitled 'Hafville (submerged voice)' presented text close to the published poems 'Hafville 5' and 'Hafville 6'.[30] In these texts repeated 't's fill two-and-a-half continuous pages before fragmented language reforms: 't go / t go off / t go off course / t go off course hafville' (42). In Bergvall's performance of these lines the multiple 't's are registered as something akin to the ticking of a clock. It is possible to detect her drawing of air. The voice becomes more and less than a tool. A means of giving body to sound, but also a way to mark the limits of signification.

As Gwendolen Muren writes, 'the poems of *Drift* have their most complete realisation in this intersection of page and performance: embodied and visualised in human pulp, the written work's struggle between fluidity and focus, between dispersed and singular subjectivity, becomes palpable'.[31] This struggle is caught in the short phrase 'Anon am I.' This is both a lament and a statement of privilege. It is an invocation of the loss of self and a recognition that, for some, that loss is only temporary, only a performance that might, in the future, come to an end. But it also recognises that performance, and a sense of anonymity, can lie at the centre of an 'I'. This is one of the tensions at the centre of *Drift*: a recognition that the historical currents that give shape to some identities subsume others. The Old English 'Seafarer' is both a source and a sounding board for this insight.

Medieval Soundings

The Old English poem called 'The Seafarer' survives in a manuscript commonly known as the Exeter Book. It is not known precisely when or by whom the poem was composed. It is generally agreed that the anthology was made c. 965–975 and that the texts themselves circulated for some time before this. The poem records a first-person account of a journey at sea. The speaker pursues 'wræccan lastum'[32] (paths of exile) before finding comfort in the Christian faith. The pains of distance are captured in the poem by the

[29] A short clip of the performance is available to view online. Caroline Bergvall, 'DRIFT excerpt 1 2013,' Vimeo video, 2:28, 12 November 2013, https://vimeo.com/79202631
[30] This performance is available online. Caroline Bergvall, 'Hafville (submerged voice),' Soundcloud audio, 5:27, 24 February 2015, https://soundcloud.com/carolinebergvall/hafville
[31] Gwendolen Muren, 'Review of *Drift* by Caroline Bergvall'. *Chicago Review* 59 (2015): 278.
[32] 'Seafarer', in Muir, *Exeter Anthology*, 233, line 15.

38 JOSHUA DAVIES

recitation of a list of absent pleasures that encodes a history of performance and identity. The speaker tells us that, for the seafarer, there is:

> Ne biþ him to hearpan hyge ne to hringþege
> ne to wife wyn ne to worulde hyht
> ne ymbe owiht elles nefne ymb yða gewealc;
> ac a hafað longunge se þe on lagu fundað.[33]

> (Not for him the sound of the harp nor the giving of rings
> nor the pleasures of women nor the glory of the world
> nor anything at all apart from the rolling waves;
> but he will always have a longing, he who journeys on the waves.)

These lines not only record socially privileged forms of masculine behaviour (poetic performance, gift giving and spending time with women) that the poem seems to value but also contain a micro-history of the text's engagement with performance. The reference to the 'hearpan' (harp) is an acknowledgement of the poem's own performance history.

It is generally accepted that it is likely that the Old English poems that survive in manuscripts circulated orally – probably before and possibly at the same time as they were copied and read in manuscripts. There are a few scenes in the Old English poetic record that seem to offer a direct depiction of poetic performance. In *Beowulf*, for instance, there are a number of moments that seem to depict public poetic performance of a highly culturally valued kind. The poem tells us that as part of festivities 'Scop hwilum sang' (a poet sometimes sang).[34] In another scene, at a heightened moment in the poem, the morning after Beowulf's fight with Grendel, the poem tells us that stories are told as part of the celebrations:

> guma gilphlæden,   cyninges þegn,
> sē ðe eal fela   gidda gemyndig,
> worn gemunde,   ealdgesegena
> sōðe gebunden[35]   word ōþer fand

> (a thane of the king's, a man laden with words, skilled at recalling songs, remembering scores of ancient stories, devised new words and cast a tale.)

Later in the same celebrations 'Hroþgares scop'[36] (Hrothgar's poet) tells another story in honour of the hero. Other Old English poems seem to

---

[33] 'Seafarer', in Muir, *Exeter Anthology*, 233, lines 44–47.
[34] *Klaeber's Beowulf: Fourth Edition*, edited by R. D. Fulk, Robert E. Bjork and John D. Niles (Toronto: University of Toronto Press, 2008), 19, line 496. All further references given in text by line number.
[35] *Klaeber's Beowulf*, ed. Fulk, Bjork and Niles, 31, lines 867–871.
[36] *Klaeber's Beowulf*, ed. Fulk, Bjork and Niles, 37, line 1066.

Medieval Soundings, Modern Movements

confirm the high-status, masculine nature of poetic performance. The poem known as *Deor* tells the story of a man who claims that 'ic hwile wæs Heodeninga scop, / dryhtne dyre' (for a while I was the bard of the Hedenings, / dear to my lord),[37] while the speaker of the poem known as *Widsith* appears to be some kind of travelling performer, or 'gleeman' (minstrel),[38] and is described as 'se þe monna mæst mægþa ofer eorþan, / folca geondferde' (he who had travelled furthest across the earth / among peoples).[39]

As these extracts suggest, poetry and its performance are bound up with ideas of masculinity in these early medieval texts. This connection rationalises the movement in 'The Seafarer' from the 'hearpan' (harp) to the 'wife wyn' (pleasures of women) as both activities share an interest in the proper performance of masculine identities. This fascination with masculinity is threaded through the most famous translation of 'The Seafarer', a text that stands in the shadows of Bergvall's work, which is Ezra Pound's hyper-archaic translation that was first published in 1911.[40] His strident work privileged sound over sense and moved between literal and figurative translations, rendering, to take just a few examples, 'siþas secgan'[41] (tell of journeys) as 'journey's jargon';[42] 'bitre breostceare'[43] (bitter heart-care) as 'bitter breast-cares';[44] 'burgum'[45] (cities) as 'burghers.'[46] Pound's bombastic transformations were often unencumbered by literal sense and grammatical rigour and attempted to reach back through Old English to produce a sense of deep-rooted and continuing masculine community. His verse is fascinated by what Chris Jones calls 'muscular vigour'.[47] His translation concludes without the final movement of the Old English

---

[37] 'Deor', in Muir, *Exeter Anthology*, 284, lines 36–37.

[38] 'Widsith', in Muir, *Exeter Anthology*, 246, line 136.

[39] 'Widsith', 241, lines 2–3. See further Emily V. Thornbury, *Becoming a Poet in Anglo-Saxon England* (Cambridge: Cambridge University Press, 2014), 16–19.

[40] Pound's 'Seafarer' was first published in *The New Age* 10 (1911): 107. I have taken the text of the poem from *The Norton Anthology of English Literature*, 5th ed., edited by Margaret Ferguson, Mary Jo Salter and Jon Stallworthy (New York: W. W. Norton and Co., 2005), 12–15. On Pound's translation see Chris Jones, *Strange Likeness: The Use of Old English in Twentieth-Century Poetry* (Oxford: Oxford University Press, 2006), 17–67 and Fred C. Robinson, '"The Might of the North": Pound's Anglo-Saxon Studies and *The Seafarer*' and 'Ezra Pound and the Old English Translation Tradition', in *The Tomb of Beowulf and Other Essays on Old English* (London: Blackwell, 1993), 259–274 and 275–303.

[41] 'Seafarer', in Muir, *Exeter Anthology*, 233, line 2.

[42] Pound, 'Seafarer', in Ferguson, Salter and Stallworthy, eds., *Norton Anthology*, 12, line 2.

[43] 'Seafarer', in Muir, *Exeter Anthology*, 233, line 4.

[44] Pound, 'Seafarer', in Ferguson, Salter and Stallworthy, eds., *Norton Anthology*, 13, line 4.

[45] 'Seafarer', in Muir, *Exeter Anthology*, 233, line 28.

[46] Pound, 'Seafarer', in Ferguson, Salter and Stallworthy, eds., *Norton Anthology*, 13, line 28.

[47] Jones, *Strange Likeness*, 35.

40   JOSHUA DAVIES

source text, which finds comfort in Christianity. Instead, Pound's version
ends with the hope that 'though he strew the grave with gold, / His born
brothers, their buried bodies / Be an unlikely treasure hoard'.[48] Where
Pound appears to read the past in terms of similarity, Bergvall insists the
meanings of medieval culture might be transformed to give form to other
identities. Language and cultural history move in both directions in her
text, opening up and changing past and the present.

Modern Movements

Bergvall's lines and their historical intertexts are written over in the next
sections of the book, which present a short series of grainy images before a
new section begins, entitled 'Report'. The new section begins with a short
paragraph:

> On March 27 2011 a ~10 m rubber boat overloaded with 72 migrants
> departed the port of Gargash adjacent to the Medina of Tripoli, Libya. This
> vessel was bound for Lampedusa Island, Italy 160 nm (nautical miles) to the
> north northwest.[49]

This introduces the second movement of the text. Bergvall's source material is the case of the so-called 'left-to-die boat'. After seventy-two migrants
were forced into a boat by Libyan soldiers in Tripoli and set course for
Lampedusa, the boat was allowed to drift across the Mediterranean Sea for
fourteen days, under the gaze of the NATO naval blockade of Libya and
numerous other military and commercial ships. After they ran out of fuel
and lost their satellite phone, the passengers in the boat were washed up
again on Libya's coast, although only eleven survived the journey and two
died shortly after.

'Report' is based on the work of Forensic Architecture, a research
agency based at Goldsmiths, University of London, that describes itself
as an interdisciplinary team of investigators that includes 'architects, soft-
ware developers, filmmakers, investigative journalists, artists, scientists
and lawyers'.[50] Their work uses surveillance technologies to interrogate
acts of violence, often carried out by governmental actors. In the case
of the 'left-to-die boat', Forensic Architecture's work was able to piece
together the movements of the vessel, its proximity to and engagement
with governmental and commercial boats and planes, and some of the

[48] Pound, 'Seafarer', in Ferguson, Salter and Stallworthy, eds., *Norton Anthology*, 14–15, lines 97–99.
[49] Bergvall, *Drift*, 71.
[50] Text taken from Forensic Architecture, at www.forensic-architecture.org/about/agency

experience of the people on the boat. 'Report' is not Bergvall's account of or response to Forensic Architecture's work; instead, it is an insertion of their work in to her project.[51] She uses their language and the 'Report' is their report. This means that the language of the survivors is recorded and, in performance, spoken by Bergvall. This is another act of writing that speaks to Bergvall's earlier work. In the project titled *Via*, for example, Bergvall printed forty-seven English translations of the opening tercet of Dante's *Inferno* as text and installation.[52] As Brian Reed writes of that project, in the 'Report' section of *Drift*, she 'lets herself dwindle to what one might call a content provider, a cut-and-paste language processor, and a rote reciter of others' words'.[53] This is not an unproblematic position to assume when the words spoken document such an extreme experience, and come from people who have been systematically mistreated and exploited. The power axis between speaker and poet is so imbalanced the appropriation is provocative. Indeed, some critics have chastised Bergvall for her use of the case.[54]

The possibility of exploitation is hard to ignore. But for Bergvall to produce a work on seafaring without acknowledging the death and despair that defines so many contemporary maritime journeys would be distasteful. She acknowledges the extremes of twenty-first century seafaring later in the text:

> These days travelling great distances by sea is mainly done for luxurious leisure, or as a last resort. It is the last option. How many overfilled open boats fleeing war zones and political oppression have resorted to dangerous, clandestine crossings of the Mediterranean Sea, of the Sicily Channel, of the Aegean Sea, of the Caribbean Sea, of the Red Sea, of the Gulf of Thailand, of the South China Sea.[55]

The story of the 'left-to-die boat' could never not be cruel and it is impossible to give the story of the death of sixty-four migrants the attention it requires without the possibility of exploitation. Yet for Bergvall to write about the cultures of the seas of Europe without writing about such stories would be negligent and unethical. In her attempt to produce a politically

---

[51] See further 'The Left-to-Die in a Boat'. Forensic Architecture, accessed 13 January 2022, www .forensic-architecture.org/case/left-die-boat/

[52] See Caroline Bergvall, *Fig* (Cambridge: Salt Publishing, 2005), 63–71. See further Sheppard, *The Meaning of Form*, 85–86.

[53] Brian Reed, *Phenomenal Reading: Essays on Modern and Contemporary Poetics* (Tuscaloosa: University of Alabama Press, 2012), 86.

[54] See for instance, Dana Levin, 'Get Lost,' *Boston Review*, 3 February 2015, http://bostonreview.net/ poetry/dana-levin-caroline-bergvall-drift-get-lost

[55] Bergvall, *Drift*, 148.

and ethically engaged account of the maritime cultures of Europe, Bergvall had to risk accusations of unethical and distasteful instrumentaliszation of the migrants' story. The cruelty of the 'left-to-die boat' is not Bergvall's. Or at least not just Bergvall's, in the sense that the event was allowed to unfold under the watchful gaze of international peacekeepers, government organisations acting in the name of their European citizens, it belongs to all those who would call themselves European.

Some of the complexities of Bergvall's use of the 'left-to-die boat' can be further drawn out through Rebecca Schneider's work on re-enactment. Schneider's work, like Bergvall's, is interested in the perception of time and 'artworks and re-enactment events that question temporal singularity'.[56] Schneider's study of the temporalities of performance, *Performing Remains*, uses American Civil War enactors as its central case study. This means that throughout her study what she delicately terms 'questions of the Confederacy' hang in the background.[57] While Schneider is clear about how her own political commitments do not align with those of the Confederacy or its belated supporters, nevertheless the possibility of her work engages racist thinking in the past and present.[58] As in Bergvall's work the relation between violence and its representation is unresolvable.

In field notes made during her research, which Schneider includes as part of her book, she gives an account of witnessing a Civil War battle re-enactment and acknowledges the problematic absence of non-white participants:

> Maybe twenty minutes in, a horse without a rider gallops out the woods and heads toward the ambulance. We can hear gunshot and muffled yelling. We see puffs of smoke.
>
> I don't know quite what I'm seeing, I think. That's not true, I tell myself: I'm seeing puffs of smoke. Again I don't feel like a spectator (there's nothing to see), but am I a witness to the nothing I see? What I'm witnessing is a mystery to me. Whatever it is, I can't see it. This event, it's very clear, is not given for me or to me, nor does it concern my ability to see. It is taking place elsewhere. I am a witness *to* the elsewhere of the event, and is that, in part, the reality that is touched here?? Elsewhere goes on, here and now?
>
> I begin to stare at a woman in front of me. I could reach out and touch her but I do not. I am riveted by her large handbag. The bag has the words, over and over again in faux Louis Vuitton style: Cherokee Cherokee Cherokee Cherokee Cherokee Cherokee Cherokee.

---

[56] Rebecca Schneider, *Performing Remains: Art and War in Times of Theatrical Reenactment* (Abingdon: Routledge, 2011), 19.

[57] Schneider, *Performing Remains*, 2.

[58] See, for instance, Schneider, *Performing Remains*, 9.

Medieval Soundings, Modern Movements

Nowhere, at any Civil War re-enactment I have attended so far, has the issue of 'Indian Removal' or 'Trail of Tears' – a veritable entr'acte for the Civil War itself – been anywhere recounted. Except here, on this faux European knock-off, among the detrital ghosts from the future. Who more properly owns the twitching inconsolable after-effects? The actors or the onlookers? And who is on which side of what? Where are the secessionists? Where the union? Which are the terrorists? Which the terrorized?

I begin to feel dizzy, and literally sick.[59]

It is worthwhile comparing Schneider's thoughts here with another account of a visit to a Civil War battlefield. This is what Ta-Nehisi Coates writes of one of his trips to Gettysburg, when he reflected on the history and continuing meanings of the Civil War from the farm of Abraham Brain, a black man whose property overlooked part of the battlefield:

Standing there, a century and a half later, I thought of one of Faulkner's characters famously recalling how this failure [the Confederate defeat at Gettysburg] tantalized the minds of all 'Southern' boys – 'It's all in the balance, it hasn't happened yet, it hasn't even begun...' All of Faulkner's Southern boys were white. But I, standing on the farm of a black man who fled with his family to stay free of the South, saw Pickett's soldiers charging through history, in wild pursuit of their strange birthright – the right to beat, rape, rob, and pillage the black body. That is all of what was 'in the balance,' the nostalgic moment's corrupt and unspeakable core.[60]

For Schneider it is the absence of violence that prompts an affective and somatic charge; for Coates it is the threat of continuing violence. Their different responses are conditioned by the different ways in which their bodies are positioned within the narratives of the past.[61] While the temporalities of re-enactment may be open and changeable, the narratives of race that define the American Civil War are closed and resolute.

Coates's reference to Faulkner's work is also worth thinking through. The scene he has in mind is from the 1948 novel *Intruder in the Dust*:

It's all now you see. Yesterday won't be over until tomorrow and tomorrow began ten thousand years ago. For every Southern boy fourteen years old, not once but whenever he wants it, there is the instant when it's still not yet two o'clock on that July afternoon in 1863, the brigades are in position behind the rail fence, the guns are laid and ready in the woods and the

---

[59] Schneider, *Performing Remains*, 59.

[60] Ta-Nehisi Coates, *Between the World and Me* (Melbourne: Text Publishing, 2015), 102.

[61] My phrasing here is borrowed from Stuart Hall, 'Cultural Identity and Diaspora', in *Identity: Community, Culture, Difference*, edited by Jonathan Rutherford (London: Lawrence and Wishart, 1990), 225, where Hall writes of 'the different ways we are positioned by, and position ourselves within, the narratives of the past'.

> furled flags are already loosened to break out and Pickett himself with his long oiled ringlets and his hat in one hand probably and his sword in the other looking up the hill waiting for Longstreet to give the word and it's all in the balance, it hasn't happened yet, it hasn't even begun yet, it not only hasn't begun yet but there is still time for it not to begin against that position and those circumstances which made more men than Garnett and Kemper and Armistead and Wilcox look grave yet it's going to begin, we all know that, we have come too far with too much at stake and that moment doesn't need even a fourteen-year-old boy to think This time. Maybe this time with all this much to lose than all this much to gain: Pennsylvania, Maryland, the world, the golden dome of Washington itself to crown with desperate and unbelievable victory the desperate gamble, the cast made two years ago; or to anyone who ever sailed a skiff under a quilt sail, the moment in 1492 when somebody thought This is it: the absolute edge of no return, to turn back now and make home or sail irrevocably on and either find land or plunge over the world's roaring rim.[62]

In Faulkner's invocation of '1492' we meet that secular divide between medieval and modern again. For Faulkner, unlike Bergvall, historical change is absolute. Even though his most famous meditation on historical events claims that 'the past is never dead. It's not even past', in the passage above it appears to be unchangeable.[63] In Bergvall's work, however, the past is open. Open to re-interpretation. Open to appropriation. A space of progressive cultural potential as well as histories of suffering. A resource. But she is alert to how different bodies are affected by the tides of history.

A quarter of a century before Faulkner published *Intruder in the Dust*, Alain Locke offered another meditation on the meanings of the medieval/modern divide in the United States. Writing on the mass black migration from the southern states of America, Locke described it as 'a deliberate flight not only from countryside to city, but from medieval America to modern'.[64] The power of Locke's statement resides in part in his use of the term medieval to signify the uncivilised cultures of the southern states, but he offers a broader and deeper insight as he suggests that people can move between temporal environments.[65] As *Drift* demonstrates, sometimes the

[62] William Faulkner, *Intruder in the Dust* (New York: Vintage Books, 1972), 194–195.

[63] William Faulkner, *Requiem for a Nun* (London: Vintage, 2015), 85.

[64] Alain Locke, 'The New Negro', in *The New Negro: Voices of Harlem*, edited by Alain Locke, with an introduction by Arnold Ramparsad (New York: Maxwell Macmillan International, 1992), 6. I owe this reference to Cord J. Whitaker's paper, 'Touching the Past in the Harlem Middle Ages', delivered at *Touching the Past Again*, George Washington University, 3 March 2018.

[65] On the temporal, spatial and racial meanings of 'the medieval' see Kathleen Davis, 'Time Behind the Veil: The Media, the Middle Ages, and Orientalism Now', in *The Postcolonial Middle Ages*, edited by Jeffrey Jerome Cohen (New York: Palgrave, 2000), 105–122.

Medieval Soundings, Modern Movements

boundary between the medieval and the modern is the boundary between the abject and the subject.[66] But as both Locke and Bergvall suggest, these boundaries are relational, in flux, even as they are violently enforced.

Locke's thinking engages with the kind of 'peculiar temporal inversion' that Forensic Architecture uncover. For example, they explain of their work with the United States' drone programme, that:

> According to US executive regulations, targeted assassinations cannot be justified as retributions for crimes that individuals have perpetrated in the past – this is the role of the judiciary and requires habeas corpus, the presentation of evidence, and a fair trial – but rather can be employed only in a predictive manner in order to stop 'imminent attacks' that otherwise would be committed in the future. Gradually, the category of imminence has become elastic and its applicability has been pushed back in time, losing its sense of immediacy.[67]

Similarly, the 'seafarers' of the 'left-to-die boat' were rendered un-immediate, beyond the here and now, when boats, planes and helicopters observed but did not save them. In its use of Forensic Architecture's work on the 'left-to-die boat', *Drift* asks its readers to reorient their perceptions of imminence to reveal new ways of imagining the meanings of the presence of the immediate, how we share time with others, who may be near or far to us, in time or space. This concern with what Eyal Weizman terms the 'threshold of detectability' brings together the judicial, the territorial and the cultural.[68] Like Weizman, Bergvall recognises that this threshold is not stable but situated in time and space, intersecting with cultural ideals and preoccupations. Bergvall asks her readers to consider who lives below the textual record, what kind of violence sustains that threshold and how the threshold might be moved.

'Language Started Shaking'

Following 'Report', the reader encounters a series of ten abstract images that resemble stargazing maps. After the images comes a new series of poems, 'Shake', which again draw on medieval sources, in this case the Old Norse 'Hávamál', a verse collection of wisdom and advice. Bergvall's

---

[66] The relationships between performance, environment and translation were the focus of a series of three workshops Lees and I organised in the summer of 2016, structured around contributions from Forster and Heighes, Laura Ferrarello and Bergvall.

[67] Eyal Weizman, *Forensic Architecture: Violence at the Threshold of Detectability* (Cambridge, MA: MIT Press, 2017), 31.

[68] Weizman, *Forensic Architecture*, 31–32.

five-line poems, like the source text, are concerned with relations with others, the transience of life and the social meanings of movement and travel.[69] Following fourteen short poems a series of drawings brings the section to a close. These drawings are hand-renderings of the letter 'þ' (thorn), an archaic and obscure relic of the written languages of the medieval north.

In the next section of the book, 'Log', Bergvall provides an account of her working process and unlocks, to a degree, some of the ambiguities of the text. She explains the line drawings which open the published text,[70] her use of 'The Seafarer', her encounter with the story of the 'left-to-die boat' and her decision to incorporate it into her work,[71] the paradoxes and tensions of her subject, and the obscure images, which are revealed to be magnified surveillance images of the boat.[72] The 'Log' is both a record of Bergvall's work and a partial map of it. It provides glimpses into the everyday labour of such work. The reader is told of Bergvall's struggles with the 'largely incomprehensible' Old English (130), how a domestic disaster threatened to de-rail her work,[73] of the exhaustion she feels after a day's rehearsal[74] and the 'blankness' of the writer's struggles.[75] It insists on the presence of the author's own lived experience within the work as it invites the reader to join in the navigation of this strange territory and re-imagine the textual and spatial journeys that give form to the modern subject.

The final two sections of the book continue to reflect on processes of making and unmaking. The penultimate text, 'NOÞING', is a meditation on the materiality of the body and language, working and re-working a discovery and rediscovery of 'some þing' that proves elusive: 'catch yourself look down but no theres no þing there'.[76] Bergvall's play here is on the wide semantic range of the Old English word 'þing' which gives us the Modern English word 'thing', but in Old English could signify either a material or immaterial object, such as a 'thing that is done', 'a circumstance' or 'a meeting'.[77] The short poem circles around these meanings as it moves from Modern English to Old English and, as a result, the meanings of the text solidify and disperse.

---

[69] See further David A. H. Evans ed., *Hávamál* (London: Viking Society for Northern Research, 1986).
[70] Bergvall, *Drift*, 146.
[71] Bergvall, *Drift*, 134.
[72] Bergvall, *Drift*, 157.
[73] Bergvall, *Drift*, 141–142.
[74] Bergvall, *Drift*, 129.
[75] Bergvall, *Drift*, 144.
[76] Bergvall, *Drift*, 171.
[77] See Bosworth, 'þing', in *An Anglo-Saxon Dictionary Online*, https://bosworthtoller.com/31866

Medieval Soundings, Modern Movements

The final section of the book draws the reader's attention tightly to the single graph 'þ', which is named 'thorn'. Bergvall locates the letter in linguistic, cultural and her own family history, from its use across northern Europe in the earlier Middle Ages to its redundancy in the age of the letterpress. She reads its 'success and ultimate demise' as a reflection of 'the contingencies and accidents of writing': 'it is a mysterious and tantalizing marker of the completely buried inscriptive and syntactical realities at the root of the English that we live within. It functions as an indice, a compressed reminder of the slow and radical overhaul towards greater simplification, mechanization and spelling chaos to which the language in both spoken and written modes would be submitted.'[78] The section and the book end with a description of the bodily pressures of producing the sound signified by 'þ'/'th', 'an unvoiced fricative [...] one of the most specific and difficult [sounds] of the language'. Bergvall notes that 'among late learners of the language [...] it remains a vexing and more or less chronic obstruction'.[79]

Who are those 'late learners of the language'? What other 'chronic obstructions' might they have faced? How have their bodies been positioned by the linguistic and cultural tides that swirl around those things we call 'English' and 'Europe'? What stories of migration give shape to, or discount, their experience? When – or where – is their now? Or then?

These are the question I am left with as I leave *Drift* behind. Its great historical, geographic and linguistic expanse is situated, finally, precisely, in the body of an unknown language learner, in their everyday experiences of translation and performance, trying to give voice to unfamiliar sounds. In that moment the medieval and modern histories and movements Bergvall invokes are left open as sites of cultural potential, of new means of initiating contact and belonging, of new ways of knowing the self and others. But the fragility of this possibility is recognised. *Drift* does not imagine that the ideological weight of the past is escapable, but it asks its readers to work towards a world in which it might be navigable, translated and given new voice.

---

[78] Bergvall, *Drift*, 180.
[79] Bergvall, *Drift*, 180–181.

CHAPTER 2

Transcolonial Performance
Mohamed Rouabhi and the Translation of Race on the French Stage

Olivia C. Harrison

How does one translate race?[1] This is a problem of translation in the narrow sense: what word should one choose in the target language to adequately render the denotations and connotations of a particular term in the source language? Should one attempt to remain faithful to the historical and geopolitical context of the source text, or adapt more freely to the cultural context of the target audience? This is also a problem of translation in a metaphoric sense, indeed in a sense close to the etymological meanings of both translation and metaphor: *transferre, metapherein*, to carry across or transpose in Latin and Greek, respectively. What is lost, what is gained, when we translate race? This is a problem of comparison, of relation, of commensurability and incommensurability. How does one translate race also begs the question: how does one speak of race comparatively?

In this chapter I explore the ways in which theatrical performance makes possible a mode of translation that does not substitute itself for the original, but brings the original back into circulation in a comparative, relational and transitive sense. This performative understanding of translation is, in fact, quite close to one of the primary meanings of translation, the act of displacing a person or thing from one place to another.[2] Translation does something; it is performative in the sense that is transitive. As Sandra Bermann has argued, this meaning is present, too, in the notion of interlingual translation.[3] Translation represents, aesthetically and politically,

[1] An earlier version of this chapter appeared in *Comparative Literature* 73, no. 4 (2021), with permission from the author and publisher. All translations are the author's own except where specified.
[2] According to the Trésor de la Langue Française, *traduire* means 1) to transfer, to put in prison; 2) to cite (citer) or compel to appear (*appeler à comparaître*) before the law. The legal definition of translation, first recorded in 1480, precedes the notion of interlingual translation (1520).
[3] In her essay on the performativity of linguistic translation, Bermann suggestively offers 'translation acts as a model for political and ethical relationality'. Bermann, 'Performing Translation', 294.

Transcolonial Performance 49

the original, even as it displaces it in translation.[4] To translate is to make appear for a second time, to represent, albeit in necessarily altered form, and for a different public. What if, taking Bermann's insights one step further, we were to think of translation as an embodied practice that requires the co-presence of both terms? How might performance allow for a more complex, multidirectional articulation of transcolonial identification, the process of speaking for and as the (post)colonized other?[5] Does theatrical performance – in French, *la représentation théâtrale* – make it possible to take on the role of the other without at the same time taking her place?

In order to begin answering these questions, I turn to the work of French-Algerian playwright Mohamed Rouabhi, whose plays elucidate the political and ethical stakes of translation in, and as, performance. Born in Paris in 1965 to Algerian migrants, Mohamed Rouabhi is the author of more than a dozen plays, most of which engage in the translation of race in some way: across imperial contexts (France and its empire, indigenous America, Palestine-Israel), languages (French, English, Arabic), and media (theatre, video, dance, music). The comparative dimension of his productions makes it particularly fruitful to think of them in, and as, translation. How does one translate race on and for the stage? What are the ethical limits and political stakes of performing Blackness in translation? To gesture toward an example I analyse later, what does it mean for a Black French woman to perform the role of a Black American woman in a French theatre? I explore these questions through a comparative reading of two recent plays by Rouabhi that stage the catachrestic translation of Blackness in France: *Vive la France* (Long live France, 2006) and *All Power to the People!* (2014), a play that interpolates the history of French empire in its denunciation of anti-Black racism in the United States. In my readings I draw attention to the ways in which Rouabhi's multimedia performances translate race across (post)colonial contexts, and also to the subtle fashion in which interlingual translation operates in his plays. As we will see, to think of race across imperial formations also requires the viewer/listener to translate race across languages.

---

[4] On the bifurcated meaning of representation in German as aesthetic (*darstellen*) and political (*vertreten*) representation, see Gayatri Spivak, 'Can the Subaltern Speak?', in *Marxism and the Interpretation of Culture*, edited by Cary Nelson and Lawrence Grossberg (Urbana: University of Illinois Press, 1988), 275. As David Lloyd has persuasively argued, in German *vertreten* includes the possibility not only of speaking for or standing as, but also of displacing those represented. David Lloyd, 'Representation's Coup', *Interventions* 16, no. 1 (2014): 8–9.

[5] I borrow the neologism *transcolonial* from Françoise Lionnet and Shu-mei Shih, who first used the term *transcolonialism* to describe the network of relations between formerly and still colonized sites across heterogeneous imperial formations. Françoise Lionnet and Shu-mei Shih, 'Introduction: Thinking through the Minor, Transnationally', in *Minor Transnationalism*, edited by F. Lionnet and S-M. Shih (Durham, NC: Duke University Press, 2005), 11.

50   OLIVIA C. HARRISON

Transcolonial Performance

Vive la France opened at the Canal 93 theatre in Bobigny, in the out-
skirts of Paris, on 1 December 2006, just over a year after urban rebel-
lions broke out across the disenfranchised communities in the peripheries
of France's cities, known collectively as *la banlieue*. Rouabhi had been
working on a play about France's colonial history when the death of two
adolescents, trapped in an electric transformer in Clichy-sous-Bois during
a police chase, sparked an urban uprising that radiated out from Seine-
Saint-Denis – the sprawling *département* that includes some of the poor-
est neighbourhoods of greater Paris – to the major cities of France. The
2005 *émeutes* (riots), as they were dubbed in the mainstream media, were
only the most recent manifestation of the social unrest that has periodi-
cally erupted in the disaffected *banlieues* of France since the early 1980s,
when the French-raised children of migrants from France's former colo-
nies in North and West Africa began to rise up against structural racism
and police violence in postcolonial France. This fraught context became
the framework of *Vive la France*, which opens with the now iconic photographic portraits of Zyed Benna and Bouna Traoré, the two boys whose
deaths sparked the uprising. In a series of tableaux drawn from French
colonial and postcolonial history, including the recruitment of colonial
troops, the Indochinese war and police violence in the contemporary *banlieue, Vive la France* offers a genealogy of the events that were unfolding
in real time when it premiered, and that continue to structure a deeply
divided France today.

An urgent indictment of French racism, *Vive la France* paints a complex
portrait of the legacies of French colonialism, drawing on a rich archive of
colonial and anticolonial documents.[6] The curtain opens to reveal a TV
monitor bearing the image of Zyed and Bouna, smiling for the camera. For
the nearly three hours that follow, a cast of some twenty actors, singers and
dancers perform scenes from France's colonial history and postcolonial

---

[6] In its use of extant documents, Rouabhi's dramaturgy is close to the documentary theatre of Peter
Weiss, which uses a montage of press, film, radio, music recording and other archives in order to
lift the 'artificial fog' of mainstream media and official discourses and provoke a critical response to
current events. The translation of extant documents on the theatre stage becomes a way to re-litigate
the recent past and present, in a way that hews closely to the juridical notion of translation found
in the French expression 'traduire en justice' ('to bring to justice'). Through 'a condensation of the
evidence', writes Weiss, 'documentary theater may become a tribunal'. Peter Weiss, 'The Material
and the Models: Notes Towards a Definition of Documentary Theatre', translated by Heinz
Bernard, *Theatre Quarterly* 1, no. 1 (1971): 41–43. On 'translational justice', see Emily Apter, 'Armed
Response: Translation as Judicial Hearing', *e-flux* 84 (2017), accessed 10 April 2020: www.e-flux.com/
journal/84/149339/armed-response-translation-as-judicial-hearing/

Transcolonial Performance 51

present in a multimedia tableau of violence: two female sign language interpreters translate the oral testimony of women protesting media representations of *banlieue* youth; a child recites the surrealist anticolonial manifesto, 'Ne visitez pas l'exposition coloniale' (Do not visit the colonial exhibition), as black-and-white photographic portraits of colonized subjects – the kind use by anthropologists and racial scientists – flash up on the screen behind him; a Black Marianne draped in the tricolour flag is paraded on stage as a voice recites excerpts from the first chapter of Frantz Fanon's classic work on anti-Black racism, *Black Skin, White Masks*. As this selective summary of scenes indicates, the contiguous and continuous experience of racism is the thread that links France's (post)colonial subjects, from Martinique to Vietnam, Algeria, and the *banlieue*, translating race across these disparate yet overlapping historical and geographic contexts. But the play also brings the memory of racism in the United States to bear on the history of antiracist struggle across the French empire, in a startling illustration of the political stakes of transcolonial performance.

Rouabhi's plays stage a complex critique of colonialism and racism, one that draws on the vocabulary of race in other contexts, and in particular, the language of Blackness in the United States. I begin my reading of *Vive la France* with a scene that interpolates American Blackness into the staging of French racism. Following a triptych of tableaux devoted to police brutality and media representations of the 2005 riots, this scene occupies a pivotal place in *Vive la France*, and serves as a transition between contemporary forms of racism and the scenes of colonial violence dramatized in the remainder of the play. It is also the only scene in the play that directly gives voice to a racialized subject, who confides to the audience in a haunting soliloquy reminiscent of Fanon's account of 'l'expérience vécue du Noir' ('the lived experience of the Black man').[7] I will tease out the Fanonian resonances of this monologue – in particular the translation of *noir* and *nègre* in late twentieth-century France – before addressing the interpolation of US racism into the scene of French racism in my reading of Rouabhi's play on the Black Panthers, *All Power to the People!*

In the penumbra of the stage, we see a Black man slowly don the uniform of a CRS (riot police) officer, while newspaper reports on 'bavures policières'

---

[7] Translated as 'The Fact of Blackness' by Charles Lam Markmann, 'L'expérience vécue du noir', the fifth chapter of *Peau noire, masques blancs*, begins with a classic scene of racial interpellation: 'Look! A Negro!' I follow Richard Philcox's literal translation of the title of chapter 5, 'The Lived Experience of the Black Man', which retains the phenomenological echoes of the original. Frantz Fanon, *Black Skin, White Masks*, translated by Charles Lam Markmann (New York: Grove, 1967), 109; Frantz Fanon, *Black Skin, White Masks*, translated by Richard Philcox (New York: Grove, 2008), 89.

(police killings of unarmed suspects) and video footage of police brutality flicker before our eyes to the tune of a melancholy cello, oral testimony about police violence, and, jarringly, Annie Cordy's 1977 upbeat hit 'Mon CRS' (My CRS). This audiovisual montage prepares the viewer for the translation of race that unfolds in this scene. In the aftermath of the global protests against police killings in summer 2020, this scene calls to mind countless citizens' videos of violent, often deadly, police interpellations in the United States, as well as relentless reports of police violence in the French *banlieue*. Indeed, it is chilling to read the newspaper clippings about police brutality projected onto the stage as the Black police officer changes into his uniform, and even more so to hear and see the raw footage of police interpellations that form a poignant sonic prelude to his monologue about racialization. By the time this ironic audiovisual montage is over, the 'petit policier' (little police officer, more idiomatically, rookie cop) is fully dressed. He loads his gun, faces the audience and begins his monologue, accompanied at intervals by melancholic string music by Shostakovich and the faint gurgling of a walkie-talkie in the background. Now fully decked out in police attire, the rookie cop begins to explain, in rhyming, colloquial French, his discovery of racism:

Dans le temps	Back in the day
On disait pas	No one used
Tous ces mots-là	Those words
Renoi, kebla,	*Renoi, kebla* [noir, black]
Pour parler d'moi.	To talk about me.
On disait rien, d'ailleurs	No one said anything, actually
Et c'était bien. . . .	And that was good. . . .
j'étais rien. . . .	I was nothing. . . .
Et même plus tard	And even later
Quand tout çà passe	When all that's over
Il est bien rare	People keep
Qu'on n'te parle pas	Talking to you
De ta race.	About your race
Qu'on n'te dise pas	People keep telling you
Qu't'as pas ta place	You're not in your place
Qu't'es comme la peste	You're like the plague.
T'es une menace	You're a menace.
Faut pas qu'tu restes	You can't stay here
Y faut qu'tu t'casses.	You gotta split.
T'as pas honte	Aren't you ashamed
Négro?	Negro?[8]

The rookie cop's soliloquy betrays a crisis in language, one that is commensurate with the process of racialization described by Fanon in *Black*

---

[8] I am citing the unpublished typescript of *Vive la France*, obtained courtesy of Mohamed Rouabhi.

Skin, White Masks, even if the nomenclatures have changed. Note the use of three separate terms to denote Blackness: 'renoi' (*noir* in French back slang or *verlan*), 'kebla' (black in *verlan*) and 'Négro'. Associated with the present ('après', later) rather than the past ('dans le temps', literally, in time), the first two terms are contemporary colloquial nomenclatures for Blackness in France. Paradoxically, their articulation in *verlan*, the slang of the disenfranchised *banlieues*, does not suffice to make them ascriptive identities – and this despite the appropriation of a US term, *Black*, associated with pride. In France, these words remain ways of 'talking … / about race', of 'telling you / you're not in your place'. They are the markers of a violent process of racialization that culminates with the first modern racial slur: *negro*, the Latin term for the colour (or rather absence of colour) black, translated throughout racial modernity as the name of human abjection. That the term *Négro* also bears the weight of the history of Black emancipation in the United States and of Negritude in the Francophone diaspora does not assuage the bite of this term in its French accented articulation, which since the heyday of slavery is inextricably linked to the darkest days of race-making in the French empire. 'Négro', here, is a modern-day translation of *nègre*, with all the violent associations of that term.

The Black man's transformation into a CRS officer was meant to defy the violence of naming made manifest in these derogatory terms: 'Même si ma peau / Elle est pas rose / Dans l'uniforme / Tu ressembles à tout / Même à un homme' (Even if my skin / Isn't pink / In uniform / You look like anything / Even a man). But the performance fails. His soliloquy reveals that he is not done with race, that he is still not in his place. In a jarring twist on the French lullaby, 'Maman, les petits bateaux' (Momma, the little boats), the rookie cop asks, 'Momma, why do the little boats drifting over the water have negroes in the hold?' The use of Guadeloupean Creole, 'tou cé ti mal' (all these brothers, a phrase that denotes affection and intimacy) anchors this evocation of the middle passage in a distinctly French colonial history, albeit one that is metonymically connected to British and US histories of slavery. The history of slavery is doubly intimate in this refrain, which uses the form of the lullaby and the mother tongue of Afro-Caribbean slaves to question the institution of slavery from the perspective of a child. In a spin on a popular children's song, the rookie cop recalls the question he used to pose his mother as a child:

> Dis-moi maman pourquoi les petits bateaux qui vont sur l'eau ont des
> négros, dans la cale
> Dis-moi papa c'est pas normal
> Y vont couler comme du papier imbibé d'eau
> Tou cé ti mal

54 OLIVIA C. HARRISON

Tell me, momma, why do the little boats floating on the water have
    negroes in the hold
Tell me, papa, it's not right,
They're going to sink like paper soaked in water
All these brothers

This question ushers in a dream-like vision of the middle passage that blurs
the boundaries between past and present, US plantations and European
metropoles:

> Et puis j'ai vu un homme
> Qui s'approchait
> Qui tenait
> Un verre de rhum
> Qui murmurait une chanson
> Du temps où les bisons
> Courraient sur la terre
> Du temps où le coton
> Naviguait sur les mers
>
> And then I saw a man
> Approaching
> Holding
> A glass of rum
> He was humming a song
> From the time when the bison
> Ran over the earth
> From the time when the cotton
> Sailed over the seas[9]

In this scene, the last in the opening sequence on police violence in the
banlieue, a Black police officer summons the vision of a man from the land
of bison and cotton before disappearing 'into the darkness'. Reminiscent of
Fanon's 'vieux nègre pris entre cinq whiskies, sa propre malédiction et la
haine raciste des Blancs' (old Negro who is trapped between five glasses of
whisky, the curse of his race and the racial hatred of the white men), this
figure beckons to the protagonist across time and space, anchoring the lived
experience of the Black man in France to the history of deportation from
Africa and the colonization of the American continent.[10] As if on cue, a
young woman enters stage, singing William L. Dawson's spiritual 'Soon Ah
Will Be Done' in accented English. She embraces him tenderly and slowly
escorts him off stage (Figure 2.1). The images of colonial America – bison,

[9] Rouabhi, *Vive la France*.
[10] Fanon, *Les damnés de la terre* (Paris: La Découverte, 2002), 231; Fanon, The *Wretched of the Earth*,
translated by Constance Farrington (New York: Grove, 1968), 243.

Figure 2.1 'Soon Ah Will Be Done'. Scene from *Vive la France*. Photograph by Eric Legrand. Courtesy of Mohamed Rouabhi.

cotton, and trees that hold the promise of hanging – and the soothing voice of a Black American woman are the vehicles for a transnational critique of racism in the play, one that implicates both France and the United States.

Before I elucidate the appearance of a Black American woman on the stage of French metropolitan and colonial racism, I'd like to pause on the critical silence surrounding this scene – a silence that is all the more puzzling given the accolades Rouabhi has received for his plays on Blackness in the United States. Although sympathetic reviewers praised Rouabhi for exposing the darker side of French history ('l'histoire, occultée, de la France'), the transcolonial dimensions of *Vive la France* were lost on most critics of the play.[11] Others condemned the play as a call for 'colonial repentance' and sui generis attack on the values of the French Republic.[12] Take, for example, the thoroughgoing critique delivered by historian and amateur playwright Gérard Noiriel, who takes Rouabhi to task for attacking the institutions of the French republic – the police, the national school

---

[11] Marie-José Sirach, 'Vive la France, et cetera', *L'Humanité*, 28 November 2006.
[12] On the polarizing notion of 'colonial repentance', see Daniel Lefeuvre, *Pour en finir avec la repentance coloniale* (Paris: Flammarion, 2006).

OLIVIA C. HARRISON

system, the government – and goes so far as to indict the play as a preachy 'lesson in civic destruction'. Even more problematic than its anarchism and didacticism, for Noiriel, is the fact that *Vive la France* constitutes an example of 'identitarian' theatre, a product of the commodification (read: Americanization) of identities in the 1980s, pithily packaged as *black, blanc, beur*. According to Noiriel, Rouabhi's play aggravates rather than remedies 'les clivages identitaires' (identitarian rifts), indulging in the memory of a particular group at the expense of others and, more gravely, at the expense of the project of *vivre ensemble* (living together).[13]

Noiriel's critique is unfounded on a number of scores, not least because Rouabhi's aim is to expose the violence of the state, past and present, rather than advocate for its destruction.[14] More seriously, the charge that *Vive la France* is a vehicle for US-style identity politics, unsurprising within the universalist, Republican discourse that dominates discussions of racism in France, completely ignores the multidirectional, relational analysis of race in the play, and its critique of racism in France via the memory of other racialized subjects, in particular Black Americans. In order to elucidate the transcolonial dimensions of *Vive la France*, I turn to a play that deals explicitly with the question of race in the United States, *All Power to the People!*

Translating Blackness

To date, Rouabhi has produced three plays on race in the United States: *Malcolm X* (2000), *Moins qu'un chien*, on Charles Mingus (2004) and *All Power to the People!* (2010).[15] None of these plays have elicited the kind of controversy occasioned by *Vive la France*, even though the discussion of race and racism in these plays is candid, and often bracing. This should not surprise us. The Black American condition often serves as a foil to shore up France's putative racelessness, while, paradoxically, African-American culture, music especially, has long been an object of fascination in France.

---

[13] Gérard Noiriel, *Histoire, théâtre et politique* (Marseille: Agone, 2009), 150–151. Noiriel culls from the Internet to evidence widespread popular condemnation of *Vive la France*. Although I have only been able to locate one of the sources he refers to, the Republican outrage expressed in the citations he gives is perfectly credible. Clochette, 'Vive la France de Mohamed Rouabhi', 29 February 2008, accessed 9 April 2020. http://passiondeslivres.over-blog.com/article-17196493.html

[14] Olivier Neveux makes a related argument, speculating that the violent reaction to plays like *Vive la France* is linked to the repression of racialized voices in France. Olivier Neveux, *Politiques du spectateur: les enjeux du théâtre politique aujourd'hui* (Paris: La Découverte, 2013), 116.

[15] *Un enfant de Dieu*, a play about the segregation of the first electric chair in the United States – Edison made a second chair for white death row inmates – was never realized. Email to author, 22 April 2017.

Transcolonial Performance

Rouabhi's plays about race in the United States were not controversial – but they should have been. Let me state this quite clearly: performing US racism on the French stage is a way to translate the question of race in France; it is a way to smuggle the question of racism back into a purportedly colour-blind society.

As Sara Ahmed reminds us in her work on the figure of the stranger, it is important to be wary of 'the violence of translation'.[16] The 'Black condition' is not identical in France and the United States, far from it.[17] But to suggest that Rouabhi's plays appropriate American Blackness to identitarian ends would ignore the multidirectional effects of transcolonial performance. As my readings will show, translation is not a one-way street in Rouabhi's plays. On the contrary, *Vive la France* and *All Power to the People!* stage Black American bodies, voices and archives that are themselves already engaged in transcolonial performance, bringing the history of French colonialism and the experience of racialization in France to bear on the experience of race in the United States.

Rouabhi's most recent play, *All Power to the People!*, is a genealogy, in ten scenes, of the Black condition in the United States, from chattel slavery to the election of the first Black president.[18] Like *Vive la France*, *All Power to the People!* has a didactic function: the annex materials that accompany the play include an exhaustive bibliography on anti-Black racism and Black liberation movements in the United States, as well as teaching materials for use in the classroom. The play itself is a multimedia repository of documents: a young man, interpreted by the play's choreographer, Hervé Sika, leafs through photographs of civil rights activists and victims of racist violence, including Emmett Till; an all-female cast dressed in slacks, leather jackets and black berets dances to Public Enemy's classic track 'Fight the Power', while excerpts of a Shirley Temple film, a Blaxploitation movie, and footage of the Black Panthers are projected on a screen behind them (Figure 2.2); Rouabhi, in full Panther gear, opens the 1970 Revolutionary People's Constitutional Convention in Philadelphia, flanked by heavily armed Panthers; a video recording of Barack Obama's 2008 election victory speech in Chicago plays while a white supremacist,

---

[16] Sara Ahmed, *Strange Encounters: Embodied Others in Postcoloniality* (London: Routledge, 2000), 83.

[17] I borrow the expression the 'Black condition' from Pap Ndiaye, whose book compares the experience of Blackness in France and the United States. Pap Ndiaye, *La condition noire: essai sur une minorité française* (Paris: Calmann-Lévy, 2008).

[18] My reading of *All Power to the People!* is based on the video uploaded on the Vimeo site of Rouabhi's theatre company. Les Acharnés – Mohamed Rouabhi, 'Power In entenso', Vimeo video, 1:31:50, 16 August 2014, www.vimeo.com/103497634

Figure 2.2 'Fight the Power'. Scene from *All Power to the People!* Photograph by Pascal Gély. Courtesy of Mohamed Rouabhi.

also played by Rouabhi, lurks at the back of the stage and loads his handgun. As we will see, these multiply framed documents are not merely objects of sympathetic consumption for Rouabhi's audience. If *All Power to the People!* translates documents of US (anti)racism for French (post) colonial subjects, it also makes present, through translation, an archive that has direct bearing on the history of racism in France.

I focus in my reading on two scenes that deploy extant documents to translate race on the French stage. Each scene is structured around sound recordings of poems by Black American artists – June Jordan and the Last Poets – recited in English and translated on stage through bodily performance and French text projected on a screen at the back of the stage. As I will show, multimedia performance is what makes apparent the co-imbrication of French and US racism in these scenes, translating the experience of racism in the United States to, and in, a French context.

The only explicit mention of France in *All Power to the People!* comes in a scene titled 'Black is Beautiful'. In the penumbra of the theatre we barely distinguish a female form, prostrate on the ground, slowly dragging herself toward a white rose. We hear a female voice recite June Jordan's 'Poem

Transcolonial Performance

About My Rights', a chilling indictment of racial and sexual violence, while a nearly complete translation is projected onto the screen behind her. Invoking the literal violence of sexual assault as well as the metaphor of colonial rape, Jordan's interpreter summons France to denounce colonialism, racism and sexism in the language of pan-African anticolonial resistance:

> and in France they say if the guy penetrates
> but does not ejaculate then he did not rape me . . .
> which is exactly like South Africa
> penetrating into Namibia penetrating into
> Angola . . .
> Do You Follow Me: We are the wrong people of
> the wrong skin on the wrong continent. . . .
> I am not wrong: Wrong is not my name
> My name is my own my own my own
> and I can't tell you who the hell set things up like this
> but I can tell you that from now on my resistance
> my simple and daily and nightly self-determination
> may very well cost you your life.[19]

Can it be a coincidence that French custom is what ushers in the image of colonial rape and plunder in a US poem performed in postcolonial France? It's hard to witness this scene without conjuring up the French colonial conquest of Africa, or to listen to Jordan's poem without hearing echoes of Aimé Césaire's *Notebook of a Return to the Native Land*, or thinking of the condition of the (post)colonial migrant in the metropole: 'we are the wrong people of the wrong skin on the wrong continent'.[20] Despite obvious differences between the trans-Atlantic passage, the plunder of Africa and trans-Mediterranean migration – they cannot be said to be 'exactly like' one another – Jordan's poem reveals that the lived experience of Black Americans is connected to a multidirectional history of colonial racism in which France plays a central role. The cruel irony that has made the descendants of deported African slaves American since the time of the bison and

---

[19] I am citing the unpublished typescript of *All Power to the People*, obtained courtesy of Mohamed Rouabhi. The recording used for the play is by New York-based performer Dawn Harden. For a complete version of 'Poem About My Rights', see June Jordan, *Passion: New Poems, 1977–1980* (Boston: Beacon Press, 1980), 86–89.

[20] The echoes of Césaire in Jordan's poem should not surprise us. Césaire's poem places Black America at the heart of Negritude, paying special tribute to the 'sanguineous, consanguineous land' of Virginia, Tennessee, Georgia and Alabama. 'ENOUGH OF THIS OUTRAGE!' clamours the poet, before taunting the colonizer: 'put up with me, I won't put up with you!' Aimé Césaire, *Notebook of a Return to the Native Land*, translated by Clayton Eshleman and Annette Smith (Middletown, CT: Wesleyan University Press, 2001), 16, 23.

Figure 2.3 'Die Nigga!' Screen capture of video recording of *All Power to the People!* Courtesy of Mohamed Rouabhi.

cotton fields, to borrow an image from *Vive la France*, cannot but summon the colonial histories that have turned Africans into French citizens for the French audience of a play about racism in the United States. The poet's claim to her own name can also be read, intertextually, as a rejoinder to the 'petit policier' who preferred to be 'nothing' rather than take on the name of racial abjection, be it a name subverted through *banlieue* slang ('renoi', 'kebla'). In a *mise en abyme* of transcolonial performance, the remediation of a poem that translates the experience of race across empires stages the very act of speaking for the colonized. Like the scene I analyse next, it also marks the birth of a new racial subject, one that takes place, I argue, in translation.

The scene that follows the performance of Jordan's poem, titled 'The Black Panther Party', is less about the transcolonial linkages between France and the United States – though, as I will suggest, the Last Poets' mention of Vietnam in the extract can be read in this way – than it is about the interlingual translation of Blackness in France. On stage, Black Panther leader Huey P. Newton, played by Sika, slowly rises from his chair as an original recording of the Last Poets' 1971 spoken word poem, 'Die Nigga!', plays offstage (Figure 2.3). Although I focus in my analysis on the crescendo of the poem's final verses, it is important to capture the rhythm and flow of the recording the audience hears, in English, in this scene:

> Walkin' down on 42nd Street
> Heard some white folks talkin'
> Had a riot yesterday
> Ten niggas died
> DIE NIGGA

Transcolonial Performance

Say what?
Ten niggas died?
Yeah
DIE NIGGA
Went down to Whitehall Street
Heard the sergeant reporting
Lots a Niggas dying in Viet Nam
DIE NIGGA
DIE NIGGA
NIGGA DIE
...

Go on and die Nigga
Been dying for 400 years.
Niggas know how to die
Niggas don't know nothing else but dying
Niggas dream 'bout dying
Niggas plan beautiful lives
For when they're dead
DIE NIGGA
Nigga preachers tell niggas 'bout heaven
Got to die first
DIE NIGGA
Niggas love dying
Niggas watch dying on TV
They love it
Niggas watch other Niggas die
They love it
DIE NIGGA
NIGGAS WATCH EMMETT TILL DIE
NIGGAS WATCHED MACK PARKER DIE
NIGGAS WATCHED JAMES CHANEY DIE
NIGGAS WATCHED BOBBY HUTTON DIE
NIGGAS WATCH NIGGAS DIE
NIGGAS WATCHED MEDGAR EVERS DIE
NIGGAS
WATCH
NIGGAS
DIE
NIGGAS DIE
NIGGAS...
DIE
DIE...
NIGGAS
DIE NIGGAS...
DIE NIGGAS!

62
OLIVIA C. HARRISON

DIE NIGGAS!!
DIE NIGGAS!!!
DIE NIGGAS!!!!
DIE NIGGAS!!!!!
DIE NIGGAS!!!!!!
DIE NIGGAS!!!!!!!
DIE NIGGAS!!!!!!!!
So BLACK FOLKS can take over![21]

A powerful critique of internalized racism, this poem takes the racist cliché of the passive victim – Fanon's drunken Negro, drowning his sorrows in the blues – and turns it on its head. Through a cadenced, hypnotic call and response, the ventriloquized racist taunt 'die niggas' turns into a command to kill the racial epithet itself, and make way for politically conscious 'Black folks'. Rouabhi's audience, it is important to note, has direct access to this poem through the audio recording in the Last Poets' own voice. But how is it translated on and for the stage? As Newton rises up, hypnotized by the Last Poets' mesmerizing recital, partial translations flash up on the black screen behind him. These are the final two verses projected on the screen: 'Les nègres crèvent pour que les noirs puissent prendre leur place.'

How does one translate race? What is lost, what is gained in translating *Black folks* as *les noirs*? What is lost, minimally, is the reference to W. E. B. Du Bois, and an entire corpus of antiracist thought leading up to the Black Panthers and beyond. What is gained, I want to argue, is transcolonial performance. Remember that the audience hears the Last Poets recite the mantra 'die niggas / so Black folks can take over', even as the French translation is projected on the screen: 'Les nègres crèvent pour que les noirs puissent prendre leur place.'[22] Even an audience not familiar with the modulations of these terms in English can hear that there is a difference, that a translational choice has been made. The rhythm of the spoken word performance parses out the Last Poets' differentiated use of *nigga*: from racial epithet to racialized subject, caught in the racial dialectic. The translation of *nigga* as *nègre* and of *Black folks* as *les noirs* in a French play about the Black condition makes evident the relational production of racial nomenclatures, even as it smuggles the question of

---

[21] Unpublished typescript of *All Power to the People!*, obtained courtesy of Mohamed Rouabhi. The sound recording used by Rouabhi is from the 2012 compilation *Listen Whitey! The Sounds of Black Power, 1967–1974*, and is freely available on YouTube. CargoRecordsGermany, 'The Original Last Poets – Die Nigga!!!', YouTube video, 3:17, 16 February 2015, www.youtube.com/watch?v=plcKB8H9jYY

[22] The translation used in the typescript places even more emphasis on the performative utterance of a new racial identity: 'CREVEZ NEGRES!!! / Pour que LES NOIRS puissent prendre leur place!'

Transcolonial Performance

race back into a language that forecloses it. It also crafts a transcolonial language of 'resistance' and 'self-determination', to echo the final verses of June Jordan's poem. An antiracist rallying cry delivered at the height of the United States' Vietnam war conjures up Fanon on the French stage, and brings us back to *Vive la France* via the first Indochinese war – one of the key moments in the play's fresco of French colonial violence – and the appearance of a US blues singer, whose song is a balm to the man who became a police officer so he could stop being a 'renoi', a 'kebla', a 'Négro'. Rouabhi's critics fail to register this performance of race in translation: an African-American woman sings away the troubles of a Black French man wearing a white mask.

What, then, is the place of translation in the kind of transcolonial performance exemplified by Rouabhi's plays? In closing I would like to suggest that Rouabhi's multimedia performances make possible the co-appearance of both terms of translation, in the source and target language, in a way that a literal, textual translation does not. Unlike the dual language typescript of *All Power to the People!*, its performance requires a simultaneous act of reading and listening, an act of translation in spectatorship. In this way, performance makes manifest the very process of translation, the co-appearance of the terms of translation.

Without exempting theatrical translation from a critique of appropriation, I have sought to mine transcolonial performance for its transformative possibilities and performative insurgencies, against the (neo)colonial policing of social roles and political identities. The fact that the performer sings a blues song with a French lilt should not distract us from her transformation into a Black American. Nor should the majority-female cast of a play about the (male) Black Panthers foreclose transcolonial identification. On the contrary, this displacement, this translation of racial identities is what constitutes transcolonial performance. Rouabhi's plays are about anything but the memory of a particular identity. They are about the comparative production of race. They are about the relational resistance to overlapping processes of racialization. They are about translating race on the French stage.

CHAPTER 3

Experiments in Surtitling
Performing Multilingual Translation Live and Onscreen in the Contemporary Theatres of Singapore, Taiwan and Berlin

Alvin Eng Hui Lim

Introduction

Live surtitling acts as a performative intersection between live performance and written text. Surtitles are often translations of an originally written text or transcribed from the spoken text. They appear as blocks of text on cue above, on or at the sides of the stage as part of the performance, though they may not always be synchronized with what is spoken onstage. This chapter critically explores the implications of including surtitles in: 1) live performance; 2) a multilingual performance archive; and 3) live streaming of a live performance. The discussion focusses on the subjective experience of translation through a live forum theatre piece, *Exit* (2018) by Drama Box (Singapore), online video recordings of *Macbeth* (2007) by Tainaner Ensemble and *Li Er Zai Ci* (2001) by Contemporary Legend Theatre, and both a live staging and YouTube streaming of *Beware of Pity* (2017) by Complicité and Schaubühne Berlin. The latter two case studies will shift into a critical review of how vertical text in comparison to horizontal text performatively calls into question how audience members access language through both hearing and seeing it as surtitles. This extends to how textual display and spoken language can combine to determine the subjective experience of a multilingual performance. In that respect, some of the observations in this chapter rely on my own subjective experience to gain insights into how hearing affects what one sees on stage, and vice versa, particularly in a context where translation plays an important role.

The case studies share the stage with English surtitles and perform what Enoch Brater calls a 'linguistically based cultural migration'.[1]

---

[1] Enoch Brater, 'Beckett, "Thou Art Translated"', in *Theatre Translation in Performance*, edited by S. Bigliazzi, P. Kofler and P. Ambrosi, 131.

Experiments in Surtitling

Similarly, Yvonne Griesel argues that surtitling is a form of 'translation hybrid' that performs 'an interlingual transfer', signalling notions of movement and travel.[2] Much has also been discussed about the function and hybridity of surtitling as translation and as complementary to live performance.[3] Moreover, surtitling for multilingual situations complicates a performance's reception: 'Who is the surtitling being done for?'[4] As Jennifer Lindsay points out, inside a theatre, audience members are always within earshot of the language spoken on stage. When they cannot read as quickly as they can hear, how would one describe the phenomenological dimension to the experience of watching a performance with surtitles?

Audience (Latin: *audire*, 'to hear') members may or may not listen to several voices and languages on stage. To view English onstage at the same time as listening to the Mandarin would immediately complicate both bodily activities of hearing and seeing. As a bilingual speaker of Mandarin and English, I am often caught between 'two minds' as the two languages (or more) meet in performance. In the context of encountering both languages in theatre, this chapter emphasizes hearing as an approach, for example, hearing the cadence and particular tones of Chinese languages as they are spoken vis-à-vis surtitles on screens. As audience members, we are always within earshot of the language spoken on stage and our hearing of this language becomes all the more complex when this spoken language is translated and displayed as surtitles. In reading the surtitles, text translates into a form of 'silent speech', an oxymoron that implicates the hearing of any spoken language on stage. Moreover, surtitles perform their own imprints via screens, where languages oscillate (or vibrate) between 'shores', as Hélène Cixous would say, translating the spoken into the written.[5] When I recall the various experiences of viewing surtitles and listening to sounds I am familiar with and not, I will explore these vibrations and direct the reader's attention toward the points of resonance and

---

[2] Yvonne Griesel, 'Surtitling: Surtitles an Other Hybrid on a Hybrid Stage', *Trans* 13 (2009): 120.

[3] See Estella Oncins, 'The Tyranny of the Tool: Surtitling Live Performances', *Perspectives: Studies in Translation Theory and Practice* 23, no. 1 (2015): 42–61.

[4] Jennifer Lindsay, 'Performing Translation: Hardja Susilo's Translation of Javanese Wayang Performance', in *Between Tongues: Translation and/in/in Performance in Asia*, edited by Jennifer Lindsay (Singapore: Singapore University Press, 2003), 152.

[5] Hélène Cixous, *Three Steps on the Ladder of Writing*, translated by S. Cornell and S. Sellers (New York: Columbia University Press, 1993), 3.

66 ALVIN ENG HUI LIM

limits between languages and examine the relationship between hearing and sight as they intercede through surtitles.

When languages switch back and forth, 'interlinguality' as a concept fails to fully encapsulate the relationship between hearing across languages. I would also like to add another question which Jean-Luc Nancy asks in *Listening*: 'under what conditions, by contrast, can one talk about a *visual sound?*[6] As I sense the sounds on stage, and as I read the surtitles and the sounds of that written language I understand resonate within me, I follow Nancy's inquiry into the 'appearance of phenomenology' and consider in this chapter whether surtitles are to be listened to rather than seen.[7] Whether one can comprehend the words or not, the flashing words in quick succession, I suggest, perform a palpable presence, a disembodiment and a trembling discrepancy, more so when multiple languages appear and varied voices percolate. Multilingual surtitling in particular draws attention to the asymmetries of our senses operating in several permutations: when sounds envelope the encounter and the text competes with the staged performance for attention; when the surtitles are ignored because the spoken language is understood; or when the eyes shift side to side in an attempt to see both the text and the performance in order to *listen* to (instead of spectating) the live performance. Hence, the performance of language (performed as speech and surtitles) plays out onstage as a constant tension between what the audience members see and hear, and consequently between what they listen to and comprehend, *or not*, as languages oscillate during the performance. When this experience is reproduced online as in the case of *Beware of Pity* (as I experienced it on YouTube)[8] and *Li Er Zai Ci* (on the Asian Shakespeare Intercultural Archive or A|S|I|A; a-s-i-a-web.org),[9] the interlingual transfer extends

---

[6] Jean-Luc Nancy, *Listening*, translated by Charlotte Mandell (New York: Fordham University Press, 2003), 3.

[7] Nancy, *Listening*, 4.

[8] Schaubühne Berlin and Complicité, 'Beware of Pity Live Stream', YouTube video, 12 February 2017. Accessed 30 January 2021. www.complicite.org/live-stream.php#

[9] Yong, Li Lan et al., *Asian Shakespeare Intercultural Archive* (A|S|I|A), 2nd ed., National University of Singapore, 2015. In English, Chinese, Japanese and Korean. Accessed 5 April 2018. http://a-s-i-a-web .org/en/home.php. The *Asian Shakespeare Intercultural Archive* (A|S|I|A) project is part of three successive research projects supported by the Singapore Ministry of Education (Relocating Intercultural Theatre, MOE2008-T2-1-110; Digital Archiving and Intercultural Performance, MOE2013-T2-1-011; and Digital Performance Scholarship, MOE2018-T2-2-092).

Experiments in Surtitling 67

to the digital medium, where the English translation lands as captions on a web browser. For the online version of *Li Er Zai Ci*, three language options (English, Mandarin and Japanese) in surtitles produce an expanded visual soundscape to which one may listen and read.

Live Surtitling: *Exit* (2018)

'Writing changes languages', writes Cixous, and the iconographic Chinese writing placed alongside English can bring about a marginal subjectivity that affects the way an audience member hears languages.[10] This involves both being excluded from and included in a performance when several writings appear with the performance. This is exemplified in the performance of *Exit* (directed by Rei Poh, 2018), a forum theatre performance staged in a makeshift space in Telok Blangah, a residential estate in Singapore. Open to the public, the performance was part of 'Both Sides, Now', co-presented by Lien Foundation, Ang Chin Moh Foundation, Drama Box and ArtsWok Collaborative and in collaboration with community partners Yishun Health (Wellness Kampung) and Montfort Care (Good Life!). The purpose of this project is to engage a community by bringing the theatre experience to residential spaces and to use the medium to address end-of-life issues.

The performers speak in several languages: some actors speak in English, others speak in Mandarin and Hokkien in varying competencies, and one of the actors speaks in Bahasa Melayu. One mounted screen (stage left) displays both the simplified form of Chinese characters and English surtitles, which appear when English is not spoken. Another screen (stage right) displays Bahasa Melayu almost throughout, corresponding to the language spoken by the character of the male nurse (Adib Kosnan) in his opening monologue and when he converses with the elderly Chinese character, Ah Po (Jalyn Han) who is multilingual. This is not often seen in Singapore, where productions provide only English surtitles when the performance is in another language. For *Exit*, the screens show three languages as surtitles.

The short play tells of two stories in a hospital ward – a 38-year-old man goes into a coma when cancer rapidly advances through his body. As his condition deteriorates, the oncologist suggests surgery. The man's

---

[10] Cixous, *Three Steps on the Ladder of Writing*, 3.

son opposes this as he feels that his father no longer wants to suffer in pain. His mother, however, insists on giving her spouse one last chance to fight the cancer. The parallel story tells of an elderly woman who is also diagnosed with cancer. She decides that she would rather return home to live out her last days. Tensions arise when her daughter refuses to accept her decision, believing that the doctors can treat the cancer. The characters constantly code switch, depending on the situation and the characters onstage. When Ah Po speaks to a Malay nurse, she speaks in a mix of Hokkien (her native language) and loosely uses some Bahasa Melayu words. In fact, her vernacular Hokkien often has loan words from Bahasa Melayu, such as 'suka' (or 'to like'). The nurse somewhat understands her and replies in Bahasa Melayu. When the son speaks to the elderly woman, he speaks to her in Mandarin but she replies to him in a mix of Hokkien and Mandarin.

This cross-cultural encounter results in a combination of gestural transfer, vocal communication, and translation and mistranslation. The nurse somewhat understands the Malay language spoken by Ah Po, who often struggles to find the right words and switches back to Hokkien instead, assuming that the nurse can understand her Hokkien due to her lack of Bahasa Melayu vocabulary. Audience members mediate both the familiar and the unfamiliar sounds, shifting as it were as Ah Po and the nurse move between languages and gesture what Paul Rae would call a 'stutterance'.[11] Rae's term encapsulates the phonological difficulties embodied in tongues that do not quite communicate yet move regardless, that is, as an utterance that stutters. In this case, the sounds multiply as both visual text as well as utterance. Alongside the spoken languages are the surtitles, which somewhat reflect the multilingual context of Singapore's linguistic environment but not necessarily the languages written in public spaces – only English is used on the signboard of Singapore's public hospitals. Linguistic difficulty arises when mixed visual sounds are sometimes abandoned for a singular lingua franca, which in the context of Singapore is English. Code switching is complicated by the presence of multiple languages as text, rapidly appearing and disappearing as the speech ensues and dissipates.

---

[11] Paul Rae, 'In Tongues: Translation, Embodiment, Performance', in *Translation in Asia: Theories, Practices, Histories*, edited by Jan Van Der Putten and Ronit Ricci (Manchester: St Jerome Publishing, 2011), 160.

Experiments in Surtitling

Bahasa Melayu 'Keluar' [As I am not a Bahasa Melayu speaker I am unable to provide a translation in Malay. This echoes my own experience seeing the Bahasa Melayu text on the screen during the performance of *Exit* but I was unable to read it. Instead, when Bahasa Melayu was spoken, I instinctively moved my eyes to the other screen with English and Chinese. I'm also assuming that most of my readers will read and understand the text in the middle column.]	*English* 'Exit' At some level, one is cognitively and affectively compelled to listen (depending on your first language) to the language one understands, while being aware of the languages on screens. As a multilingual speaker, I was able to read and listen to the English and the Mandarin. At the same time, I was acutely aware that the Chinese text is not a transliteration of the Hokkien language but a translation (from Hokkien to standard Mandarin). *If you understand Chinese characters, you'd realize that I didn't translate this sentence into Mandarin.*	*Mandarin* '出口' 从某个角度来看,每个人会随着各自的第一语言而偏向自己最熟悉最能理解的语言。他人同时也会意识到荧幕上的语文。由于我会三种语言,我能看懂英文和中文字幕,听得懂英语和新加坡华语。同一时间,我发现荧幕上的中文字幕并不是福建话的音译而是它的华文翻译。

At a performative level, the shifts of perception – from reading the text on the screens to returning my gaze to the performance – facilitates a supposed crossing of languages. At a cognitive level, when we read, as psychologist Keith Rayner argues:

> we continually make a series of short and rapid movements, called saccades, to bring new text into the centre of vision [...] Between saccades, our eyes remain relatively still for a brief period of time, called fixations, and during fixations the new information is processed.[12]

'To bring new text into the centre of vision' would be the task of surtitles, as saccades between words or characters, and between the spoken word

---

[12] See Keith Rayner, 'Eye Movements in Reading and Information Processing: 20 Years of Research', *Psychological Bulletin* 124 (1998): 372–422; Keith Rayner, 'The Thirty-fifth Sir Frederick Bartlett Lecture: Eye Movements and Attention in Reading, Scene Perception, and Visual Search', *Quarterly Journal of Experimental Psychology* 62 (2009): 1457–1506; and Erik D. Reichle, Keith Rayner and Alexander Pollatsek, 'The E-Z Reader Model of Eye-Movement Control in Reading: Comparisons to Other Models', *Behavioral and Brain Sciences* 26 (2003): 445–476; quoted in Chuanli Zang, Simon P. Liversedge, Xuejun Bai and Guoli Yan, 'Eye Movements during Chinese Reading', in *The Oxford Handbook of Eye Movements*, edited by Simon P. Liversedge, Iain D. Gilchrist and Stefan Everling (Oxford: Oxford University Press, 2011), 963.

and the surtitles. Nevertheless, when a language remains untranslated, or when the text is not equivalent to the spoken word, potential faultlines or 'stutterances' emerge that highlight similar ones present in Singapore's everyday linguistic landscape. While I 'hear' in multiple languages, including hearing my own voice reciting the texts that I read on the screen, my eyes may not be 'fixated' long enough to process the new information 'between saccades'. Surtitles, while facilitating an understanding for audience members who cannot understand the performance language, highlight the supposed interlingual transfers occurring at a rapid yet unequal pace, sometimes resulting in a dissonance. At an embodied level, an operator attempts to synchronize the surtitles with the live performance, at times missing the mark – either the text appears faster or slower than the speech, or sometimes an actor may ad lib. The former anticipates the yet to be spoken, while the latter distracts an audience member who has to wait for the text to appear before comprehending what an actor has already said.

Between languages, or rather the saccades of one's gaze – does one privilege the text or the human performer? – wavelike undulations of language voices percolate through the live event. Enveloped by the voice of a speaking performer, as well as the visual sounds of the flickering subtitles (often at the peripheries of the stage), a live performance produces an affective event that forces one to shift attention constantly. Taken together, as opposed to viewing it as 'an other hybrid',[13] surtitles are in fact the uneasy supplement to liveness, performing their own presence yet they are entangled alongside the bodies in performance, mediating language as a parallel to and a translation of the spoken. Notwithstanding the body behind the scenes operating the surtitles, cue by cue, these moving blocks of text demand a reading, a response in the shape of silent voices in the head, assuming one can read the text. At some point, even if one does not understand the words, the voices on stage haunt the text and vice versa, producing an echo chamber where one inevitably links the text to the speech, as fixations even if they do not actually correspond. In effect, there are moments of language learning, especially when one sees the text and attempts to reproduce the sounds and match the text with what is spoken. But there can also be moments of uncomfortable hearing as the language eludes comprehension. In my case, I read the Bahasa Melayu and I am able to some extent to recognize the sounds signified by the Romanized alphabetic language. However, meaning (and the correct pronunciation) eludes me. I have to shift my gaze to read

---

[13] Griesel, 'Surtitling: Surtitles an Other Hybrid on a Hybrid Stage', 119.

the screen with the English and Mandarin surtitles. Even then, I cannot assume that there is 'a high level of permeability between' Hokkien and Mandarin.[14] The Hokkien words do not fully correspond to the Chinese characters on the screen. As Lindsay points out, 'the gap between sound and sign of Chinese writing permits a specific kind of multilingualism in performance, both in the utterance of a script, and in the presentation of utterance to an audience.' *Exit*, however, exemplifies the difficulty in providing a 'common visual representation of words across sonic difference' and in fact, performs a 'unique kind of translation … between written sign and utterance, both by audiences and performers'.[15] The arrangement of the Chinese characters and the language-specific vocabularies (sometimes with loan words from other languages) complicate the translation between the written language and the spoken one. As a bilingual (English and Mandarin) speaker, reader and writer, I am always caught in a perpetual crossing between the two. Furthermore, as a trilingual (including Hokkien) speaker, the crossing, if any, raises the question about the porosity between languages (English, Mandarin, Hokkien and Bahasa Melayu). As a non-Malay speaker, I am constantly aware of my distance from the language. As a Hokkien speaker, I am engaging in my own act of translation as I figure out how the Chinese characters sound in Mandarin and in Hokkien.

There is a technical difference in the two terminologies of describing the capacity to cross languages. Describing this process as 'infiltration', Tong King Lee's argument embraces metaphors of hydrology, soil filtration and the passing through of liquid through a stratification of soil:

> English is the hegemonic language in Singapore, and thus possesses greater symbolic capital (Bourdieu, 1991) than Chinese, the mother-tongue language of the ethnic Chinese community. If we accept Bakhtin's view that language embodies socio-ideological contestations through its stratification, one may extend the argument that in a heterolingual text written in English and Chinese in Singapore, the Chinese language represents the social voice of the Chinese-speaking Chinese.[16]

This language, borrowed from the English translation of Bakhtin's claim that 'language is heteroglot from top to bottom', suggests a hierarchal and

---

[14] Jennifer Lindsay, 'Translation and/of/in Performance: New Connections', in *Between Tongues: Translation and/of/in Performance in Asia*, edited by Jennifer Lindsay (Singapore: Singapore University Press, 2003), 1–32, 21.

[15] Lindsay, 'Translation and/of/in Performance', 21.

[16] Tong King Lee, 'Asymmetry in Translating Heterolingualism: A Singapore Case Study'. *Perspectives: Studies in Translatology* 17 (2009): 72, https://doi.org/10.1080/09076760902825925

72 ALVIN ENG HUI LIM

vertical movement in the context of language code-switching.[17] Others, however, describe this as a crossing:

> An equally important concept is the juxtaposition between crossing and code-switching (Rampton, 1998). The latter is always between in-group languages, namely, languages for which there are well established speech communities to which the interlocutors belong. However crossing takes place between discrete speech communities such that a new linguistic space is created where identities can be re-negotiated. Whereas in crossing, the speakers are only aware of the superficial features of the language into which they are crossing, code-switchers tend to be bilingual.[18]

Code-switchers, as Vaish and Roslan argue, are the insiders and crossers are the outsiders; this presents a different movement – one that crosses horizontally between the inside and the outside. Nevertheless, they provide an intriguing perspective on the performativity of 'crossing', which connects to the movement of surtitles directed at gazes of audience members and, though not explicitly, sound waves that touch their eardrums:

> Finally, the idea of 'performance' is not as applicable to code-switching as it is to crossing. In crossing the speakers are staging an identity that requires them to pretend as if they are acting in a play. Code-switchers live multiple identities in their homes, schools, and other domains so the act of dramatization is not part of a bilingual's sociolinguistic behavior.[19]

The idea of 'performance' applies to bilinguals not because it is 'dramatization' that underpins what performance is. Rather, it pertains to lived identities that one struggles to enact in a situation that demands this, as it was for the production of *Exit*. It is not just the tongue that code-switches. Surtitles are, to begin with, a performative tool to provide translation of meaning when it cannot be conveyed in reality. At the fundamental level, *Exit* performs multilinguality not just at the level of speech but with surtitles, a process that pits text against speech, body against digital screens. This 'performance' lends itself to all the potential pitfalls and failed performances of 'crossing' – at the core of it is a performance of our inability to communicate across generations and even within supposed 'in-groups'. Instead of structuring the two as distinguishable units, that is, as inside and outside, *Exit* reflects the layered embodiments and shifts of text and speech, sometimes grasping for understanding while at other times paying full attention to the contradictions of identity formation.

---

[17] Michail M. Bakhtin, *The Dialogic Imagination: Four Essays,* edited by Michael Holquist, translated by Caryl Emerson and Michael Holquist (Austin, TX: University of Texas Press, 1981), 67.

[18] Viniti Vaish and Mardiana Roslan, '"Crossing" in Singapore', *World Englishes* 30, no. 3 (2011): 319.

[19] Vaish and Roslan, '"Crossing" in Singapore', 319.

Experiments in Surtitling

Displaying Translated Scripts with Video

While live surtitling carries all the above permutations of mistranslation and misperformance, surtitles in an online medium do something else to the assembly of text and performance. Transferred to a digital medium, the haptic connection (between the touchpad or mouse and the digital representation of 'touch' in the shape of a cursor) sets up the digital stage for the body and screen. On the subject of translations of Shakespeare's plays, Yong Li Lan argues that:

> Shakespeare's plays are irreducibly double wherever they are read or performed in translation, in that the English original acts as the presence of an echo or trace. When the play is performed in translation, if one remembers the original well and the production follows the original plot sequence, an English-speaking spectator can simultaneously 'hear' the words in Shakespeare's English and in another language being spoken, slightly out of sync with each other. The echo is heard as one follows the rhythm of interactions between the characters and the progress of the action. The experience becomes more complex if one remembers the play in a third language; either in addition to English, in which case one may hear two echoes doubling each other while the lines are spoken; or instead of English, when the original is rendered almost soundless.[20]

These echoes become pronounced when they appear as surtitles. The 'original' might be rendered 'almost soundless' but they can still reappear as surtitles. For Yong, surtitles perform 'translation as a paratext at the margins of the stage'.[21] Whether it is watching a live event in the theatre or a video recording on the Internet, 'the synchrony of surtitles doubles the spoken with a read text, making visible, by bridging, gaps between an audience member's linguistic and cultural community and the stage performance.'[22] Nevertheless, this 'bridge' may not always be visible to an audience member/viewer on the Internet.

This question of 'bridging' comes to the fore when I consider how Hokkien is compared to the Chinese common language (*Putonghua* / 普通话 or Mandarin). A dissonance in languages come into play again when what one hears does not correspond to what one sees (titles). In the production of *Macbeth* (2007) by Taiwanese theatre company Tainaner Ensemble, Shakespeare's text

---

[20] Yong Li Lan, 'Translating Performance: The Asian Shakespeare Intercultural Archive', in *The Oxford Handbook of Shakespeare and Performance*, edited by James C. Bulman (Oxford: Oxford University Press, 2017), 3, https://doi.org/10.1093/oxfordhb/9780199687169.013.37

[21] Yong Li Lan, 'After Translation', *Shakespeare Survey* 62 (2009): 285.

[22] Yong, 'Translating Performance', 9.

ALVIN ENG HUI LIM

Figure 3.1 Lady Macbeth's death scene, *Macbeth* (dir. Lu Po-Shen), Tainaner Ensemble (2007). Courtesy of the Asian Shakespeare Intercultural Archive (A|S|I|A, http://a-s-i-a-web.org).

is translated into Taiwanese *Minnanyu* (different from Singaporean Hokkien). The video recording comes with Traditional Chinese subtitles, a written style that allows both a Mandarin reading and a Taiwanese reading.

As the individual viewer, I would inevitably compare the Mandarin text to the Taiwanese speech through listening and translating between the two languages to work out the tonal differences. This is partly because of the multiple displays of text that highlight the plurality of languages. In Figure 3.1, the English text runs horizontally from left to right, then vertically from top to bottom. The Traditional Chinese subtitles, superimposed onto the video, reads from left to right, one line at a time. These transitions of text recall the contrast with older Chinese texts where characters run from top to bottom and across the page from right to left (see Table 3.1).

Table 3.1 shows the translated scripts (Chinese, Japanese and Korean). In reproducing the excerpts from the scripts, I recall that the East Asian languages were once commonly displayed as vertical texts. Changes in language policy in the 1950s saw the radical shift from vertical arrangement of characters to the horizontal style for all three language groups. A 1956 report in the *Far Eastern Survey* attempts to explain this shift in China:

Experiments in Surtitling

Table 3.1 *Excerpts from the translated scripts of Tainaner Ensemble's Macbeth in Chinese, English, Japanese, and Korean. Courtesy of the Asian Shakespeare Intercultural Archive (A|S|I|A, http://a-s-i-a-web.org).*

Macbeth.	Out, out, brief candle! Life's but a walking shadow; a poor player, That struts and frets his hour upon the stage, And then is heard no more. It is a tale Told by an idiot, full of sound and fury, Signifying nothing. (*Exit Lady Macbeth.*)[23]	人生只是白癡嘴裡的一段故事，又嚷又鬧。找不到一點意義。（馬克白夫人退場。） 一個可憐的演員上臺，又蹦又跳。過了一會兒，就再也聽不見他了。 馬克白。這短暫的燭光。人生不過是一個行走的影子。 馬克白夫人。去睡。 馬克白。熄滅吧。 馬克白夫人。去睡 馬克白。熄滅吧。
マクベス。	消えろ、消えろ、束の間の灯火！ 人生とは歩く影、哀れな役者にすぎない、 自分の出番のときだけ舞台の上で気取ったりわめいたり、 その後はもはや聞いてもらえない。狂人の物語、響きと怒りに満ちているが、 意味は全くない。（マクベス夫人退場。）	
맥베스.	꺼져라, 꺼져라, 덧없는 촛불이여! 인생은 그저 걸어 다니는 그림자에 지나지 않는다. 변변일 없는 배우가 거들먹거리고 또 안달을 내며 한 시간을 무대 위에서 떠들어대지만, 결국 아무도 듣는 이가 없구나. 이는 바보가 늘어놓는 이야기, 소음과 분노로 가득한, 아무 것도 중한 것 없는 이야기. (맥베스 부인 퇴장.)	

[23] Excerpts of trilingual script courtesy of Asian Shakespeare Intercultural Archive; Tainaner Ensemble's English translation of Chou Din Ban's Chinese translation; Japanese translation by Yami Sato, edited by Ken Takiguchi. In Yong Li Lan et al. (2015). *Asian Shakespeare Intercultural Archive* (A|S|I|A).

but the language experts in China recently concluded that Chinese should now be written like Western languages, horizontally, from left to right. This renovation is based upon the assumptions that it would be easier to insert Arabic numerals and foreign words in the text and that it would be less difficult and tiring to read, since the speed of perception and the width of eyespan is correlated. From January 1, 1956, a new way of horizontal typesetting has been adopted by practically all important newspapers, periodicals and other publications.[24]

This directional change coincided with the overall push for language simplification that went as far back as 1935, when the Republic of China officially accepted a list of 324 simplified characters, which were withdrawn the following year due to opposition.[25] The complete reformation of Chinese writing came after the establishment of the People's Republic of China, when Mao Zedong stated that 'Chinese writing must be reformed; it should follow the common direction in the world of phonetic spelling.'[26] The direction refers to both the move to simplify the Traditional Chinese script by decreasing the strokes in a character, as well as to introduce an alphabetical system. More a phonetic system to help with spelling and sound annotation,[27] the Pinyin was first introduced to move Chinese writing in this new direction, a direction that aimed to propel the language to match up to the Western alphabetical systems of writing – the left to right, horizontal arrangement of texts.

In lieu of surtitles in Simplified Chinese for the video recording, I now render the text from Traditional to Simplified for those who read in Simplified Chinese:

麦克白。　　　　熄灭吧。
麦克白夫人。　　去睡。
麦克白。　　　　熄灭吧。
麦克白夫人。　　去睡。
麦克白。　　　　这短暂的烛光。人生不过是一个行走的影子。
一个可怜的演员上台，又蹦又跳。过了一会儿，就再也听不见他了。
人生只是白痴嘴里的一段故事，又嚷又闹。找不到一点意义。

[24] Tao-Tai Hsia, 'The Language Revolution in Communist China', *Far Eastern Survey* 25, no. 10 (1956): 145–154, 149.

[25] Youguang Zhou, 'Language Planning of China: Accomplishments and Failures', *Journal of Asian Pacific Communication* 11, no. 1 (2001): 9–16.

[26] C. Cheng, 'Language Reform', in *Language and Linguistics in the People's Republic of China*, edited by W. Lehmann, (Austin: University of Texas Press, 1975), 41–54, p. 51.

[27] Shaomei Wang, 'Chinese Writing Reform: A Socio-psycholinguistic Perspective', in *Reading in Asian Languages: Making Sense of Written Texts in Chinese, Japanese, and Korean*, edited by Kenneth S. Goodman, Shaomei Wang, Mieko Iventosch and Yetta M. Goodman (Abingdon, UK: Routledge, 2012), 48.

In a study on the reading rates for reading both vertical and horizontal Chinese text, Sun, Morita and Stark found:

> for vertical Chinese text that the average saccade length (approximately 1.2 characters) was only about half that for horizontal Chinese text (approximately 2.6 characters), mean fixation duration was longer for vertical Chinese text (approximately 290 ms) than for horizontal Chinese text (approximately 260 ms), and consequently, reading rate was slower for vertical Chinese text (approximately 260 characters per minute, 170 equivalent words per minute) than for horizontal Chinese text (approximately 580 characters per minute, 390 equivalent words per minute). The vertical text was clearly read more slowly, and this was probably due to participants' increased skill in reading horizontal compared to vertical text.[28]

The rate of reading surtitles has a direct influence on how a viewer perceives the performance alongside the surtitles – one may choose to pause the video in order to finish reading the text, or another viewer may let the text run on, focusing instead on the recording. Either way, the experience of watching a recording in A|S|I|A challenges the viewer to visually connect two panels of viewing, with the eyes moving horizontally and vertically.

This affects a viewer's notion of time, where conventionally, the vertical typeset of Chinese characters relates to spatial constructs of time. As Benjamin K. Bergen and Ting Ting Chan Lau explain, 'we use language about space to describe time […] and English often is not explicit about the direction of the metaphorical motion it ascribes to time.'[29] Moreover, Lera Boroditsky summarizes that:

> In Mandarin,
> shàng [上]
> always refers to events closer to the past, and
> xià [下]
> always refers to events closer to the future.
> The same is true in English for
> earlier
> and
> later

---

[28] Fuchuan Sun, Michon Morita and Lawrence W. Stark, 'Comparative Patterns of Reading Eye Movement in Chinese and English', *Perception and Psychophysics* 37 (1985): 502–506; quoted in Zang, Liversedge, Bai, and Yan, 'Eye Movements', 964.

[29] Benjamin K. Bergen and Ting Ting Chan Lau, 'Writing Direction Affects How People Map Space onto Time', *Frontiers in Psychology* 3 (2012): 1.

terms. This is not true, however, for the other
English terms for time. Terms like
before/after, ahead/behind,
and
forward/back
can be used
not only to order events relative to the direction of motion of time, but also
    relative to the
observer.[30]

Through three experiments, Boroditsky shows how English and Mandarin speakers conceive time differently through language. For example, in one experiment, Boroditsky shows a sequence of white and black fish in a horizontal spatial prime and in a vertical spatial prime. For English language speakers, the white fish that is placed on the left of the black fish appears to be behind it. For those with Mandarin as their first language however, the vertical spatial prime of a black fish above the white fish produces the same temporal sequence:

Events closer
to the past were always said to be
above
or
higher than,
and events closer to the future were
always said to be
below
or
lower than.[31]

Studies in cognitive psychology suggests that the alignment of text has significant bearings on the viewing experience of it. Does a shift of alignment cause languages to read differently, or does it largely privilege the now commonplace left to right eye movements, as suggested by the subtitles superimposed onto video recordings and film? To echo the older convention of reading from top to bottom, the video and text layout of the A|S|I|A video interface arranges the video above the text. The panel design of the video player sets up a circular movement for the viewer; one 'touches' through the digital cursor and chooses the language; the

---

[30] Lera Boroditsky, 'Does Language Shape Thought?: Mandarin and English Speakers' Conceptions of Time', *Cognitive Psychology* 43 (2001): 511.
[31] Boroditsky, 'Does Language Shape Thought?', 17.

video plays (sometimes with subtitles) and the performance language envelops the listener and channels either a familiarity or unfamiliarity that predicates which language button to press in order to access and understand the performance despite the 'foreign' language. Eventually, the eyes choose to move between panels, between displays, but the sounds continue to perform. In that sense, the experience demands one to consider the relationship between writing and speech as it does in a live performance. However, in the most direct way, the scripts on the archive are not always matched to the performance: the performer ad libs, or the script provided by the theatre company to the archive is Shakespeare's text rather than the performance script. In most cases, the English translation is a translation of the production script, which is already a translation of Shakespeare's text. The overall effect is that the eyes and ears are put to the test, like the Boroditsky's experiments, where conceptions of time and space collapse to bring about an encounter with a video.

The weight of listening is signalled in the iconographic writing of Chinese: '听不见' (loosely translated as 'cannot be heard' or, in Macbeth's line, 'hear no more'). In a more literal translation, the above expression is a combination of:

'听' [to hear] + 不 [not] + 见 [to see]

Taken together, it somewhat means being unable to see what one hears. Being unable to hear negates the seeing. There is a stronger connection between the two senses as indicated in the expression. Macbeth's lines allude to the witches' prophecy, which is later proven to be true: when Birnam Wood appears to invade his castle, time collapses when the witches' prophecy that forewarned the optical illusion and Macbeth's fall comes into play. In that Chinese expression, sight and hearing negate each other, such that what is not heard is felt as a loss of sight.

Before switching languages on the A|S|I|A video platform, I am at a loss when I can hear the language but cannot read the language, most often the iconographic East Asian languages. But I can 'hear' when I see [听得见] the surtitles. So, I switch to the language I am familiar with. The platform works on this premise.

Before the script of *Li Er Zai Ci* goes into text display in the video player (see Figure 3.2), the three languages in the trilingual script are broken into blocks of text to facilitate the transfer from a Word document to cells in an Excel worksheet:

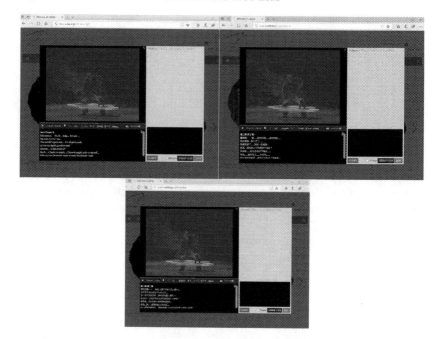

Figure 3.2 Viewing *Li Er Zai Ci* (dir. Wu Hsing-Kuo), Contemporary Legend Theatre (2001), in English, Mandarin and Japanese. Courtesy of the Asian Shakespeare Intercultural Archive (A|S|I|A, http://a-s-i-a-web.org).

Gloucester.	My eyes cannot see …
	it hurts …
羅斯特。	我的眼睛，看不見了…
	痛煞我也……
グロスター。	目が見えなくなってしまった…
	痛い…
	The candle's gone out … it's all pitch dark,
	It hurts …
	蠟燭熄滅了……眼前一片黑暗，
	痛煞我也……
	ろうそくが消えた…目の前は真っ暗だ。
	痛い…
	Oh heavens… oh heavens…
	It hurts…
	上天的，上天的…

痛煞我也……
神よ…おお、神よ…
痛い…[32]

I wonder how the text would be read if I were to follow the older publishing convention where text is printed from top to bottom, and how alphabetic language (English) would be read if it were to follow East Asian writing:

Gloucester. My eyes cannot see … it hurts …	痛い…	なってしまった…	グロスター。目が見えなく	痛煞我也……	了…	羅斯特。我的眼睛，看不见

To cite Vilém Flusser, a reconstruction such as the one above is about 'bringing material to a surface [...] to construct forms (e.g. letters)'.[33] This gesture of writing is but 'scratching at a surface [...] a penetrating, pressing gesture'. 'To be able to write', however, as I have done for this chapter, we require the following: a surface (an LED screen), a tool (a keyboard), characters (letters), a convention (the meaning of the letters and the QWERTY arrangement of letters on a keyboard), a message to be written (ideas) and writing.

Moreover, this gesture extends to preparing for the surtitles to be displayed on a screen, and in the case of a live performance, operated by presumably pressing on a key to move one block of text after another, cue by cue. Drawing from Flusser, we may argue that the complexity of writing 'results not so much from the number of essential factors as from their heterogeneity'.[34] This no doubt adds to the complexities of writing

---

[32] Excerpts of trilingual script courtesy of Asian Shakespeare Intercultural Archive; Chinese production script by Wu Hsing-Kuo, English translation by Lee Chee Keng, edited by Alvin Lim and Yong Li Lan; Japanese translation by Watanabe Satoko, edited by Ken Takiguchi. In Yong Li Lan et al., *Asian Shakespeare Intercultural Archive* (A|S|I|A).

[33] Vilém Flusser, 'The Gesture of Writing', in *Gestures*, translated by Nancy Ann Roth (Minneapolis: University of Minnesota Press, 2014), 19.

[34] Flusser, 'The Gesture of Writing', 20.

digitally. If the typewriter is 'a materialization of a whole dimension of Western existence in the twentieth century',[35] the computer and its digital tools are a materialization of a whole dimension of crossings between ocean cables that connect Internet users to those surfaces of writing. It is an expanded machine that, for Flusser, might perhaps permit freedom by changing the rules.

The multilingual textual display in the case of A|S|I|A, I argue, permits multiple directions. On one level, there is communicative potential in crossing languages. As Lindsay illustrates, 'the non-phonetic ideograms of Chinese characters, made visible to the audience as surtitles, allow for varied sound delivery in performance to be conveyed as a single text, and thus for relatively easy presentation of text-based performance in Chinese across Chinese language audiences.'[36] On another level, it is a device that works on the syntactic without semantics – at least, one acknowledges the presence of other languages without having to understand them because the visual sounds are predicated on its appearance; sounds that one may not be able to reproduce for non-phonetic languages. By arranging the text in relation to the video recording and with the options to play, pause, fast forward and rewind, one can seemingly manipulate time through the syntactics of the surtitles, video and notepad placed in panels. Where is the sound then? Fixation helps me to understand that I am at once taking up a position when I press a language button to reveal the translation. I see the sounds streamed as lines and digits, straining as it were to both listen and watch the streaming performance.

Streaming Lines and Digits

This strain, however, is a fixation that helps me to understand the 'absorptive qualities'[37] of hearing/not hearing surtitles as 'the taking up of a position as a subject of'[38] hearing (as opposed to vision). Here I am differing from Maaike Bleeker's position and analysis of vision and visuality in theatre. In my scenario, the hearing subject is absorbed by the visual sounds, resulting in a sense of difference when one hears and sees the polyglossia

---

[35] Flusser, 'The Gesture of Writing', 20.

[36] Jennifer Lindsay, 'Performing across the Sound Barrier', in *Babel or Behemoth: Language Trends in Asia*, edited by Jennifer Lindsay and Tan Ying Ying (Singapore: Asian Research Institute, 2003), 152.

[37] Here, I am adapting Maaike Bleeker's idea of 'focalization' in relation to seeing Chardin's paintings (1753). See Maaike Bleeker, 'Step Inside!', in *Visuality in the Theatre: The Locus of Looking* (Basingstoke, UK: Palgrave Macmillan, 2011), 33.

[38] Bleeker, 'Step Inside!', 33.

Experiments in Surtitling

through the syntactical relationship of text, video and digits. The digit, or digital, thus evokes all the performativity of gesture when I trace its etymological and anatomical parts – fingers and toes pointing to the abstract. Web browsers nevertheless function with a 'scroll' – either to flip your fingers up or down the touchpad, or to move the cursor of your mouse in order to facilitate a 'scrolling' of text and performance, perhaps after a search with a search engine. In other words, when I cannot listen to the performance language, my point of view moves to the surtitles of the online recording. This describes my second viewing of Complicité and Schaubühne Berlin's *Beware of Pity* (2017) on YouTube.[39] When I caught the performance at the Barbican Centre in 2017, I was able to relive my experience a day later when it was streamed live on 12 February 2017. Time no doubt collapsed spatially as I did not have to make the trip back to the Barbican to watch the performance; I watched it in the comfort of my bedroom. But in both cases, surtitles played an important role. Having studied German for two years, I could somewhat understand the performance, assisted for the most part by the English surtitles. In my second viewing on YouTube, the surtitles appeared at the bottom in two lines, superimposed (soft-subtitles) on the video. The performance was reminiscent of Complicité and Simon McBurney's *The Encounter* (2016) as *Beware of Pity* playfully mediated the inner voice of the protagonist, Anton Hofmiller, by having the ensemble members speak his inner monologue and project his speech into microphones. In both cases, the surtitles were often slower than the spoken words; the voices are not quite the character's. But the comparison of English surtitles and the spoken German reveals a fundamental difference. As the first conjugated verb (*schlafen* or 'to sleep') must be in the second position, the other verbs appear at the end of the line (*liegen* or 'to lie in a horizontal position'):

> Sie schläft. […]
> Nun erst, da sie mit geschlossenen Augen *liegt*, widerstandlos und reglos, kann ich das ein wenig eckige und gleichsam noch unfertige Antlitz *betrachten*.[40]
> She is asleep. […]
> Only now that she lies there with her eyes closed, can I really contemplate that face.

---

[39] Schaubühne Berlin and Complicité. 'Beware of Pity Live Stream'. The live stream and on-demand video are no longer available on YouTube.
[40] Stefan Zweig, 1939, *Ungeduld des Herzens*, Projekt Gutenberg. Accessed 5 April 2018. www.projekt-gutenberg.org/zweig/ungeduld/chap007.html

84 ALVIN ENG HUI LIM

Without the comparison of both the German text (that was faithfully adapted from Stefan Zweig's novel) and the English translation, this difference in language rules would have eluded my analysis. Language discrepancy remains between the two visual sounds of English and German. It strains to think in and between the two languages, but the delay in transitions between text and performance, surtitles and speech, echo the grammatical rule of German. The meaning of the verb, that is, the action or transitive verb is delayed, and the full meaning is only expressed at the end as punctuation. This is also the case when different voiceovers crowd around the single actor and punctuate our hearing of his inner thoughts, one voice at a time. Writing and speech conjugate, temporarily united in order to exchange cultural material; translation becomes embodied.

There is no unitary point of view but an expansion of perspectives, absorbing the bilingual into a reaction – do I carry on hearing or do I carry on seeing? Speaking on Jean Rousseau's *Essay on the Origin of Languages*, Jacques Derrida writes that 'the visible gesture, more natural and more expressive, can join itself as a supplement to speech, which is itself a substitute for gesture.'[41] Derrida offers a way of thinking of the supplementarity of gesture and speech, contingency and convention:

> This graphic of supplementarity is the origin of languages: it separates gesture and speech primitively united in the mythic purity, absolutely immediate and therefore natural, of the cry … Gesture is here an adjunct of speech, but this adjunct is not a supplementing by artifice, it is a re-course to a more natural, more expressive, more immediate sign … But if gesture supposes a distance and a spacing, a milieu of visibility: then speech supplements gesture. Everything in language is substitute, and this concept of substitute precedes the opposition of nature and culture: the supplement can equally well be natural (gesture) as artificial (speech).[42]

At the corporeal level, Derrida goes on to state that:

> Speech excites attention, the visible exacts it: is it because the ear is always open and offered to provocation, more passive than sight? One can *more naturally close one's* eyes or distract his glance than avoid listening.[43]

I would like to reformulate Bleeker's question in order to consider the supplementarity of speech and gesture vis-à-vis visuality: 'What kind of subjective

---

[41] Jacques Derrida, 'III Articulation: "That Movement of the Wand…"', in *Of Grammatology*, translated by Gayatri Chakravorty Spivak (Baltimore, MD: Johns Hopkins University Press, 1997), 235.
[42] Derrida, 'III Articulation', 235.
[43] Derrida, 'III Articulation', 235–256.

Experiments in Surtitling 85

point of view is implied by what is' heard?[44] When I hear the German language and view the English surtitles, I am engaging in an immediacy that requires my gesture of hearing. It may well be that I move the cursor to scroll or move my eyes rapidly from left to right and read the text, suggesting my agency and full use of my senses. It may also well be that the machine continues to run the digits, hidden in programming codes that build the frame of my experience, thus determining my attention on digital sounds and pixels, rendering me a more passive audience member than I was in the Barbican theatre. But if I were to pause, could I really contemplate that face of supplementarity: the muted voice? Later, the live streaming video of *Beware of Pity* turns into a recording streamed for a while longer for others to watch on YouTube. Going back to the video and being able to pause it, the experience of watching a streaming video becomes 'a symptom rather than an ontological given; a symptom that indicates not a match between the desires, expectations, presuppositions and anxieties that characterize an actual viewer and characteristics of the subject position implied by what is seen'.[45] There is an irreconcilable immediacy of speech and gesture, hearing and viewing, and then of a listening that is contingent on what remains unseen and absent.

Conclusion: 'Listen Up for the Cracks'

Returning to Nancy, listening:

> can and must *appear* to us not as a metaphor for access to self, but as the reality of this access, a reality consequently indissociably 'mine' and 'other,' 'singular' and 'plural,' as much as it is 'material' and 'spiritual' and 'signifying' and 'a-signifying'.[46]

Nancy reminds us that this presence, in the sense of an 'in the presence of' that is not 'in view of' or 'vis-à-vis', is 'rather a *coming* and a *passing*, and *extending* and a *penetrating*'.[47] This, I sense, gesticulates surtitled performance as emitting a resonance at the point of its dissonance. One's mishearing can effectuate a split present, which is at once made up of absent sounds (when I see the text but it is not performed) and present visuals (when I hear the voice but do not see the text), a sudden expansion of the states one can translate into and out of, or be alienated from when a visual sound is illegible. In sum, surtitling highlights this phenomenological dimension.

---

[44] Bleeker, 'Step Inside!', 37.
[45] Bleeker, 'Step Inside!', 37–38.
[46] Nancy, *Listening*, 12.
[47] Nancy, *Listening*, 13.

This chapter is an attempt to illustrate how performance and the performativity of surtitles can foreground the intricate movement of visual sounds in everyday lived experience, especially in a theatre as well as onscreen. In turn, the difficulties of negotiating language differences in a pluralistic society offers grounds for creative work to explore the tensions and intersections of languages in everyday speech and writing. My final concluding heading, 'listen up for the cracks', is a phrase from Baz Kershaw's epilogue in *Theatre Ecology*.[48] For me, it performatively points to the capacity of surtitled performance to reveal the cracks of theatre, not to insist on the impossibility of comprehension because of language differences, but to imply the points of hearing that make explicit the cracks, as if visualized through hearing. This hearing can become a form of listening, a discursive gesture that contemplates the subjective experience of translation. Given the vibration of shores and substitutions between gesture and speech, and between languages, surtitling is an entry point to think through the performance of translation at its immediacy, as we simultaneously hear and see the cracks.

[48] Baz Kershaw, 'Epilogue: Listen Up for the Cracks', in *Theatre Ecology* (Cambridge: Cambridge University Press, 2007), 320.

CHAPTER 4

Translating an Embodied Gaze
Theatre Audio Description, Bodies and Burlesque Performance at the Young Vic Theatre, London

Eleanor Margolies and Kirstin Smith

The 'differences' between images and language are not merely formal matters; they are, in practice, linked to things like the difference between the (speaking) self and the (seen) other; between telling and showing; between 'hearsay' and 'eyewitness' testimony; between words (heard, quoted, inscribed) and objects or actions (seen, depicted, described); between sensory channels, traditions of representation, and modes of experience.

W. J. T. Mitchell, *Picture Theory.*

Jess reaches up and runs a finger between Beauty's breasts and down her stomach. Beauty turns around and leans on the banister, baring and rippling her bottom, as Jess sprays it with a perfume puffer. [Bell tolls] Beauty sweeps down, robe hanging loosely around her, and sits at the table. With a confident strut, Beast makes his way down the stairs, his robe hanging open. They hold each other's gaze.

Eleanor Margolies and Kirstin Smith, audio description (AD) script for *Beauty and the Beast*, Young Vic Theatre, 2013.

This chapter explores the translation between images and language in live performance and the implications for the representation of bodies. It springs from our experiences of working together as audio describers of theatre for blind and partially sighted theatre-goers for over ten years, collaborating with each other and many other describers, while at the same time working in performance research. Writing about theatre as part of access provision has raised many questions for us around representation and embodiment. We consider AD as an embodied translation practice, and examine how it constructs a theatrical gaze. We analyse a production that we jointly audio described, Julie Atlas Muz and Mat Fraser's *Beauty and the Beast*, before considering how attending to the gaze in burlesque can help us to develop what we will term 'critical audio description'. As an example, we discuss Amelia Cavallo's cabaret act, 'Scarf Dance', which generates its own AD. This performance suggests some ways in which a theatrical gaze can be constructed and deconstructed, with implications in terms of ethics, collaboration, register and embodiment.

From Images to Language

Giving a verbal description of people and things is an everyday practice that usually only comes to attention when we have difficulty in finding the appropriate word. The stakes are much higher for written descriptions. In many contexts, from museums to police stations, the accuracy of a description can determine the fate of an object or subject.[1] The term 'audio description' was coined in the 1980s to refer to an access service for blind and partially sighted people, typically characterised as 'a verbal commentary' on 'visual elements'.[2] We'll refer to this as 'AD' to distinguish the professional practice of describing for blind and partially sighted audience members from 'description' in literary and everyday contexts.

For the production of *Beauty and the Beast* we focus on here, we followed the standard model of AD for theatre, in which a pair of describers working together create three distinct texts for each production. The first is a **written introduction** to the set, characters, costumes and style of a production. This is recorded and distributed to bookers a week or two ahead of the date of the described performance. The introduction may also be made available for download, and it is usually read aloud just before the performance, in a version adapted for live delivery. The second text is the **live description**. This is written in advance, with reference to a script and a recording of the production, with the text fitted into gaps between words and any sound effects. The timing of the live description is adjusted to the syllable in a live rehearsal in which the describers listen to each other and give feedback on

---

[1] Each profession has its own system for describing objects, defining the features relevant in a particular context. Clare Waterton suggests bringing attention to the way classifying practices are performed in her account of an experiment in which she and Nigel Stewart taught each other how to deploy their respective botanical and choreographic schemas, in the process 'making strange' their habitual practices and systems of classification. C. A. Waterton, 'Performing the Classification of Nature', *The Sociological Review* 51, no. 2 (2003): 111–129.

[2] 'Theatre Audio Description FAQs', Royal National Institute of Blind People, last modified 13 March 2015, www.rnib.org.uk/nb-online/theatre-audio-description-faqs. AD is also provided in cinemas, galleries, museums, heritage sites, sporting events and on television. While AD was developed primarily for blind and partially sighted people, there is increasing interest in how it can be used by anyone who experiences difficulty in following or accessing a work of art – people on the autistic spectrum may find the description of expressions and body language helpful, for instance.

choice of words and delivery. During the described performance, users listen through individual wireless headsets, able to hear both the sound from the stage and the AD. The live description alters from one performance to the next, as describers respond to changes in the actors' timing and any unexpected events.[3] In addition to these written texts, a more improvised verbal description accompanies a **touch tour**. Touch tours take place an hour or so before the described performance and give audience members a chance to explore the set, costumes and props, with the participation of cast and crew. They can embrace a range of sensory experiences according to the production and the interests of participants: handling props and costumes; walking around the set to understand its dimensions and layout; experiencing the speed of a revolve; learning a specific gesture or dance movement and the vocabulary associated with it; handling and listening to musical instruments. The descriptive conversation during touch tours is informal and dialogic, involving questions about the production, as well as the experience of performing in or working on the show. Blind and partially sighted audience members may make use of all three elements of the AD service, or any combination thereof, according to their own needs and preferences.

The first of these three texts, the **written introduction**, is the most formal, tonally and structurally. A description of a set or costume can be treated as an example of *ekphrasis*, defined by James Heffernan as 'the verbal representation of graphic representation'.[4] Ekphrastic writing takes a scene or work of art (real or imagined) as a starting point for the creation of a verbal work. The scene is not necessarily static, and the writing often includes non-visual elements. For example, Homer's account of the pictorial decoration on the 'immortal' shield made for Achilles describes a boy playing 'a tune of longing' on a harp, and cattle 'lowing' and 'bellowing', as well as the texture of the garments worn by dancers, and their intimate gestures, 'linked, touching each other's wrists'.[5] Similarly, an AD introduction needs to suggest how the visual world will be experienced in movement, considering how a costume is worn by an actor and how changes in the configuration of the set create new locations. The growing corpus of 'audio descriptive introductions' commissioned by museums and galleries, of objects as diverse as medical equipment and geological samples, would reward consideration in terms of ekphrasis, but it is a less

---

[3] This is the prevailing UK practice. In France, the leading provider of AD, Accès Culture, records the AD as individual sound cues, triggered live by a specialist stage manager. Some British theatre companies are experimenting with recorded AD as a way to make description available for every performance.

[4] James A. W. Heffernan, 'Ekphrasis and Representation', *New Literary History* 22, no. 2 (1991): 299.

[5] Homer, 'Book 18', *The Iliad*, translated by Robert Fitzgerald (London: Everyman, 1992), 453–454.

productive notion for AD in theatre, particularly live description, since it does not encompass the embodied nature of the spoken words.[6]

Research into AD has so far taken place mainly in the context of translation studies. Roman Jakobson defines three categories of translation: intralingual (paraphrase, commentary), interlingual (from source language to target language) and 'intersemiotic' (the 'interpretation of verbal signs by means of signs of nonverbal sign systems'). Giving examples of this last category such as the translation of a novel into a film, Jakobson also refers to it as *transmutation*.[7] AD can thus be considered as a form of intersemiotic translation. As with any form of translation, this demands a knowledge of the semiotic codes of both the source and target language. Poet and translator Fiona Sampson characterises translation as a type of 'active listening', in which the classificatory practice of 'thinking about' is replaced by an encountering practice of 'thinking through'.[8] We argue that writing an AD is a process of active observation, in which describers allow sensory experiences to work upon them in order to produce a new text. Submerged impressions are brought to explicit attention as describers typically work in pairs; they are engaged in discussion about the overall meaning and intention of the performance and the salience of particular visual signs, as well as considering the intelligibility and connotations of the language they use. They collaborate on the writing; in rehearsal, they alternately deliver and listen to the live description.

An important difference between the examples Jakobson gives of intersemiotic translation and the practice of AD in theatre is that the latter always exists alongside the visual signs that it 'translates'. Rather than seeking to replace entirely what is described, AD is an adjunct text, parts of which may circulate independently from the visual object but are always designed to make sense in relation to it. A comparison might be made with parallel texts for interlingual translation: while some readers make no direct use of the source text, others use the translation to deepen their understanding of the source. Users of AD employ it in individual ways depending on their particular needs: some use the touch tour to gain a detailed impression of props that would otherwise appear as blurs of colour; others use the live description to help orientate their

---

[6] The critical literature on ekphrasis is particularly helpful in thinking about narrative structure of a visual description, and decisions about sequences and the hierarchy of elements. Recent research considers the wider uses of the process of 'guided looking' involved in audio descriptive visual arts. See A. F. Eardley et al., 'Enriched Audio Description: Working Towards an Inclusive Museum Experience', in *Inclusion, Disability and Culture*, Inclusive Learning and Education Equity, vol. 3, eds. S. Halder and L. C. Assaf (Basel: Springer International Publishing, 2017).

[7] Roman Jakobson, 'On Linguistic Aspects of Translation', in *Selected Writings II: Word and Language*, vol. 2 (The Hague: Moutin and Co., 1971), 261.

[8] Fiona Sampson, 'Mind the Gap: Translation as a Form of Attention', British Centre for Literary Translation Research Seminar, 21 February 2018.

Translating an Embodied Gaze

gaze towards key moments on a crowded stage.[9] Recognising that vision is not a homogenous sense, and that performance is multi-sensory, has important implications for AD. The relationship between the senses and the theatrical gaze becomes apparent and problematic in writing a live description. For example, a describer considers the interplay between the aural and visual on stage, and also how to mark shifts in the relationship between performers and audience (through eye contact, changes in lighting or touch).

The **live description** is interspersed between the dialogue and other elements of the soundscape. It is not made available as a text published apart from performance. In theatre, describers write with their own performance of the words in mind, planning how pace, pitch and intonation can support the meaning. In a dance piece, the AD may be a continuous description that responds to the rhythm and structure of the music. Although a neutral, unemphatic tone of voice is usually adopted for productions where dialogue predominates, some performances demand greater vocal dynamics, interpretation or mimicry of a visual effect (a pratfall in pantomime; the unexpected reveal of a weapon in a thriller). AD is always a translation into an embodied verbal text.

If linguists and semioticians previously paid little attention to matter, producing a linguistics that 'treated the handwritten and the printed sentence, the sentence written in the sand and the sentence carved in stone, as identical for the purposes of linguistic analysis', social semiotics brought new attention to matter.[10] As Kress and van Leeuwen put it, when a voice reads out a written text, the speaker's 'bodily articulation also communicates *directly*', adding unanticipated meanings, which are 'often difficult to describe in words [...]. They are nevertheless perceived distinctly, and responded to both cognitively and affectively'.[11] Accounts of AD as intersemiotic translation also need to consider the media in which the words are produced: is the voice human or synthesised, live or recorded, vocally dynamic or constrained, whispered into an ear or received through a headset, digitally clipped or interrupted by static? AD can thus be described as intermedial translation: visual semiotic resources, addressed to the eye, are translated into aural semiotic resources, addressed to the ear.

---

[9] As Annalisa D'Innella writes, 'Blindness is not binary. It is a rich and fascinating spectrum. Visually impaired people come in many different variations. Some of us have central vision but no periphery. Some have periphery but no central. Some see the world through a window stained with blobs. For others, it is all a blur.' Annalisa D'Innella, 'The Way I See It: Living with Partial Blindness', *The Guardian*, 14 November 2016, www.theguardian.com/lifeandstyle/2016/nov/14/the-way-i-see-it-living-with-partial-blindness-rp

[10] Gunther Kress and Theo van Leeuwen, *Multimodal Discourse: The Modes and Media of Contemporary Communication* (London: Arnold, 2001), 69.

[11] Kress and van Leeuwen, *Multimodal Discourse*, 66.

But translation into words is only one of many possibilities for conveying visual sensory information by means of another sense. The pre-show touch tour offers another modality, and other experiments include the use of haptic tools to direct audience attention towards sites of interest in immersive performance, as has been traditionally done with lighting or movement, and the use of sound design to give additional information about characters' location, movement and actions.[12] As with touch tours, in these new forms of creative access, verbal description often supplements the information provided in a non-verbal form.

Constructing the Gaze

Ideas about the nature of the theatrical gaze are implicated in the practice of describing theatre for blind and partially sighted audiences. Existing definitions of AD often construct 'the visual' as an unproblematic, homogenous category that pre-exists the describer. This constructs vision as an uncontested provider of positivist nuggets of experience. Though 'seeing' is an embodied process, in this account vision appears as a disembodied phenomenon. The technology of theatrical AD, which is usually delivered through a headset, with a describer positioned in a soundproofed box at the rear of the auditorium or elsewhere in the theatre with a monitor, exacerbates the construction of a disembodied voice and, by implication, a disembodied gaze. Amelia Cavallo writes in a review of an audio described performance, 'as an audience member, I find headsets extremely isolating and frustrating.'[13] In this way, description contributes to the construction of a gaze that does not allow room for subjectivity, plurality and embodied experience.

The second substantial critique of this model of the visual relates to the way that by downplaying the connection between vision and other senses, it supports a hierarchy of senses in which the visual is privileged. At a 2016 conference about AD, describer and scholar Louise Fryer asked: 'does description reinforce the primacy of sight?' She continued, citing

---

[12] Extant Theatre Company has pioneered the use of haptics in performance. A detailed account of the environment and the use of the 'animotous' haptic device in Extant's *Flatland* can be found in Lynne Kendrick, *Theatre Aurality* (London: Palgrave Macmillan, 2017), with the production website at http://flatland.org.uk The principal investigators of the Enhancing Audio Description project using sound design are Mariana Lopez and Gavin Kearney: enhancingaudiodescription.com

[13] Amelia Cavallo, 'Audio Description: Ramps on the Moon', *Exeunt*, 27 June 2016 http://exeuntmagazine.com/features/audio-description-ramps-moon Cavallo is a blind performance scholar, performer (specialising in circus and aerial) and musician, interviewed for this chapter as both a user of AD (including as an audience member for *Beauty and the Beast*) and as a performer developing creative access, www.quiplash.co.uk

the translation scholar Lawrence Venuti's insight that translation is always 'ethnocentric', with power situated in the dominant culture, to ask whether describers are in fact 'the bastions of an ocular-centrist point of view'.[14] The emphasis in definitions, such as the one provided by the Royal National Institute of Blind People (RNIB), upon AD providing visual information audiences would otherwise 'miss' defines the visual negatively as 'whatever the blind or partially sighted person cannot perceive', as scholar and blind theatregoer, Harshadha Balasubramanian has pointed out.[15] This concept of vision foregrounds the supposedly 'disadvantaged position' of those audience members in the theatre.[16]

Such constructions of the gaze connect to a potential power imbalance in conventional theatrical AD between audience members and describers. The service aims to equalise access to a production, but can risk concentrating power in describers, whose interpretation is elevated to an objective status. Fryer quoted Hannah Thompson's provocation: 'audio description is designed to give blind users independence and yet blind cinema-goers or theatre-goers are reliant on choices made by sighted describers. It raises issues of trust and authenticity, subjectivity, power and dominance, and reliability.'[17]

While the discourse around AD often characterises vision as objective and self-evident, the practices involved in AD tend to work against that conception. Balasubramanian reported back on interviews with audio describers who instead of focusing on what was 'missed', aimed to create descriptions that worked with the audience members' vision and other senses, maximising their participation in the show as a whole. The conceptualisation of vision as a singular viewpoint is belied by the practice of working in pairs: describers often find they have conflicting interpretations of facial expression and gesture, or that one fails to recall a detail or colour that the other finds crucial.

A third critique of the notion of 'the visual' in AD, central to the examples we will go on to discuss, is that it neglects the ideological nature of the interpretation of highly coded visual material, particularly when translated into verbal discourse. The task of audio describing a stage production frequently affords access to the political nature of appearance both on stage and off. It demonstrates that a stage picture is, in Mitchell's words, 'a complex

---

[14] Louise Fryer, Keynote speech, The Art of Access, London, Young Vic Theatre, 21 October 2016.
[15] 'Theatre Audio Description FAQs'.
[16] Harshadha Balasubramanian, '"Not Just Images": Other Ideas of Vision in Theatre Audio Description'. The Art of Access, London, Young Vic Theatre, 21 October 2016.
[17] Fryer, Keynote speech.

interplay between visuality, apparatus, institutions, discourse, bodies, and figurality'.[18] On stage, a person is rendered a visual text as well as a material body; in AD, a person is rendered discourse as well as a material body. The difference between these things parallels what Mitchell describes as the difference between images and language in the epigraph above. A describer becomes aware of their '(speaking) self' in relation to a '(seen) other' – a person on stage – and aims to reproduce that construct in language. In a stage picture, bodies are made to mean in a manner related though not identical to their interpretation elsewhere in everyday life. In description, that process and the debates that spring from it come to the fore.

AD can encourage an abstraction of vision which solidifies the implicit power imbalance between the speaking self and seen other, as well as between describer and audience members. By stepping away from an embodied gaze, AD turns upon performers a gaze that potentially facilitates observation as a form of surveillance, a normative gaze that demands that all aspects of their bodies create verbal meaning. The descriptive gaze, produced in language, risks being a one-way phenomenon, rather than a reciprocal one, not only for audience members, but also for the performers described.

On the other hand, because it involves the estranging process of translating image into verbal language, AD can also enable a *deconstruction* of a theatrical gaze, and the process by which bodies on stage, as well as other visual elements, construct meaning. In doing so, AD has the potential to deconstruct the assumed objectivity of the gaze, disrupt a potentially imbalanced power structure between audience members and describers, and more broadly, to de-stabilise the ordinary workings of theatrical spectatorship. The developing practice of what might be called 'critical audio description' suggests that, as Mitchell contends: '*spectatorship* (the look, the gaze, the glance, the practices of observation, surveillance, and visual pleasure) may be as deep a problem as various forms of *reading* (decipherment, decoding, interpretation, etc.) and that visual experience of "visual literacy" might not be fully explicable on the model of textuality.'[19] Attending to the distribution of power in AD not only means considering AD in its institutional contexts (where it usually occupies a low status in theatrical hierarchies), but also analysing what verbal expression does that renders it distinct from the visual. These differences connect to the differences between spoken and written language, and formal and informal registers. By throwing sustained attention onto the theatrical gaze, the process of creating an AD

---

[18] W. J. T. Mitchell, *Picture Theory* (Chicago and London: University of Chicago Press, 1994), 16.
[19] Mitchell, *Picture Theory*, 16.

demonstrates that the gaze is not neutral or disembodied, but rather always potentially pleasurable, erotic and exploitative. The following section analyses description in neo-burlesque and burlesque-influenced theatrical performances, in order to attend to their framing of the gaze not only as erotic, but also as reciprocal and multisensory.

Deconstructing the Gaze

We analyse here a production that we jointly audio described, Muz and Fraser's *Beauty and the Beast*, before discussing Cavallo's burlesque performance, 'Scarf Dance', which contains a mechanism for generating description within the performance text. Both of these performances were created or co-created by disabled artists, and are concerned with an intersection of disability politics, eroticism and burlesque aesthetics.[20]

Beauty and the Beast is a combination of autobiography, fairytale, erotic spectacle and puppetry, creating a humorous, touching and celebratory performance. The conventional descriptive approach to this performance in some ways succeeded, and in other ways failed. The reasons for this failure point to the tensions between a disembodied descriptive gaze and the experience of eroticised performance. Beyond this particular production, there are implications for AD more broadly: the importance of informality and reciprocity, and acknowledgement of the erotic and potentially exploitative aspects of the theatrical gaze.

The written introduction for *Beauty and the Beast* raised questions about how to describe performers' bodies. All four performers are naked at different times, sometimes in a matter-of-fact way, sometimes eroticised, while the theme of physical appearance links fairytale and 'real-life' sections, allowing them to comment on each other. During an autobiographical section of the show, Mat refers to the appearance of his arms, and his mother's experience of being prescribed Thalidomide in pregnancy. He jokes about playing the 'Beast' as a way of exploring ideas about disability. Similarly, Mat's discussion about his own attitude to prosthetic arms is implicitly contrasted with scenes in which the puppeteers animate false arms for the character of Beast, and a burlesque moment in which Julie is stripped of her clothes by a 'possessed' hand (her own, gloved hand

---

[20] *Beauty and the Beast*, directed by Phelim McDermott, has been performed in New York, Adelaide and London, and we described it at the Young Vic in 2013. Julie Atlas Muz is a performance artist and dancer, and shortly before creating *Beauty and the Beast*, had been crowned Miss Coney Island and Miss Erotic World for her burlesque performance. Her husband, Mat Fraser, is an actor and radical theatre maker. They were joined on stage by puppeteers Jonny Dixon and Jess Mabel Jones.

behaving as if it were an independently animated prosthesis or puppet). Thus, the actors' bodies were heavily thematised; the performance drew our attention to them. The written introduction needed to provide information without imposing an ableist body norm. We settled on the following descriptions, in conversation with the performers:

> Mat is a wiry, lean figure in his 40s, with grey-blue eyes, a strong jaw, dimpled cheeks and full lips. His grey hair is shaved at the sides and spiked up in a Mohican in the middle. As Mat explains early on, he has very short upper arms and no forearms, and his hands join his arms just below the elbow bone. He is nonetheless highly dexterous. When we first meet Mat, he wears an old blue t-shirt with a 'Coney Island Lager' logo on it, rusty-red trousers and grubby white trainers. He has a showman's style, often looking out to us with a twinkle in his eye.
>
> Julie has a heart-shaped face with large eyes and shoulder-length blonde hair. Also in her 40s, Julie's look is larger-than-life glamour: her hair falls in tumbling, bouffant curls and she wears thick sparkly blue eye-shadow, long false eyelashes, and luscious red lipstick flecked with glitter. When she first appears, she wears a black corset and an asymmetrical black miniskirt, ruffled at the hem. She walks with ease on high black heels. Julie has a joyful bearing, smiling broadly and playfully at us.[21]

The AD introductions provided by Vocaleyes, a leading provider of AD in the United Kingdom, include a standard note asking listeners to be aware of the distinction between actor and character. Autobiographical performance typically blurs but does not erase this distinction. We had decided not to describe the performers' unclothed bodies in the written introduction, since they would only be revealed later in the piece, but concerns about the boundary between performer and character clearly influenced our decision too.

The live description, in contrast, reflected the playful tone of the wordless sections of the piece, as in this erotic sequence between Beauty and the Beast involving fruit and vegetables:

> Beast picks up another half passion fruit, and holds it in his palm. He sticks out his tongue and works it back and forth against the fruit, keeping his eyes trained on Beauty. With excitement, she picks up a banana, and peels it. She takes almost all of it in her mouth in one go. She gags, eats the banana and

---

[21] From the authors' copy of the introduction to *Beauty and the Beast* at the Young Vic Theatre, 2013. The text was provided to bookers at the time as a Word document and in audio form as an MP3 file, but is not archived on the theatre's website or elsewhere. We would write this introduction differently today, notably with awareness of how the use of concessive connectors ('He is *nonetheless* highly dextrous') can insidiously construct an ableist (racist, sexist etc.) perspective. We're grateful to Rachel Hutchinson and Hannah Thompson for this insight.

Translating an Embodied Gaze 97

chucks the peel aside. Frantically, Beast licks at the passion fruit, flicking his tongue against it. Beauty holds up a pair of cherries on a stalk and dangles them above her mouth. She sucks each one, swapping quickly, one to other. Beast slams a papaya on the table and buries his face in it. Beauty picks up a courgette, jerks it off between her breasts, lightly slaps her face with it. They stop, and look at each other, fruit smeared on their faces. Beast stands up.[22]

But describing the performers' bodies in the live description turned out to be problematic, in part because the moment at which a naked body was first revealed was accompanied by spoken dialogue, and in part because of our concern about verbally objectifying bodies at precisely the moment when nakedness was being presented as liberating and unsensational. However, in informal feedback following the show, some audience members commented on the lack of detail about the performers' bodies. The first time Mat appeared naked on stage, Amelia Cavallo's companion whispered, 'Holy shit, Mat is hung like a horse.' Cavallo reflected that 'none of that was in the description. And I was like, "I feel jipped, man. What the fuck?"'[23] The spontaneous description provided by Cavallo's friend was colloquial, implicated in an embodied experience, and expressed between people who had a shared register and, additionally, knew the performers as colleagues and friends. While Cavallo's comments made us reflect on how we could add more 'body' to our live description, we also wondered about how to strike the right note for all the audience members listening to the AD, and how our words might be received, as a disembodied but intimate voice, via a headset.

The questions raised by *Beauty and the Beast* are indicative of wider issues in describing bodies in theatre AD, including, but not limited to, the description of age, race, ethnicity and ability.[24] Failing to describe physical traits that are thematised by the performance would be a failure to provide access. However,

---

[22] From the authors' copy of the script for the live, through description of *Beauty and the Beast*, Young Vic Theatre, 2013,

[23] Amelia Cavallo, interview by Kirstin Smith, 1 March 2018.

[24] Amelia Cavallo recalls a fellow actor's response to a written audio descriptive introduction that mentioned that he 'had a gut'. The actor referred to was 'offended, but like jokingly offended and so surprised'. He said 'You have to change that – do not tell a bunch of blind people that I have a gut.' And it's like, 'But you do!' Cavallo expressed surprise that this was such a sensitive issue for the actor, saying that it was just a matter of 'describing his body' alongside other facts such as 'is a wheelchair user'. Cavallo, interview by Kirstin Smith, 1 March 2018. The Describing Diversity project, a collaboration between Royal Holloway and Vocaleyes, launched after this chapter was written, was a response to discussions between providers, users and performers about including information about disability, ethnicity, age and body shape in AD (https://vocaleyes .co.uk/wp-content/uploads/2020/09/Describing-Diversity-Report-September-2020.pdf). A follow-up project, Inclusive Description for Equality and Access, has produced workshops and resources for use by theatres as well as an online course for describers: www.futurelearn.com/courses/ creating-audio-description-for-equality-diversity-and-inclusion

AD – precisely because of its transmutation from visual to verbal – risks not just reproducing a normative visual appraisal of bodies but consolidating it.

Neither AD nor theatre performances exist in a vacuum, but in their societal contexts, which create conditions for how bodies mean. In a manifesto on 'gender abolitionism' discussed in Helen Hester's *Xenofeminism*, Hester notes that 'the traits associated not just with gender, but also with race, class, able-bodiedness, and so on, are unevenly loaded with social stigma' and should be 'stripped of their social significance, and therefore of their ability to act as vectors of discrimination'. She continues: 'The struggle must continue until currently gendered and racialized characteristics are no more a basis of discrimination than the colour of one's eyes.'[25] The aim of this project is not, as M. Menon argues, to stop seeing 'differences among peoples and cultures and colours and sexualities and identities – as if that were even possible. But it does mean that we interrupt the chain of causality that all these categories imply in their formulation'.[26] In writing such as Hester's, the gaze is politically re-evaluated, a project which might fruitfully draw on critiques of vision in Disability Studies. Once such a critique is taken seriously, little about the process by which bodies are seen (by sighted, blind and partially sighted people), or described by describers, becomes obvious.

The translation from visual to verbal exacerbates the demand on bodies to mean, making it particularly conducive to producing gendered, classed and racialised assumptions. Verbal expression relies on narrative to create meaning, a trait that Heffernan observes in ekphrasis. The 'history of ekphrasis', he writes, 'suggests that language releases a narrative impulse which graphic art restricts, and that to resist such an impulse takes a special effort of poetic will'.[27] AD may share this tendency, because narrative (causation, consequence, foregrounding and backgrounding), along with function ('this lever causes this wheel to turn'), are some of the key principles that AD follows. Such dramaturgical devices are vital to the verbal construction of sense, as well as pleasure, even when the artwork resists such a narrativizing impulse. Theatre AD is also working with visual material that is highly citational, and shaped by genre conventions. As Judith Butler suggests in *Bodies That Matter*, theatrical performances are scripted by normative behaviour and public rituals outside theatre.[28] AD is thus largely dependent on the performance it describes for the rules by which it constructs meaning.

---

[25] Helen Hester, *Xenofeminism* (Cambridge and Medford: Polity, 2018), 29.
[26] Madhavi Menon, *Indifference to Difference: On Queer Universalism* (Minneapolis: University of Minnesota Press, 2015), 41.
[27] Heffernan, 'Ekphrasis and Representation', 7.
[28] Judith Butler, *Bodies That Matter* (New York and London: Routledge 1993).

Translating an Embodied Gaze

What would a 'critical audio description' sound like? One approach to the introduction to *Beauty and the Beast* might have been to ask the performers to describe each other's bodies, perhaps through a recorded interview rather than a written description, and to employ the resulting vocabulary in the live description. In the past, introductions were written and recorded without much input from the creative team, but producers and directors are now paying more attention to them. Introductions increasingly make use of interviews: at the Unicorn Theatre, the written introduction is scripted in the first person and recorded by the performers in character; at the Almeida Theatre, a conventional introduction is supplemented by a group interview with company members, which allows for their personal interpretation of costume and their own physicality to emerge. Where the cordon sanitaire between 'access' and 'art' is broken, as in the 'aesthetics of access' movement, performers and audience have potentially much more say about what they want to hear in the AD.[29]

In the burlesque performance 'Scarf Dance', Amelia Cavallo employs a device that places the responsibility of description on the audience.[30] Cavallo's act centres on the dynamic of tease – concealing and revealing – using a large scarf to alternately cover and expose parts of their body: a foot, a hand, an elbow. While doing so, Cavallo describes their own actions. The spoken element of the performance was initially developed to provide access for blind and partially sighted audience members, but has become central to the subversive nature of the piece. Cavallo comments: 'the movements that I do in themselves are not that interesting. It's the fact that I'm describing what I'm doing as I do it that's interesting. And that in a burlesque space is already subversive because nobody ever talks.' As they explain in interview, Cavallo asks the audience to describe their appearance:

> I start off with yes or no questions. Or things that seem simple, so 'what colour is my hair?' 'You're seeing my eyes now — do they smoulder?'

---

[29] The move to integrate and experiment with AD as both an access provision and artistic practice has been spearheaded by Maria Oshodi, Artistic Director of Extant, as in the theatre production and online film *Flight Paths*, integrating aerial, song, narrative and live description: https://extant.org.uk/access/is-it-working/. The company commissioned a report on integrated description in the United Kingdom from Louise Fryer and Amelia Cavallo available at https://extant.org.uk/access/is-it-working/. Theatre company Graeae is a leading proponent of the 'aesthetics of access' movement, integrating AD and sign language from the start of a process to create a 'radical dramatic language'. http://graeae.org/about/our-artistic-vision/

[30] 'Scarf Dance' was created in workshops alongside Jenevieve Chang, an actor and dancer with an interest in burlesque as a mode of exploring intersectional identity. It has been performed in cabaret, queer, burlesque, academic and corporate spaces since 2007.

'You're seeing my nose — is it cute?' So they're quite prescriptive, but still allow some kind of agency, because you can say no. But nobody ever does.[31]

They then ask the audience to describe parts of their body, starting with the shoulder and moving on to breasts and bottom. This kind of dialogic exchange is not usually found in a burlesque setting. Not only do performers tend to be silent, but audiences are used to giving no more than an affirming whoop in the expected places. Cavallo encourages audience members to take on a more active role, to risk utterances that in another context might be construed as a heckle or judgement. In performance, they make it a rule to accept any description offered and improvise with it. This creates a pluralistic construction of the gaze, which inevitably contains disagreements and idiosyncratic impressions. The responsibility for describing the performer's body is shared within the group and the descriptions are spoken aloud for everybody to hear.

Cavallo's performance plays with burlesque conventions of the gaze and meaning. In photographer Katherine Liepe-Levison's study of stripping, she emphasises the importance of 'eye-contact' and 'dances of the eyes', arguing that the gaze must be reciprocal rather than one way, rendering the performer active rather than passive.[32] In 'Scarf Dance', Cavallo creates a version of this mutual gaze that is accessible to both blind spectators and performers. As a performer, Cavallo can gauge the reactions of audience members, drawing attention to the gaze and becoming an active participant by constructing the framework in which they are seen. Burlesque, Maggie Werner argues, engages in 'sign play', in which performers shift 'who they are and what they are communicating', so that the performances 'resist and disrupt stable meaning'.[33] Cavallo disrupts their body's function as a sign, by isolating its parts and inviting multiple interpretations of its appearance.

At the climax of the performance, Cavallo suddenly shifts persona, destabilising all that has come before. Just as they reach the ultimate reveal of the whole body, they drop the large scarf, and signal that this wasn't intentional. They begin to search for the scarf, exaggerating the effort by crawling and running their hands over the floor, a moment Cavallo describes as 'cripping up a little bit'. Instead of the scarf, they find a mirror, at which point they turn to the audience, saying: 'I've got a thing that reflects my

---

[31] Amelia Cavallo, interview by Kirstin Smith, 1 March 2018.

[32] Katherine Liepe-Levison, *Strip Show: Performances of Gender and Desire* (London and New York: Routledge, 2002), 120.

[33] Maggie M. Werner, 'Seductive Rhetoric and the Communicative Art of Neo-Burlesque', *Present Tense* 5, no. 1 (2015), 1, 3–4.

Translating an Embodied Gaze

body which I can't see.' They begin to ask questions again, but the charming persona has dropped and the questions are more confrontational: 'Do I look normal?' In Cavallo's words, discussing 'Scarf Dance' in interview: 'at the end I'm basically standing in front of them naked, going, "What do I look like?" The attitude drops as well, and suddenly it's not funny anymore, and I'm not playing anymore.'[34] For the audience, the end can be moving or shocking. Cavallo re-casts the questions about appearance in relation to their disability, and abandons the coy persona that invited a heteronormative, appraising gaze. Cavallo's performance could be categorised, in Kay Siebler's terms, as 'underground burlesque', 'a radical offshoot of neo-burlesque'. By disrupting or queering the traditional scripts of striptease, Cavallo's performance demands that the audience 'think about the complexities of desire, sexuality, and identity'.[35]

In terms of AD, Cavallo disrupts both a singular, disembodied conception of vision and the potential for a normative, descriptive gaze identified above. By initially framing the description of their body as an appraising, enjoyable game, and then disrupting that game, Cavallo demonstrates that such appraisal is at work in the act of looking (particularly, but not exclusively in burlesque performance), and then replaces it with a new kind of mutual gaze: one that challenges rather than simply acknowledges the audience. Though it was not Cavallo's intention, one of things highlighted by this performance is the ethics, pleasure and difficulties of casting a gaze upon bodies on stage, and putting it into words.

Cavallo's 'Scarf Dance' is one of a growing number of performances exploring 'integrated access' and 'the aesthetics of access'. Integrated AD techniques need to be developed as part of the conception of the performance. They might involve performers describing themselves and their own actions: Clare Cunningham has discussed how the choreographic exercise of verbally articulating points of attention or actions can be adapted to give access to the dancer's process.[36] They might involve the creation of a new character with a commentary function, as in the production of Nikolai Gogol's *The Government Inspector* presented by Birmingham Rep in association with Ramps on the Moon, 2016. The Almeida Theatre has established a project to pair audio describers with assistant directors, to give the describers greater access to the concepts behind the design and

---

[34] Amelia Cavallo, interview by Kirstin Smith, 1 March 2018.

[35] Kay Siebler, 'What's So Feminist about Garters and Bustiers? Neo-burlesque as Post-feminist Sexual Liberation', *Journal of Gender Studies* 24, no. 5 (2015), 566.

[36] Cunningham was part of a panel discussing 'Creative Approaches to Audio Description' during the Unlimited Festival, Southbank Centre, 8 September 2016.

staging, and to increase directors' knowledge about how audiences with sight loss experience their work and feed into future considerations of how productions might be made more accessible through additional semiotic resources that enlist other senses. Even within the 'add-on' model of AD, increasing use is being made of questionnaires in which performers are invited to describe the look of the character(s) they play. Collaborative, integrated description methods, in Fryer's words, 'liberate the user from the tyranny of the describer'.[37] In doing so, we argue, they also usefully deconstruct the dynamics involved in a theatrical gaze.

Conclusion

It is somewhat perplexing that analysis of AD has largely remained within the field of translation studies, rather than performance studies. While translation provides important tools for unlocking some of the difficulties encountered in AD (the myth of equivalence, for example), to develop a full account of the embodied nature of AD here, we needed to turn to social semiotics, art theory and performance studies analyses of burlesque. Rather than being textual in its operation, AD is an intermedial, embodied and situated translational practice.

As a result, it both produces and reveals ethical problematics relating to the theatrical gaze. In the case of *Beauty and the Beast*, the production thematised the body and describing it raised questions about how to represent another's body in words without objectifying it. While Cavallo's technique of generating AD from the audience offers one approach to describing the performer's body without imposing a singular, potentially normative gaze, it will not be appropriate for every production. Nevertheless, it has helped to define the principles of an emerging 'critical audio description': understanding of the gaze as embodied and plural; recognition of the multiplicity of audiences; attention to the distribution of power between artists, audiences and describers. These principles are congruent with a wide range of radical translation practices.

Inherently, AD incorporates different voices, which disrupts the assumption that visual information is a given. However, we can go further: the ethics of description in terms of access and the politics of representation would be better served by greater collaboration between describers,

---

[37] Fryer, Keynote speech, The Art of Access, 2016. Louise Fryer's 2018 article 'The Independent Audio Describer Is Dead: Long Live Audio Description!' discusses many examples of integrated access and their strengths and limitations.

Translating an Embodied Gaze

performers and audience members in the creation of descriptions. Such collaborations bring in new registers and vocabulary, in voices that reflect the range of voices on stage and in the audience, and help to avoid the construction of a disembodied gaze.

You keep saying that the practice of audio description involves at least two gazes, but this is typically erased, dissolved (as in this joint chapter) into a singular voice.
Oh yeah, why have we done that?

Institutional practices. There's a continuum, isn't there, between the authoritative AD voice and the de-personalised academic voice?
What if this section itself is a pretend dialogue? How do I know it's not just been written by one person?

But if it starts to break down the idea that an adequate description can be provided by a singular disembodied voice, then it doesn't really matter.
If we started to use some of the marks of intonation that we use in writing AD in academic writing about the practice…

Is that an ellipsis to suggest a tentative action…? Or a continuing action…?
Important to remember that AD text is often fragmentary, supplementary to a multi-modal performance text.

[*fast*] >> She grabs the thought. Looks for markers of 'voice' in academic writing. Finds more refs.
It's a conversation.

Between describers. ⇊
Yes. And increasingly, with theatre makers and audiences too. ⇈

CHAPTER 5

Performative Accents
Bilingualism, Postcolonialism and Francophonie in Michèle Lalonde's Poster-poem 'Speak White'

Kélina Gotman

C'est ça, relativiser la langue française. Elle peut être ou devenir langage pour celui-ci, 'composante' pour celui-là, langue d'appoint pour un autre. Par là elle entrera dans la relation multiple au monde. Accepter cette relation, l'enseigner, c'est ouvrir le possible sans imposer la fixité tyrannique.

[That is how you relativise the French language. It can be or become language for one person, 'component' for another, support language for yet another. That is how it enters into a multiple relationship with the world. To accept this relationality, to teach it, is to open up the possible without imposing tyrannical fixity.]

Édouard Glissant, 'Langues, langage'.

Moi j'aime ma langue. Mais c'est quoi ma langue? [I love my language. But what is my language?]

Régine Robin, *Le Deuil de l'origine. Une langue en trop, la langue en moins.*

Postcolonial critic and poet Édouard Glissant (1928–2011), in the epigraph just cited, suggests that the French language can be 'relativized', so that it is not 'tyrannically' 'fixed' but constantly in a relation of alliance or renegotiation with other languages, sites, and people, all the time. Language in this relational sense is not only translational, I am arguing further, but performative: it is constantly rearticulated in live encounters within which speakers demonstrate reaffiliations with or resistance to aspects of the languages they speak, within the immediate context of a given act of interlocution. They may do this through an inflection or a shift in accent (a flash of code-switching), or through a deliberate and systematic decision to withhold a form of accentuation to the extent habits of speech allow. Gilles Deleuze and Félix Guattari posit notions of

Performative Accents

minor literature to describe ways language worlds are co-composed within a given global order: it is not the same, at one moment or another, to write in Greek, Latin, English, or Romani, for example; yet 'major' and 'minor' are not absolute distinctions but relations or tendencies, always in motion. Drawing from this, I attend here to ways acts of accentuation, ways languages are performed, co-compose major and minor moments of micro-languaging – offered at the level of soundscapes, grammatical and anti-grammatical codes, performed at a granular level within even 'a' language as such.[1]

Thus, acts of languaging are translational: they perform movements between languages and variations within singular languages, to dramatize points of passage and impasse. To explore these relational and performative acts of translation, and suggest I hope a way forward in thinking about performative utterances also in this way as translational acts (for example between major and minor moments of accentuation) – not only as semantic types of phrase (that should performatively attest or enact a given state of affairs, for example, as J. L. Austin proffers[2]) – this chapter closely examines Québécois poet Michèle Lalonde's (1937–2021) now iconic broadsheet-poem [*poème-affiche*] 'Speak White' (1968).

Without being able to do full justice to the context of Québécois resistance to anglophone hegemony from the 1950s to the 1970s, and the resultant rise to political power of the French Canadian majority in Québec, as well as ongoing tensions and affiliations across language worlds within francophone Canada and the global *francophonie* in the period of decolonization and counterculture that characterized the second half of the twentieth century – or to the many writers and poets with whom she collaborated and alongside

---

[1] Gilles Deleuze and Félix Guattari, *Kafka: Toward a Minor Literature*, translated by Dana Polan (Minneapolis: The University of Minnesota Press, [1975] 1986), 17. Significantly, Deleuze and Guattari discuss Lalonde's 'Speak White' in Gilles Deleuze and Felix Guattari, *Capitalisme et schizophrénie 2: Mille Plateaux* (Paris: Les éditions de minuit, 1980), 127–129, where they note that alliance with 'grammaticality' is alliance with social normativity, social laws (127–128), and that the 'unity of a language is first of all political' (128); every dialect includes a zone of transition and variation, indeed every minor language has a zone of dialectal variation (128). In the case of Québécois language – they cite here Lalonde as writing – there are so many regional accentuations and modulations that musical notation might best be employed to preserve it, rather than a system of orthography (128–129). See Michèle Lalonde's performative, mock sixteenth-century-French 'La deffence & illustration de la langue Québecquoyse', in Michèle Lalonde et al., *Change Souverain Québec* (Paris: Collectif Change, Seghers/Laffont, 1977): 105–122, 113. Thanks to Craig Moyes for a clear-sighted read of an earlier draft, and for pointing me in particular to Jenny Salgado's rendition. An early version of this work was given at the Mellon symposium on Theatre and Translation | Performance and Multilingualism at the Rhode Island School of Design, organized by Avishek Ganguly, as 'Performance, Politics and Code-switching'; thanks also to Patricia Ybarra for chairing.

[2] Austin, *How To Do Things with Words*.

106 KÉLINA GOTMAN

whom she wrote – I do hope that renewed attention to this iconic poem here will offer it a long overdue place in the annals of performance poetry and, as event, performance history more broadly.

Speaking 'Speak White' ([1968, 1970] 1974)

Written in the context of the 'Quiet Revolution' (*Révolution tranquille*), an initially primarily cultural and soon political resistance movement in the 1960s against the domination of a small demographic minority of Protestant English speakers over the majority of Catholic French-speaking inhabitants of Québec, Lalonde's 'Speak White' has been reprised and reperformed numerous times by key cultural players in the Québécois landscape. Because the poem makes strategic use of English throughout (including in the poem's title, 'Speak White'), the way speakers enunciate the English – and, to an extent, the particular pronunciation of the French that they offer – perform a set of relationships to both these differently historically dominant linguistic powers. (The French had initially colonized the indigenous territory now known as Québec in the sixteenth century, before it was taken over by the British following French defeat in the Seven Years' War, 1756–1763.) The stakes, in some sense, are widely shared. Poet Rita Dove highlights the colossal stakes of pronunciation of the letter 'r' in her poem 'Parsley' (1983): she remarks in a note accompanying the poem that 'On October 2, 1937, Rafael Trujillo (1891–1961), dictator of the Dominican Republic, ordered 20,000 blacks killed because they could not pronounce the letter 'r' in *perejil*, the Spanish word for parsley'[3]. One small word (one letter) becomes synecdochal for an entire system of repression and violence – the peril in *perejil* a matter of life and death. The way the poem is said then matters a lot, as a performance of position relative to these enunciative histories. In 'Speak White', Lalonde draws attention to English and other forms of 'correct', 'grammatical' speech (Franco-French, Russian, German) as global languages of imperial power – major languages, in the sense of Deleuze and Guattari: to be told (while francophone) to 'Speak White' was at the height of British colonial rule in Québec to be told to speak the language of the master, to speak English.

Lalonde's poem, first performed by the actor Michelle Rossignol 27 May 1968 at an event organized at the Gesù theatre in Montreal, 'Chants et poèmes de la résistance' ('Songs and poems of the resistance') to support political prisoners and activists of the Québec separatist movement, was

---

[3] Rita Dove, 'Parsley', in *Selected Poems* (New Delhi: Hemkunt Press, 1993): 133–136, 136.

Performative Accents 107

performed again numerous times and particularly at a landmark event, *La nuit de la poésie*, by Lalonde herself 27 March 1970, again at the Gesù theatre in Montreal, this time before an audience of 4,000. It went on to be repeated and rehearsed, reconfigured, disfigured and republished on walls, in pamphlets, and in cafés, until Lalonde finally published the authorized version in 1974, as a large fold-out broadsheet, in bold red letters on off-white.[4] The poem virulently pushes back against not only anglophone Canadian, but also US and British imperialism, and every other sort of imperial power, including German and Russian (all identified as 'speaking white'). These are pit against the Black-identified, French-speaking demographic majority in Québec, and all peoples and nations oppressed by capitalist, wealthy, authoritarian, and/or establishmentar-ian cultures, made to 'Speak White' (in this context, to 'Speak English'). Of 104 lines, or 105 including the title, thirty-seven (thirty-eight with the title) deploy English expressions, proper names or place-names, from 'Shakespeare' and 'Longfellow' to 'Little Rock', 'Watts', 'how do you do', 'crumpets', 'Boston Tea Party', 'big deal', and 'be civilized'. 'Speak white' is repeated, including with the title, twelve times, also including variations 'speak white and loud' and 'ah! / speak white'; use of English expressions is intensified in the middle stanzas of the poem ('speak white / tell us that God is a great big shot / and that we're paid to trust him / speak white')

---

[4] There is some contention as to whether Lalonde herself eventually performed the poem in 1968 in Rossignol's stead or not; Lalonde's indication in a prefatory note to *Speak White* suggests Rossignol said it. In Michèle Lalonde, *Speak White* (Montréal: L'Hexagone, 1974). The poem is republished among others in Lalonde et al., *Change Souverain Québec*, 100–104, followed by Lalonde's 'La deffence & illustration de la langue Québecquoyse', 105–122, which while wondering whether it is possible to express oneself in one's own language, performs *joual* acts of bilingualism, with terms like 'switcher' (to switch), and 'watcher' (to watch), or 'flipper' (to flip), and spells 'Québécois' in variations indicating supposed pronunciation, from the old French to the current street speech ('Québecquoyse', 'Québécouayse', 'Kébékouaze', and finally 'Kébekway', which in its anglicizing twang most closely approximates spoken *joual*) (106–107). She also deploys classic *joual* terms like 'pantoute' ('not at all'), again dramatically contrasting with and at a granular level diverting and interrupting the mock Old French. This performance of Québécois (or Kébekway) *'parlure'* (rotten speech), genealogically born out of mixtures of sixteenth-century French, English, American, Algonquin, and many more modes of languaging, contrasts any and all languages either aiming towards Latinate purity or suffering accusations of vulgarity with the dazzling virtuosity of this code-switching. As she puts it, all the 'acrobatics and eccentricities' of current literature, from 'fonetik' writing to experimental Franglais literature, attempt to resolve the still enormous, somewhat devastating, certainly viscerally sorrowful, gulf between graphic writing systems (modernized Franco-French with its use of orthography) and the lived experience of speech (112–114). For a brilliant reading of the question of translation in – and of – *Speak White*, as well as of Québécois diglossia, code-switching and of Québec as a *'culture traduite'* (or translated culture), see especially Kathy Mezei, 'Bilingualism and Translation in/of Michèle Lalonde's *Speak White*', *The Translator* 4, no. 2 (1998): 229–247. On 'culture traduite', see Simon Sherry, *Le Trafic des langues: tradition et culture dans la littérature Québécoise* (Montréal: Éditions Boréal, 1994).

and in the two penultimate stanzas, where Lalonde tips the use of English on its head, and rather than interpellate the anglophone masters ('tell us again about Freedom and Democracy'), responds, in the English language, ventriloquizing her compatriots: when asked politely 'how do you do', and when the response given is (in English) 'we're doing all right / we're doing fine / We are not alone', she is calling for an uprising locally and globally – calling everyone in the room to stand by and to join forces with those in the Congo, in Algeria, who know that '*liberté est un mot noir*' ('freedom is a Black word'), just as misery is Black ('*comme la misère est nègre*'). She is calling on her compatriots to stand together, 'from Westminster to Washington', and rise up against violence, repression, and monopoly.

The performance at the famous *La nuit de la poésie* concluded an evening of poems and performative interventions given by some of the literary luminaries of the day, including Gaston Miron, Nicole Brossard, Claude Gauvreau, Gérald Godin, the singer Pauline Julien, and many others, including also the buffoonishly costumed DADA-esque, Beats-inspired free-jazz collective l'Infonie orchestra directed by Walter Boudreau; a clearly 'cool' crowd, with thick glasses and trendy haircuts, captured in the National Film Board of Canada (NFB/ONF) film by Jean-Claude Labrèque and Jean-Pierre Masse (1970), shows feverish excitement – the sense of being on the cusp of something that has been growing, and that is also fresh and new. In fact, as Canadian critic Sherry Simon points out, the anglophone scene in Montreal, as also the Yiddish scene, were feverishly themselves at this time in leftist, experimental, and/or countercultural effervescence creatively and socially. Montreal had just been in the international spotlight with the famous Expo67 events, bringing together an international cast of artists and audiences to Montreal's buzzing venues and streets. Although Montreal's neighbourhoods hardly crossed over, between the anglophone, francophone, and Jewish communities (the latter of which were largely anglophone, but distinctly separate from the Protestant English-speaking minority Lalonde criticized), they were geographically close – adjacent worlds not yet overlapping or entwined. (Simon attends to one cultural icon, Leonard Cohen [1934–2016], who right around the time of Lalonde's activism was experimenting with francophone and indigenous, specifically Mohawk, histories as well as anglophone genealogies, in his song and poetry, as well as his writing, such as in the experimental novel *Beautiful Losers* [1966].[5]) An extraordinary influx of

---

[5] Sherry Simon, *Cities in Translation: Intersections of Language and Memory* (Abingdon: Routledge, 2012): 144–146.

Performative Accents

immigrants over the ensuing decades continued to offer further grounds for perpetual acts of performative translation over the years, also as captured in a famous retort to Lalonde, Italian-Canadian (or Italo-Québécois) poet and playwright Marco Micone's (b. 1945) 'Speak What' (1989), as I detail later.[6] So while most immigrants to Montreal in the nineteenth century were largely British (Irish and Scottish in particular), reinforcing the anglophone sphere, by the early twentieth century other, mostly southern Europeans began to immigrate in large numbers, and after the Second World War a new influx of immigrants joined increasingly from all over the world, including, eventually, with policy to reinforce French language in Québec, from the global postcolonial *francophonie*, including Haiti and, paradoxically perhaps, increasingly over the past decades the Franco-French, who see in Québec a slice of the United States with linguistically accessible *joie de vivre*. (It is worth noting that in Québec, the designation 'francophone' is employed to differentiate primarily French-speaking people from those who speak primarily English, designated 'anglophones', and also from 'allophones', who may speak English and/or French but whose first language(s) may be neither. In this context, 'francophone' and 'anglophone' are complementary and opposite, saturated with centuries

---

[6] Marco Micone, *Speak What. Suivi d'une analyse de Lise Gauvin* (Montréal: VLB Éditeur, 2001). First published as 'Speak What', *Cahiers de théâtre. Jeu* 50 (March 1989): 83–85. Erin Hurley reads Micone's 'exiguity' – his way of performing an 'aperture onto difference' as effected through a strategy of 'simulation'; he 'approaches the issue of ethnic difference from this immigrant space of exiguity and in the mode of simulation. His work writes back to the centre of the Québec literary institution – including *le nouveau théâtre Québécois* – in a process that not only de-centres the centre but uproots it'. For Hurley, the issues of the 'Neo-Québécois' such as 'animate Micone's œuvre' operate a series of double negatives, displacing the stability of a centre. 'Neo-Québécois' she writes, 'are not fully Québécois (hence the qualifier "neo"). Yet neither are they *not*-Québécois (their new-ness is hyphenated with "Quebec"). The issue then is in what respect and to what extent are neo-Québécois Québécois? Can one convert from being "Italian", for instance, to being "Québécois"? How does one move along the national identification axis from "not Québécois" to "not not-Québécois"? By what means? And is that double negative (the not-not-Québécois) as far as an immigrant can go?' In Erin Hurley, *National Performance: Representing Quebec from Expo 67 to Céline Dion* (Toronto: University of Toronto Press, 2011), 89–90. See François Paré, *Les littératures de l'exiguïté* (Hearst: Le Nordir, 1992). On Micone and the 'Speak White' / 'Speak What' 'simulation' and attendant historico-political and cultural context, see especially Hurley, *National Performance*, 89–106. See also Erin Hurley, '*Devenir Autre*: Languages of Marco Micone's "*culture immigrée*"', *Theatre Research in Canada / Recherches théâtrales au Canada* 25, no. 1–2 (2004), https://journals.lib.unb.ca/index.php/TRIC/article/view/4650/5510 accessed 26 April 2018. See also N. Novelli, 'Pour une nouvelle culture et une langue de la migration: entretien avec Marco Micone', in *D'autres rêves: les écritures migrantes au Québec. Actes du séminaire international du CISQ [Centro interuniversitario di studi quebecchesi] à Venise, 15–16 octobre 1999*, edited by Anne de Vaucher Gravili (Venice: Supernova, 2000), 163–182; Dervila Cooke, 'Hybridity and Intercultural Exchange in Marco Micone's "Le figuier enchanté"', *The French Review* 84, no. 6 (2011): 1160–1172; and Beatrice Guenther, 'Refracting Identity in "l'écriture migrante": Marco Micone's "Le figuier enchanté"', *The French Review* 84, no. 6 (2011): 1173–1185.

of political grievance and contestation. Indigenous languages offer a further set of political questions of presence and erasure this chapter will not dwell upon, but which have to be understood as the violent terrain on which these language wars have been performed.[7] Québécois usage of 'francophone' is thus distinct from, though related to, the notion of a global *francophonie*, employed to describe a postcolonial language world marked by French.)

To come clear, my own situation is complex in this: born in Montreal, with roots that sprawl – most immediately, in the United States (via Ireland, Scotland, Wales, and laterally Germany and England) and France (via East European Ashkenazi Jewish worlds in what are now Poland, Lithuania, and parts of the Ukraine), raised partially in the Franco-French educational system, I spoke and speak a mixture of 'standard' (Franco-French) French, and (ever so slightly) Québécois, as well as North American English; in each language and setting, I 'passed' and 'pass' more or less equally as native – though most awkwardly in Québec, for sounding a bit too Franco-French among Québécois francophones (I was always embarrassed by my accent – addressing a bus driver, for example, when going to see good friends in the *joual*-dominated east of Montreal, before contemporary Franco-French had become quite so present, mixed into today's even more multilingual urban soundscape), and in France for sounding foreign also, when speaking terms I hardly realize are Québécois, eliciting surprise or chuckles (Québécois French sounds 'quaint' to Franco-French ears). I come to this poem thus as an outsider and insider, both; as someone for whom the 'language question' has always been gallingly personal, a difficult thing to think through, full of embarrassment, pride, and impasse. Thus if Simon describes the triangulation of three languages in Montreal: French, English, and Yiddish, three cultural worlds that defined modernist cultures in the 1940s and beyond, and though the situation has changed radically, and a deep and lasting détente since the referendum for Québec separation in the mid-1990s characterizes the far more boisterously and peacefully multilingual space within which languages mesh and bilingual wordplay defines everyday life, the genealogies are complex and politically as well as emotionally loaded. And while such intermixture might be par for the course in Montreal and many other bilingual or multilingual cities, the feeling of toggling, of a perpetual *entre-deux*, or 'between-two' – between

---

[7] On performance and indigenous and French language histories in Québec, see especially V. K. Preston, 'A Dictionary in the Archives: Translating and Transcribing Silenced Histories in French and Wendat', *Performance Research* 21.5 (2016): 'On Trans/Performance', 85–88.

Performative Accents

many – in small and sometimes nearly insignificant ways (a word use, an inflection) stays strong, not least when one continues to migrate (what was that last stopping point? Where is one really from?). Language becomes the cypher for the occasional (and perhaps constitutional) failure of the performative 'outing' and 'passing' that one does all the time. Neither quite one sort of national nor another, one feels, when something between major and minor, part of and always just outside both the dominant and the *'petites cultures'* or 'little cultures' Lalonde and Denis Monière describe in their manifesto *Cause commune* (Common Cause) (1981) – this way of thinking what one could call minor-national causes (Catalonia, Québec), not quite the otherwise perhaps still uncategorizable multimigratory multiplicities, but allied ways of being constantly slightly foreign, not entirely; almost French, but not quite; almost Québécois, but not quite; almost this and that, each *branlant*, off-kilter.[8] Yet as I am suggesting here, there is not such a far cry from the nomadism of migratory languaging, and the call for unicity within the 'petite culture', itself also a site of linguistic chaos, a *pullullement* of languages or a teeming – clutter and clatter.

The theatre of these negotiations, whether we are capable of performing them purposefully or not (accents are very rarely performable except in jest or, never quite entirely accurately, even with many years of highly qualified training), suggests a common and I think still undertheorized approach to thinking about the performance of speech in the everyday. This is speech when it dramatizes – performatively enacts – relationships of power between provisionally major and minor variations, 'little' and 'big' cultures, as these are constantly moving genealogically, shifting, engaged in acts of *translatio* as empires and modes of discourse shift.[9] 'Major' speech in Montreal is now Québécois French, and Franco-French is minoritarian, but saturated with the feeling of majoritarianism and cultural ascendency still (France as 'old world', etc.), though Franco-French has infinite variations, minoritarianisms within it, dialects and non-'standard' accents in the south, in the north, in the banlieues, everywhere. These inheritances emerge in heightened form with performed poetry, not least when the subject is power, translation, and speech, as is the case so powerfully with Lalonde.

Lalonde herself was, ironically perhaps, acutely aware of her own comparatively Franco-French mode of speech within Québec and the impossibility of a 'pure' Québécois language, as much as her poem came

---

[8] See Michèle Lalonde and Denis Monière, *Cause commune. Manifeste pour une uébécoiseal des petites cultures* (Montréal: L'Hexagone, 1981).

[9] See Gotman, *'Translatio'*.

to stand as a rallying cry for Québécois separatist activism. As I will detail, this helps to rethink *francophonie*, as postcolonial critic Michel Laronde also suggests: it is imperative, he writes, to 'deconstruct the French versus francophone binary opposition by [...] [including] "Franco-French" literature and cultural production, together with postcolonial French, under the label *francophone*'.[10] Francophone literature is not just from the 'rest of the world', but co-composed with and adjacent to 'standard' French; to decolonize French, one has to cease to erect an opposition. It is not just that Franco-French and postcolonial *francophonie* could be mashed together globally within the designation 'francophone' (perhaps finely tuning ways in which inflections *do* power relations), but lived histories of performative inflections, I am suggesting, further worry these distinctions every day. Relations between 'minor' and 'major' accents performatively take place within phrases, languaging acts, that individuals do. What I aim to unravel then here is how lived speech occurs as a set of displacements by which one may not only attempt to erase non-normative speech ('accents') to approximate something 'pure' but also the reverse: to erase or draw obliquely attention to 'standard' speech where, in context, it is felt as imperial, oppressive, other – alien, awkward – skin that is too pale, speech that is too 'French', or not in the right way. This is the experience of *xenophony*, as I will describe further, after Rey Chow, who notes with Jacques Derrida that the heart of a language is never one's own; language is so plural, it is necessarily uncountable. Many languages do not equal more than one monolanguage, since language can never be singular[11]: there are a hundred-thousand 'Frenches'. One is constantly accounting for one's language, and yet it cannot be taken to account.

Lalonde's poem in fact performs a near constant state of code-switching, between English and French. Educated briefly in the United States and the United Kingdom during study periods at Harvard, in Baltimore and in London in the mid-1960s, with a degree in Philosophy from the Université de Montréal, Lalonde's English is fluent, her pronunciation of the English words and phrases she deploys strategically offered as phonetically 'correct' (anglophone-passing). She is a master poet and virtuosic public speaker, script writer, and performer; eventually Professor of the History of

---

[10] In H. Adlai Murdoch and Anne Donadey, 'Introduction: Productive Intersections', in *Postcolonial Theory and Francophone Literary Studies*, edited by H. Adlai Murdoch and Anne Donadey (Gainesville: University Press of Florida, 2005): 1–17, 5. See also Michel Laronde, 'Displaced Discourses: Post(-)coloniality, Francophone Space(s), and the Literature(s) of Immigration in France', in *Postcolonial Theory and Francophone Literary Studies*, 175–192.

[11] Chow, *Not Like a Native Speaker*, 31. See Jacques Derrida, *Le monolinguisme de l'autre: ou la prothèse d'origine* (Paris: Éditions Galilée, 1996), 55.

Civilizations at the National Theatre School of Canada as well as, in 1984, President of the International Federation of French-Language Writers, Lalonde's poetics deploy absolute sensitivity to the granular movements of language codes and accents in and beyond Québec and to their performative power. Language in Québec has been the primary rallying point for political grievance, and Lalonde offers her capacity – her decision I think – performatively to point to and to complicate, and paradoxically perhaps to globalize '*parlure*' via recourse to her own more standard French, the 'lesser enemy', as critic Dianne Sears points out (relative to the reviled and yet nevertheless well-incorporated English).[12] If Québécois films, for example, are frequently subtitled in French for global audiences not able to follow the Québécois accents and dialect, Lalonde's intended audience has to be understood similarly to gesture towards the global francophone listeners she also speaks of – a deferred audience – as well as the few thousand fellow Québécois gathered at the Gesù.

Grammatical correctness is state power, she argues forcefully, orthography a manner of judging fitness to speak and be heard by an institutional yardstick aligned with political power; and while Québécois French boasts a distinctive grammar and accentuation relative to 'standard' French, including heavy use of English, American, and to an extent genealogically Algonquin and local patois tones and expressions (as well as, in compensation, hyper-Gallicisms), anglophone modes of pronunciation and syntax, longer vowels, frequently rolled rs, and wetter consonants, as well as tenses conjugated non-normatively relative to standard French (the first person singular for example may be conjugated in speech with the second person singular, as in *je vas*, contracted to *j'vas*, pronounced *j'vaw*, rather than the standard *je vais*, pronounced *jə veh*, etc.), Lalonde does not speak for the most part with this Québécois idiom, nonetheless used strategically by other poets and writers and by herself in some works; but articulates the poem with a comparatively 'white' French, barring one or two instances where she strategically deploys Québécois slang ('*notre parlure*' ['our (rotten) speech']).[13] This 'rotten' speech is in fact, she suggests, literally dirty, dirtied by oil and sludge. In contrast, even Franco-French is 'white',

---

[12] Dianne E. Sears, 'Défense de parler: Language on Trial in Michèle Lalonde's "La deffence et illustration de la langue québecquoyse" and "Outrage au tribunal"' *The French Review* 68, no. 6 (1995): 1015–1021, 1018. See also French philosopher and poet Jean Pierre Faye's preface to Lalonde's *Défense et illustration de la langue Québécoise, suivie de prose & poèmes* (Paris: Éditions Seghers/Laffont, 1979), where he aligns '*parlure*' with the language and aims of Hölderlin, Yeats, Synge, Joyce – particularly in *Finnegan's Wake* – and Rabelais, among others, situating Lalonde at the heart of an emerging movement to forge a new poetic language, 'insurgent' and 'free'.

[13] See also Lalonde, 'La deffence', 108.

and though she writes 'we are a resentful people / but do not reproach anyone / their monopoly of the correction of language' (*'nous sommes un people rancunier / mais ne reprochons à personne / d'avoir le monopole / de la correction de langage'* [in French in the original]), she goes on to rebuke a string of majoritarian cultures for this monopoly. In my translation, 'be at ease with your words / [...] in the sweet language of Shakespeare / with the accent of Longfellow / speak a pure and atrociously white French / as in Vietnam and the Congo / speak an impeccable German / a yellow star between your teeth / speak Russian speak call to order speak / repression / speak white / it is a universal language / we are born to understand it / with its tear-gas words / with its words that bludgeon.' Grammatical language ('white' speech) is not only the language for giving orders but also, perhaps tragically, a literary language where this aligns with political rule – Shakespeare and Longfellow, Byron, Shelley, and Keats, even as fellow poets, are associated with cultural capital; nothing escapes the stain of English, powerhouse of world domination culturally as well as of ongoing global economic and political ascendency.

Lalonde is clear: the alternative is not necessarily to hunker down into another form of majoritarianism. She aims to work through what language is – what her language can be. In her distinctively performative essay, 'La Deffence et illustration de la langue quebecquoyse' ['Deffense and illustration of Quebecquois language'(*sic*)] (1977) – a mock imitation and trenchant cultural translation of Renaissance poet and visionary Joachim du Bellay's (1522–1560) *La Deffence et illustration de la langue francoyse* (1549), which sought to argue for the possibility of a French-language literature that might equal that of Greece and Rome – she toggles between mock sixteenth-century French, in effect at the roots of Québécois French, current street speech or *'parlure'*, littered with anglophone terms, and standard literary French, shifting spellings constantly, as was practice before the regulation of orthography. This suggests, as she writes with some dismay, that being colonized as she is, she doesn't know where to turn to express herself. I quote in her performative French, and will paraphrase: 'Quant à moi', she writes,

> affollée comme tous à la pensée d'estre colonisée et anxieuse comme quiconque de me défendre de cette calamité, je ne sais où trouver refuge, ny en quel sophisme donner de la teste, ny au forsaille en quelle langue me battre à visière levée… Car si je m'exprime en Français très correct et contemporain de France, je risque de bien mal illustrer l'originalité de la Langue Québécoyse, voire de me ranger à droite avec ceux qui la méprisent injustement. Et si au contraire, je me tourne la langue sept fois à gauche

Performative Accents

> pour ramasser tous les anglicismes, barbarismes & vices de syntaxe qui font l'orgueil du Kébecway moderne, je risque de prendre parti comme la langue-à-ma-mére, qui après tout parlait plus traditionnellement et compréhensiblement Français.

Though she speaks a fairly standard French, as she states, risking thus not sufficiently well enough to illustrate the originality of Québécois French, it is not much better to turn to the 'vices of syntax', 'anglicisms and barbarisms' that current 'Kébecway' street speech is so proud of, and which risk another sort of nostalgism for the mama's tongue ('*la langue-à-ma-mére*' – the diacritic 'é', rather than 'è' indicating Québécois pronunciation and, for her, skirt-gripping provincialism). She turns playfully to this sixteenth-century style, as an alternative linguistic 'root', older and thus (falsely) truer, perhaps stylistically less pure also and thus more adequate for resistance: it is not yet national, not state-sanctioned, closer to a 'freer' era, as she puts it, when language was spoken on Canadian terrain without the painful complications of the present day. (Again, one might counter that French speech also violently imposed upon indigenous speech in devastating systems of re-education at the time – an era 'free' only for a minority.) Lalonde's commentary is slightly tongue-in-cheek, as her own linguistic performance suggests the impossibility of returning to any sort of sixteenth-century mode, and although she deploys this picturesque orthography to offer a counterpoint to current-day Americanisms, Canadian-Anglo anglicisms and standard French, it is clear that all these form the still distinctive intermixture with which she writes; there is no pure speech or condition.[14] While this text is printed alongside the manifesto of the separatist Front de Libération du Québec (FLQ), as well as government responses to the organization's actions, which had been designated terrorist and triggered declaration of the war act (October 1970), and alongside writings on Ireland and Portugal, as well as feminist writings and others attending to language, and a new manifesto co-signed in 1976 by Lalonde, Hubert Acquin, Gaston Miron, and Pierre Vadeboncoeur, situating the victory of the Parti Québécois that year not in a 'folkloric' but a 'global' movement towards 'disalienation', her own performative writing finds the global within a crafted and hyper-contemporary false folklorism: speech and writing uttered as non-grammatical, and thus distinctively embodied, vibrant and alive.[15]

---

[14] Lalonde, 'La deffence', 105, 110. See also n4.
[15] Hubert Acquin et al., 'Réflexion à quatre voix sur l'émergence d'un pouvoir québécois', in *Change Souverain Québec* 5–10.

In a short text published in 1980, Lalonde reflects further on this 'anti-grammaticality': she had been, at the outset, an expert poet, she writes, playing with words joyfully, but these were floating in the air, she herself lived in a glorious and glamorous bubble, she was called a 'poet', a high priestess of language, but unconnected to the lived reality of the everyday – her own street, her home. She began to reject this 'purer style', 'empty', and 'strictly grammatical', with which, she writes, she had been 'used', by 'them', a mere literary court jester, insignificant, and suddenly people began to pay attention: her every word was surveilled, every breath on the phone tracked. When she refused the rules of syntax, raised her voice, became merely 'intelligible' to those around her, to her children, while peeling a potato, suddenly it mattered, a lot. The tone in this 'Little Testament' (*Petit Testament*) is playful, still; writing with the hindsight of her central role in the new politico-cultural landscape, some of her peers imprisoned, she could offer a mock naivety here and recognition that the 'few banalities' she lined up on the page had all the power of breaking, sabotaging, exploding, and invalidating the instrument – language – she had mastered.[16]

With 'Speak White', Lalonde directly denounces the violence of colonial oppression through the lens of speech: this was not just government rule but language power translated into and indistinguishable from the broader global violence of racist oppression and classicism. Lalonde references the race riots in Watts, the African-American majority neighbourhood of Los Angeles where in August 1965, the arrest of Marquette Frye sparked a massive uprising against housing, employment, and educational system discrimination, as well as against police violence, resulting in the death of over thirty and the arrest and injury of thousands. 'Speak white' then was a cypher for a cultural and capitalist system of injustice waged through the orthographic rule of 'law' keeping entire peoples – here, the Québécois, alongside those in the Congo, Haiti, Little Rock, and elsewhere – among the perennially downtrodden, the janitors (she describes a *'peuple-concièrge'* or 'janitor-people'), the ordered about, those who die at the workplace, and those for whom a day of strike action lasts an eternity;

---

[16] Michèle Lalonde, 'Petit Testament', *University of Toronto Quarterly*, 50, no. 1 (1980): 66–68. Glissant was similarly preoccupied with the notion that grammar came in the form of dictation, and so quite literally a form of power over, articulated in writing, through speech; in *Le discours antillais* (Paris: Gallimard, 1997), a collection of writings within which he also treats the question of Québec and Montreal, and the dictum 'Speak white', noting as in the epigraph to this chapter that in Québec, the French language was claimed, demanded, while in the Caribbean, it was imposed (401–413, 452, 553–555).

for whom the 'standard of living' and '*gracious living*' (the latter in English in the original) are bitter and laughable aims. Ironically, once again, her audience was an educated, cultured, comparatively empowered one at the time of her performance; but the cultural strides made during the period from the 1940s to the 1960s, which at once made such a gathering possible, still smarted from the wounds of poverty and humiliation. Lalonde's reference to the 'not very brilliant' people to the east of her implied interlocutor's empires – always on the receiving end of grand discourse about the Magna Carta, the Lincoln Memorial, the 'grey charm of the Thames' – is contrasted to the secure knowledge that they nevertheless boast, quietly, the hoarse songs of their ancestors, the sorrow of Émile Nelligan (1879–1941), one of the first renowned French-language Québécois writers, who at the turn of the twentieth century wrote an extraordinary number of modernist poems before being institutionalized at the age of nineteen for paranoid schizophrenia. Nelligan himself, born between languages and cultures from an Irish immigrant father and a French-Canadian mother, was already caught culturally and emotionally in the linguistic crossfire, ultimately identifying with the French. As an adopted forefather, his bilingualism is translated strategically into a willed francophonie. It does not matter so much what language (or languages) one was 'born' with: what matters is what one chooses to speak. This approximates Jacques Derrida's notion, in a footnote at the end of *Le monolinguisme de l'autre: ou la prothèse d'origine* (1996) (*Monolingualism of the Other; or, The Prosthesis of Origin* (1998)), that identity might best be defined by the place one chooses to end up, rather than where one was born: we are most from the place we desire to be, that which we gesture towards, or lean into. Rather than speak of migrants 'going back to where they are from', one can speak of cultural and linguistic identity as privileging those chosen affiliations, those deliberate and cultivated arrivals.[17]

Performatively, as I have noted, Lalonde offers her capacity in speech to pronounce all of the English place names and terms impeccably – to have learned the master's speech. Her audience at the Gesù would have been a French-speaking audience equally versed in this terminology and for the most part well capable of understanding the bitterness and rage contained in her not-so-gentle depictions of how 'lovely it is to hear' her implied English-speaking interlocutor tell of Paradise Lost. Reference to the accent of Milton and Byron and Shelley and Keats, to the sonnets of Shakespeare,

---

[17] Derrida imagines, after the idea was put to him, one day dedicating a symposium to language, nationality and cultural belonging not based on natality but on death. Derrida, *Le monolinguisme*, 30.

offer images of intertextual negotiation where the pronunciation of the poet's names – for Shakespeare, with a Franco-French grated r, in this case – announces a prior relationship, a form of domination and mastery, and a rupture. These poets who would have been kindred spirits are instrumentalized in the poet's view, by the violence with which their language has been imposed; the violence is double, uncountable, aligned with massacres in Vietnam, with working-class poverty in Saint-Henri, a neighbourhood of Montreal south of the wealthiest, anglophone sections to the west, and where workers would have gone home at night, as she depicts, at the hour when the sun comes crashing down on the alleyways – but, as she notes, it is rising, also, and that hope is what fuels the changing set of political relations globally that she announces and depicts. To come back to Glissant, the French language is relativized – as much with regard to ('white') Franco-French as to white British, white American, and white Canadian English. Lalonde is white – blonde – strikingly so – yet the whiteness she depicts is relational here, aligned with the anti-colonial struggles and anti-racist activism of the time.[18] As a member of a worker people in a context where to be told to 'speak white' is to be told to get into line, that one's people is uncultured, ungrammatical, a backwater people not fit for anything better than slavish work, Lalonde offers a picture of defiance and transformation: her poem is cultured to the highest degree, impeccably aware of global history, literature, and language – and as such it is arguably an entire speech act, a performative utterance, a way of doing oneself in and through translation, where the act of translation transforms the relationship to language by refusing the power relation that has been enacted up to this point. She enacts this most directly in the final lines, where it is clear she wants to be certain her audience understands both the English and French: that the English is not decorative to some people's ears, clear to others'. She states: 'We are not alone/ / nous savons / que nous ne sommes pas seuls', the first instance of a direct self-translation in the poem, emphasized by the repetition of 'we are not alone', effectively stated three times: in English, in French, and again in French, with added emphasis: 'we know that we are not alone.' Lalonde thus subverts 'speak white' into 'we are not alone', retorting that the polite responses will continue but there is a global mass of people and peoples tired of this, who are beginning to refuse. Her compatriots' landmark *Refus Global* manifesto ('Global

---

[18] On studies depicting the 'whitening' of demographic groups previously not considered 'white', see especially Noel Ignatiev, *How the Irish Became White* (London: Routledge, 2009); and Karen Brodkin, *How Jews Became White Folks and What That Says about Race in America* (New Jersey: Rutgers University Press, 1999).

Performative Accents 119

Refusal'), signed in 1948 by a group of sixteen Montreal-based artists, had effectively sparked what came to be known as the Quiet Revolution, first of all attacking the hegemony of the Catholic church, and with that Christian hegemony more globally.[19] Although much further activity took place between the *Refus Global* movement and resultant outcry and Lalonde's performative interventions, the relationship of Québec to a global imperial order was being radically and now systematically questioned, alignments and hierarchies redefined. While *Refus Global* offered an anarchic vision of the world finally opened up to others for exchange and emancipation, 'Speak White' brought the site of the revolution back home to Québec, and to Montreal, where on the street a granular battle with power had to be waged at the level of language and dialogue, poetry and speech first of all. Lalonde comes back onstage following the performance of her three-part *Panneaux-réclame* (Advertising Billboards) at the same *La nuit de la poésie* event where she gave 'Speak White' – amid ecstatic cheers and clapping – with the phrase 'poetry will be total, or it will not be' ('La poésie sera totale ou elle ne sera pas'), the last line / 'epilogue' of the dramatic poem, offered here as a performative utterance directly in response to this historic event: poetry, like philosophy, does not merely describe but transforms the word – and world.[20]

Paradoxically, as Micone has pointed out, in his now classic retort, 'Speak What' (1989), the French-speaking, Catholic Québécois majority, quickly ascending to power after the Quiet Revolution of the 1950s to 1970s, just as quickly forgot its own roots in the back rooms of industrial factories and imposed its own linguistic hegemony over a new wave of immigrants coming to Québec from Greece, Italy, and elsewhere. These new immigrants – now required by law to learn and to prioritize French following the institution of the Loi 101 (in 1977) and the Loi 178 (in 1989) respectively enshrining French signage and French-language education in Québec as ways to curb the continued, increasing ascendancy of English in this part of North America – were, he pointed out, effectively

---

[19] Paul-Émile Borduas et al., *Refus Global* (Shawinigan: Anatole Brochu, 1972 [orig. publ. 1948]). *Refus global* is also excerpted in Lalonde et al., *Change Souverain Québec*, 238.

[20] *Panneaux-Réclame* is published in Michèle Lalonde, *Défense et illustration de la langue québécoise, suivie de prose et poèmes* (Paris: Éditions Seghers/Laffont, 1979): 59–78. It was performed 29 March 1970 at the *La nuit de la poésie* event at the Gesù theatre, by Lalonde, Rossignol and Michel Garneau. Lalonde's instruction suggests the poem should be 'performed ['*joué*'], sung, screamed, whistled'. The three performers form a dramatic tableau onstage, not performing any action except sonically: they are observers of a trompe l'œil theatre, the text characterized by abrupt stylistic shifts (60) – as with 'Speak White', though more theatrically here, a characteristic marker of Lalonde's critique through collage, juxtaposition, and code-switching.

culturally denied an equal right to their own mixed-heritage Québécois narratives. Their broken accents, and memories of war, displacement, and exile, marked them as threatening to a majority still experiencing itself as fragile in its new-found ascendency, and susceptible to outside influence as it continued to stake claims to national unicity founded in the myth of *'pure laine'* (pure wool) Québécois culture. What Micone forcefully points out, in his reappropriation of Lalonde's iconic poem, is that francophone Québécois literature and culture had become majoritarian and hegemonic in turn, so that by the time of his writing in the late 1980s, a new minoritarian literature had to rise up to complicate and further displace this new hegemony, reminding the now firmly entrenched francophone Québécois majority that they too were 'not alone'. (Québécois government funding in the 2000s began to recognize some of the ironic reverse disparity and to offer arts council grants for organizations specifically working within anglophone contexts, now seen as near suddenly minoritarian and in need of subsidy, an unsettling but necessary reversal in this country [and nation] shifting power dynamics across language and cultural groups.)

Performative *Xenophony*: Speaking a Language While Bilingual (of Other Versions)

My aim in coming back to 'Speak White', and its political and cultural entanglements in Québec and the global *francophonie*, is thus to examine how performative speech enacts politics within performance poetry. Here, the performance of Anglo speech emerges in 'Speak White' as a marker of reterritorialization (Québec recuperates English language and terminology) but also as an interruption, an excrescence, an act of presencing the 'master' within a divided, but constitutionally translational self. Spoken language secretes moments of pronunciation that enact, at a granular level, relationships to multiple languages and/or codes. 'White' language, articulated by Lalonde in English but also in her own comparatively standard French, emerges as the poet's manner of negotiating linguistic power relations, just as the speaker theatrically divests herself of this aspect of her own speech, this manner of having been linguistically and culturally colonized – points to it, dramatizes this onstage as an utterance. Québec, although emerging as a 'new' nation, is forged in a multiplicity of power relationships between Frenches and Englishes, degrees of symbolic 'whiteness' and 'Blackness', a *métissage* that constitutes a distinctive singularity. Separatist action in Lalonde's work then comes paradoxically as a singularizing but also a radically relational linguistic condition, performative in tone and

Performative Accents 121

expression, not to reproduce the imagined 'monolingualism of the other' (or the imagined monolingualism of the self), as in Derrida's formulation, but to replace this with a messy '*parlure*' enabling subjects to pass between registers not only to obey a master, but as a precondition for a plural, genealogically complex, and ultimately potentially anarchic – certainly rhizomatic – political possibility. This is consistent I think with poet and statesman Léopold Sédar Senghor's concept of Négritude (ironically also often seen falsely as a singularity) as a heteroglossic, mixed condition, radically plural and always moving – what philosopher Souleymane Bachir Diagne further describes as a condition of co-birthing/co-knowledge (*co-naissance*) and of rhythmic adjacency.[21] Race and nation are always, at their core, at the outset, and after, intermixed.

At a granular level, performative acts of rejection and incorporation constitute (co-compose) *co-naissance*, knowledge-together, and ultimately knowledge and care of self (and even one's reviled others), thus eventually, perhaps, I think, plural politics – a 'common cause', made up of little and perhaps of bigger cultures. This genealogical xenophony – this way language moves in its alliances and affiliations with 'other' sounds, producing a perpetually shifting linguistic turf – resounds in further versions of 'Speak White', each time showcasing the granularity of performative utterances and the million ways accents are conjugated to perform relations of distance and refusal: performative utterances offered at the level of the phoneme complicate linguistic genealogies and national archives. In an NFB/ONF short directed by celebrated Québécois filmmakers Pierre Falardeau (1946–2009) and Julien Poulin (b. 1946), and narrated by Marie Eykel (b. 1948) (1980), as well as a remixed version spoken by Falardeau himself, and in a far more recent performance by Haitian-Canadian poet, producer, composer, and musician Jenny Salgado at the Moulin à Paroles in the Plaines d'Abraham in Québec City in 2011, the heightened presence of English does not just distance the speaker from this particular master culture, but performs a negotiation within which the capacity for incorporating English terminology is shown as violent, assailable, a forced imposition, *dressage* and, ultimately, an irrelevance. 'Shakespeare' with a rough France-French 'r' in Lalonde's version signals 'I am – unwittingly or not – speaking something of a "pure," "white", literary, heightened French, in spite of and also importantly alongside my call to Québécois revolt'; as I detail above, she was aware of her Franco-French manner and was

---

[21] See especially Souleymane Bachir Diagne, *African Art as Philosophy: Senghor, Bergson and the Idea of Negritude*, translated by Chike Jeffers (Calcutta: Seagull Books, [2007] 2011).

displaying that inheritance on this ground for contestation. 'Shakespeare' with a sliding, American 'r' (in Eykel's version) signals 'I am able to speak imperialist English, this hated white speech, even though I also reject it; I reject that part of myself that has been colonised, and that pronounces this word this way.' 'Shakespeare', forcefully, with a background of electric guitar, enunciated with all the passion and musicality of a rolling Québécois 'r', sign of the deepest *joual* pronunciation, in Falardeau's case, suggests that 'Shakespeare' has been for good or ill folded into Québécois idiom: a cultural import spit back out, almost seamlessly said alongside 'jurons' (swear words), spoken with all the pride of a language founded in poverty. These versions perform relationships to English language and 'correct' grammar such as saturate Lalonde's text, theatricalizing the polyphonic relationships to English that Québécois French possesses, and the inextricable intimacy with which these languages produce a plastic and morphing Québécois speech (as well as, one might be at pains to add, eventually a Québécois English – and mixed-up *franglais* – saturated with Québécois Gallicisms). In Jenny Salgado's recent performance, whiteness takes on another hue: she begins by greeting her audience as 'brothers and sisters', and saying that she is delighted to be among them (*'parmi vous'*, 'among you' or 'with you') and then adds, quite emphatically, that she is even more delighted to be 'among us' (*'parmi nous'*). Spoken by a Haitian-Québécois woman, whose musical career as J.Kyll, with the band Muzion, sets Haitian-Québécois life at the heart of a constant negotiation with roots, culture, and race (for example in her song 'Mal à ma culture' [Pain in my culture or My culture hurts]), Lalonde's 'Speak White' here comes to be thickly ghosted by the spectres of anti-Black racism that Lalonde conjures and which were always in the 1970s distinctively materially outside the room. Forty years later, the gestural rapprochement Salgado performs highlights the genealogy at play, and with this, a complex national-affective archive. Blackness in Lalonde's poem may have been material and symbolic – an epithet, an alliance, not epidermal, or not in the same way – while with Salgado the performance becomes materially and epidermally charged. Her accent is distinctively francophone, and now the English words are nearly an afterthought; this is no longer the battle being waged. That battle has gone quiet, Québécois French heavily dominates Québec, in a general détente between anglophone and francophone worlds, and in the gesture of togetherness Salgado performs at the start, it seems that even racial harmony has been won, were it not indeed for how pale-skinned and slightly uncomfortable and perhaps jaded her overwhelmingly white audience at this event appears to be, from what

I can see on the video record.[22] Nevertheless, Salgado's choice to bring this particular poem to the setting – one of her favourite in the Québécois literary canon, as she states – presences, performatively, the still difficult and charged history of comparative Québécois nationalism still recent in many people's memories. As Micone suggested in his retort, to remain culturally vibrant, Québec had to continue to recognize and nurture migration and allophony in new generations of underclasses and new waves. Postcolonial language, including Québécois language, requires one perpetually to reimagine how language is and is also not 'one's own'; how in embodying, uttering, sounds and phrases, within specific rooms or performative sites, one hosts (re)alliances. Salgado does this in coming back to 'Speak White', offering another moment of performative re-alliance.

As her performance of the poem suggests, now, the Québécois were distinctly white, but not so white they could not also find an asynchronous but comparatively affectively shared history of dispossession. Salgado's French is strewn with Québecisms and other anglicisms, like 'so', etc., just as anglophone speakers in Montreal strew their speech with Gallicisms in a general give-and-take characteristic of the Montreal cityscape; more than suggest antagonism, this scene offers a moment within which translingualism is possible, in granular speech acts where the 'other' language is not only a language of power, but also awkwardly a shared inheritance. Salgado's commentary is paratextual, in the performative presence she offers and her gesture at the start. By *not* inflecting the poem, she performs a decision to be with it, in the sheer historical irony and alliance represented by her skin colour in relation to this term, 'Speak White'. We are all Québécois, and this history is mine also, she says implicitly to her audience. Nonetheless, Québécois critic Lise Gauvin suggests in conversation with Glissant that a poetics of 'disquiet', after Portuguese poet Fernando Pessoa, might best describe the slippages and anxieties of multilingualism in a postcolonial age. Referring to the work of Moroccan novelist, playwright, and critic Abdelkebir Khatibi, Gauvin suggests that, in Khatibi's words, a 'chiasma' falls between languages in the process of translation from one to another, a process that might also be said to characterize writing as such.[23] As Gauvin further argues, Algerian novelist and critic Assia

---

[22] Jenny Salgado, 'Speak White au Moulin à Paroles', https://jennysalgado.ca/videoclips/mes-articles-video/60-speak-white-au-moulin-a-paroles accessed 19 May 2022.

[23] Abdelkebir Khatibi, 'Lettre-préface', in M. Gontard, *La Violence du texte: études sur la littérature marocaine de langue française* (Paris: L'Harmattan, 1981), 8. Cited in Lise Gauvin, 'Entre rupture et affirmation: les manifestes francophones'. *Études littéraires africaines* 29 (2010): 13, https://doi.org/10.7202/1027490ar accessed 2 April 2015.

124 KÉLINA GOTMAN

Djebar employs the metaphor of the 'veil', the 'double', the 'lost shadow', the '*entre-deux-langues*' (between-two-languages), and 'langage-tangage' to suggest discomfort, loss, anxiety, and disquiet in the process of toggling between tongues.[24] Multilingualism is not just a tactic of slippage, a positive 'poetics of relation', as Glissant posits, a way constantly to circumnavigate authoritarian or majoritarian race and class, political and language relations, but also a constant source of affective displacement and an uncanny sense of being never quite 'at home' in one's 'own' language or in another's. In other terms, the mother language or mother tongue (in French, 'language' and 'tongue' are both signified by the single word '*langue*', as in '*langue maternelle*', 'mother tongue') always recedes, disappears. It is constantly uncanny and unbecoming, constantly needing to be rebuilt. It also constantly haunts the speaker and writer, who is not only lost trying to find her way through a maze of foreign modes of speech, even while these may be partially adopted, familiar, or quotidian and banal. Rather, this mother tongue spectrally grounds – pins – the writer to an imagined sense of an original language that would be reachable, just as a mother nation, a *terre natale*, a land of origins, might (or might not) be. In *Le monolinguisme de l'autre*, Derrida argues that it is a logical and performative contradiction to suggest that one might speak a language that is not one's own – that one might have one's own original language, and that this is completely distinct from that of the master. All language is one's own, he writes, including language that has been 'imposed' on one.[25]

Put another way, wresting another one's language from oneself denies one one's own quite powerful and constitutional foreignness to oneself. For Julia Kristeva, both Bulgarian and French, in different ways, foreignness to oneself is the most formidable and truthful figure for conceptualizing the possibility of plural politics, multiple affiliations.[26] We are always a bit uncanny, a bit awkwardly in one's skin, in one's tongues and accents – at least, I might add, when, as for so many, there is not a singular 'one' that is the language one might speak. This linguistic homelessness (or feeling

---

[24] Assia Djebar, *Ces voix qui m'assiègent: en marge de ma francophonie* (Paris: A. Michel, 1999), 51. In Gauvin, 'Entre rupture et affirmation', 13–14.

[25] Derrida, *Monolingualism of the Other,* 39–40. For Derrida, it is a 'performative contradiction' to suggest that white and black speech, colonized and colonizing discourses, can be entirely separated. It is significant that he uses the term '*performative*' in English, after J. L. Austin, when he writes of the '"*contradiction performative*"' (quotation marks and emphasis in the original) of the idea that one might speak a language that is not one's own. Derrida, *Le monolinguisme*, especially 16–18. This chapter among other things worries this claim to a performative contradiction, suggesting that one always speaks one's own language, yet it is inflected performatively with 'others' – which are of course in this respect *also* 'one's own'.

[26] Julia Kristeva, *Étrangers à nous-mêmes* (Paris: Fayard/Gallimard, 1988).

Performative Accents

of homesickness), mythifies (and mystifies) the linguistic 'home' within which one might supposedly find refuge: where one might speak as if lucidly, transparently, without drawing attention to the awkwardness, the mis-grammaticality, or hyper-grammaticality, the accents, the words or turns – all these things by which one is perpetually always infelicitously, perhaps, or else companionably, 'out'. For philosopher and philologist Barbara Cassin, language is impossibly and crucially where 'home' resides: reading Hannah Arendt, she suggests that language may feel *more* like 'home' than any land or physical territory. If one is nostalgic for a lost terrain, one is also through this in pain: 'nostalgia' can be understood – in relation to Odysseus's near ceaseless voyaging (though he does arrive!) – etymologically in terms of a dual movement: *nostos* suggests 'return', and *algos* signals 'pain'. Seventeenth-century French and German physicians first diagnosed Swiss military officers as suffering from *oder Heimweh*, '*le mal du pays*' (homesickness), a painful longing for their homeland.[27] Nostalgia signifies at once rooting and uprooting, and their temporal (temporary) mismatch; it is the affective register that describes a state of fluctuation.[28] At the same time, translation can be seen as the space of negotiation between these that enables the exilic condition to be situated at the forefront of pedagogical practice and what Cassin hopes may herald a new paradigm, after nation: recognition that languages are always composed of negotiations – errors of history, echoes and correspondences, relations and differentiations.[29] For Deleuze and Claire Parnet, bilingualism is a perpetual stammering, a way of worrying one's 'own' language with interjections of heterophony. They call this '[b]eing a foreigner in one's own language',[30] and see this as a necessary state of gestural plurality, a way of being complex and open to others, as well as constantly open within oneself: 'We must be bilingual even in a single language, we must have a minor language inside our own language', they write. And further,

> we must create a minor use of our own language. Multilingualism is not merely the property of several systems each of which would be homogeneous in itself: it is primarily the line of flight or of variation which affects

---

[27] In Barbara Cassin, *La nostalgie: Quand donc est-on chez soi?* (Paris: Éditions Autrement, 2013): 16–20.

[28] Cassin, *La nostalgie*, 20.

[29] Cassin, *La nostalgie*, 118–132. On the notion of translation as a pedagogical philosophy, see also Barbara Cassin, 'L'énergie des intraduisibles: La traduction comme paradigme pour les sciences humaines', in *Philosopher en langues: les intraduisibles en traduction*, edited by Barbara Cassin (Paris: Éditions Rue d'Ulm / Presses de l'École normale supérieure, 2014): 9–20, 19–20.

[30] Gilles Deleuze and Claire Parnet, *Dialogues* (Paris: Champs essais, 1996), 4.

126 KÉLINA GOTMAN

each system by stopping it from being homogeneous. Not speaking like an Irishman or a Romanian in a language other than one's own, but on the contrary speaking one's own language like a foreigner.[31]

To 'speak one's own language like a foreigner' is to speak I think always as if in stereo, as if sitting just off to the side of one of the speakers, as if hearing another voice, a split second out of synch, perpetually displacing oneself, comparing versions. One is never entirely at home in one's own language, or languages (one 'stammers'), except inasmuch as the feeling of home is doubled, tripled, ghosted, transient, a passage, translation. Like Lalonde hearing her own Franco-French, and hearing English, and hearing *parlure*, one passes through languages and registers and utterances and attempts I think to build a patchwork, makeshift space, that honours the impossibility of reaching a foundation or a root, an 'origin' – and yet feeling these also.

As Tobagonian and Canadian poet and essayist M. NourbeSe Philip (b. 1947) offers, the 'logic of language' is 'anguish': 'English/ is my mother tongue./ A mother tongue is not/ not a foreign lan lan lang/ language/ l/ anguish/anguish/ –a foreign anguish. // English is/ my father tongue./ A father tongue is/ a foreign language,/ therefore English is/ a foreign language/ not a mother tongue.' The ambivalence of the 'foreign' and the 'mother' tongue is constitutional, unrelenting: 'I have no mother/ tongue', she adds, and as the poem goes on, permutations of father, mother, tongue, language, and anguish shift the terms of discourse so that the 'logic of language', as the poem's title suggests, completely breaks down. Language is and is not one's inheritance; it is and it is not intimate violence, interior, and exterior, just as it is inextricably the articulation of aspects of one's genealogy, one's father and/ or mother and/or land.[32] This feeling of the performative loss (and finding) of an original language is compounded by an equally uncanny sense of alone-ness in the process of seeking a return, an arrival. Faced with one's alienation before another one's language(s) – though this may be the languages(s) with or within which one speaks and writes – one feels at once *sui generis*, original, strange, and not, native and foreign. The 'disquiet' Gauvin describes derives not so much from feeling unable to speak with a language that would be (in an ideal world) original, untainted, maternal (say); but rather from the sense that one is neither entirely held within language, nor can one ever break away. This is perhaps a state 'between *both* and *and*'.[33]

---

[31] Deleuze and Parnet, *Dialogues*, 4–5.
[32] M. NourbeSe Philip, 'Discourse on the Logic of Language', in *She Tries Her Tongue, Her Silence Softly Breaks* (Middletown, CT: Wesleyan University Press, [1989] 2014), 29–33.
[33] See Kélina Gotman, *Essays on Theatre and Change: Towards a Poetics Of* (London: Routledge, 2018).

Performative Accents

As I have been arguing, performative speech acts that gesture towards and so defy 'master' languages – such as Lalonde's poem deploys – are at once less romantically, and more uncomfortably, neither entirely enslaved nor do they entirely resist the power of majoritarian ('white') discourse. The granular speech act that does fluency performs its capacity for resistant intimacy within a majoritarian tongue, just as it sits awkwardly between this majoritarianism and a form of minoritarianism that may paradoxically also be becoming majoritarian in this process in turn. In other words, in Lalonde as in Micone, the inflections of speech perform an ability to 'pass over' (to translate) to the other language, and sit within it, just as they aim to resist hegemony and monolingualization; difference is intractable. Becoming-minor (or major-and-minor) is not so much to carve out a minor language from within a majoritarian linguistic space (or alongside it, or in its shadow), but to break down the division between majoritarian and minoritarian linguistic territorialities by acknowledging varying performances of identification and disidentification such as constitute every sort of linguistic act. One becomes a co-participant in the translinguistic event, performatively, just as one draws now this line, now that one, now this punctum, this slide. In this regard, the double performances of recuperation and disavowal offer moments of (micro) mimicry that set differentiation on the stage. I can speak my language and yours, the poet performs; and in this, she shows a form of linguistic and thus cultural power and possible ascendency. In a version of the 'almost the same, but not quite' relation Homi K. Bhabha iconically describes of the colonial relation,[34] Lalonde performs her capacity to be almost white, but not quite; to mimic but in doing so also potentially to subvert. Even Micone, however, with his multiethnic retort to Lalonde and to the Québécois establishment her poem now canonically spoke for, arguably repeated the minoritarian trope Lalonde had proffered, only Micone's marginality put forward a global immigrant other. This was not an oppressed machine-operating *habitant*, but a migrant Blacker, more speechless, and poorer than the now middle-class Québécois in their comfortable ('*huppé*') salons. It similarly theatricalizes the distinction between major and minor, and through discursive mimicry shows the enormity of differentiation: you are now the masters, and we are now the slaves, those who serve.

My analysis thus aims to show how language, as a set of performative gestures and relations, takes shape within aesthetico-political and poetic

---

[34] Bhabha, *The Location of Culture*, 122.

scenographies: audiences, prior speakers, and other languages are conjured in the act of speaking to people (or to an emerging class, a '*cause commune*') in a room, as well as directly or indirectly to those outside it (to what I am calling a *deferred audience*). The group is constituted by the implied interpellation – by audience members' presumed capacity to understand the particular politics of these acts of code-switching. This echoes Michel Foucault's concept of the 'scenes' within which power plays out, and the direction of the gaze performed through uses of language and discourse.[35] To employ a set of accents, grammars, translinguistic references, and phonetic modes of address to enact a political relation is to break down the notion of the 'speech act'. The speech act is not just something said but a manner of saying, a performative accentuation: it is performatively grammatical (or 'anti-grammatical') and it performs the politics of discourse inasmuch as the way of offering a particular turn – via inflection, verbal or corporeal gesture – 'speaks'. If language does not just reflect but co-composes and co-conducts power relations through the use of specific formulations and phonemes, within given contexts (theatres, scenes) – shaping not just what is thought but how people, concepts, and relations are thought – then attention to performative acts of language and translation taking place within acts of speech, with 'speech acts' understood granularly, may help to understand the critical genealogy of how relations between groups (and individuals) are theatrically and politically formed. This is also another way to think form: poetry given in speech has to be understood fundamentally as performative and as such ethopoetical.

As translational speech acts, moments of performative 'languaging' do not just 'do' (or enact) relations of alienation or proximity for example, but engage in (dramatize) the broader politics and aesthetics of genealogical wars, pointing to ways other people have said words or phrases before, sometimes with violence. This builds community, frequently from dissensus, and allows collective modes of understanding to be – with Glissant – not 'tyrannical' or 'fixed', but consciously or unwittingly, in some cases, relativized. For Chow, the concept of the 'xenophone' I have alluded to describes a way of understanding language as a relationship to the 'outside' – to always feeling oneself on the outside – but also through this as a way of knowing oneself in relation to others. Arguably, I am suggesting,

---

[35] See especially 'The Philosophical Scene: Foucault interviewed by Moriaki Watanabe', in *Foucault's Theatres*, translated by Robert Bononno, edited by Tony Fisher and Kélina Gotman (Manchester: Manchester University Press, 2020): 221–238. I discuss this notion of a discursive scenography also in Gotman, 'The "Scene of Discourse": Foucault and the Theatre of Truth (*on parrhēsia*)', *Cultural Critique*, no. 113 (2021): 28–71.

Performative Accents   129

this is enacted in a performatively relational (and translational) approach to language, to poetics as that which shapes language consciously. The concept of the xenophone Chow offers describes how speech can be felt as if coming from the outside, and remaining outside – a variation on Derrida's notion, which she also draws from, that language is always falsely singularized. Following Chinua Achebe, Chow muses that xenophony is thus a 'creative' possibility, 'languaging emerging', '[bearing] in its accents the murmur, the passage, of diverse found speeches'.[36] Chow's analysis responds to Derrida's ambivalence about his own French speech in relation to his Maghreban origins. Derrida, Chow reminds us, was embarrassed by his Algerian accent; he felt that 'proper' philosophical discourse had to sound standardly 'French'. At the same time, for Chow, the provocation Derrida left postcolonial theory – that language has to be understood as something first of all 'impure', relational – shows that there is no 'pure', inside language that one may nostalgically preserve or seek.[37]

In Lalonde's poem, one of the questions that is posed, as in her 'Deffence', can be phrased: how to perform one's own knowledge of this other, reviled, colonial tongue – of these many colonizing tongues? In particular, how to perform one's own relation to those colonial accents one is most intimate with, the Franco-French, with which ongoing relations of alliance and differentiation are articulated through emerging notions of *francophonie*? Geopolitics appear in flashes of language, not to impose another 'fixity' – rather, ironically perhaps, to continue to trouble the notion that any nation might be articulated entirely against the other or the old. Thus, with Chow, one has to reimagine what language is, to rethink 'the question of language' or, as Franco-Jewish Québécois writer and contemporary of Lalonde's (on another side of the French-language question) Régine Robin (1939–2021) suggests, to muse: 'I love my language. But

---

[36] Chow, *Not Like a Native Speaker*, especially 1–2, 21–23, 59.

[37] Chow, *Not Like a Native Speaker*, 33. On debates about *francophonie* as a postcolonial condition not exactly parallel to Anglo-imperial postcolonialism, see for example, Jean Bessière and Jean-Marc Moura, eds., *Littératures postcoloniales et francophonie* (Paris: Champion, 2001); Jean-Marc Moura, *Littératures francophones et théorie postcoloniale* (Paris: PUF Quadrige, 2013); and the special issue of *Yale French Studies* 103 (2003), 'French and Francophone: The Challenge of Expanding horizons', edited by Farid Laroussi and Christopher L. Miller. The literature on postcolonial *francophonie* has ballooned in the past decades, testifying to rising interest in rethinking comparative postcolonialism and the legacy of francophone literature in an era of competing concepts of world literature or 'littérature-monde'. Although relatively few analyses attend to the performativity of translation, one exception, on Maghreban voices in audio and other media, including in the work of Lebanese-Québécois playwright Wajdi Mouawad, is in Jennifer Solheim, *The Performance of Listening in Postcolonial Francophone Culture* (Liverpool: Liverpool University Press, 2018).

what is my language?'[38] And further, how does it move? As Gauvin argues, for Glissant the condition of the speaker and writer in a 'composite' world such as the Caribbean (and, one might add, to an extent in Québec, which he also wrote of), marked by colonialism, is a sort of 'torment' (*tourment*), different from the 'tranquil' mass of monolingualisms practiced among those who do not know the fragility of speech or language 'contaminable' by official grammars. He gestures towards the masses of US monolinguals, though one could contend that US speech – all speech *tout court* – is also arguably composed of infinite mono- and multilingualisms – uncountable inflections, hierarchies of accentuation and utterative violences, tyrannical relations of temporary fixity and affective reaffiliations. Until we understand 'majoritarian' languages as composed of a million minoritarianisms, we have not I think reimagined language sufficiently yet. As Glissant observes, however, minoritarianisms, spoken alongside one another, may offer a gateway to radical plurality: tranquil (self-contented) monolingualism is blind to the '*chaos-monde*' or 'chaos-world', which he describes as a 'conflictual and marvellous meeting of languages' full of 'sparks' (*éclats*) that 'spurt' (*jaillissent*) every which way. Even créolité, Glissant argues, has to be reimagined as an impure, 'networked' set of disruptions and juxtapositions, not merely another emerging monolingualism to counter to colonial ones. As with Lalonde's Québecquoys, languages miscegenated out of various mother and father tongues can and perhaps must remain mixed, non-grammatical and grammatical both, to resist the lure of fixity (of tyranny). To reimagine what language 'is' (what it might become), for Glissant, as for Lalonde I think, is to reconceptualize normative speech and créolité both as tending towards purism and chaos at once, always in different ways, to different degrees; both are and need constantly to be re-languaged, reconceived in terms of perpetual shifts, a living chaos. This is ethical and political (and as such ethopoetical) because it offers language as perpetual translation, an 'infinite multiplicity of contacts'.[39]

In suggesting that we reimagine language as performative and *xenophonic* (after Chow), I am arguing that we might reconceptualize the terms with which to discuss language also, and see this, a priori, as a performative act of translation and xenophony. This may take place between one's multiple linguistic selves (again, even monolinguals speak in variations of tone and of code) and in relation to surrounding discourses – and accents, and

---

[38] Régine Robin, *Le deuil de l'origine. Une langue an trop, la langue en moins* (Paris: Presses Universitaires de Vincennes, 1993): 7.

[39] Édouard Glissant, 'L'imaginaire des langues', in *L'imaginaire des langues: Entretiens avec Lise Gauvin (1991–2009)* (Paris: Éditions Gallimard, 2010), 11–34.

Performative Accents 131

tones – shaping culture, language, and so power. We are in the realm of the 'bi-lingue' that Khatibi describes when he suggests that bi-lingualism is always agonistic, haunted, and formed by the clash of powers that forced their way into one's body (one's speech), one's life; bi-lingualism, like multilingualism and monolingualism, arguably, involve a violent and unshakable *incorporation* of performative alterities into lived speech.[40] The affinity with race is not symbolic only. Chow writes of 'biosemiotics' to describe how 'language possession is translated into and receives its value as skin color' – in the case she describes (of Barack Obama being surprised to discover an advertisement suggesting someone should wish to lighten their skin), Blackness erased, whiteness acquired. For Frantz Fanon (1925–1961), Chow notes, the Black person of the Antilles becomes proportionately closer to whiteness as they acquire (master) French: '[t]he acquisition of (the French) language [...] becomes the acquisition of whiteness.'[41] In Québec, English was equated with more whiteness, as was standard French; and yet other diasporas mixed in with this, complicating relations of *métissage* and affective relations to displacement. This is not just the trio of cultures Simon describes: the Yiddish, Anglophone, and Francophone worlds, but myriad displacements and dispossessions, reaffiliations, and re-minoritizations (as well as re/majoritarianizations). As critic Eloise A. Brière notes of Robin's Jewish-French narrator, in her semi-autobiographical *La Québécoite* (1993), the narrator 'observes the Québécois landscape as she wanders through Montreal, hearing French but not understanding, wondering how she will ever stake out a space where her [Franco-]French-Jewishness fits into late-twentieth-century *québécité*. Robin, acutely aware of the complexities of francophone life in Montreal, where French language alone is not sufficient for integration,[42] becomes a writer celebrated within the Québécois landscape – also because of her performative articulation of the all too familiar experience of linguistic negotiation, as well as of cultural anxiety and hypervigilance. If this unsettling feeling of being at home and never quite at home within an adopted (or a birth) territory constitutes the many-generational migrant experience of postcolonial languaging par excellence, it also suggests the possibility

[40] See Steven Ungar, 'Writing in Tongues: Thoughts on the Work of Translation', in *Comparative Literature in an Age of Globalization*, edited by Haun Saussy (Baltimore, MD: Johns Hopkins University Press, 2006): 127–138, 132.
[41] Chow, *Not Like a Native Speaker*, 2–3. See Fanon, *Black Skin, White Masks*, 109ff.
[42] Eloise A. Brière, 'Quebec and France: La Francophonie in A Comparative Postcolonial Frame', in *Postcolonial Theory and Francophone Literary Studies*, 157. See Régine Robin, *La Québécoite* (Montréal: Les Editions XYZ, 1993).

of a performative re-dramatization of the discursive scenographies of power that take place throughout so much of the world all the time in speech.

As previously alluded to, one can think of this as a variation on Bhabha's famous '*almost the same, but not quite*'. 'Colonial mimicry' is 'the desire for a reformed, recognizable Other', he writes, '*as a subject of difference that is almost the same, but not quite*. Which is to say', he adds, 'that the discourse of mimicry is constructed around an *ambivalence*; in order to be effective, mimicry must continually produce its slippage, its excess, its difference. The authority of that mode of colonial discourse that I have called mimicry is therefore stricken by an indeterminacy: mimicry emerges as the representation of a difference that is itself a process of disavowal'.[43] In Lalonde's poem, as in Robin's writing, origins are performed as ill-fitting and in many ways adapted (or adapting) to the current landscape, but also as ultimately untraceable, nearly non-utterable, the relationship to the present too much in motion; there is no strict 'mother tongue', and no situation within which present and past are lined up. It is this linguistic dispossession within a complex linguistic ecology that defines the regime of the xenophone. To out oneself as a speaker of a particular language world is to perform the possibility of the sort of alliance and disavowal Bhabha speaks of – mimicry that always approaches a master tongue and fails entirely to conform.

This self-dramatization through language constitutes 'common' politics within a shared, public sphere – speech acts that subtly, sometimes falsely, 'do' one's genealogy. Xenophony, as speech that is outside and inside, may be understood as the not always settled *order* by which languages perform reaffiliation, enter into relations of (re)alliance, and are renegotiated at every event of interlocution. I have been arguing that this as a granular and translational as well as a phonemic re-understanding of the notion of the performative utterance put forward by Austin. If for Austin a speech act is a form of grammatical utterance that *does* what it is saying (to declare 'I do' in marriage, or name a ship, etc.), then the translational and phonemic speech act, attentive to accent and to a form of toggling between national languages or dialects or registers, enacts ('does') a relationship to language and discourse, and therefore to power relations as such. The speech act that attends to the language with which one is speaking, and to the relationship between languages, when two or more are deployed within a set of performative utterances, as well as to the accents deployed, is effectively (and

---

[43] In Bhabha, *The Location of Culture*, 122.

Performative Accents

affectively) dramatizing – in the act of speech – a distinctive translinguistic event (one of defiance, a call for revolution, a cultural moment of sabotage, etc.). The utterance does not merely 'describe' a state of affairs, as Austin suggests other forms of grammatical utterance do, but effectively *does* a political gesture of differentiation and affiliation, to different degrees. The political efficacy of the act is arguably all the more powerful as it is legible to the immediate audience in the room, who must be aware not only of the relative power dynamics of each language or dialect or form of accentuation alluded to, but also be called upon within this linguistic act to recognize those who are not in the room; and to recognize this as a historically significant and contingent set of linguistic relations. Thus, the speech act performed – in the declaration that for example (in English) 'we / are not alone', also translated into French ('*Nous savons / que nous ne sommes pas seuls*') calls forth a supra-bilingual state within which those who have learned the master's language effectively may begin to dismantle the master's house: if power is performed through language ('speak white', given as an injunction), then to recuperate this as a speech act is to reorganize power.

PART II

Translation, Nation-state and Post-nationalism

CHAPTER 6

Transembodiment as Translation
Staging the Włast/Komornicka Archive

Bryce Lease

For Judith Butler, translation concerns the transformation of values from multiple cultural frameworks, spheres of beliefs and historical understandings. This is not a singular exercise; translation is not a simple case of moving from one value system to another. Rather, translation is the process of moving from and between the many to the multiple.[1] In this chapter, I will consider how translation pertains to the body on stage as such a site of multiplicity. If, following Butler, the body is understood as an entanglement of biological, historical and social conditions and conditioning, it functions as a crucial nexus of ethical debates. In order to consider the relationship between translation and the movement of a body through time, culture, politics, class, gender and language I employ the neologism *transembodiment*. My intention in considering transembodiment is to analyse the effects and limitations of physical and fictional bodies as they appear within the mimetic, representational and concrete frame of the theatre space. Ultimately, I argue that the body is itself a paradigmatic site of translation, which can neither be reduced to nor fully dislodged from language, and which is both submitted to and escapes processes of mimetic representation. In this way, I do not wish to consider transembodiment as a methodology but rather as a *structure* and a *consequence* of the process of transmission in the theatre.[2]

In order to explore this line of argumentation, I will focus on a particularly rich example from contemporary Polish theatre that simultaneously engages with the *trans* of translation, transmission and transgender. In 2011, theatre makers Weronika Szczawińska and Bartosz

---

[1] Butler, *Parting Ways*, 1–27.
[2] In conceptualizing transembodiment as such, I explicitly draw on Marianne Hirsch's notion of postmemory, which she conceives as a '*structure* of inter- and trans-generational transmission of traumatic knowledge and experience' and as a '*consequence* of traumatic recall'. Marianne Hirsch, 'The Generation of Postmemory', *Poetics Today* 29, no. 1 (2008): 106. While I will not focus on trauma specifically, it is a concept that deserves further investigation in relation to transembodiment.

138   BRYCE LEASE

Frąckowiak respectively wrote and directed *Komornicka. Biografia pozorna* (Komornicka. Ostensible biography).[3] The performance attempts to place a much revered and controversial Polish poet's biography through a series of critical lenses that differently understand and interpret a transbody. Providing multiple perspectives from which to interpret the translated body, through historical and critical texts, archival objects and sources and the physical body of the actor, I argue that *Komornicka. Biografia pozorna* helps us to think through the broader implications of transembodiment and to consider the constellation of body, translation, performativity and theatricality.

Schemas of Transposition

In 1907, the writer Maria Komornicka and her mother, Anna Dunin-Wąsowicz, stopped at the Hotel Bazaar in Poznań en route to a sanatorium in Kołobrzeg. While her mother was out of the hotel room, Komornicka burned her own clothes, cut off her hair and allegedly knocked out her teeth in an effort to give her face a more masculine shape. From that day on the poet wished to be known exclusively as a man, his name Piotr Włast. The transition from Komornicka to Włast has attracted the scrutinizing gaze of the scientific community and literary critics alike since the late 1970s in Poland.

Appropriations of the transgender body in recent Polish literary criticism has found a particular focus on Włast/Komornicka,[4] whom the Polish literary scholar Maria Janion has characterized as 'the great illegal figure in the history of Polish literature'.[5] The poet moved to Warsaw and published at the young age of sixteen in the influential *Gazeta Warszawska*, two years later publishing an anthology of prose, *Szkice* (Sketches), at the age of eighteen. Komornicka's despotic father, Augustyn Komornicki, sent his daughter to study at the University of Cambridge, a period that Janion has given particular focus in her two studies of the poet, particularly

---

[3] The performance was a co-production between the InVitro Festival in Lublin and the Teatr Polski [Polish Theatre] in Bydgoszcz.

[4] I choose to use they/their as pronouns when addressing Włast/Komornicka to avoid imposing a final gendered reading on their subjectivity and I employ he/she when I speak to specific historical moments of the poet's self-described embodiment. Although many scholars ultimately attempt to suggest that it is crucial to choose Włast or Komornicka as the authentic subject, for the interests of this chapter I am more concerned with the effects of gender and translation through staging, which redirects the discussion away from such aims.

[5] Maria Janion, *Kobiety i duch inności* (Warszawa: Sic!, 1996), 253–262.

Transembodiment as Translation

emphasizing the adverse effects of England's many patriarchal constraints.[6] Returning to Poland, Komornicka became a leftwing activist and married Jan Lemański, who shot them in a fit of jealous rage, permanently injuring both of their arms. The marriage dissolved in 1900, resulting in a divorce that permanently coupled Komornicka's name to scandal and shame in the public sphere. While living in Paris at the turn of the century, Komornicka spent time in the Polish library reading up on an ancestor, Piotr Włast, a name the poet used to sign reviews for the modernist journal *Chimera*. Later, Komornicka claimed in letters home that they were Włast's familial heir – Włast was a Polish noble and voivode of the king of Poland, Bolesław III, in the twelfth century – reading the hereditary inheritance of their maternal lineage through a fatalistic lens. Both a rebel and a martyr, Włast is framed in national history as a near-legendary figure particularly honoured in Polish Catholicism for his restoration of many churches. Within Komornicka's family, and for their mother in particular, Włast was reified as brave, strong and resourceful, a bastion of masculine power and valour.

Significant new treatments starting in the 1990s resuscitated Włast, who was seen to deserve fresh readings in light of postmodern thought and more fluid notions of gendered bodies. For the most part, the interpretation of Włast's literary output has been strongly marked by biographical inferences. Scholars have obsessed over the motives for the transition, typically foregrounding an essentializing understanding of Komornicka as the authentic historical figure while sidelining Włast as 'her' uncanny alter ego, and one which offers evidence for mental instability and ill health. The literary critic Edward Boniecki argues that Komornicka's ultimate goal was not masculinity but androgyny, a preoccupation of the Polish Modernist movement, which entailed a dissolution of the egoistic 'I' in favour of an identity based on internal harmony.[7] Not acceding to this line of thinking, Janion referred to the transition as the shedding of a cocoon that enclosed the genuine inner man. This argument can be positioned in relation to the experience of many transpeople who do not understand their biological gender at birth as equivalent to their lived gender.

Queer theorist and writer Izabela Filipiak suggested another reading. The transition resulted from a fear of symbolic violence, and so Komornicka wanted to see her 'I' as 'holistic and indivisible', not the representative of a

---

[6] Janion, *Kobiety*, 257.
[7] Edward Boniecki, *Modernistyczny dramat ciała: Maria Komornicka* (Warsaw: Instytut Badań Literackich PAN, 1998), 12.

140   BRYCE LEASE

particular gender but as a member of the whole of humanity, a reading that denies Włast's wish to been recognized as a man.[8] Art historian and literary theorist Brigitta Helbig-Mischewski suggested that the desire to change sex was a resistance to the stigma of being seen as a loose woman after her divorce and affair.[9] In general, an overriding emphasis tends to be placed on providing an interpretation that gives special attention to the cultural dimension of transition, that is, the potential of cross-dressing to change not only one's physical appearance but the subject's entire symbolic field. The careful critical attention paid to every line written by the poet over their lifetime has failed to produce a consistent biography or a determining interpretation, version or understanding of Włast/Komornicka, succeeding rather in exposing the absolute anxiety produced by such a radical model of gender variance.

Labelled as everything from a mad woman in the attic, a wandering Ophelia, an original lesbian, or a martyr for freedom and women's emancipation, Komornicka's transformation into Włast is overwhelmingly regarded as either a product of psychosis, the deliberate creation of a literary persona or as an outcome of women's social subjugation. Komornicka was co-opted by Krzysztof Tomasik in his *Homobiografie* (Homobiography, 2009), a gay rereading of major Polish historical figures, and the Polish LGBTI movement in general as a queerly valenced icon. Readings of Włast's poetry that highlight eroticism, lust, sexual craving and sadomasochism unintentionally propel the poet out of the realm of flesh into the subversive signifier of the desiring female. While it is true that the desiring female, as opposed to female desire, occupied a strictly taboo subjecthood in Polish literature in the late nineteenth and early twentieth centuries, such arguments contextualize Włast as an effect or symptom of female desire rather than an autonomous subject. Similarly, it might be tempting to agree with Filipiak's argument that Komornicka's transition into a male subject allowed the poet to speak about fantasies otherwise only attributed to men, given that the adoption of the male gender prompted the production of a new language.[10] Although Filipiak introduced queer studies to the available scholarship on the poet in an effort to disarticulate gender from essentialist readings, particularly through demonstrating how

---

[8] Izabela Filipiak, *Obszary odmienności: Rzecz o Marii Komornickiej* (Gdansk: Słowo/Obraz Terytoria, 2006), 93–94.

[9] Brigitta Helbig-Mischewski, 'Warum heulen die "inneren Dämonen"? Metaphorik des existentiellen Vakuums in Maria Komornickas "Biesy"', *Zeitschrift für Slawistik* 47, no. 1 (2002): 34–49.

[10] Izabela Filipiak quoted in Katarzyna Lisowska, 'Body, Spirit and Gender in Maria Komornicka's Poetry', *The Journal of Education Culture and Society* 2, no. 1 (2011): 102.

Transembodiment as Translation

clothes play a significant role in the citation and reiteration of normative gender,[11] this reading still assumes an authentic and original Komornicka preceding Włast. Ultimately, Filipiak's approach remains partial to biography as the determining scheme of intelligibility. Staging the bodies of Włast/Komornicka however suggests that this epistemological frame is no longer adequate.

By conceiving of this act of self-determination through the point of view of Komornicka, Włast's biography is carefully dissected (and, in effect, subsumed) in an effort to unearth their motives, which is typically reduced to an act of rebellion against a domineering father and violently jealous husband. Many Polish feminist scholars persist in using feminine pronouns and only refer to Włast as a secondary figure in the narrative of the poet's life, which reinforces such transphobic positions that argue Komornicka did not wish to be Włast (a man) but that the transformation was a cry for women's equality or an act of revolt against the prevailing patriarchy. Even when Janion claims that 'transsexualism' is a desire to feel the internal arrangements of sexuality outside the state,[12] the scholar perseveres in framing the transbody as primarily a site of rebellion rather than as a coherent identity. There appears to be a refusal to privilege the figurative over the literal and a determination to suture authenticity to the naked biologically sexed body, which places many contemporary critics in a similar position to their early twentieth-century counterparts. Włast was coetaneously read as a product of Komornicka's madness, which justified detention in psychiatric institutions until the onset of the First World War and, later, relegation to the margins of society as an abject deviant. I would like to suggest that the continuing disavowal of Włast – even Tomasik and Janion write about Komornicka as a woman, exclusively using feminine pronouns, an example of how language itself is a key participant in normative oppression – and the concomitant resuscitation of the 'authentic' Komornicka beneath 'her' counterfeit gender impersonation is no less an act of symbolic violence inflicted on Włast's body than their institutionalization. When Agata Kozłowska argues that it is more accurate to define 'transsexualism' through the prism of Komornicka's (again, *her*) personal experience than to describe the transformation as an internalized struggle between gender and anatomical sex we return to the appropriation of biography as an attempt to defuse what is clearly seen as a traumatic corruption

---

[11] Filipiak, *Obszary odmienności*, 135.
[12] Janion, *Kobiety*, 250.

of female gender.[13] The transbody, highly stigmatized, is diagnosed as a symptom of mental illness, an identity that does not deserve recognition but due suspicion and circumspection centred around the effort to marry anatomical sex and gender.[14]

Ostensible Biography

Having set out the modes in which Włast/Komornicka has been interpreted and understood by literary scholars, I will now turn to the embodied staging of Włast/Komornicka in order to consider how questions of transembodiment on stage differently figure these arguments. Rather than side with Włast or Komornicka as the authentic body, I am interested in the way in which this performance example of transembodiment remaps social bonds. To rearrange Butler's argument, translation is a process of negotiating 'converging and competing ethical claims', as well as the 'condition of a transformative encounter, a way of establishing alterity at the core of transmission'.[15] What happens to the transposition of bodies in a historical moment that offers new forms of visibility (and, as a result, judgment) to transbodies? Using a theatrical term, Butler suggests that translation is a '*scene* in which the limits of a given episteme are exposed, and forced to become rearticulated in ways that do not recontain alterity'.[16] Moving from conservative, nationalist considerations of the poet to feminist and queer appropriations, *Komornicka. Biografia pozorna* sheds light on attempts to resolve alterity through containment. As I have evidenced above, the Włast/Komornicka archive is neither self-sufficient nor self-obvious. Rather, this archive opens up the very notion of selfhood to multiple figurations, bodies, images and texts. Why does it demand to be translated on stage through bodies today? What is not knowable in recognized or traditional epistemological fields that Włast/Komornicka

[13] Anita Nowak, 'Wielki sukces Anity Sokołowskiej!'. *Teatr dla Was*, 12 March 2012.

[14] What's more, Włast is frequently understood as a symptom of failure. Although both Janion and Tomasik place particular emphasis on the wilful act of transgendering, extending this act as a sign of courage that exceeds the cultural limits set out for women in Włast's historical moment, what is often found in criticism is the view that Komornicka showed exceptional aptitude as a writer before 1907 and that the subsequent transformation into Włast indicated the disappointment and eventual failure of this outstanding potential. Komornicka is positioned as the subject full of literary promise, who is intellectually curious and knowledge hungry, erotically charged and desirous, an icon of modernism and a member of the Warsaw bohemian elite, while Włast is situated as the fulcrum of Komornicka's failure: the failure to effectively cite manhood or the heterosexual 'original' as well as the decline of their profession as a writer.

[15] Butler, *Parting Ways*, 8, 17.

[16] Butler, *Parting Ways*, 8, my emphasis.

Transembodiment as Translation

143

can signal to us? If translation is not 'simply an assimilation of what is foreign into what is familiar', how might Włast/Komornicka open us to the unfamiliar?[17]

The first critical turn we come to in analysing this performance is the choice of the title, *Komornicka. Biografia pozorna*. I will treat the punctuation (full stop) as an opportunity to break the title into two parts. Firstly, there is the choice to name the poet, Komornicka. In attempt to think transhistorically, I employ the name Włast/Komornicka. Not only is my intention to undermine a chronological conception (on a historical timeline Komornicka lived before Włast), thus allowing for a diachronic mode of thinking, I also wish to confront and reconfigure an essential question concerning prioritization. Włast/Komornicka, a name that is itself a transconfiguration, is not intended to prioritize Włast. By placing them out of time I hope to draw attention to the problem of chronological historical interpretations of the poet that implicitly understand Komornicka as the legitimate historical body and Włast as a delusional or phantasmatic (disembodied) projection. The performance title *Komornicka* decides in advance who should ultimately be prioritized in representation. This gesture interprets the body beyond the spatial and temporal limits of the stage, indicating whose body is the 'original' and whose is the translated. In a process of transcoding, and following the logic of literary scholars set out earlier, does this not position the semiotics of one body against another, and in so doing attempt to produce an *original*? Is Włast only intelligible to us as a translation of Komornicka after a psychic break?[18]

The choice to title the production *Komornicka* effectively distils and crystalizes the archive in a mode that favours a particular moment of embodiment. My critique here is that the sign of Komornicka simultaneously subsumes the referent *and* the body of Włast, and with them a broader and more complex history. The second part of the title, *Biografia pozorna*, returns us to the conditions of narrative account, and what has either been deemed (im)permissible or (de)authorized. While directing *Komornicka*, Frąckowiak was influenced by Todd Haynes' *I'm Not There* (2007), the genre-defying biopic of Bob Dylan, which interrogates the many facets

---

[17] Butler, *Parting Ways*, 12.

[18] The question of chronology also impacts our understanding of gender and performativity. For Butler, repetition (for example in critical acts of drag performance) can be about displacement – the displacement of gender norms that are reiterable and come to exist through repetition. For this reason, Butler famously critiqued a notion of theatricality that assumed a stable subject who could work through mimesis to critique gender norms. This resonates with a problematic conception of Komornicka preceding and thus 'playing' the role of Włast.

of the cult US singer-songwriter that unsettled conventional forms of biography that favour chronology, historical facts and narrative coherency. Just as Haynes elided a hidden essence that most biographers attempt to uncover in their subject, Szczawińska and Frąckowiak attempted to circumvent a comprehensive, finalized or authoritative depiction of Włast/Komornicka. Through an episodic structure, *possible* as opposed to *definitive* versions of events are suggested rather than reenacted, drawing the viewer into an investigation of a (possible) life or lives. The presence of *pozorna* (ostensible) signals the theatre makers' intentions to consider the tensions between has been settled or agreed upon and which epistemological horizons might still be excavated. The staged body of the poet must also be understood as *pozorna*, as a potential form, a body that has been deemed permissible in current sociohistorical conditions.

Frąckowiak chose a female actor, Anita Sokołowska, to portray Włast/Komornicka. The consequences of this casting choice in relation to transembodiment are multiple. If Włast/Komornicka as and in relation to biography functions as a resource for audiences to consider and, ultimately, to judge the transbody, then gender plays a crucial role as evidence. Before analysing Sokołowska, I think it is productive to consider how the actor was ghosted by an earlier performance in the 1990s. I would suggest that ghosting is a fundamental aspect of transembodiment, given that this term suggests a palimpsest of bodies (past and present) that produce a stage character or presence.[19] Implicitly, *Komornicka. Biografia pozorna* offered a corrective to Aleksandra Czernecka and Dariusz Pawelec's 1995 documentary *Nadmiar życia. Maria Komornicka* (An Excess of Life. Maria Komornicka) – a title that again reinscribes the name Komornicka over Włast – that offered a troubling representation of the poet framed by academic commentary from literary experts Maria Dernałowicz and Maria Podraza-Kwiatkowska. Malgorzata Hajewska-Krzysztofik, who portrayed Komornicka in the documentary, was best known in Poland in the mid-1990s for her role as Konradowa in Krystian Lupa's *Kalkwerk* (Stary Teatr [Old Theatre], Kraków, premiere 1992), for which she received ample praise for her embodiment of madness, emotional rawness and physical frailty. Residue of this performance certainly informed the reception of Hajewska-Krzysztofik as Komornicka, who is depicted on screen in a Polish bucolic setting, striking romantic poses that stereotyped the poet as

---

[19] For a detailed discussion of 'ghosting' in relation to casting and performance histories see Marvin Carlson, *The Haunted Stage: The Theatre as Memory Machine* (Ann Arbor: University of Michigan Press, 2003).

Transembodiment as Translation

forlorn, troubled and feeble. Ultimately, the documentary was unable to disrupt the consistency of the realist field by shooting close-ups of a woman performer that visually obliterates Włast from their own biography. In fact, rather than conceiving Włast as a meaningful designator of unpredictable gender identities, or even Włast as anything other than Komornicka in drag, it is only when Hajewska-Krzysztofik dons men's clothing that we see her most conventional portrait of femininity. While Hajewska-Krzysztofik was seen as a passive and listless *woman* in the documentary, as Grace in Krzysztof Warlikowski's groundbreaking production of Sarah Kane's *Cleansed* in 2001 for Warsaw's Teatr Rozmaitości [Variety Theatre], she emerges with a phallus that she contemplates in the large metallic surface of Małgorzata Szczęśniak's vivid set.[20] While the textured surface of the mirror and its distance from the audience made the veracity of this phallus difficult to repudiate, the point is not ultimately whether we believe in the reality of the physical phallus – that is, whether the spectator treats this performance of gender transgression merely as an act of counterfeiting – but rather in the reality conditioned by *the presence of phallus as such*, that is phallic power. With her breasts bound under a surgical bandage, Hajewska-Krzysztofik's body reflected 'through the looking glass' is indeed a queer echo. This echo confronts us with the sustained exposure of the actors' bodies up until this point so we *retroactively* read these bodies as no longer original, authentic or real but, as Butler argues, 'constituted as effects'.[21] I would like to suggest that Hajewska-Krzysztofik's performance in *Cleansed* offered a retroactive reading of her performance as Komornicka that reintroduced Włast into the public field of vision. In other words, it was only in the layering of performances – and mediums – that transembodiment fully occurred.

In contrast, alterity in *Komornicka. Biografia pozorna* is inscribed through the overlaps between the archive and the body. Frąckowiak explains that the theatre he produces with Szczawińska is interested in topics that exist in public space and in the cultural memory of a collective imagination. His museum aesthetic for this performance may be called documentary or ethnographic surrealism, not a factual representation, but an investigation into biography that questions the role of witness, employing the rhetorical

---

[20] This was a co-production between Wrocław's Teatr Współczesny [Wrocław's Contemporary Theatre], Poznań's Teatr Polski [Poznań's Polish Theatre] and Warsaw's Teatr Rozmaitości [Variety Theatre].

[21] Judith Butler, *Gender Trouble: Feminism and the Subversion of Identity* (London and New York: Routledge, 2015), 200.

146   BRYCE LEASE

strategy of postmodern collage, a non-hierarchical stacking of factual dimensions from fieldwork and archives on top of fictional hypotheses.

Transembodiment

Even though Sokołowska was cast to play the eponymous figure, one of the central tensions of the performance was her resistance to fully embody the role. Defying naturalism and coherent characterization, Sokołowska primarily acted as a medium or guide in a performance lecture on the subject of Włast/Komornicka. Although the poet was largely rendered as an assemblage of particular social and cultural discourses rather than a historical person, the body of the actor was fundamental. Each episode begins with a review of old documents, archival photographs and fragments, which are projected overhead on a screen that specifies an academic setting, such as a lecture hall or operating theatre. In the performance, the interrogation of Włast/Komornicka through narratives is supplemented by objects. Non-canonical biographical symbols locked in display cabinets and exhibited on white pedestals were placed across the stage space: a little mound of loose teeth, a glass head filled with walnuts, anatomical sketches, a laundry wringer and a large naked female doll. By presenting and relying upon the archive as evidence (*dowód*) we are reminded that the constitution of Włast/Komornicka as subject is also the responsibility of the spectator.

This confrontation between the body of the actor and the detritus of the archive (text, object, image) returns us to a longstanding debate concerning gender and embodiment *qua* theatricality and performativity. By way of Gayle Rubin, theatre and performance scholar Elin Diamond uses translation in a double mode to think about gender. Firstly, 'gendering coercively translates the nuanced differences within sexuality into a structure of opposition' between men and women; and secondly, 'by virtue of entering the stage space' the body, the female body in particular, is inevitably translated through representation: 'it is not just *there*, a live, unmediated presence'.[22] Diamond thus reminds us that in theatre embodiment is always mediated. What is interesting in this argument is that theatre is suspended between two forms of representation, which Shannon Jackson has called the 'flexible essentialism' of theatricality.[23] Theatricality is troublesome because it

---

[22] Elin Diamond, 'Brechtian Theory/Feminist Theory', *The Drama Review* 32, no. 1 (1988): 86, 89.
[23] Shannon Jackson, 'Theatricality's Proper Objects: Genealogies of Performance and Gender Theory', in *Theatricality*, edited by Tracy C. Davis and Thomas Postlewait (Cambridge: Cambridge University Press, 2003), 189.

Transembodiment as Translation

147

is essentialist on the one hand (a concrete manifestation) and anti-essentialist on the other (mimetic, foregrounding construction over identity). I argue that this perplexing contradiction is precisely the tension that undergirds transembodiment; that is, the central tension that figures the concrete and mediated body on stage (the mimetic distance between Sokołowska and her characters) as well as the oppositions upholding Włast/Komornicka as historical figure *and* figuration. Employing the museum scenography, the spectator is positioned as a fellow detective and co-conspirator, confronted with a material archive that is incomplete and partial, shaped by fragments, residues, hints, where no story, rumour or material object is known beyond the shadow of a doubt. Although this postmodern tactic is useful in its confrontation of the archive as a generator of objective knowledge and as an essentializing force in historical positionings of subjectivity that is very much in sympathy with Jacques Derrida's deconstructivist methodology in *Archive Fever* (1995), the performance finds itself rubbing up against the same concern that has confounded literary scholars and historians: namely, what to do about the poet's body? Writing about testimonial-based verbatim theatre practice, performance scholar Collette Conroy has suggested that audiences are not drawn to performance to witness the 'truth' when the documentary evidence is readily available for public scrutiny. Rather, 'the bodies, and the embodiment of the testimony, are the point of [this genre of] theatre irrespective of its relationship to some separate truth.'[24] Similarly, the archives plundered by Szczawińska and Frąckowiak are not restricted or private, nor are they even particularly obscure or difficult to locate. Reviews suggest that spectators were drawn first and foremost to see what choices would be made in the corporeal representation of Włast/Komornicka. In other words, it is precisely in the theatre that the distinctions delimiting gender – through their exposure to physical bodies and the performative acts that inscribe those bodies into the social lexicons of gender – that we find the most appropriate space for this debate, not to side with an 'authentic' or originary body that implicitly favours Komornicka over Włast, but rather to force a blatant confrontation with the very discourses that obscure the body as socially marked in the literary and textual approaches to theorizing Włast/Komornicka.

Feminist theatre scholar Jill Dolan claimed that in any solo performance the audience is confronted with the question, 'Why are you listening?' and 'What does this depiction of history embodied by the single storyteller

---

[24] Colette Conroy, *Theatre & The Body* (Basingstoke: Palgrave, 2010), 39.

148   BRYCE LEASE

offer us today?'[25] Szczawińska and Frąckowiak's choice to produce a solo performance with Sokołowska as both body and voice of the archive clearly marks the poet as female, which reinforces the choice of name for the title, *Komornicka*. What's more, Sokołowska's black costume had purposefully pronounced material around her hips, thus accentuating her female figure, and very little effort is made to render the performer's gender as denaturalized, following feminist performative strategies that attempt to distance the signifier of woman from the objectifying signification of femininity. As a result, what we encounter is essentially a one-woman show with the full force of the historical and cultural values that attend this genre, primarily, though not exclusively, the very feminist-based scholarship Szczawińska hoped to critique. Sokołowska writes over or marks with graffiti historical documents, creating a palimpsest that chimes with feminist interventions into male-centred, sole-authored versions of history that make claims to objectivity and impartiality. However, this palimpsest, which is further enforced by the qualifier *pozorna* in the title, indicating a life that purposely defies narrative biography, is overwritten by the name Komornicka, an intransferable designation that Włast cannot shed, escape or undo, even posthumously. In contradistinction to the title, Frąckowiak claimed that he attempted as a director to consider how the audience might be invited to look *with* rather than *at* a transgendered body.[26]

In the opening scene, we see Sokołowska trying on gender as a role, attempting to investigate a number of gestures and actions that cannot be easily attributed to a single sexual category. This approach is clearly informed by Butler's theorization of gender as an effect of the performance of norms through the repetition of gestures and actions that accumulate the force of authority through their citation of an occluded (and imaginary) original.[27] After this initial attempt to assign the body actions that defy easy gender categorization, Sokołowska strives throughout the remainder of the performance to make her body culturally intelligible by subjecting it to certain social norms. The actor claimed that she did not identify with the character, and so a multivalent persona was produced through other means, such as mime, poetic metaphor and buffoonery. These metamorphoses were supported by Bartosz Nalazek's impressionistic lighting, a blending of light and shadow that critic Anita Nowak referred

---

[25] Jill Dolan, *Utopia in Performance: Finding Hope at the Theater* (Ann Arbor: University of Michigan Press, 2005), 67.
[26] Bartosz Frąckowiak, interview by author, Warsaw, Poland, 8 January 2014.
[27] See Butler, *Gender Trouble*.

to as 'woven lighting',[28] which at moments rendered the sculptural body as two-dimensional as the objects that are placed beneath Sokołowska's camera and projected onto the flat surface of the screen. Placing herself under the same spotlight as the archival objects suggests that Sokołowska is allowing her own body to be submitted to an equivalent level of signification, a complex translation of the actor into an object of exhibition open for inspection. While this might at first inspection be unnerving, Sokołowska *qua* archival object is not simply mute, fixed or objectified. Rather this theatrical act highlights the objecthood of the archive and its complex processes of meaning-making through the performer's ability to question the status of her co-presence as archive *and* as the archive's co-generator. While this exerted a deconstructive effect on the Włast/Komornicka archives, the performance itself redirects the intent of Butler's notion of 'gender insubordination', the break with gender assigned through performativity whose radical insubordination is reliant on subverting the very norms Sokołowska continues to reinscribe through clothing, gesture, voice and patterns of behaviour, thus leaving gender meanings within the performance essentially unchallenged. Queer literary theorist Błażej Warkocki was the most vocal critic of the casting choice. In his analysis, Warkocki argues that Włast spent forty-two years of his life trying to force his social environment to acknowledge him as a man, putting everything on the line in this effort, including his literary career. 'While Anita Sokołowska at the beginning attempts to experiment with movements *à la* a drag king, the question of gender completely disappears. Piotr is a woman in pants. TransPiotr remains (against his will) a woman.'[29] Warkocki also conjectures about future performances about Anna Grodzka, the first Polish transgender Member of Parliament. Why is it, he asks, that if the public never attempts to use Grodzka's former male name, Ryszard, the same rights cannot be extended to Piotr Włast? However, I would suggest that, by transcoding Włast into contemporary trans politics this comparison with Grodzka is uneven and even a little misleading. Nevertheless, Warkocki is astute in drawing attention to the ethical call of transembodiment. If the Włast/Komornicka archive places a certain ethical demand upon us today, as the performance convincingly

---

[28] Agata Kozłowska, 'Maria Komornicka. Nieistnienie', *Bez Dogmatu* 92 (2012). http://lewica.pl/index.php?id=26900

[29] Błażej Warkocki, *Różowy język. Literatura i polityka kultury na początku wieku* (Warsaw: Wydawnictwo Krytyki Politycznej, 2013), 195. Despite this criticism Warkocki praised the performance for the treatment of violence, which is inflicted by a heteronormative culture on those who do not wish to slavishly adhere to its ideals.

150 BRYCE LEASE

suggests, it is not the same idiom in which it is adopted. This performance makes visible the difficult, variable and internally complicated traditions that impose themselves on this archive, refreshing and renewing the political claims at different historical moments, from Janion (sexuality outside of the state) and Filipiak (symbolic violence) to Warkocki himself (transbody).

Frąckowiak claimed that until 1907 there was only Maria Komornicka. 'Which is more important before or after? Why give more weight to one or the other era? She was a public intellectual and part of the mainstream before 1907 and considered herself a public intellectual', he argued.[30] Transembodiment, as I conceptualize it, asks a similar question but offers a different answer. On the one hand, Włast was adamant in their decision to subsume Komornicka's history and wished for previous publications with that name to be republished with the author as Piotr Włast. In the *Book of Idyllic Poetry* (1914) Włast is listed as the author with Maria Komornicka in parenthesis, suggesting this was only an alias or pseudonym. On the other hand, Frąckowiak is right to challenge such a straightforward chronological view of history. The problem, as I see it, lies in the wish to create a character that is neither entirely feminine nor masculine but somewhere in between, making Włast/Komornicka a stand-in for interests in (trans)gender bodies as postmodern paradigms (fantasies, one might say) of gender fluidity. While Włast was adamant about his gender identity, Komornicka was drawn to the modernist interest in the necessity of the unification of both elements of human nature (male and female), and a sublime fusion of body and soul outside gender norms.[31] Nevertheless, in her writing, Komornicka situated her female body as the foundation of her consciousness.

One of the solutions in performance was to frustrate spectators' desire to see a dramatic staging of Komornicka's 'transformation' into Włast on the now legendary evening in Poznań in 1907. Sokołowska only indicates a requisite bibliography on the overhead projector that the audience can research the matter for themselves. This refusal to graphically portray this canonical moment on the one hand successfully moved away from hackneyed depictions of transgendered characters as signifiers of difference and disclosure, such as Neil Jordan's infamous trans thriller *The Crying Game* (1992). On the other hand, transembodiment always-already stages the crisis of identity that is articulated in such 'revelation' scenes as

[30] Frąckowiak, interview.
[31] See Boniecki, *Modernistyczny dramat ciala*, 108.

The Crying Game exploits. Casting and embodiment foreclose attempts to avoid this concern. A further challenge for the theatre makers entailed the relationship between representation of a transgendered body and current scholarly trends that posit Włast as purely phantasmatic. The transition from Komornicka to Włast is still fuelled by biographical speculation that is suspicious of the desire to change gender, and resulting accusations of madness are suggested, as is latent homosexuality and the poet's desire for recognition. Although one senses the director's intention to problematize these lines of reasoning as *causes*, the self-same anxieties that produce such interpretative attempts to find a definitive understanding of Włast's act of self-determination are inadvertently reinforced. Rather than situate this as a simple critique, I would like to suggest that this dilemma sits at the very heart of transembodiment.

In *In a Queer Time & Place: Transgender Bodies, Subcultural Lives*, Jack Halberstram considers the reception of the transgender body by multiple audiences. Halberstram argues that for some this body 'confirms a fantasy of fluidity so common to notions of transformation within the postmodern', or the 'utopian vision of world of subcultural possibilities', while for others transgender bodies confirm 'the enduring power of the binary system'.[32] Szczawińska and Frąckowiak's production has a postmodern slant that intended to think through gender as a fantasy of fluidity, which produced the expectation to see gender in more expansive or progressive ways, though in practice Sokołowska served as a reminder of a structured binary that Włast himself enforced through his determination to inhabit a normative masculinity and benefit from its concomitant social privileges. While the episodic composition of the performance allows for multiple views and perspectives that account for the pressure placed on gender in particular historical moments, the casting forcefully reminds us of the impossibility of a gender-neutral critique.

The process of transembodiment here also directly engages the ongoing debate between second-wave feminists and their third-wave counterparts in the Polish public sphere.[33] This is particularly developed in the episode

---

[32] J. Jack Halberstam, *In a Queer Time & Place: Transgender Bodies, Subcultural Lives* (New York: New York University Press, 2005), 96. Of note to a discussion of Włast, Halberstram also changed his name from Judith to J. Jack and writes about the confusion this produces, which the author celebrates rather than defuses through a final and conclusive explanation.

[33] Szczawińska identifies as a third-wave feminist, mobilizes gender stereotypes rather than working against them, which she claims is the territory of the second-wave, and pursues literary and theatre histories of female oppression by resurrecting lost voices and tracking male fantasies. Claiming to be sex positive, she invests in depictions of eroticism without shame, religious oppression or bodily taboos (Cited in Łukasz Drewniak, 'Śmierć Fredrom i Mrożkom', *Przekrój* 10, 9 March, 2012).

entitled 'Holy feminists', which implies that second-wave feminism regards itself as self-satisfied or morally superior. Janion, who devotes more than one-third of her book *Kobiety i duch inności* (Women and the Spirit of Otherness) to Komornicka, focuses primarily on two themes: mysticism, juxtaposing Komornicka's poetry with Julius Słowacki, and the poet's role as a so-called 'changeling', situating Włast as an expression of her historical social framework in which a woman had no chance to realize herself as an author, bohemian, intellectual or artist. In the mid-1990s Janion's focus on the equality of women in Komornicka's era was directly linked to the question of Polish independence after 1989 and the failed promise of women's emancipation in a newly self-governing Poland. The majority of second-wave feminists in this region at the time rightly argued that democracy was immediately determined as patriarchal after political transformation. In two primary modes Szczawińska demonstrates an allegiance to third-wave feminism in the performance. Firstly, the poet appears as a response to the collapse of the category of 'woman' that is too narrow and reliant on unification rather than coalition. And secondly, there is evidence of a move away from traditional politics towards the foregrounding of personal narratives as an intersectional and multi-perspectival vision of feminism, whose boundaries are not carefully policed. Negotiating a desire to view the poet outside a perceived outmoded feminist lens, Szczawińska actively employs its legacies even while critiquing its ostensible politics. The critique of the movement indicates its assumed and shared understanding. This position requires neither hectoring nor support, which shows a marked difference between Szczawińska's performance text and Janion and Filipiak's criticism, both of which are realigned through a concept of transembodiment. While Janion, who believed that explicit feminism is one of the hallmark values of contemporary literary criticism, builds a coherent picture of Komornicka, Szczawińska revels in the contradictions and the ignored or difficult details that challenges Janion's notion that Włast is an appropriate figure for emancipation, particularly given his sense of aristocratic superiority derived from a patriarchal line. As a result, the production offers a crucial attempt to engage the mythology around Włast/Komornicka and the discourses that have appropriated this figure as heroic 'holy martyr', patron of transgression, or icon for the rights of a 'third gender', who ultimately dared to challenge the social order and thereby expanded understandings of freedom in the Polish cultural sphere.

Transembodiment ultimately stages an encounter with inadequacies in current frames of knowledge and meaning making. The body translated through archive, history and theatrical mediation draws discourse into crisis. Where will we emerge? Which discourses will be unable to reemerge? Gayatri Chakravorty Spivak speaks about the importance and the inevitability of catachresis in translation – and here we see this with the body itself.[34] Bodily catachresis – the semantic misuses of the body – might also be productive, in the sense that the body is being applied in a way that departs from conventional usage or understanding. Through transembodiment new subjects emerge and come into being, ultimately opening up the horizons of what was not previously knowable.

[34] Gayatri Chakravorty Spivak, 'Translation as Culture', *Parallax* 6, no. 1 (2000): 13.

CHAPTER 7

Translating Triumph
The Power of Print and the Performance
of Empire in Early Modern Europe

Daniel J. Ruppel

In the early sixteenth century, the widespread adoption of the Gutenberg press and novel methods for creating reproducible images transformed the relations between performance, translation, and performance documentation. This chapter explores how one royal family, the Hapsburgs, leveraged burgeoning technologies of print and the transformations they facilitated in language and visual culture to appropriate an antique Roman ceremony known as the 'triumph', casting themselves as inheritors of the glory and majesty of imperial Rome. The Hapsburgs were far from alone in this enterprise. Echoing the medieval concept of the 'translation of empire' (*translatio imperii*), rulers throughout early modern Europe drew on triumphal imagery to claim the symbolic capital of ancient Rome, reinforced by the flourishing intellectual fashions of Humanism.[1] However, the Hapsburgs were unique in the political and linguistic diversity of their territories, and for having a relative paucity of illustrious ancestors they could claim to fill out their noble pedigree. The stakes were therefore higher for the Hapsburg rulers to stage their performative claim to be inheritors of an imperial genealogy that exceeded bloodlines, and to translate this claim to audiences throughout their disparate realms in ways that exceeded language alone.

By looking at three case studies that frame the life and reign of Holy Roman Emperor Charles V (1500–1549), the most famous Hapsburg ruler

---

[1] In distinction to the Renaissance, the idea that civilization perished with the fall of Rome and was 'reborn', the various formulations of '*translatio imperii*' contend that civilization has persisted throughout time by passing from one place to another, either from Rome to Constantinople to Charlemagne's capital at Aachen, or by passing through Rome as part of a lengthier process of westward transfer of divinely sanctioned rule. A version of this idea appears in *Les illustrations de Gaule et singularitez de Troye* (1512), by Jean Lemaire de Belges. Lemaire was an influential poet in the circle of Margaret of Austria, Hapsburg Regent of the Burgundian Netherlands and a parental figure to young Charles V; his book traces the lineage of the House of Burgundy back to Hector of Troy.

of the era, I argue that the Hapsburgs used the new possibilities of print to encourage audiences to see the family as part of what performance historian Joseph Roach terms a 'performance genealogy' of triumphant emperors,[2] while localizing their arguments through verbal and visual cues that appealed to audiences' regional pride and emergent national imaginaries. In collaboration with leading artists and scholars of the day, Hapsburg rulers created documents of triumphal performances that were also themselves performative documents, whose rhetorical and political efficacy was bolstered by what translation theorist Lawrence Venuti calls 'domesticating effects'.[3] By virtue of these performative documents, diverse reading publics could participate in political rituals translated across language, space, and time. When the documents' complex rhetorical cues were effective, they could make disparate readers across the Empire each feel right at home.

For the ancient Romans of the Republic and the early Empire, the triumph was a processional ritual that honoured a military victory, the highest honour a commander (one with '*imperium*') could achieve.[4] The army paraded before the crowds in the metropolitan capital, who feasted their eyes on the spoils of conquest and prisoners taken to be enslaved: goods and people who had been forcibly ferried over (literally, *trans-latus*) from the site of their capture. This stolen wealth and labour would beautify the metropole, building monuments to Roman greatness, including the 'triumphal arches' that served to document in stone both the impressiveness of the conquest and the opulence of the triumphal parade that made it gloriously manifest. Even in antiquity, the triumph troubled linear conceptions of time. New armies paraded past reliefs of past parades; the architects and historians responsible for documenting triumphs created new pasts that shaped rituals to come. The cultural importance of the triumph and its propagandistic flexibility made it a crucial lever in

---

[2] See Joseph R. Roach, *Cities of the Dead* (New York: Columbia University Press, 1996), 24–40.

[3] Lawrence Venuti, *The Translator's Invisibility* (London: Routledge, 2008), 6.

[4] Military parades and processional entries (e.g. the Hellenisic *epiphanos*) existed throughout the ancient Mediterranean (and persist in strikingly similar forms today). It is difficult to say when, exactly, the triumph as such came to be. As the Classicist Mary Beard has shown, the triumph was part of the Roman Republican imaginary, and monopolizing the right to perform triumphs was critical to the consolidation of power and military authority (*imperium*) under Princeps Augustus in what came to be known as the 'Empire'. The 'Roman Empire' persisted for centuries in various forms, but Rome ceased to be an Imperial capital in the late third century CE. Mary Beard, *The Roman Triumph* (Cambridge, MA: Harvard University Press, 2009), 52–53, 72–80. See also Michael McCormick, *Eternal Victory: Triumphal Rulership in Late Antiquity, Byzantium and the Early Medieval West* (Cambridge: Cambridge University Press, 1990).

156   DANIEL J. RUPPEL

the shift from Republic to 'Empire', when *imperium*, and the celebration that honoured it, was increasingly restricted to the ones who would come to be known as 'Emperors'.

For early modern rulers, the triumph itself became the spoil, captured not (only) through physical theft, but also through translation and artistic appropriation. As a titular ruler of far-flung states, successfully appropriating the triumph was crucial to Charles' symbolic legitimacy as a transnational 'Emperor'. Through the careful planning of his grandfather, Emperor Maximilian I, and various machinations of his own, Charles became Holy Roman Emperor, Spanish King, and the titular ruler of domains stretching from Bohemia to Cuzco, but as a nobleman born in Flanders, Charles was never fully accepted as 'German' or 'Spanish'.[5] Beginning with a series of 'paper triumphs' executed for Maximilian using novel printing technologies, I look at how Charles' predecessor merged visual styles and formal tropes to make an Italic ceremony the quintessential expression of a new 'German' identity, with the Hapsburgs at its centre. Witnessing how Maximilian domesticated the triumph for a Teutonic audience, the chapter then moves to documents of Charles' own 'triumphal entry' into Rome, focusing on an epistolary account translated from Italian into French, German, and Flemish.[6] Each of these translations employ domesticating effects that supplement linguistic changes with novel imagery and typographic form. Finally, I examine the *Triumph of Antwerp*, a document that appeared in Latin, Flemish, and French. Working in concert with the festival it describes, the document seeks to guarantee the 'susception' of Charles' son Philip as ruler of a united Netherlands, which never before existed. 'Susception' describes Philip's act of becoming the hereditary ruler of a territory that is also constituted by his taking-up the office. I argue that the balance of continuation and creation encapsulated in this term

---

[5] Born in Ghent, Charles grew up speaking local dialects of French *(Franchois)* and Flemish (*Vlamms/Nederlands*), with French being his primary language of correspondence. Charles inherited the Archduchy of Austria and myriad titles in the 'Burgundian Netherlands', a patchwork of fiefdoms between modern France and Germany. By convincing the Spanish *Cortes* that his mother, Joanna of Castille, was mad, he became the *de facto* ruler of Castille and Aragon (Spain), along with their territories throughout the Mediterranean and the 'new world'. Finally, once elected Holy Roman Emperor, he held symbolic sovereignty over the plethora of Germanic states in central Europe.

[6] Throughout this chapter, I use the terms 'Italian', 'French', 'German' and 'Flemish' as shorthand markers for non-specialists. These markers stand in for a complex linguistic landscape that, despite the stabilizing effects of print, remained very much in flux. The documents consulted are written in writerly forms of Toscano ('Italian'), *Franchois* (the 'French' dialect of Antwerp), *Brabanter/Vlamms* ('Flemish') also in its Antwerper variety, and the *Teutsch* ('German' of Austria and Strasbourg).

also describes the rhetorical effect the document seeks to engender: these translations, not quite fully domesticating in their effects, encourage the susception of a new 'global' reader, who merges her historical local identity, with her participation in a violent transnational, translinguistic, and transoceanic empire that is just (again) coming into being.

A Triumph of Print: Maximilian's 'Paper Triumphs'

The highest honour the Roman Republic could bestow on a military commander (an *imperator*), the triumph played a crucial symbolic role in the consolidation of power that transformed the Republic into an 'imperial' state. In turn, early modern rulers appropriated the form and imagery of the ceremony as proof of their claims to carry on the glorious mantle of the ancient Empire, its military might, and its cultural supremacy. Like their counterparts in Italy, England, and especially France, the Hapsburgs integrated triumphal symbolism into ceremonial entries, processional rituals used to celebrate the arrival of dignitaries, confirm transfers of power, and publicly embody the hierarchies of the city, church, and court. With the advent of print, these 'triumphal entries' gained a new audience, and their performative effects gained a new reach. Cleverly made documents of triumphs permitted readers distanced in space, time, and language to bear witness to these ceremonial processions and the stylized symbolism that dressed their routes. By carefully constructing the readers' experience through rhetorical invitations, visual *mise en page*, and material cues, I argue that these documents could make readers feel like they were present at the ceremonies themselves, witnesses to the opulence of the event and to the performative felicity of the treaties or rites of succession described. Thus, documents of triumphs could serve distant rulers as a type of evidence for the legitimacy of their local rule, and to ratify their broader territorial and symbolic claims. However, readers might also find these documents unpersuasive, interpreting them as propagandistic records of pageantry, rather than legitimate records of successful, 'performative' rituals. In fact, as the case studies in this chapter bear out, many of these ceremonies did *not* take place as the documents indicate. Rather, the performance 'itself' takes place asynchronously, as reading publics negotiate the embodied encounters staged by the documents. I argue that the multi-modal translation strategies of the Hapsburg 'triumphs' explored below invite local readers to step in and verify for themselves felicity of the ceremony described – even if the triumph never quite happened.

Emperor Maximilian I was the architect of Hapsburg expansion. His strategic alliances forged the massive, transnational territory that his grandson Charles would claim. However, Maximilian's Imperial status was troubled by a fateful lack. With wars wracking Italy at the time of his election, travel was impossible, and Maximilian became the first Holy Roman Emperor in nearly 500 years to forgo a Papal coronation in Rome. Therefore, he decided to bring a bit of Rome to his homeland across the Alps by performing a triumph for his vassals. In collaboration with the Humanist scholar Johannes Stabius, he conceived a new kind of triumph. To create it, he commissioned artists who had experienced the innovations of the Italian Renaissance firsthand and established themselves as innovators in the media of woodcut prints, including Hans Burgkmair, Albrect Altdorfer, and Albrect Dürer. The project sought to translate the Roman triumph, to domesticate it or make it 'German', all the while leveraging the symbolic capital of Rome to address an identity both syncretic and novel: to redefine what being 'German' meant. The resulting masterworks, known by scholars as the 'paper triumphs', allowed Maximilian to project his triumphal presence simultaneously throughout his Imperial domain.

This project relied on transformative technologies of reproduction, but also exemplifies (and exploits) their effects on reading culture, and the emergence of 'national' identities. The mechanical press played a major role in disseminating texts by Classical authors and their early-modern Humanist imitators, but the printing of translations, literature, and legal documents in vernacular languages also reified the status of these common tongues as languages in their own right. Printing encouraged a more standardized orthography and privileged the grammar and diction of those regions or classes that could support a press, while new typefaces gave vernacular languages a recognizable appearance on the page. Publishing a translation of a Classical text often meant not only substituting Greek or Latin phrases for others in codes that modern readers might call 'French' or 'German', but also creating texts that *looked* the part. The appropriation of a text through translation, therefore, was (and is) not only a matter of linguistic substitution, but also of visual and material cues – a mix of deliberate choices and practical necessity that congeal (albeit always partially) to signal a type of collective ownership. Even illiterate or partially literate readers might visually identify a text as being in a language that was more or less 'theirs', sedimenting the association of a particular style with an emergent linguistic (or linguistic-national) community. To this

Translating Triumph 159

end, in addition to the complex imagery discussed later, Maximilian commissioned a new typeface to define the look of his 'paper triumphs', based on the blackletter hand refined by his chancellery. So influential was Maximilian's project, that even a non-expert reader will likely identify this blackletter '*Faktur*' typeface, distinguishing this quintessentially 'German' font from the (Times New) 'Roman' fonts made ubiquitous by Microsoft Word.[7]

Maximilian's project encompasses five printed works, each a rhetorical and technical achievement that stretched the possibilities of genre and medium to address a new type of elite reader, whom these works also helped to bring into being. The *Theuerdank* and *Weisskunig* are richly illustrated codices printed in fine *Faktur*, whose title characters present romanticized allegories of Maximilian as an exemplary German knightking. Since the Burgundian court had long poured its immense riches into establishing its Order of the Golden Fleece as the epitome of the chivalric ideal, by blending chivalric traditions with tropes from Teutonic *alten Istorie*, these ornate, visibly *German* books helped solidify Maximilian's appropriation of the lands and heritage belonging to his wife, Mary of Burgundy.[8] Meanwhile, the *Triumphwagon* (Triumphal Chariot) and the *Triumphzug* (Triumphal Procession) inserted Maximilian in a context that visually and materially indexed the Humanist re-visioning of ancient Rome. In the former, an intricate six-leaf composite print, Maximilian and his family sit with stoic poise, ringed by allegorical Virtues competing to lay laurels on his head. The 27-foot-long *Triumphzug* depicts an enormous parade of German soldiers, exotic prisoners, spoils, and arms. The subjects are contemporary, but the form resembles the rubbings of friezes taken from ancient monuments. It appropriates the triumphal form through an act which both is (as a print) and also imitates (as the semblance of a rubbing) an act of physical transfer. Thus, it stages its claim to authenticity and 'Roman-ness' not by looking like a triumph *per se*, but by looking

---

[7] Blackletter typefaces prevailed in early Northern European printing, while recognizable 'Roman' ones were common in Italian presses. They arose from blackletter hands – textura ('Gothic'), rotunda, bastarda, and later *Faktur*, which were common throughout Europe, but generally gave way to 'humanist' hands in the south, where Renaissance scholars imitated Carolingian scribes, mistaking their work for ancient manuscripts. Though developed under Maximilian, modern readers would likely recognize the retooled *Faktur* from the late-nineteenth century, infamously adopted (then abandoned) by the Nazi regime. David C. Greetham, *Textual Scholarship: An Introduction* (New York: Routledge, 2015), 225–236.

[8] Larry Silver, *Marketing Maximilian: The Visual Ideology of a Holy Roman Emperor* (Princeton, NJ: Princeton University Press, 2008), 31.

and feeling like the authentic, indexical *evidence* of antique triumphs that artists had carried back from Rome itself.

The fifth work, the monumental *Ehrenpforte* (the Arch of Honour, see Figure 7.1), merges the technical achievements of the other pieces, as well as their dual projects of appropriating Burgundian chivalry and Roman antiquity under a legibly 'German' roof.

Figure 7.1   *Ehrenpforte* ('Arch of Honour') of Maximilian I.
Courtesy of the National Gallery of Art, Washington, DC, Accession No. 1991.200.1.

Translating Triumph 161

Though commonly called 'Maximilian's Triumphal Arch', the *Ehrenpforte* claims an explicitly hybrid heritage.[9] On the one hand, the form of the commemorative arch indisputably cites the triumphal arches of ancient Rome, of which early modern replicas had already begun to proliferate.[10] Despite being made in paper, Dürer's subtle shading and use of blank space make the *Ehrenpforte* seem like one of these freestanding monuments, standing forth from the wall it hangs on and inviting the viewer to step up and (almost) through. On the other hand, a tiled roof crowns the central arch in a distinctly northern European style, while the flanking portals carry the insignia of the Burgundian chivalric Order of the Golden Fleece in circular fields that appear, from a distance, like the clock faces that were beginning to adorn German city squares. Small figures dance on the roofs. Statuesque nudes overlook robed heralds. Between them flit satyrs – classical types whose depiction makes them almost indistinguishable from the archetypal *Wildemen* of German forests, who had, in turn, already become models for early portrayals of the Indigenous Americans some writers termed '*sauvages*'.[11] For a viewer in a German city, or a nobleman who visited many, the *Ehrenpforte* could make the Roman borrowings seem comfortably assimilated in their new locale. The foreign, the grotesque, and the monumental are awesome in their own right, but nonetheless share space comfortably with the familiar and the quotidian.

Translation scholar Lawrence Venuti, borrowing from Friedrich Schleiermacher, terms such a semblance of comfortable familiarity a 'domesticating effect'.[12] Though Venuti theorizes specifically textual effects, and the Arch signifies through iconography and architectonics, the nature of early modern printing encourages scholars to consider language in its visual and material form, viewing the relationship between printed word and image on a continuum, rather than as exclusive categories. Domesticating translations, Venuti argues, make readers experience texts *as if* they were composed by native speakers – not translations at all. These effects render the translator's labour of interpretation invisible to the

---

[9] Though the translation 'Triumphal Arch' is common in Anglophone literature, in his Colophon to the *Arch*, Johannes Stabius calls it an 'Arch of Honor, *similar* to a Triumphal Arch' (quoted in Silver, *Marketing Maximilian*, 90). For a detailed bibliography of the explicitly 'triumphal' projects, see Silver, 39.

[10] See Margaret Ann Zaho, *Imago Triumphalis: The Function and Significance of Triumphal Imagery for Italian Renaissance Rulers* (Baltimore, MD: Peter Lang, 2004), especially 46–64.

[11] On the circulation of printed images of '*sauvages*' from the old world and the new, see Stephanie Leitch, *Mapping Ethnography in Early Modern Germany: New Worlds in Print Culture* (New York: Palgrave Macmillan, 2010), 55–56.

[12] Venuti, *The Translator's Invisibility*, 6.

reader, even though producing such domesticating texts usually requires the greatest interventions. By contrast, 'foreignizing' texts make fluent reception difficult, creating interruptions that, like Berthold Brecht's *Verfremdungseffekt*, render the work of interpretation apparent to the audience. Analysing such effects requires a standard of fluency, an understanding of what a given audience would perceive to be familiar or 'native'.

In his work *Translation and Subjectivity*, Naoki Sakai questions whether such a standard exists, objectively, or whether it is in fact interlingual translation itself that produces an illusion of languages as bounded spheres in which communication occurs without hindrance. By contrast, he proposes the 'heterolingual address', a practice that views 'homolingual' interpretation and interlingual translation on a continuum – never expecting pure, objective transmission of thought. Attending to the domesticating and foreignizing effects of the *Ehrenpforte*'s imagery and text requires an acknowledgement that both the 'original' and 'target' standards are (re)constructed in this virtuosic composition; the impression that there is a coherent German identity to which the arch is appealing is an effect of the impressive print itself. Time and linguistic difference make modern viewers such as you or I imperfect surrogates for the arch's original audience, but the arch has always addressed an imperfect audience, inviting them to play a more perfect role. Given the fluctuating linguistic landscape of early modern Europe, the extant records of printed text and imagery allow for probabilistic assessments of what peoples of different linguistic communities would expect to see *in print*, provided one acknowledges that these works both reflect and re-form the linguistic landscape in which they participate.

The dichotomy of 'domesticating' and 'foreignizing' usefully breaks down in cases where interruptions of fluent reception signal the virtuosic instantiation of a new register, a mark of cultural capital or even genius. This process of drawing on legible traditions, and through a virtuosic gesture, exceeding them, is crucial to the work of early modern triumphs. The *Ehrenpforte* does not produce a uniform effect. Rather, by integrating elements that would be familiar to audiences throughout Maximilian's domains with others that are deliberately distancing, it manifests a novel cultural imaginary that claims symbolic superiority over more common linguistic and visual vernaculars used throughout the realm. Thus, the hybrid elements of the *Ehrenpforte* are not simply a mix of traditions, but a sort of sublation of them. The viewer might see Roman columns as the foundation supporting German roofs, or the German roofs overshadowing the Roman past, but in either case, they are both subject to the imprimatur of Maximilian's imperial majesty.

Translating Triumph 163

The larger visual programme of the Arch explicitly opposes vignettes of Maximilian's 'triumphal' accomplishments as emperor (those which expanded the realm) with those of his 'chivalric' deeds as knight-king (those which magnified his personal glory), giving each pride of place on the two flanking portals. The distinctions are sometimes different than expected. Maximilian was a belligerent hunter (chivalric), but his successful conquests (triumphant) privileged the marital over the martial. Under his rule, Hapsburg expansion was a masterwork of strategic dynastic alliances. So it follows that the centrepiece of the monumental image yields to the knotted doubling of two genealogies. Like the Arch as a whole, it merges traditions to fabricate new pasts and imply virtual futures.

The first of these genealogies depicts the 'lineage' of elected Holy Roman Emperors, while the second depicts the bloodline of the Hapsburgs, back to the differently elected (i.e. invented) ancestors of Troia, Francia, and Sicambria. Shown as allegorical grandmothers, these personified sites of origin offer a Classical and Imperial history that circumvents Rome, but hews close. 'Francia' serves to appropriate Charlemagne; the quasi-legendary Sicambrians fought with and against Julius Caesar along the Rhine; and 'Troia' reflects a contemporary myth of Trojans other than Aeneas founding civilization in German lands.[13] Thus, the Arch makes clear that Maximilian claims the Roman legacy not by direct, biological descendance, but by a sort of elective affinity. It is a performative gesture – not a claim to truth, but an effort to bring a new status into being – and in its workings, it resembles what the performance historian Roach terms 'performance genealogy'.[14] Roach uses this term to trace the circulation of processional ceremonies throughout what he terms the 'circum-Atlantic world'. He focuses on funerals, modelling his theory on performative utterance that grounded the ritual of French royal succession in the early modern period: *'Le Roy est mort. Vive le Roy!'* (The King is Dead. Long live the King!).[15] This phrase, for Roach, encapsulates the strange way by which a new body comes to inhabit a persistent office, or theatrical role. The new body 'surrogates' for the deceased; the King dies and also lives on. Like a translation, the surrogation is always imperfect. The inheritor inhabits the office, but the office is not unchanged. Still, the new body 'passes'. So does Imperial majesty pass on, Maximilian claims, in his monumental arch. The arch passes for Roman, even as it passes Rome by; it passes for German, even if Germany does not yet exist.

---

[13] Silver, *Marketing Maximilian*, 56–57.
[14] Roach, *Cities of the Dead*, 24–40.
[15] Roach, *Cities of the Dead*, 24–40.

Maximilian's Arch also projects acts of surrogation yet to come. Amidst the overabundance of constructed and conflated pasts, the Arch also contains remarkable, intentional gaps: empty seats at the end of the line of Emperors, a space among Maximillian's grandchildren for others not yet born, and a final panel in his 'triumphal' history, where the next Emperor might step in to add an image of Maximillian's funeral. As the Arch achieved its first edition in 1517–1518, Maximilian leveraged his diplomatic might to ensure that his two genealogies would remain interwoven. The marriages Maximilian arranged ensured his grandson Charles would inherit the Hapsburg lands in Austria, the 'Burgundian Netherlands' from the English Channel to the Franche-Comte, the Aragonese Kingdoms in Iberia, Sicily, and Naples, and the co-rule of Castile, with its expanding claims in the New World. Charles' election as Emperor, however, was far from guaranteed. By delivering copies of the Arch to the Imperial Electors (along with substantial gifts of borrowed gold), Maximilian encouraged these privileged spectators to ensure the felicity of the performative passing, literally 'filling the blank' with Maximilian's chosen successor. These blanks create a space of uncertainty, but they also serve as an invitation for the spectator to step in and surrogate for the Electors themselves, retroactively affirming the genealogical claims the Arch makes, and bearing witness to the futures it scripts in advance.

Unlike many of the titles he inherited, taking up the office of Holy Roman Empire and (co-)King of Castile required Charles to prove that he could perform roles of 'German' Emperor and 'Spanish' King, even though, like the empty spaces in the Arch, these roles were virtual, not yet fully fleshed-out. Indeed, other historical rulers vied to fill these roles – Francis I of France and Henri VIII of England for the Empire, and Charles' own mother for the throne of Castile – and even today, the Arch seems to invite others to step in, and see themselves as the 'surrogate' for Empire. It is this invitation to surrogate, and thus, to participate as living 'effigies' in the 'performance genealogy' of this triumphal form, which I argue, makes the propagandistic claims of Maximilian's Arch *feel* so persuasive.

Thus, Charles was chosen as 'King of the Romans', a sort of 'Emperor-elect'. Yet to gain the true Imperial crown, he would have to go beyond the German lands, to Rome itself. In so doing, he would fulfil his grandfather's virtual script, but he would also take it in a new direction, because Charles was not very German at all. In fact, born in Burgundian Ghent, he was not *not* French. The remainder of this chapter considers the way Charles V surrogates as transnational Emperor, and how he attempts to ensure the performative felicity of his own surrogation by his son Philip.

Translating Triumph 165

Considering francophone texts from his homeland of Flanders and neighbouring Antwerp, it explores the tactics of translation employed to ensure performative acts of surrogation 'pass' in new contexts, forming the role of a 'global' reader/spectator that cannot be divorced from the violent legacies of Empire.

Plus Iterum: Charles Enters Rome

Maximilian provided his vassals and, even today, provides viewers the opportunity to experience his triumph by virtue of a complex process of surrogation, through which he marks his Imperial virtues on the walls and on the bodies of those who take up his legacy. However, as Maximilian's chosen surrogate, Charles would not be contained by his grandfather's ambitions. Maximilian's motto was '*Halt Mass*' – hold the measure; Charles chose '*Plus Ultra*' – further beyond. The shift to Latin indicated his ambitions to carry his Empire far beyond Germany. In his crest, he drapes it across the 'Pillars of Hercules', symbol of the Strait of Gibraltar, to indicate his transoceanic reach. Still, this 'New World' reach was present in Europe largely by virtue of circulating paper: printed accounts, painted maps, and promissory notes drawn against future shipments of plate. Charles' ambitions were centred in the old world, in the 'Eternal City'. He sought to go beyond by going back, by reenacting a Roman triumph on the site of its origins. Nevertheless, this embodied 'back-translation' reaches us as it did Charles' own surrogates and subjects: translated into complex documentary surrogates, which like maps, debt, or 'paper triumphs', ask us to see multiple, overlapping presences.

Charles' road to Rome was rocky and circuitous. 'Charles' reached Rome early on, albeit via an unfortunate surrogate. In 1527, after capturing the French King Francis I at Pavia, a restless and unpaid Imperial army under the French turncoat Charles de Bourbon ventured to Rome – and sacked it, leaving Pope Leo X to flee by night. The Emperor Charles reconciled with the Papacy only after a new pope, the Medici Clement VII, took St. Peter's throne. The Emperor used his influence and his army to expand the Papal domains and install Clement's 'nephew' Alessandro (rumoured to be his son) as the first Duke of Florence. In recompense, Clement anointed Charles, carrying out the precedent set by Charlemagne and ritually affirming Charles' surrogation as Holy Roman Emperor. Yet to avoid further tensions with a Roman populace still reeling from the sack and subsequent bout of plague, the coronation took place in Bologna. Only in 1535 did Charles dare to enter Rome. Following an expedition to the African coast,

166   DANIEL J. RUPPEL

where his army overwhelmed an immensely outmatched Ottoman garrison in Tunis (the site of ancient Carthage), Charles demanded a triumphant reception – a ceremony to prove that Charles was not only a surrogate of Charlemagne, but also that of the most triumphant *imperatores* of all time.

Numerous sources attest that Rome received the Emperor with imperial pomp, but two extant documents go *plus ultra*. Deploying visual form to extend or even displace their verbal content, these documents construct sensory experiences that invite their anticipated readers to surrogate for live spectators of Charles' reception through the act of reading itself. The first is an anonymous itinerary, *Ordine, Pompe, Apparati, et Ceremonie Della Solenne Intrata Di Carlo V, Imp. Sempre Aug. Nella Citta di Roma* (The Order, Devices, and Ceremony of the Solemn Entry of Charles V, Ever August Emperor, into the City of Rome). The *Ordine* appears studiously 'Roman', appealing to an audience versed in Humanist reimaginings of the classical past by using print technology to create a visual and haptic sense that antiquity is pressing into the present day. Though the title mentions only Rome, the account describes Charles' processional entries into Rome, Siena, and Florence. The second is an epistolary account by the Florentine Zanobio Ceffino, addressed to Alessandro, the newly created Duke of Florence.[16] Ceffino's account survives in Italian, Flemish, German, and French. None of these editions approach the rich layering of the *Ordine*, but collectively, they demonstrate the power of domesticating effects to make Charles' Roman triumph resonate for communities throughout his Empire.

Though the author of the *Ordine* goes unnamed, the Emperor is present on the first page by virtue of his device (see Figure 7.2): *plus ultra*, winding around stylized Columns of Hercules. The verso features a Latin poem celebrating Charles' victory in Tunis (*'ex Lybiae'*) and reconciliation with the Pope, and below it, an antique medallion with a laureled Caesar shaking a spearman's hand.[17] A close analysis reveals this Caesar to be Marcus Aurelius, called 'Germanicus', an erudite suggestion to

---

[16] Zanobio Ceffino, *La triumphante entrata di Carlo V. imperatore augusto innelalma citta de Roma: con el significato delli archi triomphali [et] delle figure antiche, in prosa [et] versi latini* ([Rome]: s.n., 1536).

[17] This appears to be a rendering of an actual antique artifact, rather than a new medallion celebrating Charles in an antique style. The inscription identifies the Emperor as Marcus Aurelius (IMP VIII), whose successful campaigns in Germany earned him the title *Germanicus* – Charles, of course, is a 'German' Holy Roman Emperor. The handshake could be read as symbolizing the reconciliation with the Pope, but also, the Imperial relationship with the newly instated Duke of Florence. 'DE GERMANIS IMP VIII COS III P P', in Seth William Stevenson, Charles Roach Smith, and Frederic W. Madden, *A Dictionary of Roman Coins, Republican and Imperial* (London: George Bell and Sons, 1889). Searchable database at NumisWiki, www.forumancientcoins.com/numiswiki/

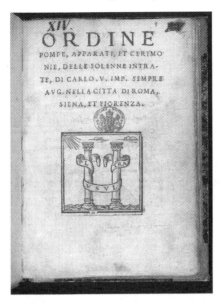

Figure 7.2 Title Page of *Ordine Pompe, Apparati, et Ceremonie Della Solenne Intrata Di Carlo V., Imp[erator] Sempre Aug[ustus] Nella Citta Di Roma* (1536), and verso.

consider the 'German' Emperor Charles as surrogate for the famously erudite Roman. For a less-learned reader, however, the illustration nonetheless conveys a *sense* of the poem that precedes it: a sense of military victory, a sense of reconciliation, and above all, a sense of ancient Rome, all shown as the physical flip-side of Charles' transcendent device. Bleeding through the page, this device persists ghost-like in the antique imagery. Thus, this leaf performs Charles' surrogation of and as a Roman Imperator on several mutually reinforcing, but independently accessible levels. Before the reader even enters the text and its elegant, distinctly *italic* typeface, she has already joined Charles in his reenactment of a Roman Roman Triumph. This interplay of significant layers in the formal *mise en page* is common among finely crafted ceremonial documents of this period, which instantiate the opulence of the festivals they describe, allowing even illiterate users to see and feel the prestige of the event through its surrogate, while inviting more erudite readers to delve further into the mysteries of surrogation that they stage.

Notably, despite emphasizing Charles' status as 'ever august Emperor' (*imp. sempre au[g].*) and terming him a 'Caesar', the *Ordine* does not term Charles' procession into Rome a 'triumph' *per se*, but rather a 'solemn entry' *(solenne intrata)*. As an 'entry', the ceremony recalls a ceremony of surrogation especially prominent in Charles' native Netherlands and northern France: the 'Joyous Entry'. The early modern entry was a formal ceremony of surrogation that also effected a type of translation. Typically occurring on a sovereign's first visit to a polity, the entry was a sort of reenactment of the coronation, a 'localization' of the act of succession that renegotiated the abstract relation between sovereign and polity by concretizing it in the physical encounter of the corporeal monarch with the corporate body of the city. While the famous 'Joyous Entry' (*Joyeuse Entrée, Blijde Inkommst*) of Duchess Joanna of Brabant (1356) was a constitutional document outlining the respective powers of the Duchess and the privileges of the Brabanter cities, entries could also be demonstrations of asymmetrical power, in which military parades and other 'triumphal' citations called into question who was enjoying the rites and rights of entry, and at whose expense. Scholars have generally focused on how triumphal imagery travelled northward throughout the sixteenth century on the wave of Humanism, giving the ceremonies the gloss of Italic cultural prestige. Many contend this Italicization distanced the form from its roots as an efficacious political ritual, replacing it with theatricalized pomp.[18] By contrast, Charles' triumph in Rome manifests how the ceremonial entry itself inverts the ancient triumphal formula in which wealth stolen from afar enriches the metropole. Enjoying a series of lavish gifts and costly theatrical displays, Charles performs the repertoires of a sack without the (physical) violence. The spoils travel only in documents.

Reading Ceffino's 'original' account, *La triumphante entrata di Carlo V*, reveals the complexity of the inversion.[19] Charles passes through a palimpsest of Romes; the reader passes with him, past ancient monuments erected in stone to honour the triumphs of emperors past, as well as ephemeral arches and 'theatres', newly erected with great haste and at great cost to construct a narrative that persists only on the page. The victory happened in Africa, but Rome itself is the site of extraction, the ruined city as well as the Papal See. Royal entries in this period are always to some degree parasitic, but by coercing the Romans to amass their meagre financial capital to produce a hybrid display of opulence on the actual ruins of their city, Charles proved himself determined to extract the last of Rome's symbolic

---

[18] Richard Cooper, 'French Royal Entries and the Antique (1515–65)', in *Writing Royal Entries in Early Modern Europe*, edited by Marie-Claude Canova-Green, Jean Andrews, and Marie-France Wagner (Turnhout: Brepols, 2013), 153–176; Margaret M. McGowan, *The Vision of Rome in Late Renaissance France* (New Haven, CT: Yale University Press, 2000).

[19] Ceffino, *La triumphante entrata di Carlo V. imperatore augusto innelalma citta de Roma.*

Translating Triumph 169

significance and attach it to himself. In lieu of celebrating the arrival of the riches of conquest, in this 'triumph', Rome celebrates a reenactment of its own defeat, a celebration at its own expense.

La triumphante entrata di Carlo V stages Charles as a Roman *imperator*, a living effigy of ancient *imperatores*, and an equal to the current Pope. As the reader moves along the parade route with Charles, the narrative slows, dilating into ekphrasis as Charles approaches the ancient Porta San Sebastiano, newly outfitted as a triumphal arch. An inscription, reproduced in indented capitals that make it *appear as* an inscription on the page, proclaims Charles to be *Tertio Africanus* (Third Africanus), successor to the conquerors of Carthage, Scipio the Elder and Younger, whose deeds Charles ostensibly reenacted on the ruins of that ancient city.[20] Yet the first two *Africanii* were elected citizens defending a Republic that had overthrown its tyrannical kings. By contrast, in the prior decade Charles' troops had quashed one Republic (Florence), threatened another (Venice), and overrun Rome itself. The arch, as described by Ceffino, elides this issue by collapsing Rome's long history upon the present. First, the reader encounters Charles' imperial title, rendered on the page as if inscribed on the arch. Below (in the text and on the arch) are the first three 'Kings' of Rome, with Romulus, the mythical founder, 'formed so carefully and naturally ... as to seem almost lively (*ressemblant quasi au vif*)'.[21] Flanking the central portal, the reader 'sees' the two Scipios, each standing above their painted names. The Younger rides a triumphal chariot pulling Syphax and Numidia, two allies of Carthage, as prisoners, while the Elder also steps through time, 'seeming to return through the same portal (*porte*) right now'. In fact, it is Charles who passes through the arch, passing as the third Scipio by filling the space between them, under the title of Emperor and under the approving gaze of the quasi-living Kings. As with Maximillian's Arch, he fills a gap seemingly *made* for him, and as he does so, his live body, too, becomes inscribed by the inscription, overarching all the other captioned bodies that surround him. In this visually and haptically engaging experience of reading, Charles passes as emperor by merging with the

---

[20] Scipio Africanus 'the Elder' defeated Hannibal in the Second Punic War, ending Carthaginian expansion. Mercantile competition triggered a Third Punic War, in which Scipio's grandson ('the Younger') breached the wall, razed the city, and enslaved the remaining citizens. Carthage became the Roman province of 'Africa'. Both Scipios earned triumphs, parading captured Carthaginian elephants, goods, and persons through Rome.

[21] Zanobio Ceffino, *La triumphante entree de lempereur nostre sire Charles le cincquieme tousjours auguste, faicte en sa tres noble cite de Rome, avec ses significations des epitaphes triumphantz & figures auctenticques &c.* (Antwerp: Johannes Steelfius, 1536), sig A2r. Literally, 'to the life', '*au vif*', appears interchangeably with '*vive*' (lively), but may also give the sense of a figure drawn 'after life'.

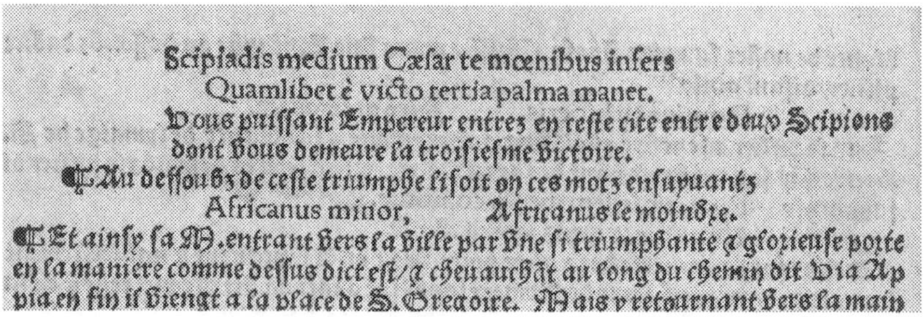

170 DANIEL J. RUPPEL

Scipiadis medium Cæfar te mœnibus infers
Quamlibet è victo tertia palma manet.
Vous puiſſant Empereur entrez en teſte cite entre deux Scipions
dont Vous demeure ſa troiſieſme Victoire.
¶Au deſſoubz de ceſte triumphe ſi ſoit on ces motz enſupuantz
Africanus minor,   Africanus le moinſ/ʒe.
¶Et ainſy ſa M⁹.entrant Vers ſa Ville par Vne ſi triumphante & glorieuſe porte
en ſa maniere comme deſſus dict eſt/q̃ cheuaucha̅t au ſong du chemin dit Via Ap
pia en fin il Vient a ſa place de S. Greaoire. Mais r retournant Vers ſa main

Figure 7.3   Ceffino, *La triumphante entree de lempereur nostre sire …* (f°2r).

medium of the passage itself, but particularly in the French edition, the
reader physically passes, too. Fortuitously, this moment of passage occurs
where the French reader turns the page, reading (in two languages) at the
top of the next one, 'You powerful Caesar enter between [lat. *medium*] two
Scipios, of which you maintain the third victory' (see Figure 7.3).

The 'You' here addresses Charles, but also seems to address the French
reader, suddenly asked to 'step in' as Charles. By framing the account as a
letter to Alessandro, the Duke of Florence, Ceffino draws the reader into
his text using an ancient rhetorical sleight-of-hand, which works in each
of the several languages. Like more substantial dedications that preface
longer works, naming a powerful addressee displaces responsibility for the
contents and publication of the letter onto a higher authority, but the gesture also casts the reader as a surrogate for the addressee. The epistolary
form permits the repetitive deixis of a personal address – the hail of the
pronoun 'you' – prodding the reader for her attention and participation.
Moreover, Ceffino's text refers substantial gaps in his description to the
Duke's 'imagination' (Fr. *ymagination*). These elisions 'work' insofar as
his reader (whether the Duke or, more likely, a surrogate) shares the commonplace knowledge to fill in these gaps, to pass fluently over them and
make the description pass as perfect(ed). In turn, by letting her probable
knowledge flow into the gap between herself and this figure of authority,
the reader's own theoretical, 'imaginary' experience serves as a guarantee
for the probity of the addressee for whom she steps in. Such theoretical
substitutions reinforce the performative claims of many ceremonial documents, making their structuring of society seem true – verisimilar and
virtually real. Taken together, these two effects cast the reader who buys
into this publication as the Duke.

Crucially, Alessandro played a particularly complex role in the Medici
genealogy, complicating the operations of surrogation at play. Born to an

Translating Triumph 171

unmarried African woman serving at the Medici court, Alessandro was known as '*il Moro*' (the Moor). While scholars continue to debate the Duke's relationship to his mother, let alone to any specifically 'African' identity, Ceffino nonetheless chose to address to him a document of a ceremony, which centres on 'African' identity in another sense. Charles enters Rome as the victor at Tunis, but the ceremony, in Ceffino's telling, stages him as another conqueror of Carthage: another Scipio 'Africanus', whose triumphs were a popular subject for paintings and tapestries. At the very least, Ceffino's readers would be attuned to the coincidence that the 'you' they repeatedly encountered in the text was a 'Moor' who owed his title to the 'African' Emperor Charles, whose conquest of 'Africa' (Tunis *qua* Carthage) had also installed another semi-autonomous vassal. While a full discussion of Alessandro's historical identity and the identity Ceffino constructs is beyond the scope of this chapter, it is an important reminder that the act of surrogation does not simply eclipse other bodies who have held the 'office' in question; a legacy of embodiments persists throughout the performance genealogy, as translations trace new meanings onto their 'original' sources.

While the 'role' of the Duke is nominally fixed, each translation of Ceffino's text forms a unique stage, addressing itself to distinct reading publics. The Italian original opens with a composite title page that does not read *as* Italian at all, making its own origin appear unstable, as if it were already in the process of translation.[22] The title is in blackletter typeface, while the arrangement of decorative elements resembles the layout of Simon Vostre's hugely popular books of hours, keystones of early French printing.[23] Neither of these elements precludes an Italic origin, but they contrast with the Humanist aesthetic of the text that follows, let alone the refined antiquity indexed by the anonymous *Ordine*. It seems as if the title page were added belatedly (though technicalities of printing suggest otherwise) just to destabilize the origins of the book.[24] The book addresses a wider audience than the linguistic signs it contains. Even a reader incapable of understanding the dense Italian

[22] Like the 'French' kingdom, 'Italy' was home to many 'nations'. The common tongue of Florence, home to the Medicis, is called 'Tuscan' in this era. This 'Italian' text lists no date or site of publication, though the letter concludes 'From Rome, MDXXXVI'.

[23] Vostre commissioned over seventy editions of the *Heures* between 1493 and 1525. Beginning in 1508, these books included one of the earliest French depictions of a classical triumph: a marginal illustration featuring the 'Triumph of Julius Caesar' with descriptive captions in French, See *Ces presentes Heures a lusaige de Chartres: avec les miracles nostre Dame / et les figures de lapocalipse et de la Bible et des triumphes de Cesar* (Paris: Philippe Pigouchet for Simon Vostre, 1508).

[24] An eight-page quarto would be printed on a single sheet. It would be uncommon to 'add' an eighth page.

172 DANIEL J. RUPPEL

dialect on the following pages – say, a German or Spanish speaker in Charles' retinue – could appreciatively 'read' the *varietas* of the opening page. Whether for the large Imperial coat of arms at the centre or the hunting scene (the chivalric complement to conquest) at the base, these readers might desire to possess such an 'original' document.[25] For the Italophone, on the other hand, the alienating destabilization performed by the initial *mise en page* instantiates the foreign *Kaiser* translating himself through Rome.

While the 'original' edition stages a defamiliarizing opening, the translations make the text – and the event – appear right at home. The German (*Teutsch*) edition, printed in Strasbourg, displays the most adept printcraft.[26] The finely formed *Faktur* lettering gives the edition striking elegance. It opens with a woodcut depicting Charles atop a throne, the centre of adulation from the clergy and bourgeois both. However, despite the content of the book (a 'Roman' Triumph in Rome), the image displays Charles wearing a royal (i.e. 'German'), not imperial crown.[27] Together with the style of the figures, it gestures more towards Charles' first coronation at Aachen than the Italic Imperial citations referred to in the text.[28]

The 'Germanizing' performance of the Strasbourg edition becomes even more clear alongside the Flemish (*Nederlands*) edition.[29] The Antwerp-based printer Jacob van Liesvelt commissioned a woodcut that shows Charles on horseback, wearing an Imperial crown, preparing to pass through a generalized but unmistakable triumphal arch.[30] The motif is a double citation.

---

[25] Similar hunting scenes were common elements in books of hours, including Vostre's Book of Hours [*Heures*] discussed above, where they precede the depiction of Caesar's Triumph.

[26] Zanobio Ceffino, *Ein Sendbrieff, so der edel Herr Zanobio Ceffino, dem druchleuchtigen Fürsten unnd Herrn, Hertzogen zu Florentz, dem triumphlichen einzug deß aller durchleuchtigisten, großmechtigisten Römischen Keyser, Caroli des Fünfften … ordentlich zugeschriben Mit allem fleiß auß Welsch ins Teutsch gebracht* (Strasbourg: Frölich, 1536).

[27] That is, an open circlet (Ducal, Royal), rather than a closed cross (Imperial).

[28] Printers often recycled quasi-relevant woodcuts they already owned, but given the quality of the printing and the prestige of the subject, this appears to be a deliberate appeal to the expectations of a 'Germanic' readership.

[29] 'Flemish' was one of a plethora of local dialects of *Nederlands* spoken in the Seventeen Provinces (Burgundian Netherlands), and is the common term for the modern language spoken in Antwerp. I use it now, as I use French, German, and Italian, with implicit quotation marks, using '*Nederlands*' where a specific distinction from the County of Flanders is required.

[30] Zanobio Ceffino, *Die blijde en[de] triumpha[n]te incoe[m]ste des aldermoghensten […] Heere Kaerle van Oostenrijcke en[de]van Spaingen […] Rooms keyser die vijfste van die[n] name […] geschiet de[n] v. dach in april binnen Roome[n] anno xv.c.xxxvi* (Antwerp: Jacob van Liesvelt, 1536). Famous for printing the first Flemish (*Nederlands*) translation of the New Testament, Jacob van Leisvelt was influential in establishing Antwerper *Nederlands* as a printed language. Antwerper printings in '*Franchois*' skew towards the increasingly standardized orthography of the Île de France, with notable exceptions (like '*Franchois*').

Translating Triumph 173

The arch draws on the reader's associations with Roman antiquity but the arrangement of horses indexes the visual history of Burgundian 'Joyous Entry' documents.[31] The reader witnesses the Emperor entering Rome *as* a Netherlandish ruler, as if Rome *itself* were a city in Flanders or Brabant. The doubling is echoed in his title, *Die blijde en[de] triumpha[n]te incoe[m] ste des [...] Heere Kaerle* (The joyous and triumphant entry of [...] Lord Charles), which folds the 'triumph' into the local tradition of 'joyous entries' (*joyeuses entrées, blijde incoemsten*).[32] These translations *performatively* address 'German' and Flemish/Nederlands identities, a performative gesture that becomes felicitous in the presence of an accepting reader.

The French edition, also printed in Antwerp, presents the least overt appeal to the eyes.[33] A steel-cut initial 'T' is all that separates this text from a news bulletin.[34] Nonetheless, the relatively unadorned octavo format and blackletter '*bâtarde*' typeface was common for many printed French entry accounts at this time, giving it a fitting appearance for its audience and its subject matter.[35] The French edition subtly extends its domesticating effects in the way it renders Latin inscriptions, which appear on monuments throughout Charles' parade route. The *mise en page* separates the inscriptions from the rest of the text block, placing the Latin words in a humanist 'Roman' typeface alongside French translations in *bâtarde*.

The visual separation afforded to these inscriptions allows them to operate both as image and text. While translating the inscriptions presumes a reader who cannot interpret the Latin, this presumption is itself performative. It stages the French language as capable of interpreting classical inscriptions.

---

[31] Gordon Kipling, *The Triumph of Honour: Burgundian Origins of the Elizabethan Renaissance* (Leiden: Leiden University Press, 1977).

[32] The relation of the *Joyeuse Entrée* and the 'constitutional history' of Brabant (the Duchy including Antwerp) is discussed later.

[33] Another Anterwerper edition, *Dye triumphelike incomste ons ghenadichs Heeren des Keysers Caerls de vyfste ... ghedaen in ... Roome*, published by Michiel van Hoochstraten, is unillustrated, and closely resembles the French edition in looks and linguistic choices. It may be a translation of Steelfius' (or vice-versa). I have only been able to consult a poor digital facsimile.

[34] Hélène Visentin, 'The Material Form and the Function of Printed Accounts of Henri II's Triumphal Entries (1547–51)', in *Writing Royal Entries in Early Modern Europe*, edited by Marie-Claude Canova-Green, Jean Andrews, and Marie-France Wagner (Turnhout: Brepols, 2013), 1–30, 17; see also William Kemp, 'Transformations in the Printing of Royal Entries during the Reign of François Ier: The Role of Geofroy Tory', in *French Ceremonial Entries in the Sixteenth Century: Event, Image, Text*, edited by Hélène Visentin and Nicolas Russell (Toronto: Centre for Reformation and Renaissance Studies, 2007), 111–132.

[35] Blackletter typefaces based on the '*bâtarde*' hand were common in printed francophone texts of all registers throughout the mid-sixteenth century, when they were displaced by 'humanist' typefaces of Geoffroy Tory and his imitators. The *bâtarde* script was also the basis for *Fraktur*, discussed earlier.

174 DANIEL J. RUPPEL

Ceffino's narrative structure gives a temporal order to the theoretical experience of this symbol-laden archway, constructing a weighted relationship between Emperor Charles and the Pope (now Paul III). King Romulus holds in his right hand the 'realm' and arms of the Pope, and in his left, the 'empire' and the arms of Charles. Locating the papal insignia in the right hand privileges the Pope, but the order of the *description* privileges Charles. The 'realm' and the 'empire' Romulus holds likely refer to the royal sceptre and imperial orb (*globus cruciger*) typically held in those hands, but the description again seems to link Pope Paul III to the role of a King, *subordinate* to Charles' Empire. Overseen by the balanced figure, 'naturally formed' (Fr.)/ 'natural seeming' (Ita.) of this quasi-live re-founder of Rome, Charles' triumphant passing is more than an efficacious enactment of the reconciliation between the Papacy and Emperor. In the time of reading, it becomes an ekphrastic re-presentation that re-originates the histories it tells. Despite the ordered nature of the description, the festival does not present a dramatic arc, but a progressive overwriting. Soon after, St. Peter (in effigy) is figured on St. Peter's Bridge, requesting in his inscribed 'voice' that the reader/listener place his '*chaire*' here. It is impossible in French not to sound this word doubly: '*chaire*' (throne) and '*chair*' (flesh), as the reader of the book physically steps in for the 'live' reader of the archway's inscription.

The flesh virtually overwrites the office. Ceffino's texts operate by allowing 'you' – in each case – to approach a familiar text that addresses 'you' as (if) part of a community that extends beyond linguistic intelligibility. The *chaire* renders itself appropriate to the *chair*, and 'we' pass as happily as the Duke of Florence in Tuscan as in German, Flemish as in French *bâtarde*. This present-passing, the feeling a performance is 'sound', gives each translation the power to instantiate the 'same' virtual relationship between probable viewer and probable event, but to potentially quite different ends. The sameness lies in the familiarity itself. It is a type of 'gentlemen's bargain' through which you (*vous/Sie/u*) may pass into another language, another present, another I.

If the rhetorical address allows the reader to 'double' as the Duke even as the reader reads the part in multiple, *domesticating* scripts, this documentary act reflects the unsettled duplicity of the festival programme itself. Charles' triumphal entry into Rome happens multiple times at once. The event itself is a multiplication, an overdetermined surrogation of a new imperator returning to the original site, a 'return' that the performance declares to be 'same'. Yet the 'original' event is seen only through multiple lenses of translation, which guarantee its performative claims to

Translating Triumph 175

identity by inviting readers to experience an event almost as if it were live (*quasi au vif*). The translations of Ceffino's text clearly address themselves to homolingual communities. By employing forms made probable to French, German, and Flemish readers through habituated modes of reading text, image, and codices, these 'domesticating' editions make the event 'pass' for each audience as if their reading experience were unmediated, even 'original'. The visual and textual form of these translations serves as a type of proof of the performative efficacy of the ceremony by producing a legible 'felicitous' context for each readership. At the same time, a probable reader in Antwerp could well encounter both the French and the Flemish edition, witnessing the triumph's trans/heterolingual address as she sees the ceremony operating at the level of image and textual form. The same sign – 'triumph' – slips across languages and media, as if to remind the reader that translation is possible, and each translation probable, for translation is all the triumph ever was. Passing in each language, the triumph surpasses the limits of language, nation, or empire. It passes *plus ultra*.

The Triumph of Antwerp: The Susception of Philip and Susceptible Readers

In 1549, Prince Philip entered Antwerp. The rich city, couched between Flanders and Brabant, was a central node in the circulation of wealth, learning, and printed books throughout his father Charles' disparate Empires. Since Duchess Joanna's 'Joyeuse Entrée' in 1355, entries in the Low Countries had served as performative rituals that guaranteed succession, embodying the performative subjugation of the corporate body of citizens to a new corporeal body, while also providing space for renegotiation of the terms that constituted the polity. Moreover, since that first Joyeuse Entrée, 'entry' had always referred to both a ceremony and a document. As the ruler instantiates a virtual office vacated by her predecessor's passing, so does the document offer the reader a chance to surrogate for an audience that was once 'live'.

Charles, however, had neither died nor stepped down. Rather, Charles had issued the 'Pragmatic Sanction', declaring Philip the heir apparent to a unified Netherlands with Antwerp as its capital – a state that did not yet exist.[36] This made the Entry untimely – subjunctive, if not quite conditional. Philip would, probably, take up the new title, but Charles wanted to oversee

---

[36] The Pragmatic Sanction of 1549 declared that Philip would receive the 'Seventeen Provinces' of the Burgundian Netherlands as a single inheritance, with Antwerp as their *de facto* capital.

176 DANIEL J. RUPPEL

this *probable* triumph while he still had the power to *guarantee its perfor-mative felicity*. Therefore, Cornelius Grapheus, the designer of the Entry and its official documentarian, chose a peculiar word to describe the peculiar event. He called it a 'susception' – literally, a 'taking-up', or the first instance of what would subsequently be called a 're-ception'.[37]

As Grapheus' ornate document scripts its probable readers to actualize the triumph, it suggests Philip is not the only susceptible party. The earlier discussion explored how Antwerper printers processed Charles' multi-layered acts of surrogation in his triumphant entry into Rome by addressing 'national' audiences through 'domesticating' *mise en page*. The documents of Philip's entry extend this project to a novel audience. Though Grapheus composed in the transnational language of Latin, translations of *Spectaculorum in Susceptione Philippi Hispan ...* in the two 'national' lan-guages of Antwerp demonstrate both domesticating distinctions as well as translingual continuities, limning a role for a new cosmopolitan reader, waiting to be 'suscieved'.[38]

The title page of the Latin edition claims authority before an established international community. Designating Grapheus as 'City Secretary', offi-cial representative of the polity, it states that the triumph is 'described both truly and accurately to life' (*Et verè & ad vivum accuratè descriptus*). The page contains neither printer's name nor printer's mark, but asserts 'Caesar's privilege', indicating a level of official approval (and intended dis-tribution) that far exceeds Antwerp's limits.[39] The page employs three type-faces, each indexing the book's connections to a Roman past in a different way. The title appears in antique capitals, resembling antique inscriptions

---

[37] The rare nominal form of 'susceptible', 'susception' appears in medical and religious literature in Latin and French, describing the bodily assimilation (or uptake) of certain substances, and the 'taking up' of a religious '*ordre*'. This is the only instance I have found in a festival context, while '*réception*' becomes common later. As the religious usage especially suggests, the middle-voiced 'susception' confuses subject and object, as one takes up the practical rules of the order, but also, thereby, becomes part of it. As I will suggest below, this ambivalence characterizes the contempo-rary performance of translation into '*Franchois*'.

[38] The editions are as follows: Cornelius Grapheus, *Spectaculorum in Susceptione Philippi Hispan. Princ. A. 1549 Antverpia Aeditorum Mirificus Apparatus* (Antwerp: Gillis van Diest, for Pierre Coeck d'Allost, 1550); Cornelius Grapheus, *De seer wonderlijcke, schoone, triumphelijcke incompst, van den hooghmogenden prince Philips, prince van Spaignen, Caroli des vijfden, keyserssone. Inde stadt van Antwerpen, anno M.CCCC.XLIX.* (Antwerp: Gillis van Diest, for Pierre Coeck d'Allost, 1550); Cornelius Grapheus, *La Très admirable, très magnificque & triumphante entrée de très hault et très puissant Prince Philipes, prince d'Espaigne, [...] traduicte en franchois* (Antwerp: Gillis van Diest, for Pierre Coeck d'Allost, 1550).

[39] 'Privilèges' (in this sense) were a sort of early modern 'copyright' afforded to the publisher (usually the primary bookseller). They offered a monopoly within the jurisdiction of the issuing body, so an Imperial privilege conveyed greater benefit, but required stricter vetting.

Translating Triumph 177

(like those on the arches depicted in the woodcuts that follow). Slanted 'Italic' for Grapheus' name and serifed 'Roman' lettering for the short epigraph indicate, respectively, the Humanist credentials of the author and the Classical pretentions of the verse. These marks of authority could be read even by one who was incapable of reading Latin for 'sense'. They mark the book as intellectual and political property of the highest order, addressing a heterogenous, translingual readership.[40]

By contrast, the interplay of textual form and verbal meaning in the Flemish and French editions addresses these distinct linguistic communities. With the exception of iconic Latin inscriptions, the Flemish edition is printed in Gothic type. Domesticating the text, it translates the description into a form that increasingly read as 'Germanic'. Meanwhile, the French text forgoes the blackletter font used in the French translation of Ceffino's account in favour of the Humanist typefaces popularized by printers like Geoffroy Tory, linking it to the prestigious *avant-garde* of French design.[41]

Despite these domesticating traits, these two vernacular editions also stage a bilingual Antwerper identity. Explicating what the Latin edition claims through typographic form, each appends a paper cover with a new title that identifies the ceremony qua book as a '*Triumphe*' (spelled identically in Flemish and French), framing the words in a grotesque '*a l'anticque*' design.[42] Though it indexes Rome, this design differs from the *type* of 'Roman' citations visible in the Latin edition and from the 'Roman' architecture attributed to the city's 'nations' (ethnic or expatriate communities), illustrated in subsequent woodcuts. In a deft deployment of visual rhetoric, this *anticque* aesthetic reappears in the 'Figure of the Stage (*Eschaffaulx*) of the City on the Meerbruge'. By virtue of this repetition, the vernacular books appear as surrogates for that already metonymic stage. Antwerp stages the triumph; Antwerp is the stage; the book is (seen as) the stage of the city; the book stages the triumph of Antwerp. The Flemish edition distils the claim, placing only the words '*De Triumphe van Antwerpen*' (The Triumph of Antwerp) in the cover-page frame. The French edition, more verbose, announces the triumph was 'performed

---

[40] More subtly, the Latin text includes accent marks, visible on the final ès, which would be rare in Classical manuscripts, but represent a heightened erudition and attention to limiting linguistic ambiguity, similar (but less formalized) to the 'vowelling' of the written Torah or Qu'ran. Thus, the text casts itself as Romanesque through the stylized behaviour of its titular letters.

[41] Tory's 'Humanist' fonts notably appeared in his accounts of the coronation of Charles' sister, Eleanor of Austria, who married King Francis I, and became Queen of France. His work inspired a transition to 'Roman' typefaces throughout the francophone world.

[42] These forms recall the distinctive Franco-Italic décor of Francis I and Henri II at the palace of Fontainebleau.

(*faicte*) on the susception of Prince Philips [sic], prince of Spain'. While the former effaces Philip, claiming the triumph for the city alone, the latter emphasizes that Philip 'of Spain' is not or not yet *Anversois* (Antwerper). Thus, these vernacular covers appeal to local knowledge and local sentiments about civic pride and 'foreign' rule, (literally) papering over the titular claims of the international Latin edition.

Attending to typeface, titles, and paratexts in Grapheus' books, gives depth to seemingly superficial continuities between the experience of 'live' spectatorship and the live experiences of reading these performance documents. Records of historical readers for such documents are sparse, but those that do exist suggest the books might be owned by members of the bourgeoisie of Antwerp, local nobility and clergy, and diplomats in the Imperial retinue, while the consistency within the genre makes it clear that festival designers regularly consulted – and tried to surpass – each other's work. The propensity for Grapheus and his peers to explicate the cleverness of their historical or allegorical symbolism at length suggests that these authors appealed to readers desiring to participate in an erudition greater than their own, but also that they were uncertain that the live experience would be sufficient for spectators to grasp the full complexity of the festival and its performative claims. In order for the festival to do its work of appropriating the symbolic capital of ancient Rome on behalf of the ruler (and the city), the festival required an audience appropriate to the task of evaluating and affirming the arguments it made across languages, materials, and visual forms. Thus, the books effectively stage an experience of the festival that is not a diminished or partial form of the real, 'original' event, but rather an elaboration thereof, in which both event, and the readership, may be perfected through the performance of reading the book invites. The French edition makes such an appeal explicit in an epigraphic poem, which follows the title page described earlier. Through word and form, it tempts readers with a chance 'take up' the symbolic capital of Humanism by purchasing (and presumably reading) the book.

> Friendly reader, if you take delight
> in hearing or seeing something most marvelous
> [in] this triumph, as if you were even there,
> then by you this book must be bought right away
> For in this you'll see in the antique manner
> 　　Triumphant arches, magnificent theatres,
> Gates, columns, stages, buildings
> 　　Wherein are hidden many most excellent Arts.

What's more you'll see (as for literature)
Grave devices, very subtle aphorisms
Arduous sayings, obscure inscriptions
   Which (as for sense) show themselves most difficult
That nevertheless are useful (*utile*) to all humans
   To buy it, do not think yourself useless (*inutile*)
For the saying of the proverb is well known (*courant*)
   No knowledge is hateful, except what one knows not.

The poetic epigraph to *Le triumphe d'Anvers* (Figure 7.4) casts the book in the mould of Maximilian's *Ehrenpforte* – a virtuosic balancing of vernacular forms and antiquarian citations – and casts the reader in the role of one who, with amiable generosity, will do the work to be worthy of it. The vernacular now is not German, but Franchois, a dialect of langue d'oïl spoken in Flanders and Brabant – yet the 'vernacular' is also apparent in the form of the document itself. Unlike the oblique rhetorical deixis in Ceffino's account of Charles' triumphant entry into Rome, this epigraph addresses the present reader directly, as a friend. Such prefatory addresses in verse or in prose became increasingly common in French books throughout the latter half of the century, but like the 'humanist' typeface, could still be seen as a novel addition that elevates the book. The poem also tempts the reader with a chance to elevate herself, at least within the particular framework of prestige the book seeks to embody.

The first stanza addresses the reader at a sensory level, promising the reader who takes sensuous delight (volupté) in seeing and hearing a marvellous experience that would make them feel as if they were present at the event. Though it poses a condition ('if you take delight'), it resolves in

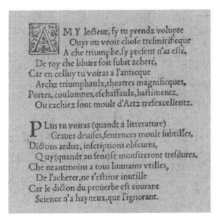

Figure 7.4   Epigraph to *Le triumphe d'Anvers* (1550) (sig. A2v).

180   DANIEL J. RUPPEL

the subjunctive (soit). 'By you this book shall be bought', has a different impact from the imperative phrase modern marketing might use in its place (you must buy this book!). The book shall be bought by those who delight in a bevy of spectacles – triumphant arches, magnificent theatres, portals, columns, stages, buildings – that cannot help but bring sensory satisfaction, particularly since they are depicted 'a l'anticque', a phrase which, as art historian Rebecca Zorach has shown, meant both being in the style of antiquity, and also being antic, almost overflowing with perceptible energy.[43] This double reading echoes in the verbal excess within the list itself. Arches and portes, theatres and eschaffaulx are used interchangeably in earlier entry documents – essentially synonyms, except in their register. An arch may be a decorated portal, but it is one with cachet. The concluding line brings this home for the reader – within these spectacles, 'most excellent Arts are hidden (cachiez)'. The capitalization of Arts emphasizes the sense of the ostentatiously hidden.

The second stanza moves the reader from the visual to the verbal (though as this chapter has shown, the two are hardly separable). Another list confronts the reader – mottos, aphorisms, sayings, inscriptions – a catalogue of 'literary' genres shorter than a line of verse, but which like the fragments of texts and ancient inscriptions that they imitate, were believed to yield an abundance of arcane wisdom to those who knew how to unravel their mysteries. The poem offers friendly encouragement to the reader, albeit again with the condition of purchase: 'To buy [this book], do not think yourself unworthy (inutile)', for even if this literature is very difficult (tresdures), its secrets will be 'profitable (utile) to all humans'. The pairing of 'utile/inutile' whose connotations exceed the English 'useful/ useless', is still odd in French. However, such a 'foreignizing' interruption of fluency is exactly what is at play, and the poem suggests that the reader will reap a utility greater than voluptuous physical delight. In case the reader hailed by this poem still doubts herself up to the task, the final couplet ends with an example, a proverb that is both familiar and apt (courant) for the reader to parse. The contemporary reader of the poem, and potential buyer of the book, is told that no knowledge is hateful, but that of which one is ignorant. To sound out the 'saying' (diction) of this 'proverb' (proverbe) – another deliberately imperfect doubling – the reader must question whether she is ignorant and hateful of the elevated knowledge this book has on offer, and if not, the logic of the poem insists

---

[43] Rebecca Zorach, *Blood, Milk, Ink, Gold: Abundance and Excess in the French Renaissance* (Chicago: University of Chicago Press, 2005), 1–2.

that she will take up (or susceive) to the position of a reader both worthy of the book and friendly towards its rhetorical overtures.

Passing as ruler through the arches and theatres of a polity that existed only by virtue of a performative declaration, the reader and/as Philip perform a new relationship between Antwerp and its sovereign in a familiar, familiarizing context. The reader moves as if she were Philip through the Humanizing scenes of the document, a series of spectacular archways, (ap)proving the felicity – or at least, the *utility* – of the new order. It is a performance of translation. Unlike his father, who was always most comfortable around Flemings and francophones, Philip was truly 'of Spain'. This was new, strange, and ultimately unhappy. The advent of this Spanish monarch-to-be onto the Antwerpian scene initiated a long and often violent transition of Antwerp from a global centre of maritime trade and cosmopolitan knowledge production to a bilingual backwater dammed off by increasingly nationalized boundary disputes.[44] Myriad individual choices and accidents led to this outcome, but if for a moment one takes up the role of a late sixteenth-century Humanist, indulging in a little belated prognostication, she might read some ominous portents in the way that Philip's Entry unfolded – at least, the first time. So great were the gaps between the happy future projected by the festival and the actual, lived events of the day, that Grapheus inserts a disclaimer after the title page: '*Quaedam hîc ante omnia necessariò obseruanda*' (that which here, before everything, must be observed).[45]

The first 'observation' tells the reader that, most sadly (*tristissima*), a heavy rain pelted Antwerp at the moment the Entry was to begin. Under this 'dense onslaught', most of the 'apparatuses' – ephemeral architecture, decorations, set-pieces, costumes, and live performances – 'either were seen in minimal perfection, or had no opportunity to be shown'.[46] Indeed, like Maximilian's 'paper triumph', Philip's *entry* celebrates an act of subjunctive surrogation still to come (*a-venir*), which never transpired as it is presented

---

[44] Antwerp would revolt against Spanish rule twice in the next decades (1576, 1585), and each revolt was brutally suppressed. The latter began with a sumptuous 'Ducal Entry' for the French prince François d'Anjou, and ended, along with Antwerp's economic and cultural dominance, when d'Anjou fled before the arrival of German and Italian troops under Alexander Farnese. Farnese sacked the city and blockaded the Scheldt river, suspending Antwerp's rich international trade, and initiating Amsterdam's ascent. Stijn Bussels relates that pious persons wondered whether their ostentation (including, he suggests, Philip's Triumph) was a trigger for their downfall. Stijn Bussels, *Spectacle, Rhetoric and Power: The Triumphal Entry of Prince Philip of Spain Into Antwerp* (Amsterdam: Rodopi, 2012), 231–232.

[45] Grapheus, *Spectaculorum in Susceptione Philippi Hispan.* sig A2v.

[46] Grapheus, *Spectaculorum in Susceptione Philippi Hispan*, sig. A2v.

182   DANIEL J. RUPPEL

in this elaborate document. But perhaps, by the happenstance of an earnest, generous reading, it *does*. The multilingual editions of Grapheus' text aid such probable reading and produce their own probity by scaffolding the reader's experience with domesticating *mise en page*, rendering the refined defamiliarization of Humanist *utility* slightly more palatable to the vulgar public(s). Yet as their readers affect a Humanist gaze, these books invite them to participate, affectively, in Antwerp's probable assumption of a new, triumphant role.

Taking Up the Globe: The Susception of Antwerp on the World Stage

The formal citations describe above theatricalize a (now-counterfactual) future for a city on the verge of 'going global'. In the multi-nodal Empire that reiterated Rome as German, Italian, Spanish, Netherlander, and not *not Franchois*, the triumph was not the culmination of a unidirectional translation of spoils, but a modular performative claim to centrality. In the Triumph of Antwerp, a city of merchants and lenders, even hypothetical claims to future spoils could serve as virtual leverage in an Empire whose orientation and fortunes were in flux. Thus, the sequential stages the reader encounters in Grapheus' books stage the translation of the 'globe' itself, balancing the Hapsburg desires for transoceanic, global hegemony with Antwerp's aspirations to be the nexus of the Empire's mercantile, financial, and intellectual exchange.

Four '*globes*' stand out among the architectural vignettes. Two feature iconic portrayals of continents (the world as depicted in mid-sixteenth-century maritime maps), and two seemingly blank ones, described as orbs of pure gold.[47] Framed by triumphal arches, these globes translate the new world into the Empire of Christ, effecting this translation through a metamorphic *jeu d'images*. The globes-as-maps manifest newly 'discovered' knowledge.[48] The first, on the centre of the Genovese Arch (Figure 7.5), depicts the 'circum-Atlantic World' as a Philip-esque Hercules lifts the

---

[47] In the French edition, they are found on the Genovese Arch (sig. F1r), *Arch publique … au pont de la vigne* (sig. I1r), the *Arch de l'haute rue* (sig. L4r), and the German Arch (*des Allemans*, sig. N1r). The arches of the 'nations' were built by expatriate communities (though the idea of *patria* – and authorship – is complicated in these renderings).

[48] Globes and painted maps were both produced in great numbers in the sixteenth century, and beginning with illustrated translations of Ptolemy, print maps followed suit. The loose woodcuts produced in Grapheus' edition resemble the outlines in Gemma Frisius' correction of Peter Appian's *Cosmographie* (Antwerp, 1592), gesturing towards the interweaving of navigation, cartography, and festival documentation.

Figure 7.5   Arch on the Pont de la Vigne from Le triumphe d'Anvers (sig. I1r).

'burden' of Atlas (sig. F2r).[49] The second depicts the Ptolemaic continents in updated forms, highlighting the new circum-African trade route. This enormous world 'all around lively (*vivement*) and artificially portrayed' is held between effigies ('*images*') of Charles and Philip 'so lively (*au vif*) that it seemed [one was] seeing the Emperor and his Son themselves' (sig. L4v).

Meanwhile, the golden globes 'figuring the world' resemble the *globus crucius* that formed part of the Imperial regalia, in which a cross surmounting a sphere represents Christ's dominion over the world.[50] The first appears in the triumphal procession between the 'old world' and the 'new', indexing the

---

[49] See Roach, *Cities of the Dead*. The details of the globe are difficult to see in this figure. What would be far more evident to the viewer would be the 'Tupi' headdresses that are worn by the two naked men, whom the description designates as Genovese Rivers. Tupi accessories were often read as indicative of an undifferentiated new world people. See William Sturtevant, 'The Sources for European Imagery of Native Americans', in *New World of Wonders: European Images of the Americas, 1492–1700*, edited by Rachel Doggett, Monique Hulvey, and Julie Ainsworth (Washington, DC: Seattle: Folger Shakespeare Library; Distributed by University of Washington Press, 1992), 25–33; Leitch, 'Chapter 2', in *Mapping Ethnography in Early Modern Germany*. The headdresses worn by the 'Rivers' undoubtedly have European heritage as well, but they obviously participate in an intentional doubling, which we may suspect from the '*satyres*' and other '*nudz*' people featured throughout this festival/book, in the tradition of '*hommes sauvages*'.

[50] On the Pont de la vigne, it is *a 'globe ou boule figurant le monde'*, and later, '*clobe (sic) ou monde*', (sig. I1v). The German Arch reads similarly.

bullion extracted from the Western Hemisphere by Spanish *Conquistadors* – triumphant spoils in the most traditional sense. However, being almost identical in size and visual prominence to the 'old world' supported by Charles and Philip, it seems as if this golden manifestation of sanctified Empire were the actual flip-side of the empirical Empire, which was translated from the ancients by the iterative citation of the triumph and its synecdochal arch. The reappearance of a smaller globe on the penultimate 'German Arch' (*Arch des Allemans*), with the Imperial Eagle in lieu of the *cruciger*, cements the perception of this virtual palimpsest, and the pregnant layers of over-sight to which it lays performative claim. The 'translation of Empire' and the ongoing translation of stolen wealth are conflated into a single gesture of surrogation, the virtuosic artifice of which brings it home to the live spectators. Yet the translation/transformation is completed by the viewer, who must with her mind's eye fill in the virtual colours that bring these objects truly to (seeming) life, even as the material lack of colour facilitates the rhetorical conflations described.

The final Arch brings the reader's experience home, while introducing transcendence besides. The figure displays a celestial 'round', depicting the world as cosmos. Such depictions are commonly found in both cosmographies (similar to modern atlases) and above the doors of churches. Located by the doors of the Monastery of St. Michael the arch fuses the 'medieval' and the '*renaissant*'. It allows the reader to 'see' Philip's performance as most felicitous Prince (*Prince tresheureux*) in a context at once otherworldly and quotidian, besides. To the probable Antwerper reader it suggests the centre of the cosmos and its king-to-come are right before your eyes, and look – you're right next door.

As the globe transforms throughout the reader's procession through the pages, these concatenating figures embody a hope that Antwerp will continue to be a primary beneficiary of the circulation of Imperial wealth, that its nations will continue to translate the bullion of the world into fine wares, financial instruments, scientific publications, and maps. The globes represent only one of the ways the Antwerp triumph reaches out beyond Europe, and asks its readers to fill in. Grapheus' festive theatricalization of the 'global' world would seem of peripheral importance, but that an imitation of this allegorical archway appears as the frontispiece to a work that would shape how the world was seen for centuries to come.[51]

---

[51] One could argue whether Ortelius and his publisher were simply responding to general trends in the high-end book market, where frontispieces increasingly featured 'theatres' and 'triumphal arches' (the distinction being minimal in this sense). The contention is self-defeating, however, since this trend clearly developed from a desire to index the virtue and opulence associated with triumphal culture, and Grapheus' work was the most important instantiation of this *topos* in what was then the most important centre of printing in Philip's domains, if not the whole world.

Translating Triumph 185

In the *Theatrum Orbis Terrarum* (Theatre of the Whole World), first printed in Antwerp in 1570, Abraham Ortelius displays cartographic knowledge gleaned from dozens of contacts across Europe, making it widely considered the first atlas.[52] Dedicated to Philip and his father, the work cites the form of the festival book epitomized by Grapheus' edition.[53] The capitalized text of the dedication mirrors the form of Roman inscriptions in earlier festival books, and the frontispiece features an engraving of a 'theatre' similar to the Arch in the Via Vaccaria (*Rue de la Vache*; sig. K1r). In Grapheus' depiction, Prince Philip (in effigy) stands framed by two historical Princes, crowned with omens that preceded their kingship. Below them are three women, described as 'of color brown', 'black', and 'white', representing Asia, Africa, and Europe. Four female figures frame the title text of Ortelius' *Theatrum*. Each wears the garments (or lack thereof) representative of the 'four parts of the world': Africa, Asia, America (in effect, Brazil), and Europe. Sitting atop the lintel, Europe wears a closed Imperial crown. To her right and left are mounted globes showing the celestial and terrestrial cosmos (the latter now spun to show the Atlantic); at the centre, Imperial Europe rests her hand on a golden *orbis cruciger*, the largest globe of all.

Grapheus' book scripts a new performance of an 'old' world, which can incorporate a Spanish King (or surrogate reader) entering Antwerp, passing through his streets, and viewing, in its triumphal theatres, a microcosm of the whole earth. In Ortelius' *Theatrum*, the transformation from globe to theatre qua book is made complete. The bourgeoisie of Flanders and beyond could now enter into the *Theatre* itself, staging their own theoretical journeys, or their next commercial (and inherently, colonial) expedition. Grapheus' book asks its readers to buy (into) its projection of a festival that never quite happened, for despite the difficulty of the task, they may uncover in its scholarly citations worlds of ancient knowledge. The book stages the cosmopolitan city which turn by turn, stages the world in microcosm. Ortelius' projections invite the reader to expend their energy (and their *livres)* to implicate themselves in a world born anew. Still, the performance of Triumph remained an uncertain protection for the Antwerpers. In 1576, Philip's troops sacked the city and blockaded its ports. The centre could also become provincial. As the triumph was translated, so were the sites of extraction.

---

[52] Thanks to Leo Carrio Cataldi for introducing me to the complexities of Ortelius' projects.

[53] The text was approved for publication by the Imperial representatives in the Netherlands (the privilege is printed in *Nederlands*), but is dedicated to Prince Philip and his father, described as 'August Emperor, King of Spain and India, etc. for all time and in all the world the greatest (*amplissimi*) imperial monarch'.

CHAPTER 8

From Novella to Theatre and Opera
Translating 'Otherness' in Cavalleria rusticana

Enza De Francisci

Introduction

This chapter focuses on early translations of *Cavalleria rusticana*, a novella written in 1880 in Sicilianized Italian by Giovanni Verga, which the author adapted into an Italian play only four years later for the interpretation of the *grande attrice*, Eleonora Duse.[1] The success of Duse's performances caught notable critical attention, and, arguably, the attention of Pietro Mascagni, who, in 1890 was inspired to turn the play into an opera, which he also composed in Italian, excluding the prelude 'La Siciliana'. Both theatrical and operatic versions were subsequently included in the international repertoires of a variety of nineteenth-century and early twentieth-century stars, such as the French soprano Emma Calvé and the dialect actors Giovanni Grasso and Mimì Aguglia – the only actors to interpret the drama in Sicilian. The dialect performers enjoyed a reputation for naturalistic immediacy and impulsiveness readily associated with their Sicilian identity. Early critical reviews ventured a romanticized, sentimental portrait of the Italian South (or *Mezzogiorno*), while simultaneously co-opting a condescending vocabulary of rustic primitivism and animalism: cultural stereotypes about Sicily's African and Arab heritage that the performers both exploited and resisted.

Within the cultural context of Risorgimento Italy, which coincided with this emerging stereotype of Sicily as the 'Africa of Italy', the present chapter explores what it meant for each translator (the writer-translator, composer-translator and actor-translator) to *perform translation* in response to Sandra Bermann's question: 'What does it mean to perform translation?'[2] In reconstructing the reception of early performances of *Cavalleria rusticana* through close analysis of newspaper reviews that record the first

---

[1] Unless specified, all translations are author's own.
[2] Sandra Bermann and Catherine Porter, eds., *A Companion to Translation Studies* (Chichester, UK: John Wiley and Sons, 2014).

From Novella to Theatre and Opera 187

critical responses to the play and subsequent opera, I argue that performing translation meant, for the celebrity star actors, generating and circulating an exoticized 'brand' of Sicilian-ness in and outside the Italian peninsula shortly after political unification in 1861. In the ethnographic context of late nineteenth-century Italy, and given Sicily's perceived 'otherness' to mainland Italy, I argue that for the actors, especially the Sicilian actors, this meant not only synthesizing the multilateral cultural threads (Italian, African) of the 'rustic' Sicilian but also partnering this racial alterity with a new dramatic language of realism and immediacy. In so doing, this chapter intends to elucidate a new performative (and translational) concept (and practice) of nation-building, shed light on issues related to translating Italian/Sicilian 'otherness' on stage, and illuminate the cultural politics of performing in the standard language or dialect.

Cavalleria rusticana: From Novella to Play

Based on what Verga allegedly witnessed from outside his window in his hometown of Vizzini, *Cavalleria rusticana* brings to life the triangular relationship involving husband (Compare Alfio), wife (Lola) and lover (Turiddu). Turiddu returns from military service to find his betrothed Lola married to the wealthy cart driver, Compare Alfio. He begins to court Santa (called Santuzza in the play and subsequent opera) and, much to his plan, this makes Lola jealous. The two former lovers rekindle their relationship, leaving Santa/Santuzza full of envy. She subsequently enlightens the betrayed Alfio to his wife's adultery and he kills Turiddu in a duel.

What is striking about Verga's original novella is its dialogic technique. In the prelude to his short story 'L'amante di Gramigna' (Gramigna's Lover) (1880), where he exposes the principles of *verismo*, the author sheds light on his intention to create his narratives as though they were 'human document[s]', composed of 'simple and picturesque terms of popular narrative', so that the reader is confronted by the 'plain and simple facts rather than having to go searching for them between the lines with the lens of the writer'.[3] Verga maintained that 'the triumph of the novel' lies in 'the sincerity of its reality'.[4] To achieve this, the author felt the need to see the action through his characters' eyes, removing the 'hand of the artist' from his works.[5]

---

[3] Giovanni Verga, *Cavalleria rusticana and Other Stories*, translated by G. H. McWilliam (England: Penguin, 1999), 93.
[4] Verga, *Cavalleria rusticana*, 94.
[5] Verga, *Cavalleria rusticana*, 94.

188   ENZA DE FRANCISCI

To mimic his characters' spoken language, Verga adopted the use of free indirect speech, a blend of direct and indirect speech. According to the linguist Giulio Herczeg, Verga's narrative contained more direct speech than indirect speech, recounted by the popular narrator who represents the choral voice of the villagers.[6] Moreover, Verga wrote in a sort of Sicilianized Italian – a form of Italian with a heavy Sicilian dialectal imprint superimposed, like a sort of 'popular' or 'Regional' Italian.[7] This idiosyncratic register allowed Verga to both retain the local colour in his narrative and enable his Italian readers to taste the Sicilian flavour of his stories. In so doing, the newly united Italian readership would be able to gain an understanding of Sicilian without having to read dialect.

Significantly, Verga's dialogic style of writing has been linked with the theatrical genre. In a letter to the author Nicola Scarano of 12 March 1915, Verga postulated that *veristi* writers aimed to 'paint the picture with suitable colours, in other words, from top to bottom, in the actors' spoken language and in their description of the scenes as they see them, in order to live in them and with them'.[8] By withdrawing the author's hand from his fiction and allowing what he called the 'actors' to execute their 'scenes' independently, Verga thus produced a kind of 'theatrical effect', to use Sergio Blazina's words.[9]

However, though Verga's technique might have led him to write for the theatre, he had a problematic relationship with theatre audiences, overall, because of his treatment of language. Verga was well aware that his Sicilianized-Italian could not be so easily adopted on the nineteenth-century stage. The average spectator would not have expected to decode the register on a night out at the theatre, and if the author had targeted a purely Sicilian audience by writing in dialect, he would have considerably reduced his spectatorship.[10] As a result, Verga produced his play in Italian, thus depriving the characters of speaking in their mother-tongue dialect.

So why did Verga choose to adapt *Cavalleria rusticana*? It would seem that the main reason was Eleonora Duse. In a letter to his contemporary Giuseppe Giacosa of 8 October 1883, he explicitly asked whether the actress

---

[6] See Giulio Herczeg, *Lo stile indiretto libero in italiano* (Florence: Sansoni, 1963), 28.

[7] For a definition of Regional Italian, see Anna Laura Lepschy and Giulio Lepschy, *The Italian Language Today*, 2nd ed. (London: Routledge, 1991), 13–14.

[8] Giovanni Verga, *Lettere sparse*, edited by Giovanna Finocchiaro (Rome: Bulzoni, 1980), 404.

[9] Sergio Blazina, *La mano invisibile: Poetica e procedimenti narrativi del romanzo verghiano* (Turin: Tirrenia, 1989), 67.

[10] For more on Verga's reservations about the theatre, see in particular his 1894 interview now in Ugo Ojetti, *Alla scoperta dei letterati*, postface by Nicola Merola (Milan: Fratelli Dumolard editori, 1895), 70–71.

From Novella to Theatre and Opera

would be willing to perform a drama of his in one act or two.[11] Giacosa certainly played the intermediary and encouraged Verga to include a part for Duse, promising that, with an actress like Duse, 'wonders' could be made.[12] In spite of her initial reservations, Duse eventually accepted the lead part of Santuzza. The biographer Alfred Alexander has argued that, following her acceptance of the role, Verga felt the need to develop Santuzza's character, which was only thinly sketched in the narrative, in order to give the star actress 'the opportunity to show her art'.[13]

Such collaborations were especially desirable because of the crucial role played by actors in the theatre system in late nineteenth-century Italy. The influence of the actor was exceptionally strong during this period, arguably because of Italy's peculiar linguistic situation. Before political unification in 1861, Italy had been dismissed by Prince Metternich at the 1815 Congress of Vienna as no more than a 'geographical expression',[14] an agglomeration of unstable regions and states: the Austrian-controlled North, the Papal States of Central Italy, and the Kingdom of the Two Sicilies in the South. Political fragmentation was also mirrored linguistically. Despite efforts by the Cinquecento humanist Pietro Bembo to establish the Florentine of the *tre corone* (three crowns) (Dante, Boccaccio and Petrarch) as the Italian literary standard, after 1861 the majority of Italians spoke in dialect. Tullio De Mauro has estimated that, during this period, only 2.5 per cent of the population was able to speak Italian,[15] and little changes if we consider the correction of Arrigo Castellani who has suggested that the percentage was approximately 10 per cent.[16]

As a result of the socio-linguistic phenomenon, New Italy came to acquire a state of diglossia, which has been defined by Charles Albert Ferguson as '[o]ne particular kind of standardization where two varieties of a language exist side by side throughout the community, with each having a definite role to play'.[17] This meant that the 'high' variety of Italian (literary Italian used predominantly in public spheres) coincided with the 'low' variety of Italian (the regional dialect), a spoken language used

---

[11] Verga, *Lettere sparse*, 146–147.

[12] Quoted in Federico De Roberto, *Casa Verga e altri sagi verghiani*, edited by Carmelo Musumarra (Florence: Le Monnier, 1964), 196.

[13] Alfred Alexander, *Giovanni Verga: A Great Writer and his World* (London: Grant and Cutler, 1972), 110.

[14] Giuseppe Fumagalli, *Chi l'ha detto?* (Milan: Ulrico Hoepli, 1989), 361–362.

[15] Tullio De Mauro, *Storia linguistica dell'Italia unita* (Rome: Laterza, 1995), 41.

[16] See Arrigo Castellani, 'Quanti erano gl'italofoni nel 1861?', *Studi linguistici italiani* 8 (1982): 3–26.

[17] Charles Albert Ferguson, *Socio-linguistic Perspectives: Papers on Language in Society 1959–1994*, edited by Thom Huebner (Oxford: Oxford University Press 1996), 25.

190   ENZA DE FRANCISCI

instinctively in informal occasions.[18] It has been jocularly but appropriately stated by Max Weinreich that 'a language is a dialect which has an army and a navy'.[19] The distinction between a language and a dialect is thus based on social and political factors rather than linguistic ones. The Italian language and regional dialects are, linguistically speaking, separate Romance languages, or 'sister' languages, each deriving from spoken Latin with a specific role to fill.

This political and linguistic disunity directly influenced the development of the Italian theatrical tradition. For a medium so reliant on speech, the lack of a common spoken language would seem to inhibit the growth of an early national theatre, a growth hindered further following the collapse of public subsidies for the performing arts in unified Italy.[20] As a result, many theatre companies of the nineteenth century favoured touring in Europe and in North and South America.[21] In fact, only two forms of Italian drama met with any notable success when, subsequently, they were taken out into a global market. These were the *Commedia dell'arte* and the opera, both of which subordinate the importance of the spoken word to, respectively, body language and music.[22] Even though there was some early attempt to fill in this gap, such as by Verga and his contemporaries, including Marco Praga and Giuseppe Giacosa, ultimately, nineteenth-century Italy was not producing its own major playwrights in this period, equivalent to Alexandre Dumas, for example.[23]

The lack of a common tongue consequently lent added importance to gesture over speech on stage, and helped cultivate the so-called Theatre of the Actor in which audiences were drawn not by the play per se but by the star actors, such as Adelaide Ristori, Ernesto Rossi, and Tommaso Salvini, whose performances became the central ingredient of any production.[24] Hence, because of the lack of a common spoken language, more importance was placed on the *actions* of the performers to convey the meaning

---

[18] See Lepschy and Lepschy, *The Italian Language Today*.

[19] Quoted in Giulio Lepschy, *Mother Tongues and Other Reflections on the Italian Language* (Toronto: University of Toronto Press, 2002), 36.

[20] See Axel Körner, *Politics of Culture in Liberal Italy: From Unification to Fascism* (New York: Routledge, 2009).

[21] See Marvin Carlson, *The Italian Shakespearians. Performances by Ristori, Salvini, and Rossi in England and America* (Washington: The Folger Shakespeare Library, 1985).

[22] See Pietro Trifone, *Malalingua. L'italiano scorretto da Dante a oggi* (Bologna: Il Mulino, 2007), 51–65.

[23] See Roberto Alonge, *Teatro e spettacolo nel secondo Ottocento* (Rome: Laterza, 1988).

[24] See Cesare Molinari, 'Teorie della recitazione: gli attori sull'attore. Da Rossi a Zacconi', in *Teatro dell'Italia unita. Atti dei convegni Firenze 10–11 dicembre 1977, 4–6 novembre 1978*, edited by Siro Ferrone (Milan: il Saggiatore, 1980), 77.

From Novella to Theatre and Opera 191

of the play, as opposed to the actual *words* of their script, a technique for which Duse became renowned.

Dramatic and Operatic Performances of Santuzza: Duse and Calvé

Following the première, *Cavalleria rusticana* gained phenomenal success. In just one act, with no spectacular scene changes and uncomplicated dialogue, Verga managed to convey Sicily's peculiar traditions to the recently united Italian public. As the contemporary critic Cesare Levi put it, the play was a breath of fresh air that blew through the Italian stage, sweeping away the last residues of tragic Romanticism and the conventionalism of bourgeois theatre and, as a result, Verga offered New Italy 'its first Realist play'.[25]

The *Corriere della Sera* attributed a large part of the play's success to Duse, who allegedly made the spectators shiver and weep.[26] Owing to her triumph, Verga confided to the actress that *Cavalleria rusticana* belonged 'more to you than to me'.[27] Indeed many, like the biographer Cesare Molinari, have argued that it was Duse herself who *created* the role of Santuzza.[28] The actress was said to have moved her body just as the character would have done herself. Arthur Symons in his review threw light on her 'unconscious hand', which appeared to instinctively fold over Turiddu's sleeve.[29] Another critic, the German Herman Bang, also recollected how the actress seemed to spontaneously twist her handkerchief while leaning against a wall.[30] Duse herself admitted that, at the end of her performances, the most tired parts of her body were her hands.[31] In his article 'Eleonora Duse: Actress Supreme', first published in *The Century Magazine* shortly after the actress's death in 1924, Luigi Pirandello referred to her hands as 'divine hands, that seemed to talk'.[32] Mirella Schino has associated Duse's 'un-necessary gestures' on stage with what Stanislavsky would later call objectivization.[33]

---

[25] Cesare Levi, *Autori drammatici italiani: Giovanni Verga, Roberto Bracco, Marco Praga, Sebatino Lopez* (Bologna: Zanichelli, 1921), 4–5.

[26] See De Roberto, *Casa Verga*, 209–210.

[27] Quoted in Clemente Fusero, *Eleonora Duse* (Milan: dall'Oglio editore, 1971), 102.

[28] See Cesare Molinari, *L'attrice divina: Eleonora Duse nel teatro italiano fra i due secoli* (Rome: Bulzoni, 1985), 72.

[29] Arthur Symons, *Eleonora Duse* (London: Elkin Mathews, 1926), 131.

[30] Herman Bang, 'Menschen und Masken', in *Eleonora Duse: Bildnisse und Worte*, edited by Bianca Segantini and Francesco von Mendelssohn (Berlin: Kaemmerer, 1926), 66.

[31] See Giulio Piccini (Jarro), 'I nervi della Duse', in *Eleonora Duse*, edited by Leonardo Vergani with the collaboration of Luigi Pizzinelli (Milan: Aldo Martello, 1958), 98.

[32] Luigi Pirandello, 'Eleonora Duse: Actress Supreme', *The Century Magazine*, June, 1924, 247.

[33] Mirella Schino, *Il teatro di Eleonora Duse* (Bologna: Il Mulino, 1992), 55–100.

192   ENZA DE FRANCISCI

Several others noticed how Duse appeared so fused within her roles that her physiological features allegedly changed during her performances. Her facial expressions were said to powerfully convey Santuzza's profound remorse as she betrayed Turiddu. Her fellow actor Luigi Rasi remembered her contorted face, her eye flickering and her cheeks which changed colour from red to pallor, enabling her to give an authentic portrayal of characters of what he called 'a hysterical temperament'.[34] As a result, scholars such as Susan Bassnett have concluded that the actress's seemingly natural responses on stage represented how she felt 'totally at one with her character'.[35]

A *verista* writer, however, who was unconvinced by Duse's interpretation was Luigi Capuana. Recalling a production he had seen in his native Sicily, he argued that the non-professional actress performing the role of Santuzza in her mother-tongue dialect appeared more genuine and authentic than the star actress: '"Santuzza-Duse", therefore, seemed to my Sicilian eyes to be a sort of falsification of Giovanni Verga's passionate creature, in her gestures, in the expression of her voice, in her costume'.[36] Verga, nonetheless, was evidently pleased with Duse's interpretation, praising her performances in a letter to a friend Gegè Primoli of 24 January 1884.[37] Indeed, it could be argued that it was only a matter of time before one of the most naturalistic writers in nineteenth-century Italy met one of the most naturalistic actresses to emerge from the Italian stage. The pair aimed to convey a sort of *mimesis* through their art, seeing the action through the characters' eyes and expressing their suffering in the characters' own words, both engaged in what Donatella Orecchia has called a 'parallel search' for portraying reality in their art.[38]

Much to Verga's disappointment, though Duse kept the role of Santuzza in her early national and international repertoire, her interest in his theatre soon came to an end. According to William Weaver, 'Duse's tastes did not coincide with the harsh realism of this literary movement.'[39] Likewise, Giovanni Pontiero explained that following the triumph of *Cavalleria*

---

[34] Luigi Rasi, *La Duse: Con 55 illustrazioni* (Florence: R. Bemporad & Figlio, 1901), 38.

[35] Susan Bassnett, 'Eleonora Duse', in *Bernhardt, Terry, Duse: The Actress in her Time*, edited by John Stokes, Michael R. Booth and Susan Bassnett (Cambridge: Cambridge University Press, 1988), 142–143.

[36] Luigi Capuana, *Teatro dialettale siciliano*, 3 vols. (Palermo: Alberto Reber, 1911–1912), I, x–xi.

[37] Verga, *Lettere sparse*, 156.

[38] Donatella Orecchia, *La Prima Duse: Nascita di un'attrice moderna (1879–1886)* (Rome: Artemide, 2007), 127.

[39] William Weaver, *Duse: A Biography with 53 Illustrations* (London: Thames and Hudson, 1984), 43.

rusticana, 'Duse soon lost interest in plays with a regional flavor.'[40] Indeed, Duse was constantly looking out for new roles and by the late 1880s she was beginning to collaborate with Arrigo Boito on his experimental adaptation of *Antony and Cleopatra*, after which she began working for Gabriele D'Annunzio, both engaged in developing a new type of non-realistic, Symbolist, Italian theatre.[41]

Just as Duse was catching considerable critical attention for her interpretation of Santuzza, so did the French soprano Emma Calvé, whose operatic version of the same character became one of her greatest. Interestingly, Duse's 1893 London tour coincided with Calvé's own London tour and, from a close reading of critical reviews and early accounts, it seems that most critics, at least at the outset, tended to prefer the operatic version. Perhaps what may have hindered early international performances of the play, especially in the on the London stage, was the use of Italian. In the nineteenth century, Italian was not generally understood, as Henry Knepler has indicated:

> French was the language of culture generally and Italian the language of opera, both of them more euphonious to foreign ears than German or English, both in vogue as cultural assets with the middle class, even if one only pretended to know them.[42]

So while Calvé, in Mascagni's opera, could rely on the universality of music, Duse, in Verga's drama, had to rely on the scripted (foreign) word. Indeed, according to *The Standard* on 31 May 1893, had it not been for Mascagni, 'Verga's tragic sketch would scarcely have been heard outside of Italy.' The critic goes on to state that 'Signorina Duse made no particular impression last night in the opening piece', and felt that the role of Santuzza was not substantial enough for the star actress, in spite of the fact that the original role was actually written for *her* interpretation.[43] The impression that emerges

---

[40] Giovanni Pontiero, *Eleonora Duse: In Life and Art* (Frankfurt am Main, Bern, New York: Peter Lang, 1986), 53.

[41] For more on Duse's collaboration with Verga in both *Cavalleria rusticana* and *In portineria*, the second and last play by Verga, which Duse included in her repertoire, see Enza De Francisci, 'Verga and Duse: Transposing Silence in "Il canarino del n. 15" and *In portineria*. A Prelude to Symbolism?', *The Italianist*, 34, no. 1 (2014): 73–87; Enza De Francisci, 'Verga and Duse: A Silent Partnership in *Cavalleria rusticana* and *In portineria*', in *Eleonora Duse and Cenere (Ashes): Centennial Essays*, edited by Maria Pia Pagani and Paul Fryer (Jefferson, NC: McFarland and Company, Inc., 2017), 41–55; and Enza De Francisci, *A 'New' Woman in Verga and Pirandello: From Page to Stage* (Oxford: Legenda, 2018).

[42] Henry Knepler, *The Gilded Stage: The Lives and Careers of Four Great Actresses: Rachel Félix, Adelaide Ristori, Sarah Bernhardt and Eleonora Duse* (London: Constable, 1968), 4.

[43] Author unspecified, 'Signora Duse', *London Evening Standard*, 31 May 1893, 3, The British Newspaper Archive. www.britishnewspaperarchive.co.uk accessed 2 January 2018.

here is that London audiences were expecting the 'diva' to be positioned under the spotlight throughout the course of the play but the star of the show is effectively withdrawn as soon as Santuzza informs Compare Alfio of the affair – unlike in the opera where Santuzza is kept on stage in the grand finale. Furthermore, the acting styles of both actresses also differed. While the French prima donna was known for being 'intensely dramatic and impulsive',[44] the Italian *grande attrice* was renowned for her small gestures, quiet voice, and minimalistic approach, which might explain why critics felt that she did not make much of an impression.

A year later, contemporary critics continued to agree that '[t]he music of Mascagni is much more beautiful than the words of Verga's spoken dialogue'[45] and that '[w]ithout the music, the [dramatic] plot seems a little thin'.[46] In contrast to this, William Archer seemed to value the stage actress more than her singing contemporary. While in 1893 he admitted that he had not entirely appreciated Verga's work, ('[Duse's] Santuzza in *Cavalleria rusticana* is a fine and impressive performance; but the play is a sketch, a mere incident, a scenario, rather than a developed drama'[47]), a year later, he revised his views:

> Why then does the vocalist, on the whole, take lower artistic rank than the actor? Compare Calvé with Duse in Santuzza, and I think you will see the reason. The actress is far more of a creator; she brings far more of her own observation, invention, thought, and feeling to her work. The singer's whole expression is prescribed for her, so that her achievement is more technical than intellectual.[48]

According to Archer, there was more craft required in a dramatic performance than in an opera. The stage actress Duse had to invent her own role, independent of the playwright, and to consider the thoughts and feelings of her character in order to convey Santuzza's psyche to her audience, different from the soprano Calvé who had merely to follow the music and words prescribed to her by her composer. As a result, Archer concluded that there was more invention and skill on the part of the actress as opposed to the opera singer, thus favouring Duse over Calvé.

[44] Stanley Sadie, ed., *The New Grove Dictionary of Music and Musicians*, vol. 3, Bollioud-Mermet-Castro (London: Macmillan, 1980), 629.

[45] Author unspecified, 'Signorina Duse', *The Standard*, 24 May 1894, 3, The British Newspaper Archive. www.britishnewspaperarchive.co.uk accessed 2 January 2018.

[46] Author unspecified, 'The London Theatres', *The Era*, 26 May 1894, 9, The British Newspaper Archive. www.britishnewspaperarchive.co.uk accessed 2 January 2018.

[47] William Archer, *The Theatrical 'World' of 1893* (London: Walter Scott, 1893), 148.

[48] William Archer, *The Theatrical 'World' of 1894*, with an Introduction by George Bernard Shaw, and a Synopsis of Playbills of the Year by Henry George Hibert (London: Walter Scott, LTD, 1895), 164.

From Novella to Theatre and Opera   195

Significantly, George Bernard Shaw reacted to Archer's article and also drew a comparison between Calvé's *spectacular* interpretation of Santuzza (noting that 'her performance was unmistakably an opera in Covent Garden') and Duse's more *realistic* rendition:

> Now I confess that the illusion created by Duse was so strong that the scene comes back to me almost as an event which I actually witnessed [. . .] I pitied Santuzza as I have often pitied a real woman in the streets miserably trying, without a single charm to aid her, to beg back the affection of some cockney Turiddu.[49]

Here, it appears that Duse's naturalistic acting went even further than it had done previously and drew her audience's attention, despite the language barriers. She ultimately enabled audiences to read Santuzza's complex psychology without having to rely on the universality of music, a luxury that operatic actresses like Calvé could exploit.[50] Moreover, placed within Italian socio-linguistic history, it seems that Duse's privileging of physical techniques of expression has its roots in practical necessity: the absence of a common spoken language in the newly unified Italy compelled actors to exploit their use of gesture and mime in order to render their plays accessible even to a 'home' audience – a technique exploited, above all, by the Sicilian dialect players.

Sicilian Dialect Players: Aguglia and Grasso

Despite the fact that Verga never produced a version of the play in dialect, believing that targeting a purely Sicilian audience would be a 'diminution',[51] and insisting in a 1909 interview that he had no intention of composing the play in dialect,[52] he nevertheless allowed theatre companies to translate his plays into Sicilian.[53] The dialect players thus adapted the drama from the 'high' variety of Italian into the 'low' variety of dialect. If, therefore, translation is 'a field of power',[54] then what emerges here in this translation shift, in the first instance, is Verga prioritizing the dominant

---

[49] George Bernard Shaw, 'Mr William Archer's Criticism', in *Our Theatres in the Nineties*, vol. 1 (London: Constable and Company Limited, [1932] 1954), 91.

[50] For more on the British reception of Duse and Calvé, see Enza De Francisci, 'Eleonora Duse in *Cavalleria rusticana*: Santuzza on the London Stage', *Italian Studies* 69, no. 1 (2014): 95–110.

[51] De Roberto, *Casa Verga*, 295.

[52] Now quoted in Sarah Zappulla Muscarà and Enzo Zappulla, *Giovanni Grasso: Il più grande attore tragico del mondo* (Acireale, Catania: Cantinella, 1995), 133.

[53] See Alessandro D'Amico, 'Il teatro verista e il *grande attore*', in *Il teatro italiano dal naturalismo a Pirandello*, edited by Alessandro Tinterri (Bologna: Il Mulino, 1990), 25–46.

[54] Spivak, 'More Thoughts on Cultural Translation'.

Italian language in his stage adaptation (despite the fact that the characters on stage would essentially be speaking a foreign language), and the Sicilian artists subsequently replacing the 'major' language with the 'minor' – and more authentic – variety. In so doing, the performers essentially dethroned the national language in order to bring the œuvre *back* to its original cultural roots, a choice to which contemporary critics reacted extremely well: '*Cavalleria rusticana*, performed in dialect, acquired more humanity and local color compared to the famed version in Italian.'[55]

One of the first dialect actresses to perform the role of Santuzza was Mimì Aguglia.[56] As with her contemporaries, she included the part into her international repertoire and performed it in cities like London, which had already seen the interpretations of both Calvé and Duse. In the same way as critics tended to compare both stage and operatic versions of Santuzza, early accounts also compared Duse with Aguglia. As Symons pointed out, 'to see her [Aguglia] after the Santuzza of Duse [...] is to realize the difference between this art of the animal and Duse's art of the soul',[57] describing Aguglia's 'furious wrestle with her lover' and her 'unanticipated knife into his heart';[58] actions, which are not included in the original play. Indeed, the Sicilian players worked in a mostly oral tradition, improvising their lines from one scene to the next,[59] and from Symons's review, it appears that Aguglia, like Giovanni Grasso, took this tradition to the extreme.

Grasso was one of the most renowned actors to emerge from Sicily's first official theatre company, the *Compagnia drammatica dialettale siciliana* (Sicilian Dialect Theatre Company), which was founded by director Nino Martoglio in 1902. The set cast included actors such as Grasso, Aguglia, Angelo Musco and Marinella Bragaglia, and their repertoire largely consisted of plays composed by the *veristi* writers (Verga, Capuana and Pirandello), Spanish writers (Joaquín Dicenta and Àngel Guimerà), and their staple play, Shakespeare's *Othello*, which they performed in a translation by Carlo Rusconi and opened at London's Lyric Theatre in 1910 starring Grasso and Bragaglia in the lead roles.[60]

---

[55] Francesco De Felice, *Storia del teatro siciliano* (Catania: Gianotta, 1956), 78.
[56] See Sarah Zappulla Muscarà and Enzo Zappulla, eds., *Le donne del Teatro Siciliano da Mimì Aguglia a Ida Carrara* (Acireale: La Cantinella, 1995).
[57] Symons, *Eleonora Duse*, 131.
[58] Symons, *Eleonora Duse*, 131.
[59] See Antonio Scuderi, 'Sicilian Dialect Theatre', in *A History of Italian Theatre*, edited by Joseph Farrell and Paolo Puppa (Cambridge: Cambridge University Press, 2006), 257–265.
[60] See Enza De Francisci, 'Giovanni Grasso: The *Other* Othello in London', in *Shakespeare, Italy, and Transnational Exchange: The Early Modern Period to the Present*, edited by Enza De Francisci and Chris Stamatakis (New York/London: Routledge, 2017), 195–210.

From Novella to Theatre and Opera 197

Grasso's debuting role in 1902 was in *Cavalleria rusticana*. During his 1908 international tour in Paris, he interpreted the part of Compare Alfio who challenges his wife's lover to a duel. Different from Verga's original script, which concludes soon after the lover is killed by the betrayed husband, Grasso's version allegedly saw the actor return on stage, covered in fake blood, in order to give himself up to two *carabinieri*, declaring in Sicilian, 'Cca sugnu! ... Non scappu!' ('Here I am! ... I'm not going anywhere!'). Shocked by Grasso's alterations, Verga wrote to his translator, Édouard Rod, in a letter of 29 January 1908, to express his horror at what he called Grasso's 'grotesque caricature' of the Sicilian character and to order the immediate withdrawal of *all* his plays from the actor's repertoire.[61]

The Sicilian performers enjoyed a reputation for naturalistic immediacy and impulsiveness readily associated with their Southern Italian identity, and what emerges from early critical reviews is a romanticized, sentimental portrayal of Sicily together with a somewhat condescending vocabulary of rustic primitivism and animalism: racial stereotypes about Sicily's African and Arab heritage that the players both took advantage of and resisted. Indeed, in spite of Verga's disgust at Grasso's modifications to his play, Parisian audiences were struck by the image of Sicily that they saw on stage. According to the *Pall Mall Gazette* on 17 January 1908, Grasso's acting in particular touched spectators: 'Strange and marvellous is the power of this Sicilian peasant who manages to deeply move, indeed to tears, a public as sceptical and frivolous as that of Paris.'[62]

From this, it would seem that, well before debuting in London on 3 February 1908 at the Shaftesbury Theatre, the travelling artists had already been turned into celebrity star actors by the media. Their reputation had been so sufficiently established that their debut in London was even attended by members of the royal family: King Edward VII, his wife, and the Prince and Princess of Wales. What drew audiences to their performances was their reputation for being 'primitively realistic', and this portrait – one that paired clearly eulogistic terms of wonder ('strange', 'marvellous') and authenticity ('natural', 'realistic', 'authentic') with a haughty and pejorative rhetoric ('peasant', 'primitively') in an uneasy, contradictory balance – was perpetuated in their opening performances of *Cavalleria rusticana*.

---

[61] Giovanni Verga, *Lettere al suo traduttore*, edited by Fredi Chiapelli (Florence: Le Monnier, 1954), 245–246.
[62] Zappulla Muscarà and Zappulla, *Giovanni Grasso*, 97.

The *Manchester Courier and Lancashire General Advertiser* on 8 February 1908 was one of the first newspapers to note the initial success of the Sicilian dialect players in London. They debuted with Verga's *Cavalleria rusticana*, Giuseppe Giusti-Sinopoli's *La zolfara* (1895) and Luigi Capuana's *Malìa* (1904):

> The artistic success of the Sicilians is assured. When they opened on Monday at the Shaftesbury in *Malia* [*sic*] it was at once seen that they were great realists, and to-night they show that their success is not confined to one play. They gave a wonderful performance of *Cavalleria rusticana* which, minus music, is more powerful than the opera. Signor Grasso's Turridu is a very strong piece of action, and a big hit was scored by Mme. Aguglia as Santuzza. The second item on the bill was *Zolfara*, a grim little melodrama about the sulphur mines. It, too, is full of blood and fire, and shows the players to the utmost advantage both as tragic and comic actors of great skill.[63]

The review here points to the actors' realism and the play's defining atmosphere of 'blood and fire' – qualities reminiscent of those celebrated in the company's earlier performances in Paris, which suggests that the explicit use of aggression in their renditions was becoming a popular trademark. Tellingly, the critic preferred Grasso's version of *Cavalleria rusticana* to the more famous one-act opera of Mascagni, unlike earlier reviewers who favoured the music over the play. In spite of the performing artists' use of dialect, this critic was not lost in translation. Indeed, to overcome the obvious language barrier, the actors continued to rely heavily on their body language in order to communicate their script to their foreign audience: a realistic acting technique that they took one step further in their explicitly aggressive performances and which, arguably, anticipated the pioneering methods of Stanislavsky, Meyerhold and Strasberg.[64]

Significantly, these years in Italy were marked by the so-called 'Southern Question', whose roots lay in the period of the Risorgimento itself. After Garibaldi's triumphant entrance into mainland Italy in May 1860 with his 1,000 troops, an expedition that ultimately led to political unification a year later, Luigi Carlo Farini, the chief administrator of Southern Italy, wrote despairingly to Camillo Cavour, who was soon to become Italy's

---

[63] Author unspecified, 'Our London Correspondence', *The Manchester Courier and Lancashire General Advertiser*, 8 February 1908, 6, The British Newspaper Archive. www.britishnewspaperarchive.co.uk accessed 2 January 2018.

[64] Sergei Tcherkasski, 'Twofaced Giovanni Grasso and his Great Spectators or What Stanislavsky, Meyerhold and Strasberg Actually Stole from the Sicilian Actor', in *The Italian Method of La Drammatica*, edited by Anna Sica (Milan: Mimesis, 2014), 109–132. See also Gabriele Sofia, *L'arte di Giovanni Grasso e le rivoluzioni teatrali di Craig e Mejerchold* (Rome: Bulzoni, 2019).

From Novella to Theatre and Opera

first prime minister, from Molise on 27 October 1860 with the famous words: 'Some Italy! This is Africa!'.[65] From 1861 onwards, Italy faced the challenges of self-fashioning its own national identity. As the Piedmontese statesman and man of letters Massimo d'Azeglio also allegedly claimed: 'Italy has been made. We now need to make Italians.' Yet Italy remained fundamentally fractured between northern and southern spheres, with the *Mezzogiorno* (the Italian Southern sphere) branded as a kind of 'other', which popular journals, namely the *Illustrazione Italiana*, were keen to exploit.[66]

In the context of Risorgimento Italy, what is noteworthy is that early performances of *Cavalleria rusticana* were in dialogue with such questions of racial identity, especially so when this 'other' play was performed by actors from the 'other' part of Italy. Indeed, it would seem that the very image that Verga perpetuated of the Sicilian working-class villagers, particularly in his portrayal of the mafia-like rituals leading up to the duel (mainly a bite to the earlobe and the exchange of a kiss between the two rivals) is that of 'Other'. In other words, a society that treated honour as a rigid code, a kind of law for the lawless, instead of what it really was, that is a very loose and flexible set of practices and norms.[67] So despite the fact that Verga's incensed reaction to Grasso's interpretation of *Cavalleria rusticana* led him to ban the actor from performing his plays, it would appear that, to some extent, the author himself exploited the racial stereotype he resented.

Translating Sicilian 'Otherness'

In conclusion, I propose that the decision to stage *Cavalleria rusticana* in the late nineteenth-century must be placed within the wider historical and cultural framework of a newly united Italy, and needs to be understood in the context of prevailing racial stereotypes of the Sicilian. While,

---

[65] See Nelson Moe, *The View from Vesuvius: Italian Culture and the Southern Question* (Berkeley, LA: University of California Press, 2002).

[66] See Rhiannon Noel Welch, *Vital Subjects: Race and Biopolitics in Italy, 1860–1920* (Liverpool: Liverpool University Press, 2016).

[67] In an anthropological study conducted much later by Jane and Peter Schneider of a community in the west of Sicily, Villamura, over the period of two years (1965–1967) and two summers (1968 and 1971), they explained that 'the only way for cuckolds to lose their horns was to kill the people who placed them there. "Only blood would wash blood"; hence, the legendary crime of honor'. However, later on in their fieldwork, they added that 'although rigorous in theory, the code of honor was flexible in fact. Most cuckolds were not murderers and therefore not disposed to follow the rule that "blood washes blood", especially if their predicaments were not widely known in the community.' See Jane Schneider and Peter Schneider, *Culture and Political Economy in Western Sicily* (New York: Academic Press, 1976), 90, 94.

one could argue, the performers, especially Grasso, appeared to exploit the emerging stereotype of the violent Sicilian, early performative translations of *Cavalleria rusticana* skilfully introduced a new stage space as a site for transnational encounters and intercultural exchanges. Combining a veneer of a 'Southern' abandon, each performer not only placed Sicily centre stage, but was able to introduce a new form of physical performance never before seen on stage. What, then, presumably attracted author, composer, singer and actors to translate and perform *Cavalleria rusticana* was, to some degree, the opportunities it afforded them to take advantage of the associative 'otherness' of the Sicilian island, which defined many ethnographic prejudices of the time. Thus, to return to Bermann's question as to what it means to 'perform translation',[68] it would seem that, when considered in the wider context of transnational cultural practices and expectations from the late nineteenth to the early twentieth century, performing translation in *Cavalleria rusticana* meant making (indirectly or otherwise) an exoticized brand of Sicilian-ness at a time when the newly established nation-state was self-fashioning its identity – an exoticization that went one step further in forging Sicily as mainland Italy's own gestural and linguistic Other.

[68] Bermann and Porter, eds., *A Companion to Translation Studies*.

CHAPTER 9

Gestural Archives
Transmission and Embodiment as Translation in Occupied Palestine

Farah Saleh

My practice-based research the *Archive of Gestures* investigates how artists can contribute to change by exploring and problematizing cultural and political memories. My objective is to uncover Palestinian gestures and alternative narratives that have been left out of the Israeli and mainstream Palestinian accounts, by re-enacting, analysing and commenting on them and the contexts in which they were produced. Indeed, this project is an attempt to collect fragments of a gestural collective identity, and to construct an archive that the Israeli and dominant Palestinian nationalist narratives have ignored and often suppressed.

In what follows, I explore how the gestural archive retrieves stories related to my own biography as a refugee in the Palestinian diaspora, later as an occupied subject in Palestine and now as citizen of the world living in Europe. I attempt to construct the archive by engaging with private and informal archival material (videos, pictures, written documents), oral histories and imagination, exploring how using the body as archive offers ways to unearth, as well as to translate, the movements and gestures in the stories.

In order to investigate ways of archiving the stories through my own body, the bodies of my collaborators and those of the audience, first I undertook a series of artistic residencies and developed the narratives into artworks. Then, I presented the works multiple times in different settings to understand better how the gestural archive can be shared and transmitted to other bodies, and how the knowledge it carries can be embodied and translated.

In this chapter I will analyse the first four works I have developed since the beginning of this gestural-archival research. A Fidayee Son in Moscow (2014), an interactive video dance installation (also transformed into a participatory live performance in 2016), in which I re-enact, transform and deform gestures of Palestinian children, one of whom is my brother, at a Communist international boarding school in the Soviet Union during the 1980s. Cells of Illegal Education (2016) is an interactive video dance installation in which I attempt to reconstruct the movements of Palestinian students during the First Intifada, when education was banned by an Israeli military rule. Gesturing Refugees (2018), an interactive performance that attempts to archive alternative narratives of refugeehood and the gestures of these narratives using the bodies of refugee artists and those of the audience as the main form of archive. What My Body Can/t Remember (2019) is an interactive dance promenade that investigates what my body can or can't remember from performing daily gestures and dancing at home during the Israeli siege of the West Bank in 2002.

The driving force of the four works is not nostalgia, but the necessity to reflect on the past and present, and encourage the creation of social and political responsibility for the future.[1] For this reason, I include interactivity and participation with the audience, and in this chapter I explain how this helps to transmit the stories and their gestures to the audience's bodies. My aim is to allow the audience to live an experience, even if for a short period of time, which would allow them to re-enact the gestures of the stories, while understanding the context in which they were produced, transforming their bodies into a living archive of these stories. Therefore, I will explore how transmitting and embodying the gestural archive in the audience's bodies translates the gestures and their context to the audience and culturally mediates between them and the stories.

Three important caveats before starting the remainder of my analysis: firstly, in my practice-led research I work with the archive as what Michel Foucault calls a 'general system of the formation and transformation of statements',[2] which is changeable and keeps inventing itself, rather than considering the archive as a mere source, or a storehouse within which to search for documents that belong to the past. Secondly, by 'gesture' I intend a movement done by one or more parts of the body to express a personal or collective idea, which has a political power – a definition in dialogue with Judith Butler, who associates gestures to performativity, vulnerability and activism.[3] Thirdly, what I mean by translation is 'to convey the form and meaning of the original [gestures] as accurately as

---

[1] Jacques Derrida, 'Archive Fever: A Freudian Impression', translated by Eric Prenowitz, *Diacritics* 5, no. 2 (1995): 27.

[2] Michel Foucault, *The Archeology of Knowledge and the Discourse on Language*, translated by A. M. Sheridan Smith (New York, 1972), 130.

[3] Butler, *Notes*, 24–66.

Gestural Archives 203

possible' to the audience's bodies, although this does not mean that parts of them will not be lost or transformed.[4] On the contrary, the transformation of the gestures through their repetition allows people to interpret them and create their own relationship to them.

A Fidayee Son in Moscow: Experimenting with Audience Participation in Revolutionary Education

In this first work, I archive gestures of Palestinian children who were sent to the Soviet international boarding school Interdom by their leftist parents after the Israeli war on Lebanon in 1982.[5] The school was built in 1933 in Ivanovo, northeast of Moscow, to host children of revolutionary parents from all over the world as a form of solidarity between nations, including the children of Mao Zedong, Josip Broz Tito, Isidora Dolores Ibarruri Gomez ('La Pasionaria') and my brother – the son of a Palestinian freedom fighter (*fidayee* in Arabic).

The installation portrays a school day at the Interdom from a physical point of view. It provides gestures and movements students used to do in their History, Singing, Physics and Creative Writing classes, while also analysing the historical context of the school. The installation asks the public to try to embody these gestures themselves, in an attempt to make them live traces of the Interdom experience.

Using the setting of a classroom furnished with a desk and a blackboard, and after a short extract of black-and-white footage from different periods of the school, I speak from the video directly to the audience, like a teacher would do to students during a class (see Figure 9.1). Giving instructions to the audience, I encourage them to repeat the gestures that I make.

The choreography of each class was created combining archive material, testimonies that I collected throughout several months, and imagination, to fill in the gaps of the narrative and add my interpretation. The History class, for instance, prepares the body – in particular the mouth – to salute the Communist revolutionaries the students were learning about (Figure 9.2). The Singing class warms up the left arm to sing all together the Italian Communist song 'Bandiera Rossa' (The Red Flag) with a raised fist. The Creative Writing class is inspired by the content of the letters my brother sent to the family during his stay at the Interdom

---

[4] John Johnston, 'Translation as Simulacrum', in *Rethinking Translation: Discourse, Subjectivity, Ideology*, edited by Lawrence Venuti (London: Routledge, 1992), 42.

[5] Lebanon was one of the places where the Palestinian political leadership was based at that time.

Figure 9.1 History classroom in Suspended Accounts exhibition in London (January 2016), © Andy Stagg, courtesy of the Mosaic Rooms.

Figure 9.2 History class in A Fidayee Son in Moscow live performance at Dance Base, Edinburgh (February 2017), © Brian Hartely.

Gestural Archives

and reflects his nostalgia for home. The class asks the audience members to write a nostalgic letter to their distant parents. The Physics class echoes the greatest Soviet dream at that time: to go to outer space and prepares the audience members to jump into space.

This artwork is a form of self-historicization and re-appropriation of the history of a certain socio-political group, rather than a form of nostalgia for a certain era. Even if the piece evokes some nostalgia, this would be a nostalgia for the future, according to Svetlana Boym 'nostalgia is not always about the past; it can be retrospective, but also prospective.'[6] In that sense, the nostalgia present in A Fidayee Son in Moscow is one that reflects on the past and present of the children of the Left within a generation that was active in the struggle for the liberation of Palestine, while questioning the future of today's Palestinian Left. As André Lepecki suggests of re-enactment, 'in reenacting we turn back and in this return, we find in old dances a will to keep inventing.' For Lepecki, the 'will to archive' is not a result of cultural failure or nostalgia, as some performance scholars suggest.[7] On the contrary, it is the wish to embody creative corporeal possibilities that existed in previous works, by re-enacting and transforming them and therefore creating new material for the present and future.

However, the central idea behind this piece is also that, if only for a short time, the audience can live fragments of the school's life and its historical context. This happens while embodying and repeating the gestures and being affected by them, physically and emotionally. To further experiment with inter-activity, I also transformed the piece into a live performance that I brought to different contexts and countries to investigate further the concept of transmission of the physical archive to the bodies of the audience and how that helped translate the context of the story and the embodiment of its gestures.

In this new experiment, my physical presence in the space and the direct instructions I was giving to the audience enormously enhanced the inter-activity. While in the installation version the public had the choice to perform the instructions or contemplate the gestural archive, in the live performance they were almost left without any choice other than to join the classes and perform the gestures with their own bodies. Through this latter element I added a further political layer – the question of obedience in the Soviet context – and comment to the piece.

---

[6] Svetlana Boym, *The Future of Nostalgia* (New York: Basic Books, 2002), 26.

[7] André Lepecki, 'The Body as Archive: Will to Re-enact and the Afterlives of Dances', *Dance Research Journal* 42, no. 2 (2010): 46.

In both versions I was keen to create an experience for the audience members, in which they are also actors, participating in part or completely, rather than being mere spectators. My aim was to create an experience and an event through which they are touched by affect, and at the same time touch one another. This is a process that allows for the creation of inter-subjectivities and for an afterlife of the performance.

According to Brian Massumi, during an event one is always affected and affects in return.[8] For him, affect is transversal, it cuts across the subjective and the objective, and therefore the feeling process that affect provokes cannot solely be characterized as subjective or objective, since it strikes both the body and the mind at once and involves the subjective qualities as much as the object initiating them, and freedom as much as constraint: 'you could say that sensation is the registering of affect that I referred to before – the passing awareness of being at a threshold – and that affect is thinking, bodily – consciously but vaguely, in the sense that it is not yet a fully formed thought. It's a movement of thought, or a thinking movement.'[9] He suggests that when you affect something, you are at the same time being affected, making a transition from where you were before, however small it can be, which makes you step over a threshold and experience a change, opening each situation to its potential and making people remember that we do not live in isolation, but are inter-dependent on others and things around us, allowing for the fluidity of each person's subjectivity.

Translation here means gestural translation and consists of making accessible, transmitting and acquiring through the body a hidden fragment of Palestinian political history and culture. In this process of translation, audiences unfamiliar with the hidden story and its gestures are asked to re-enact the experience of a Palestinian child in an internationalist Soviet school, opening it up, like in all forms of translation, to their own interpretation of the original, and its meaning for our present and future.

Cells of Illegal Education: Interactivity as a Tool for Revitalizing the Spirit of Anti-colonial Uprising

In this second installation, I re-visit gestures of civil disobedience carried out during the First Intifada (the First Uprising) in Occupied Palestine. More specifically, I attempt to archive gestures performed by Birzeit

[8] Brian Massumi, *The Politics of Affect* (Cambridge: Polity Press, 2015), 3–6.
[9] Massumi, *Politics*, 10.

University students between 1988 and 1992 while trying to continue their education process at a time when schools and universities were forcibly closed by an Israeli military rule and students and teachers who refused to abide were labelled 'cells of illegal education'. The clandestine classes were organized in alternative spaces, such as houses, open air spaces, cafés, dorms and the university entrance.

Before going into the dance studio with the dancers (Salma Ataya, Ibrahim Feno, Hiba Harhash, Maali Khaled, Fayez Kawamleh and Farah Saleh) and starting the creation process, I researched various kinds of archival resources, in particular texts, photos and videos from the First Intifada. Additionally, I carried out interviews with scholars, former activists and students, then imagined ways of archiving gestures of the First Intifada through our contemporary bodies using an interactive video installation as an artistic form. During the intensive weeks in the studio we intertwined archival material, oral testimonies and imagination to re-visit the gestures of a group of Birzeit University students during their university closure.

I chose to work with three pictures and one painting from that historical period, studying the gestures of the students in each one and imagine, while keeping the information I researched in mind – what was before and after the moments captured by the pictures and the painting. The four constitutive sections of Cells of Illegal Education (C.I.E) were filmed and edited not as a consecutive narrative; before each section a short text appears to describe the situation narrated by the students. The first section is called 'In the shadow of the Intifada' and portrays students while attempting to secretly study in someone's kitchen. The second and third sections are entitled 'The forbidden area' and 'A historical moment' (see Figure 9.3), in which students manage to violate the Israeli military order, break into their closed university labs and organize an architecture class. In the fourth section – 'We organized a mock lecture' – students stage a mock lecture in front of the closed university's entrance in order to take a picture to be utilized to print propaganda postcards and mobilize the international community against Israel's collective punishment.

While identifying gestures and working on reconstructing them with the dancers, I kept in mind Jacques Derrida's key constituting parameters of an archive: a certain exteriority, a technique of repetition and a place of consignation.[10] For that reason, in the choreography I opted for pedestrian movements similar to those that would exist in the four situations

---

[10] Derrida, 'Archive Fever', 14.

Figure 9.3 The third section of the video 'A historical moment'. On the left, architecture students at Birzeit University in 1991, posing after they broke into their university to take a lecture in the Architecture Department lab. On the right, the re-enactment and deformation of the picture in Cells of Illegal Education, © Salem Thawaba.

of the images; added a certain repetition of the gestures and used the body as the main place of consignation of the archive, supported by other archive material. The body is treated as a privileged site of archive, since as suggested by Lepecki, it combines many levels: affective, political and aesthetic.[11]

After the video was shot at the university's old and new premises, archive material – such as photos and music – was also used in the editing. And while conceiving the final version of the installation, I turned to interactivity again, looking for ways to allow the audience to try the gestures of the students, help them translate the narrative into their own bodies and possibly re-connect with similar civil disobedience acts of the present and future. This is what Erin Manning calls a 'minor gesture': a gestural force that brings possibilities for disturbance and new ways of expression to emerge through experience.[12] The idea is that what the audience experiences and embodies would be translated through the language of gestures,

---

[11] Lepecki, 'The Body as Archive', 34.
[12] Erin Manning, *The Minor Gesture* (Durham: Duke University Press, 2016), 1–2.

into a deeper understanding of how different political cultures from different historical moments can enrich each other and new horizons of justice can be developed. In this sense, gestural transmission and embodiment constitute a form of translation of a hidden element of the Palestinian archive.

Other than recreating the setting of the kitchen table present in one of the video's sections (Figure 9.4), instructions were provided to the audience on a piece of paper hung on the door before entering the installation. The first asks them to enter the room one after the other and to leave 20 seconds between each person. This is how the students during the First Intifada used to enter a space so that the Israeli military wouldn't notice that a group of people was going to meet and study somewhere. The second instruction is to lower their head and watch for any danger before arriving at the kitchen, while I put some obstacles between the door and the table to make the audience feel the constant state of alertness of the students. The third is to have a fruit from the plate on the table while watching the video for 12 minutes looping, to make the audience live the familiar and enjoyable situation people were describing in their recounting of popular education at that time. The fourth is to leave from the back door, again one by one, to keep all suspicions away and maintain the organized secretive work until the end.

Interactivity as a tool for re-experiencing the past is crucial in this piece, since during the last ten years, at least, a strong feeling of nostalgia for the First Intifada's civil disobedience acts has been sensed in Palestine and among international activists, and calls for reactivating the political spirit of this historical moment of revolt have been repeatedly launched.[13] This was a reaction to the failure of the Oslo peace agreements signed with Israel in 1994, the disastrous outcomes of the Second Intifada (2000–2005) on the Palestinian struggle and the ongoing status quo of continuous Israeli occupation and internal Palestinian political division since 2006. C.I.E constitutes an artistic exploration of this nostalgia and an invitation for it to transform into a prospective act. As Manning suggests, being in the process and from within the experience creates different kinds of physical and affective knowledge, which leads to *the more than* of the experience itself.[14]

---

[13] Ala Alazzeh, 'Seeking Popular Participation: Nostalgia for the First Intifada in the West Bank', *Settler Colonial Studies* 5, no. 3 (2015): 1–17.
[14] Manning, *The Minor Gesture*, 33.

Figure 9.4 The kitchen setting of the installation in Granoff Center at Brown University in Providence (March 2016), © Farah Saleh.

Gestural Archives 211

Gesturing Refugees: Understanding and Challenging Exile by Embodying Archives

In this interactive dance performance I experiment with ways of archiving latent stories of refugeehood using the bodies of refugee-artists Hamza Damra, Fadi Waked and myself, and the bodies of the audience as the main archives, while also playing with other archive material, testimonies and imagination. The archives include stories of refugeehood to interrogate collective responsibility and find bridges between past, present and future refugees. The re-enactment, transformation and deformation of the alternative and personal memories of refugee-artists aims at re-appropriating the refugee narrative and developing a collective gestural identity that might challenge that of passive victimhood to which refugees are often subjected.

The piece faced many obstacles in the creation period related to visa denial to artists and the impossibility of their physical encounter. In fact, for the first creation period in May 2017, the visas of the refugee dancers (one resident in Palestine and the other in Germany) were denied by UK authorities. Therefore, we had to work over Skype, which added other formal and political layers to the performance (Figure 9.5). The impossibility of physical encounter opened up the question on how gestures can be archived and shared remotely via a digital platform and how accepting remote working, each appearing physically in a different space and location, can still be a form of acting collectively towards freedom. Freedom from stereotypes, freedom of movement and freedom of self-determination.

In our time together, we attempted to archive ordinary refugee gestures in stories told by the artist-refugees ourselves and those of other refugees, such as: Fadi making jokes with his friends during the long journey to Europe; Hamza holding his brother's shoulder after being shot by an Israeli soldier; me calling an ambulance to take me to school under curfew; and Hassan Rabah, a friend Syrian dancer refugee, performing a complex choreography of gestures in his room in Beirut days before committing suicide as a result of not being able to cope with his refugee status there. Re-enacting, transforming and deforming Hassan's gestures was a way to revive them in our own bodies and the bodies of the audience and bring them where Hassan wanted to go, but was not able to: out of Lebanon.

The following creation periods continued from afar, as a decision to transform the distance among us produced by the UK restrictions to free movement led to the possibility of a new archival form. I worked with a local video artist to connect the Messenger elaborations and transform the whole narrative into an interactive performance with the audience.

Figure 9.5 Experimenting with archiving gestures with other artists over Skype at Dance Base in Edinburgh (May 2017), © Maciej Czajka.

The performance begins with a short preparation session for the audience prior to entering the performance space, in which I guide them into becoming future refugees. I teach them some stereotypical gestures related to the refugee journey in the Mediterranean Sea towards Europe – a journey Fadi, one of the dancers, had to go through, and which are constantly produced by mainstream media. For instance, I ask the audience members to have a cup of water to prepare for long days of thirst in the sea, hand in their ID cards to me, take a last selfie at home and to put all their belongings in one plastic bag. The aim is to do all of these stereotypical gestures of refugees and then undo them along with the stereotypes connected to them during the performance, by watching and embodying alternative gestures of refugeehood. By 'alternative' I mean gestures different to those found in the narratives produced by the mainstream media, which often represent refugees as passive suffering victims.

After the preparation session, I allow the people into the performance space, where the video artist distributes Landing Cards for the audience to fill in while sitting on chairs in the centre of the space (Figure 9.6), facing a TV looping silent footage archiving our dialogues on Skype, Fadi's journey to Berlin and Hassan's dancing in Lebanon. The Landing Cards consist of ironic questions to the audience – such as the minute and second of birth, the type of shampoo they use and the size of their underpants and boxers – which amplify the very personal and absurd questions refugees have to

Gestural Archives

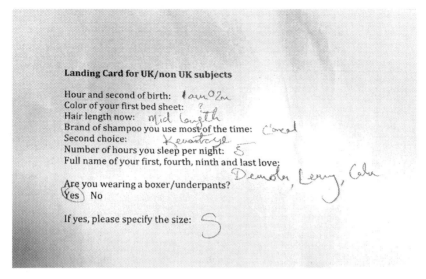

Figure 9.6 A filled-in Landing Card completed by a member of the audience, © Farah Saleh.

answer in their paperwork requesting refugee status, and in the documents we had to fill in for the dancers UK (denied) visas.

From that moment onwards, the audience experiences the performance based on their answers. For instance, the people who were born before midnight have to go to stand across the Boxer Line (a physical line created in the space with a boxer hanging on it, echoing the personal questions in the Landing Cards), and watch funny stories of refugeehood at one end of the stage. Whereas those who were born after midnight have to follow me, and watch and re-enact Hassan's gestures, based on my instructions on the opposite end of the stage. Then the groups are asked to swap, but they see partially different videos and re-enact different gestures – again to reflect on how one creates a point of view depending on the information received, who they received it from and how.

In the last part of the performance, everyone wearing underpants/boxers is invited to take a seat and I start recounting and re-enacting my personal ironically funny gestures of refugeehood, which were produced in critical situations and became funny because of the context they were produced in, such as calling an ambulance under curfew in the West Bank in 2002, to take me to school to do my International Baccalaureate exam. I do that to connect myself to the other refugee-artists in the piece and to the potential future refugees present in the room: the audience. After re-enacting, transforming and deforming my own gestures of refugeehood, I repeat and also ask the audience to repeat traces of gestures that were performed throughout the piece to enhance the embodiment of the gestures and the physical and affective knowledge acquired by the moving–thinking together.

From the beginning of the performance, I prepare the audience for the idea that they will be active members in the performance, rather than mere observers. That they are entering an event, where everyone is a co-creator of the performance. The audience members are asked to make decisions, act or refuse acting from the start, allowing them to affect and be affected by the experience, which might leave traces on them even after the performance finishes.

In his work on affect and 'the more than' that it produces, Massumi distinguishes between emotion and affect.[15] He explains that while emotion is the expression of what a person is feeling at a certain moment through gesture and language, structured by social convention and culture, affect is an unstructured and a non-linguistic bodily sensation that exceeds what is actualized by language and gesture. It stirs a sense that something is being experienced, initiates efforts to understand what was experienced and find ways to express it.

Building on Massumi's thought, Deborah Gould suggests that often when people try to grasp what they are feeling, they draw meaning from their culture and personal habits.[16] They express what they are feeling in an incomplete way that doesn't represent the affective experience, rather they merely express an approximation of what they are feeling, reducing unpresentable affective states into conventionally recognized emotions, fixed language and gestures. Gould suggests that the distinction between affect and emotions is not temporal, it is not that affect comes first followed by the manifestation of a fixed emotion. Rather affect is always there, even if not actualized, it is what makes people feel any emotion. She explains that for Massumi the non-fixity of affect provides enormous freedom, allowing it to be directed and mobilized in new ways and implies that diminishing affect into culturally conventional emotions, would reduce its potential of passing the threshold and realizing 'the more than' of what is actualized in social life.

---

[15] Brian Massumi, *Parables for the Virtual: Movement, Affect, Sensation* (Durham: Duke University Press, 2002), 27–28.
[16] Deborah Gould, 'On Affect and Protest', in *Political Emotions: New Agendas in Communication*, edited by Janet Staiger, Ann Svetkovich and Ann Reynolds (New York: Routledge, 2010), 26–28.

In that sense experiencing a performance can make us see the world differently. Witnessing bodily archives and embodying their gestures might translate later in living our lives differently. In *Gesturing Refugees* this happens for example: by people understanding better the asylum seekers' process after having to fill in the ironic Landing Cards themselves and bringing them home, where they can look at them again and keep them as physical trace of the experience; by people looking at the mainstream media on refugees with a different perspective after taking their 'last selfie at home' during the introductory section, which they can find on their phones when they are back home; by sharing and transmitting the alternative stories and gestures of refugeehood with a friend, after archiving them in their own bodies during the performance; or even by hosting a refugee at home or by contacting their MP to ask for a change in the asylum seekers' procedure.

What My Body Can/t Remember: From Witnessing a Bodily Archive to Accessing Your Own

In this promenade performance, I investigate what my body can or can't remember from me performing daily gestures and dancing at home in my city Ramallah, during the 2002 Israeli re-invasion of the West Bank. During that period, we had to stay at home for many months under curfew, which brought me back to dancing after years of interruption. In this live performance I also reflect on how moving in a private domestic space became my only mean of physical freedom.

I explore ways of archiving the story relying on my body as the main source of archive, rather than also working with physical archives as I did in my previous projects, to investigate body memory as archive and challenge the ephemerality of performance. To do that I undertook a series of artistic residencies between October 2018 and February 2019 at Dance Base in Edinburgh, through which I attempted to remember the movements I was performing in 2002. First, I invited video artist Owa Barua to help me document my daily process of remembering. Then, I decided to make my practice of remembering accessible to an audience, considering my body memory as an archive opening its doors to the public during the period of the performance, and the audience as witnesses of that archive, with whom I also exchange thoughts on body memory and I invite them to access their own living archives.

In this performance I travel back in my memory to 2000, more than a decade after the First Palestinian Intifada of 1987, when the Second Intifada

(Second Uprising)[17] erupted in the Palestinian Occupied Territories as a response to the deadlock in the so-called Oslo 'peace process' between Israelis and Palestinians. At that time, I was studying at high school and I was practicing modern dance at a local cultural centre. But the uprising exploded, and with it demonstrations, and violent clashes at checkpoints controlled by Israel, as well as bombings of Palestinian cities by the occupying military forces. In 2002, Israel took the decision to escalate and even further weaken the Palestinian Authority by re-invading Palestinian territory with troops and tanks throughout the main West Bank cities, including my city, Ramallah. I was in my last year of high school then and had stopped dancing since the beginning of the uprising, because of the political situation.

During the invasion of the West Bank, civilians were put under curfew by Israeli military rule. For several months we were confined to our homes with irregular food supplies, regular electricity and water cuts, and systematic home incursions. Also, schools, universities and cultural centres like all other services were closed. On top of that, I was home alone with my older brother, the *fidayee*'s son in Moscow of my previous piece, as my father was persecuted by the Israeli military for being a member of the Palestine Liberation Organization and my mother was stuck in Jordan, where she was attending a conference at the moment of the invasion, as all border crossings were closed.

To survive the dire situation, I started creating my own routine at home. First, dancing and playing cards in the living room, while listening to MTV music – when there were no electricity cuts. Second, sleeping for long hours during the day in my bedroom to escape time and the sound of explosions in the city. Third, cooking creatively with what was left in the kitchen, moving in it anxiously, entering and exiting it promptly, as it was exposed to the Israeli snipers on the road. In What My Body Can/t Remember, I try to re-visit all these memories, through a somatic approach to memory, in which body and mind unite to revive gestures from the past in the present moment.

To assist my process of remembering and recalling images, I decided to give myself a spatial structure and concentrate on three parts of my house in Ramallah, where recollections were more intense. Accordingly, I divided the studio space into three rooms: the kitchen, the bedroom and the sitting room. In addition, I added minimal objects in each

---

[17] The Second Intifada (2000–2005) followed a First Intifada (1987–1992), and is a popular uprising that, like the first, had the aim of putting an end to the Israeli Occupation in Palestine.

Figure 9.7 The audience watching the video documentation at the beginning of the performance, Fruitmarket in Edinburgh (February 2019). Courtesy of the Fruitmarket, © Chris Scott.

room, which appeared in my memory. Entering with my body into each reconstructed room was every time like re-immersing myself with images from the past, which my body then would transform into gestures and movements in the present.

Each day of my practice, I was trying to access again my memories of 2002, rather than remembering the gestures I enacted the day before. To make sure my practice was truthful, video artist Owa Barua was documenting the process, so that I could notice how each day was different or similar to the other, but also to connect time: me re-enacting the past in my body, while he archived the present process, for future use. Indeed, the accumulated video material was used to create a 4-minute visual archive of the process, which is projected at the beginning of the performance to invite the audience into my practice of remembering (Figure 9.7).

When the audience enters the space in *What My Body Can/t Remember*, they see me standing in the open semi-empty space with the few objects lying around in three designated areas representing the rooms. Laurajane Smith suggests that when people enter museums or memory sites, like the one I re-created of my house by dividing the gallery into rooms and placing objects in the space, the objects present in them act as tools from the past that help people remember old experiences.[18] And since remembering is an active process, it continues re-shaping the experience of memories. In that sense, when we enter a memory site, embodied performances are produced with emotional, physical and intellectual responses to how we process our understanding of the past in the present moment. This is relevant to me when I am trying to remember in the presence of the audience, but also crucially functions as an invitation to them to remember and create their own relationship to the objects in the space.

Similarly, Joslin McKinney explains, objects and scenography allow for kinaesthetic awareness to emerge and for an experience that includes the whole body of the viewer to materialize, by enabling an understanding of the spatial positioning of the self in relation to the objects.[19] McKinney claims that both the placement of the objects and their quality are crucial for the self to become a creative agent, engaging with these objects and creating a personal relationship to them.

Building on Smith's and McKinney's ideas, I chose the objects according to their particular significance in my memory and placed them in the same rooms they appeared according to my memory. First, I put a blanket in the bedroom as it emerged in my memories of sleeping and sleeplessness. This helped me to re-discover the feelings and movements performed by my body long time ago. Second, I placed two chairs and a table in the kitchen, reflecting the setting I recalled of my apartment, where I was cooking, eating and moving quickly and anxiously, which also revived the embodied memories of that situation. Finally, in the living room, I propped a mirror and a pair of socks, since I remember checking my dance movements in a mirror for corrections. The mirror helped me to remember the movements I was enacting. While the socks reflected my brother's socks, who was always present with me in the sitting room and had to change his socks a few times a day, because he could be arrested and captured at any moment by the Israeli army, simply for being a Palestinian man. And when arresting men, soldiers often put their socks in their mouths, in a gesture of humiliation and as a form of torture. For me, placing the socks in the sitting room space brought me physically and emotionally to my state of tension of waiting for my brother's an arrest, that fortunately never took place.

[18] Laurajane Smith, 'The Embodied Performance of Museum Visiting', in *The Sentient Archive: Bodies, Performance, and Memory*, edited by Bill Bissell and Linda Caruso Haviland (Middletown: Wesleyan University Press, 2018), 126–142.

[19] Joslin McKinney, 'Empathy and Exchange: Audience Experience of Scenography', in *Kinesthetic Empathy in Creative and Cultural Practices*, edited by Matthew Reason and Dee Reynolds (Chicago: The University of Chicago Press; Bristol: Intellect, 2012), 219–235.

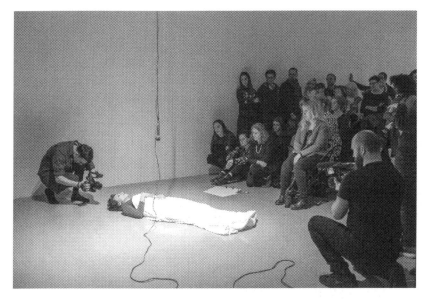

Figure 9.8 What My Body Can/t Remember, Fruitmarket in Edinburgh (February 2019). Courtesy of the Fruitmarket, © Chris Scott.

These objects-memories are both tools that allow me to remember through the body and elements that can help the audiences of my performances to become part of my archival process by triggering their own imaginative and remembrance processes. When the audience members witness me remembering the gestures of many years ago in relation to the objects in space, this also allows them to identify their own relationship to these objects and the memories that might erupt. For example, one audience member I talked to after my performance told me that he remembered the image of a dead body when he saw me covered by the white blanket (Figure 9.8). Another audience member saw the table and chairs in the kitchen as a torture room.

The Body, A Collective Repository

having explained how I approach memory in my practice, I will now look at how my body memory can act as a collective living archive, rather than a merely individual one. In order to do that, I will unfold the concept of archive and how the notion of a bodily archive, which I embrace, has emerged.

As previously noted, according to Foucault the archive is 'the general system of formation and transformation of statements'.[20] Foucault describes statements as units of enunciative function, which in oral or written language can be considered as a collection of signs, figures or marks, and defines the sum of these statements, which belong to the same system, a 'discourse'. He argues that the archive is an archaeological practice that allows discourse to emerge, enabling the statements both to survive and to transform. Derrida builds upon Foucault's thought, reflecting on the power of archive. He argues that 'there is no political power without control of the archive, if not of memory.'[21] Derrida considers the preservation of memory as the responsibility of the present and the promise of the future. In conversation with Freud's notions of the death drive, Derrida maintains that people suffer from an 'archive fever', a will to hold back death and forgetfulness by recording, repeating and recalling through texts, objects, data etc., which is the same way we archive, repress and remove memory in our bodies according to Freud's theory of memory and archive.

Linda Caruso Haviland[22] suggests that Foucault and Derrida have both contributed to the changing notion of the archive, allowing artists and scholars to consider the body as a cognitive system that can store, retrieve and transmit experiences and memories. Their take on the archive gave a certain openness to the possibility that knowledge can be embodied, therefore not only accessible through text, but also through physical states and actions. Thus, the body here can be considered as a repository of both knowledge acquired by lived experience and cognitive processes: a living archive informed by remnants of personal and cultural history and the ability to recognize, retrieve and perform its memories at unconscious and conscious levels.

Focusing on the connection between memory and archive, Derrida investigated the archive as a response to memory failure. In his work on the archive fever he analysed how the act of remembering involved a process of consigning, then retrieving and finally reproducing memories. His conception of the archive shed light on the subject and interrupted the ideas of objectivity traditionally attributed to the archive since ancient Greece, where it was conceived merely as a physical space where objects

[20] Foucault, *The Archeology of Knowledge*, 130.
[21] Derrida, 'Archive Fever', 11.
[22] Linda Caruso Haviland, 'Considering the Body as Archive', in *The Sentient Archive: Bodies, Performance, and Memory*, edited by Bill Bissell and Linda Caruso Haviland (Middletown: Wesleyan University Press, 2018), 1–21.

were organized. It also challenged the conventional role of the archivist, seen as a selected authority figure and gatekeeper of the archives, who after Derrida's work can now be considered as any individual active in the process of consigning, retrieving, reproducing and repeating, thus transforming and producing knowledge.

Laura Millar, a specialist in Archival Studies, also tries to understand the relationship between memory and archive by comparing the way memories and archives are created, stored and retrieved and investigating the concept of individual and collective memory.[23] She argues that humans see their memories belonging to the past, keep them in their brain, organize them in a certain order and retrieve them when needed, in a way similar to an archive, which belongs to the past and is kept in a storehouse where information is ordered in a certain way and retrieved when needed. The process of creating and later triggering a memory is selective; it comes with a sensation, a situation, a picture etc., similar to the process of archiving, where only some documents and narratives are acquired, preserved and made accessible. But Millar identifies an important difference between the two: memories are not static, rather when people remember old stories, they become clearer to them and may even undergo variations to the original, because the present emotions related to the past memory influence how they remember it today. This explains how memory is a process that involves emotions and where information is not merely copied into our brains and retrieved for future use, but is constantly transformed.

According to Millar, the role of emotions is absent in the physical archives, which makes them 'touchstones' of memories, rather than memories themselves. In that sense, by archiving we create pieces of evidence to allow us to remember. Also, Millar argues that when the records in the archive belong to another person's memory, they don't allow us to remember, but to know, acting as a device transforming individual memories into a collective remembering. Through this, individual memories are transmitted from one person to another, allowing the personal to become collective, creating a shared experience and collective memory. When members of the society have access to the lives of others they develop some understanding of the other and so a further sense of collectivity.[24]

Building on Foucault's theories of the ever-transforming archive, Derrida's investigation of the process of the archive in relation to memory,

---

[23] Laura Millar, 'Touchstones: Considering the Relationship between Memory and Archives', *Archivaria* 61 (2006): 105–126.
[24] Millar, 'Touchstones', 119–122.

and Millar's investigation of the relationship between individual and collective memory, I maintain that embodied memories play an important role in contributing to shared knowledge. Therefore, they should be well articulated, stored, made accessible and transmitted to other bodies, to the incipient and always transforming collectivity.

For this reason, What My Body Can/t Remember takes the form of an open practice of remembering, dealing with the body as an accessible archive that opens its doors to the audience. The recollections I use are not considered merely personal, but collective, in two ways. First, my individual recollections are part of the collective Palestinian experience under siege during the Second Intifada. They constitute painful collective moments that I reconstruct through my practice. Second, they become collective through their transmission throughout the performance to the other bodies that are situated in and share the same space.

In the performance, the audience are considered first as visitors of the archive, who enter the archive witnessing, experiencing and embodying in the present what has been said and done in the past, which might inform their actions in the future. Second, I conceive the audience as living archives themselves, subjects who carry embodied knowledge and are asked to connect with their own memories, experiences, and sense of oppression and resistance. The ultimate aim is to connect the latent Palestinian narratives and gestures under occupation to the international audience, creating a collective sense of empathy. In this sense, my archive is also an archive of the future, a way of triggering transnational solidarity that can help build a transnational future of justice.

Resisting the Ephemerality of Performance

In my research on gestural archives, I am exploring ways of creating a collective sense of solidarity by experimenting with different forms of disseminating and dispersing embodied memories to the public during the performance, so as to make that knowledge exteriorized, but also to allow it to survive beyond my body and the body of the other dancers, and after the performance finishes. Although some scholars, such as Peggy Phelan, argue that performance by definition is fleeting, transient and ephemeral and that it is realized only in the present and through its disappearance,[25] in my approach I take quite the opposite direction: how can we

---

[25] Peggy Phelan, *Unmarked: The Politics of Performance* (London: Routledge, 1993), 146–166.

consider a live performance as a living archive, which keeps on forming and transforming each time it appears in both the body of the performer and the audience? This is the key question driving my gestural archives.

When studying the knowledge creation and transmission of cultural tradition in Latin America, Diana Taylor suggests that performance is capable of transmitting embodied social knowledge and cultural memories, by leaving immaterial traces of memories and embodied knowledge from the performance experience in the audience.[26] Taylor considers the embodied memory as 'repertoire' and an extension of the material archive, which is made of stable objects. The transmitted repertoire offers another layer of knowledge, which parallels that of the material archive, and is able to leave behind tangible traces that can't be seen. Taylor's argument underlines the importance of the presence of the body in space and explains how that facilitates the embodied experience, while still considering the repertoire as ephemeral, unlike the archive. She argues that only the bones of human bodies can be considered as an archive because they carry embodied memory that endures in time; by this, she follows a habitual line of thought that defines the archive as merely material and sets fixed parameters as to how it functions.

As discussed earlier, in my research I argue that the living body is an archive, and I explore alternative methods of archiving through the body and transmitting the knowledge to other bodies through performance, allowing the continuity of the archive. As previously noted, in 'The Body as Archive: Will to Re-enact and the Afterlives of Dances', Lepecki explores the notion of the body as archive, investigating the role of the body as an archival site.[27] He analyses practices of re-enactment in dance, where the body functions as a medium for the re-enactment of past dances through archiving performances of others. By that, Lepecki bypasses the difference between the repertoire and the archive, explaining that the works archived through the body don't rest, but keep forming and transforming. He suggests that the interest of the artists in archiving stems from continued engagement with the works in the present, and creating a future for the old dance works, rather than creating an archive that is frozen to prevent a failure in cultural memory. By looking at the function of the archive from a different lens, Lepecki allows for the concept of *bodily archive* to emerge.

My research aims to push Lepecki's insights further. I don't re-enact historical dances, but instead experiment with ways of archiving hidden

[26] Taylor, *The Archive and the Repertoire*, 5–10.
[27] Lepecki, 'The Body as Archive', 28–48.

stories of the multiple narratives on Palestinian and refugee identity while re-enacting the gestures of those latent stories. For me, the bodily archive is a point of access for the ephemeral traces of the latent stories that are not archived in the material archive. The body plays the role of a privileged archival site, where a valuable and more-layered knowledge exists, in which affect and sensation, which cannot be replicated or accessed in physical archives, occupy a prominent space. In all four works, I experiment with ways of allowing the embodied archive to survive beyond my body and after the performance is finished through disseminating the knowledge to the audience members' bodies. Indeed, in the works the audience is invited to witness the gestures, re-enact them and contribute with their own gestures.

Conclusion

To physically appear and perform in public or private, as Butler argues, means that you are exposing yourself to others, therefore becoming vulnerable.[28] By inviting the audience to perform and expose themselves to gestural archives, I attempt to make them realize their own vulnerability and that of others through interactivity and live performance, acknowledging physically and emotionally that what is happening somewhere else in the world, could happen here, where they live or is even already happening. It is through bodily vulnerability, as Butler explains, that activism starts – 'I don't lose myself, but I accept to be transformed by the interdependency and vulnerability of others; thus, I begin to self-make and act in concert.'[29]

Furthermore, I believe that when an audience member embodies the transmitted gestures and translated stories into their own body, they enrich and enlarge their vocabulary of gestures and knowledge of the context where these gestures were performed, allowing the creation of new subjectivities. As Walter Benjamin suggests, translating from one language to another enriches the target language.[30] It adds to it the spirit of the source language, while also introducing to it new concepts, creating together a new transformed text. Benjamin suggests that translation not only allows people to understand the differences and similarities between languages, but also

---

[28] Butler, *Notes*, 1–23.
[29] Butler, *Notes*, 55–57.
[30] Walter Benjamin, 'The Translator's Task', translated by Steven Rendall, *TTR: traduction, terminologie, rédaction* 10, no. 2 (1997): 151–165.

Gestural Archives

how languages represent non-linguistic actions in a similar manner. This is essential in my work, as I aim to find connections between Palestinian gestures of resistance and those of others around the world.

The gestural transmission through the participatory element in my research is in conversation with Manning's concept of the minor gesture:[31] the living variation of experience that opens space for new ways of expression, allowing new tendencies to emerge by placing emphasis on experience and transforming everything into an event.

Manning suggests that the minor gesture is always political, because it awakens new ways of encounter and creates new ways of experiencing life together. It also helps the creation of the undercommons, a concept developed by Fred Moten and Stefano Harney as a collectivity born in the encounter with others.[32] They explain that the collectivity becomes a commons with time, not only because of existing together in the same space, but mostly because of the ecology of practices that the encounter generates. These are practices that aim to create conditions to reveal new ways of thinking and to understand not-solvable problems. In that sense, Manning suggests that the minor gesture allows individuals, who are in an ongoing process of self-constitution, to become researchers in the experience, led by intuition and moved by affect, activating the interval between past, present and future and invoking the *memory of the future*.[33] My research experiments with how moving–thinking together, through re-enacting, transmitting and embodying latent gestural archives, can contribute towards the creation of future responsibility.

---

[31] Manning, *The Minor Gesture*, 23.

[32] Fred Moten and Stefano Harney, *The Undercommons: Fugitive Planning and Black Study* (New York: Minor Compositions, 2013), 38–43.

[33] Manning, *The Minor Gesture*, 47.

PART III

'Translation at Large': Dialogues on Ethics and Politics

CHAPTER 10

'Translation Is Always Not Enough ...'

Gayatri Chakravorty Spivak in conversation with Avishek Ganguly

AG: I want to start off by asking what, according to you, are the stakes of translation today in the everyday, and in general.[1] And then, I would like to come to specifically the question of translation vis-à-vis theatre and performance.

GCS: What do you mean by stakes?

AG: OK, let me re-state this via the title of your most recent lecture on the topic of translation – the lecture you gave at Jamia Millia Islamia University in Delhi last month, 'What is it to translate?' today?

GCS: Did you come to the place where Harish Trivedi was trying to say that what I really was talking about was 'What is translation?' Did you go up to there?

AG: Yes, I saw that in the video recording of the lecture, and how you then corrected him by saying that what you were really talking about is 'what is it to translate?' and not 'what is translation?'.[2]

GCS: Good, because I am not interested in the onto-phenomenological question of defining something called 'translation'. Why did I say that? Because there is no such thing as the everyday. I mean the circumstances of the everyday are so diversified ... you can generalize if you are talking about something in the abstract but if you were asking what is it to translate? then it's no use trying to go the other way and define something like the everyday today. What are we really talking about? I mean in what language? I don't mean just named language but in what lingual memory is the subject placed so that the stakes can be defined? I think in terms of any idea of the everyday or any idea of today as a metaphor for this minute, *hic et nunc*, or broadly, since the electronification of the

[1] Interview conducted in Zürich, 18 April 2018.
[2] Fifth Floor, 'Prof Gayatri Chakravorty Spivak on "What is it to Translate?" Part-1'. YouTube video, 29:50, 21 February 2018, www.youtube.com/watch?v=NJ8TDXET5Qw

229

230 GAYATRI CHAKRAVORTY SPIVAK WITH AVISHEK GANGULY

stock exchanges, we really have to mark the question as a symptom coming from someone wanting to transcode academically for cultural work practice.

I would not want to answer it as a question but rather read it as a question. So that's just what I have done right now.

AG: I could not agree more with your reading of my question. But since you already brought up the idea of lingual memory in your response, I would like to move that forward from my list and ask: could you please elaborate how you use this concept of lingual memory? I know you have distinguished it from cultural memory in the past, and you have also talked about it in terms of something like underived memory, but I would like to know how you think about it in the context of translation.[3]

GCS: I am here helped by [Emmanuel] Lévinas with whose politics I am so uncomfortable ... I find it hard, being the kind of person I am, to use him but here I think he is the best person to turn to. He suggested that becoming human was to have access to a memory which is underived from anything, because there is nothing to remember. But the newly constituted subject is constituted by something called 'access to memory'. You see what I mean. So that is not really memory in the kind of literal sense, it is a catachrestic use of the word 'memory'; it's a function described. Now you can, however, find something like an empirical correlative for it, without any guarantees, because I am absolutely not relying here on the mind-brain theorists; I find that really useless because what we need here is poetry, not science. And poetry in an active sense, poetry as method. So, in fact that was my answer to your first question, which I read as a symptom rather than gave an answer to, and this is magnified manifold if you are talking about the scientific description of these things. Anyway, so we find an empirical correlative for this in the fact that language articulates itself in terms of a historicity within itself, which is not fully accessible to the individual using the language. [Émile] Benveniste – I may have mentioned him in the Jamia lecture – speaking about the Indo-European languages, but I believe this can be extended to other kinds of languaging, says that the fact that language means the possibility of the articulation of meaning – that this is something that is in the category of the transcendental, in the way in which [Immanuel] Kant uses the word 'transcendental', not

---

[3] Gayatri Chakravorty Spivak, 'Rethinking Comparativism', *New Literary History* 40, no. 3 (2009): 609–626.

'*Translation Is Always Not Enough ...*'

provable by law but absolutely necessary to be assumed in order for us to make sense of the fact that we are in language – also means that we get languaged. Again, of course, another way in which one can understand this empirically is the useful example of the mechanically digital – we can think of a memory that does not resemble the phenomenal remembering mechanism. When you 'learn' a language well, you may come to a place when you begin to sense the skeleton of the language as you read, listen, hear, speak, think. This, if you like, is the lingual memory lodged in the body of the language. You may begin, at this stage, to become your own lexicographer. Incidentally, I think we were given training in this as we were taught *shomash* as we learned Bengali, our mother tongue. It would be impossible to explain *shomash* in a footnote, do you realize that? Maybe someone could find something in Sanskrit grammars written in English, but Sanskrit is a classical language, spoken only by philosophers at Tirupati, whereas we are talking about children learning their mother tongue. And, relevant to the concept-metaphor of a lingual memory lodged in a body – although I think the relevance should be kept open here for people to think it through, in their diverse ways, depending on their situation – we remember that Derrida remarks in 'Che cos'è la poesia?' that you must kill the sound-body of the text as the initial sacrifice for translation.[4] This is not at all an exact quote, I am revising the Zürich manuscript sitting in locked-down Manhattan. And one can also go to [Sigmund] Freud's notion of the 'mnemic', that it is not necessarily just remembering what actually happened which is the function called mnemic. But for the Freud thing you have to look it up a little bit here or there.

AG: Do you remember where exactly Freud talks about this?

GCS: Well, I anticipated your question because I have not been working on Freud very recently. I think one very humble place to look is the *Dictionary of Psychoanalysis*. Look at 'memory' and see what they say.[5]

AG: There are a couple of things that immediately come to my mind from what you just said, so I will again skip the order in which I had initially thought about asking you these questions. First, regarding Benveniste's idea of language as a possibility of articulation of meaning ... I have been trying to think about the relationship between performance and translation in my

---

[4] Jacques Derrida, 'Che cos'è la poesia? [1988]', in *A Derrida Reader: Between the Blinds*, edited by Peggy Kamuf (New York: Columbia University Press, 1991), 221–237.

[5] Nandor Fodor, ed., *Freud: Dictionary of Psychoanalysis* (Redditch: Read Books Limited, [1950] 2013).

own work and recently I found myself re-reading your essay, 'The Politics of Translation', written more than twenty-five years ago now, and something that struck me there was how you begin with, and keep repeating at regular intervals, the idea that language is only one among many ways of making meaning. You talk about gestures, you talk about pauses …. So while you are not talking directly about performance, I have been wondering if these are some of the spaces in your theoretical architecture where we might be able to locate something like that – a concept of theatre or performance, maybe even of the performative, as a mode or medium which explicitly deals with ideas of agency and embodiment in terms of gestures and movements, say, or as an event that is tied up with the idea of liveness. Do you have any thoughts on that speculation?

GCS: Well, there I think I would go to Derrida's notion of 'spacing'; that what is important in understanding meaning is not the content of words and clusters of words but the spacing which allows the meaning to emerge through the articulation of sound and no-sound. You see that's why he talks about 'the work of death', because spacing is not full of words that are meaning-full. It would be difficult for someone … no, let me recast that sentence, it would be counter-intuitive for a theatre-thinker to understand the non-languaged parts of meaning-making as the work of death because you are used to not thinking that way. But to an extent, the possibility of interpreting texts is the work of death, so that there isn't a living text ever. So yes, I would say theatre is something that allows you to pay close attention to meaning-making possibilities of what I need to think of as the work of death because I am not the kind of person who has to think those good solid thoughts when it comes to theatre! You know what I mean. So yes, I therefore think that the possibility that theatre can always be different, that is for me its singularity: repeatable difference, right. I would probably say this is a much more complex cluster of ideas than simply thinking that it is in the performance. Performative, on the other hand, should not be used there because in the Austinian sense performative is 'how to do things with words', and that does not happen in theatre at all; in fact, it's exactly what is not happening in theatre, although imagining that it is happening is part of the theatre experience.[6] Even you and I, tremendously educated people [laughs], who when we go in to watch, we must in fact mingle with whatever sophistication we possess, the absolutely crude idea that this

---

[6] Austin, *How To Do Things with Words*.

is real. Not realistic, but crazily happening. Otherwise there is no theatre. So, it's like everything, like [G. W. F.] Hegel's *Phenomenology of Spirit*, which is an example of this but it happens in everything. The *Phenomenology* constantly warns against reading it as real but its structure and texture constantly ask even Hegel to read it as real. To an extent that is the theatre experience, and that's what makes the word 'performative' not useful. So, let's keep to the word performance, and the performance is carried by what I am calling that work of death. So, when people say 'Shakespeare really lives', we would say yes, because Shakespeare is dead. You know what I mean. The text is dead. That's why it can live, because it carries within it the fact of undoing it through that spacing mechanism. I hope this is not too complicated, because you know one has to really think about this. So yes, that's a useful way for me to think about it. And you see, theatre can do it whereas dance can't quite do it. Theatre actually is contaminated by both sides. Dance, to an extent, is more given over to trace – 'perhaps this means something' – than making meaning, if you know what I mean.

AG: Yes, I see how you are thinking about this. In fact, if we may take this contrast between theatre and dance that you just mentioned as an occasion to think a little more in terms of media, since that is also one of the ways we are trying to think through in this volume … because theatre or performance takes its place in more than one medium, do you think we could then begin to think of translation too as a kind of trans-medial or inter-medial act? Could re-routing translation thinking through performance or theatre open up that possibility?

GCS: But if that happens, then we must also be able to think that media is not part of meaning-making. See, the very wonderful first chapter of *Of Grammatology*, which I don't think I read correctly when I first read it … I mean when we are talking about informatics we are not talking about structures of making meaning, so therefore one should think more about the mediatic interventions … then we are talking about translation in the sense of transference, not psychoanalytic transference but the word 'carry' ….

AG: Right, carrying, transfer in the sense of bearing or carrying across ….

GCS: Yes, I mean meaning becomes … this is again annotating Benveniste as it were … Benveniste is more German classical philosophy … once we step into informatics – and Freud had a sense of that especially in *Beyond the Pleasure Principle* when the Ego is constituted from the Id as it were, a blip in the death drive, or in the unconscious, and [Jacques] Lacan is even more interesting here – we are not really talking about the making

234 GAYATRI CHAKRAVORTY SPIVAK WITH AVISHEK GANGULY

of meaning, we are talking about the mechanisms that seem to produce structures that seem to translate in that sense into signification. So that the first thing you remember is that picture in 'The Subversion of the Subject and the Dialectics of Desire', the consciousness is going round and round and round like a bicycle chain, and suddenly it clicks, something stops, signification emerges and produces the ground of the real; it's the drives that do it and a predication emerges, not necessarily 'correct': the dog says 'meow' and the cat says 'bow wow'.[7] That's the real. So, to an extent this entire poetry of Lacan, the imaginings of Freud, etc., go into this idea of the mediatic, informatics, and kind of annotate Benveniste in terms of that new perception that what is transcendental in the sense of Kant, in fact, may well be not meaningful but the possibility of meaning – *significance.* You should keep that in mind if you are thinking about media. It's not like translation in some nice metaphorical sense. I must say these are extremely interesting speculations. I am so glad you are asking me these questions because I don't have the time to put these down in writing but when someone asks me and I say something then I could edit it and it could become a part of the archive.

AG: Well, I am very glad that you think so, because as I mentioned these are some exploratory ways in which we are trying to move in this volume ... so it's really wonderful to have this conversation and to run some of these ideas by you. I do want to follow up with another question that relates directly to theatre before getting back to something else that you also mentioned in that thought-provoking lecture you gave at Jamia that we began with. This has to do with your translation of Aimé Césaire's play *A Season in the Congo*.[8] You added a foreword to that, a translator's note. But I want to hear about something that I felt was not addressed in that note. You have previously translated theory/non-fiction, prose fiction, devotional poetry, and songs, but this is the first time you have translated a play. Was there anything different in this instance? Do you have any reflections on the act of translating a theatrical text, a text meant for performance, keeping in mind the specificity of that form or genre?

GCS: You see, when I translate, I am not thinking. Yesterday at the Cabaret Voltaire I was talking about the distinction between ... because

---

[7] Jacques Lacan, *Écrits: A Selection*, translated by Bruce Fink (New York and London: W. W. Norton & Company, 2004), 281–312.

[8] Aimé Césaire, *A Season in the Congo*, translated by Gayatri Chakravorty Spivak (London and New York: Seagull Books, 2010).

they had wanted to know, it was very kind of them to put me in their 'Great Thinkers' series, and they had wanted to listen to me thinking. So, I distinguished between many things, but one of the things I began with was that thinking for me was a totally solitary thing because I am *in* thinking rather than thinking as a subject, if you know what I mean. And then I talked about different ways of clustering these kinds of activities and one of them was, of course, teaching. And I told them when I am teaching – as you know, I do not think I am a good teacher, that's my thing – but when I'm teaching, I'm just in it. It is taking me from here to there and what I'm really focusing on are the people in front of me so that they can respond in their way rather than me telling them this and that. So, to an extent it is hard for me to narrativize this, but on the other hand I do think about it later. So, in that mode I would say, it is the stage directions that really stand out; I mean, not directly during the activity so much, like I said I don't think, I am totally surrendered to what the text demands, I mean I am not making any … this comes out of practice, right? Maybe some people can do it normally, naturally, right away etc. but, as with my first experience of translation, I revised and re-did the whole translation of *De la Grammatologie* after it was completed. So that's what kind of gave it to me at first. Now thinking and re-thinking about it I would say it is the directions, and Césaire's use also … maybe this is true of all pieces, but this is the only one I have translated and you know how intimate one gets when one translates … his stage directions were really like epigraphs, they opened up to another intertextuality. I don't know if you have ever read a piece I had published in *Romanic Review* called 'Postcolonialism in France'….[9]

AG: I don't think I have.

GCS: Then I think you should try to access it because there I do talk about what is left out of Césaire. And I think that also is that work of death … the stage directions, I am thinking as I am talking about it, the work of death where the word 'death' is like a very different kind of word. Remember that piece 'Translation as Culture' where I mention how Melanie Klein talks about …

AG: … the work of translation as an incessant shuttle that constitutes a 'life'?

---

[9] Gayatri Chakravorty Spivak, 'Postcolonialism in France', *The Romanic Review* 104, nos. 3–4, (2013): 223–242.

GCS: Yes, there. Klein re-defines birth as death, which is really an extraordinary thing to do but it can't be re-defined fully as death, so it loses some of its phenomenal meaning. To an extent the stage directions are like that. This is what I was describing as the work of death which allows us to … See there is also something of Freud's which you ought to look at for this stuff – I can't give you the exact reference right now – it is the 'dream of the father's death', which Lacan also comments on. So, that 'dream of the father's death' is the continuation of life and legacy and you see that's what performance does in the sense of theatre, even where theatre is completely within an unwritten tradition, the oral-formulaic tradition … The oral-formulaic is mnemic writing. So that is something that would have to be brought in when one thinks about what was happening when I was translating theatre.

AG: Since this intriguing question of death as a condition of possibility of translation and reading and so many other things is coming up again and again, let me now ask you the question with which I had initially planned to open our conversation. And it takes us back to something really interesting that you said at Jamia, something at least I do not recollect you saying or writing about explicitly anywhere else in your body of work on translation so far, and also a point that resonated very much with our collaborative project in this volume. I want to go back to how translation takes place after the death of the sonic, or the phonic body of the text ….

GCS: Oh yes! The body … forget for a moment the sonic or the phonic, it is about the body …

AG: Yes, and that translation's first contribution is to kill the phonic (and phonetic?) body of the text?

GCS: Yes, but that is of Derrida – 'Che cos'è la poesia?' – it's in that thing as I said.

AG: So is this then a kind of new vector in your thinking on translation?

GCS: Well, Derrida has taught me many things, as I have always said, and I was very taken by that remark. It was as if I should have thought it, you know what I mean. It is in French but the title is Italian – 'What is Poetry?' That's something, isn't it?

AG: Yes, I found that a very striking thing to say and you go ahead and also talk about poetry in that lecture …

GCS: Oh yes, it is such an interesting thing to think about …

AG: I mean the idea, to walk under the shadow of its loss …

GCS: Whoa, yes! It is very, very moving. And also, you see, the idea that translation is always not enough. That it always points to something that you cannot have.

'*Translation Is Always Not Enough ...*' 237

AG: Absolutely.

GCS: Even if you had the body of the thing, that doesn't really ... again, that work of death is in the body. You see our, unfortunately Hindu, idea of *satkar* ... you know this idea of the body made *sat* in death ... otherwise it rots, but if you put it in fire it becomes *sat*, right? The *Haushaltung der Natur* will do it also.[10]

AG: Do you mean in the conventional sense of making pure?

GCS: Well, the Sanskrit word *sat* is not just about purification, that is a later imposition of meaning; It is 'being', the making *sat* of the body after death as in making it into being ... its true, correct being.

AG: So more along the lines of *sattva* (essence) than *satya* (truth) then?

GCS: Yes, so that is the death of the phonic body as also the death of the body. These are such important things to think about and theatre to an extent is an occasion for these thoughts, you know what I mean. It is not an end in itself. Remember all cultures are cultures of death. So, theatre celebrating the death of the real. In class I bring in Edgar and Lear ... there are so-called meaningless sounds there ....

AG: I think that is also how we are trying to approach theatre and performance in this volume, as an occasion to speculate on questions of sound, orality, aurality, gestures, the body ... I mean you do give the example of poetry on the one hand, you are reading aloud this nineteenth-century Bengali epic poem, *Meghanadavadha Kavya* (The Slaying of Meghanada), this remarkable re-telling by Michael Madhusudan Dutt, in verse, of a slice of *The Ramayana* from the point of view of its anti-heroes as it were, Meghanada and Ravana ....

GCS: That was funny, wasn't it?

AG: I thought it was a brilliant moment ... the performing of this sonorous epic-poetic text to illustrate theory!

GCS: And remember, that is also a sentence about death ... substitution.

AG: Yes, of course ... it begins *in medias res*, the opening verses, an invocation of the death in battle of the valiant warrior Birbahu ....

GCS: '*Paathaaila raney puna*' [পাঠাইলা রণে পুনঃ] – 'sent into battle, again' – repetition ....

AG: Absolutely. And you also spoke about the possibility of producing a Bengali-English bilingual, parallel text version, a Loeb Classical Library type edition, of this well-known text?

---

[10] George Gregory, *Haushaltung der Natur*, vol. 1 (Charleston, SC: Nabu Press, 2011).

238 GAYATRI CHAKRAVORTY SPIVAK WITH AVISHEK GANGULY

GCS: We are trying, the poet Sankha Ghosh and I are trying. Let's see.

AG: That sounds great. As I was saying, I was inspired by that moment of performance we were discussing earlier to think how we could maybe open up ways of theorizing sound and orality and aurality vis-à-vis translation, working back from theatre and performance, the question of loss, the death of the sonic ... all of those provocations. Now let me get to another thought that comes to my mind, staying with the question of the body but in a probably slightly different sense: when you showed the image of that silent young *birangana* woman who you said you had encountered when you were out working with your mother among the refugees of the Bangladesh War of Independence in 1971, you kept saying how she did not speak, how there was no way for you to read the image ... you were unable to read her ... in a sense then this was the figure of the first 'silent' subaltern for you, right?

GCS: Yes.

AG: So, I am wondering, is it too bold to suggest that from that *birangana* child to the figure of the young woman [Bhubaneswari Bhaduri] who commits suicide in 'Can the Subaltern Speak?' [CSS] decades later – that whole trajectory of your thinking about subalternity....[11]

GCS: It passes from subject to agent ....

AG: Right. But when you say that she was unable to translate herself into the world, are you entertaining, in the absence of either speech or writing, the idea of something like the ('silent') body being translated, the body in translation?

GCS: Yes, you are right but that's just my speculation. That's another thing, so that to an extent she, the child, kept the secret of subjectship without agency, if you see what I mean. And, on the other hand, Bhubaneswari [in CSS] was exactly the subaltern claiming agency, saying, 'you hear me...'.

AG: Not 'do you hear me?'?

GCS: No. 'You, hear me' – it's an imperative. Because my cousin, her intended audience and listener, didn't pick it up, I said in rage, 'the subaltern cannot speak'.

AG: I guess I am just trying to explore these various connections between ideas of subalternity, silence, the failure to be heard... while there was an imperative to listen, and then this image of the *birangana* child ... so, I am trying to think back and speculate if all of this taken together creates a kind of aural-visual pre-history of that moment in CSS.

---

[11] Spivak, 'Can the Subaltern Speak'.

'Translation Is Always Not Enough ...'

GCS: Well, you know one interesting thing is that I have never seen a picture of Bhubaneswari – there must be a photograph somewhere ... no, I am not sure if there is a photograph. On the other hand, I don't know what she looks like – so, there is no kind of death of the visual there as it were. And I want to insist that image is for me a limit to theorizing.

AG: That is very interesting. Continuing this discussion of bodies and translation, as you know questions of embodiment, the question of the body, come up in several ways in theatre and performance scholarship – so, I was wondering if you had any thoughts on the possibility of thinking ideas of translation and embodiment together?

GCS: No, because I don't read theatre theory and I probably would find notions of embodiment less interesting theoretically in my own work. I have great doubts about things like the immediacy of the body or the body even as ... I mean phenomenologically, the body does not exist. It's like the way Marx explains 'capital', there is no such thing; 'labour', there is no such thing. And I am very deeply committed to that way of thinking. Forms of appearance of the body are so different, you can't really ... embodiment, for me, and I'm saying again I do not read theatre theory so it is possible that there is something extremely cool out there that I am just not aware of, but embodiment for me, how shall I put it, the notion is pre-critical. It's the work of death I am talking about, so why would I want to ....

AG: Sure. I, too, get uncomfortable sometimes about the possible pre-critical nature of some of the concepts we work with when we talk about performance ....

GCS: I mean it is really the body as instrument there rather than embodiment ....

AG: And you are saying that its status is often under-theorized, as opposed to say something like textuality?

GCS: Well, I don't necessarily need it to be over-theorized. It's a bit like what happens with virtual reality. I mean the imagination is much more creative about virtuality than turning everything through the digital into a semblance of the empirical. That's exactly the kind of thing that happens because we cannot take the digital on the terms that it invites us to think. We have to transform it into a kind of previous semiotic in order to celebrate it. One thing I would say though, about epic performances – for instance, *kathakata* [storytelling] in India – there is no embodiment yet there is a semblance of embodiment; but everybody knows that there is an embodiment you see, and that's what makes it interesting. I guess that's all I can say.

AG: That's great, thank you. These are really all excellent points to think more about. I know we are nearing the end of our conversation but there's one thing I wanted to ask you before we finish. And that has to do with your thoughts on [performances of] *créolité*/creoleness; you have often talked about it in the context of the unsystematized, unwritten African languages, again with respect to the question of speaking and how they were taught, in the context of literacy, etc. So, I was wondering if you could tell us how your thinking on *créolité* has evolved and if there might be anything rich in there for theatre and performance folks to run with.

GCS: To an extent, if one thinks of history as *créolité* as it were ... as a noun, that which is not good ... I mean creolization is too cumbersome because then one thinks of the original, pure language, Sanskrit language, so it has to be some kind of word right in there ....

AG: Creology ....

GCS: Creoloss ... only half in jest! [laughs] But whatever that is, it is a theory of change. So, to an extent it brings us all the way back to that question of stakes, the everyday, etc., and why for me that question is symptomatic. Because ... do you remember that instance ... perhaps I have written about it somewhere ... when I was put on the Mayor's Committee in New York City to look at CUNY [City University of New York] ...?

AG: I remember you talking about it on a couple of occasions ....

GCS: Yes, because you were perhaps then a student at Columbia when I was actually doing that work ....

AG: I was.

GCS: So yes, we were asked to look at why 84 per cent of the incoming class at CUNY needed remedial English and so on ... so I went like an idiot because I didn't realize at that time that I was being used as 'well, we also consulted radical folks of color' – they had probably already made their decision by then, who knows, but I did go for one of the schools ... Lehman? Bunche? I forget which school it was in Manhattan Borough, where they had chosen this very upper class, very Americanized Taiwanese young woman, full of good intentions, but couldn't really deal with this class of West African students and Tillie Olson was being taught ... it was really a bizarre experience because I also could not interfere ... because I had so much more power than the poor Taiwanese young woman who was teaching that I couldn't tell her that 'hey come on, stop, listen, listen to what these students are saying ... don't try to turn them into New Critics.'

'Translation Is Always Not Enough ...'   241

So, their everyday, their stakes in that class ... where, in a limited sense, the attempt was being made to overcome *créolité*, right? And in their case, there was also creole, the West African ... Senegalese creole and so on. There you get a sense of the mixed empirical picture of what I was trying to say when I was reading that sentence. An attempt to generalize the subaltern as it were but the subaltern is not generalizable.

AG: Right.

GCS: So, therefore you have to admit that what happens when you start to think about *créolité*, its use in theatre, etc., that supplementation is dangerous because it really does bring in the incalculable. You have to really stand in front of it. Because when it is transformed into theatre in the technical sense, people buying tickets and so on, then no ... it is the incalculable that becomes contingent and escapes. So, therefore, we have to face that; the contingent as such, that's why the supplement is dangerous, it brings in the incalculable. I hope that was useful? Remember the unsystematized tongues of Africa are exactly not creole. And that the deliberate presentation of many languages in theatre is the creole's resistance to translation into the original.

AG: It is always useful to have a chance to talk to you about these things. I had one last question, a slight deviation from what we were discussing right now, but something you have mentioned earlier – the difference between the concepts of equivalence and equality, something that Étienne Balibar also talks about. How do we go about thinking that distinction with reference to the act of translation?

GCS: Yes, he was saying that the idea of equivalence was not a good idea, right? Like a philosopher, he was reading as he should, literally. Whereas I, like a literary person, was reading it literally as well as questioning literality because the logic is nestled in the rhetoric, right. So, what I would say is that since equality is not sameness, I mean that's exactly what we were talking about in terms of the danger of ... the incalculability, the demands of *créolité* in many different respects, the non-generalizability. Since equality is not sameness, different diachronies come into the question of citizenship where it becomes simply equivalent. We therefore have to think about equivalence because equality then becomes ... you take the metaphor simply as truth. Equivalence is the metaphoric. And therefore, if you can think of translation as the relationship between figuration and the figure that is called 'truth', it questions the idea that translation is efficient because it transports content – then it certainly is something that relates to translation. And something that I did not mention earlier, either at Jamia or at the India Habitat Centre talk in Delhi, because I have mentioned it many, many times before and it is not always useful to mention it, that the biggest industry of translation is – you have, of course, heard me say this before – the directions for using things ….

AG: Those multilingual instruction manuals … for IKEA products for instance, or medicines?

GCS: Yes. Also, all that DIY stuff. For those translations … the real rigor there is to undo the incalculable, remove it … I have talked to you about how it's done, right? Re-translated and then read again, etc. ….

AG: Yes. But isn't this also what the machine translation enthusiasts are attempting? …

GCS: Oh yes. And there the theatric confronts the question of the taxonomy shuttling between reproduction and representation, with interpretation hanging in somewhere, as well ….

AG: And they often quite openly acknowledge that their work doesn't have anything to do with literature or poetry ….

GCS: Yes, but it doesn't work. Why it doesn't work is precisely because translation is not what you must ask when you say what is at stake in the everyday. See I am bringing you back to that question. On the other hand, I mean sometimes it really doesn't work but sometimes it works but that working is not working. It's like sex and jerking off into a test tube because you are contributing your sperm … I mean I have friends who have been artificially inseminated, but it is and is not. One has to think about it because that translatability which is in the sexual encounter – which is very much in Freud and Lacan – that is in the definition of the human as inevitably self-inadequate, that is to say making more than it needs. Capital rises there, meaning rises there, mourning rises there, judgment rises there, so called libido inhabiting the sexual rises there. That is the libidinal economy, the economic rises there. So that's where you have to remember that although the biggest business … and you were also talking about the mechanical translators … is in that kind of usefulness, that is not what we will talk about in spite of everything. You know I was just in China and at the airport, where the limits of my Chinese were really tested … I was by myself … they did not know where Zürich was for example, they did not know in the domestic airport where Swiss Air was supposed to leave from … they were constantly translating on their phones and giving me instructions. So, our discussion here is put to the test in those kinds of situations. We somehow coasted through because I did know some Chinese.

'Translation Is Always Not Enough ...' 243

So Benveniste won, to an extent, rather than the mechanical translator. Because when nothing could happen, we come through with something or the other, you know what I mean?

AG: So it is the magic of the something or the other then!

GCS: It is indeed the magic of the something or the other – you've got it!

AG: That is a wonderful place to stop today. Thank you very much.

CHAPTER 11

Afterword
Can Translation Do Justice?

Sruti Bala

I write this afterword with a sense of distress in the face of the growing polarizations and rifts on the planet.[1] To think about the work of translation, about 'what it is to translate', as Gayatri Chakravorty Spivak phrases it, is, in the current moment, to think about whether and how translation can do justice. What are we asking when we ask of translation to do justice? The formulation tends to be commonly read as doing justice to the original, or 'living up' to the original, which raises questions about what originality is and what demands it places on translation as something that follows in its wake. It might be interpreted as a question of seeking equivalence. But these ways of reading the question imply translation is by definition never enough nor ever measures up to a standard that has been set before it arrives on the scene. The question 'can translation do justice?' becomes a rhetorical one, for the answer is inevitably no. The challenge is then one of pursuing the task of translation, knowing fully well that it is necessarily not enough, but necessary nonetheless, translation as catachresis, as Spivak suggests.[2] We might also read the question assuming some limited hope and scope, perhaps asking it as: 'what kind of justice is it that the work of translation might do?' Rephrased in this manner, we begin to notice how both the terms 'translation' and 'justice' are 'carried across' (in the etymological sense of trans-latio) from one terrain to another, shifting translation from its technical or formal to its ethical-political dimensions, shifting justice from the terrain of the quest for parity or alikeness (eye for an eye) to the terrain of repair, dignity, care, responsibility, a justice on terms that are yet to be ascertained. The question is not addressed to a particular instance of translation but to the work, the labour, the effort, the practice of translation itself.

[1] Parts of this text have been previously published in Sruti Bala, 'Necessary Misapplications: The Work of Translation in Performance in an Era of Global Asymmetries', *South African Theatre Journal* 32, no. 2 (2020): https://doi.org/10.1080/10137548.2020.1760126
[2] Gayatri Chakravorty Spivak, *An Aesthetic Education in the Era of Globalization* (Cambridge, MA: Harvard University Press, 2012), 242.

244

Afterword 245

For readers of this book it will be clear that the work of translation is not restricted to the linguistic, it encompasses a range of idioms and forms and urges us to consider translation as enmeshed in very local, as well as global and historical asymmetries. The work of translation is thus not about seeking equilibrium between languages or cultures or systems of thought, but about finding ways to acknowledge and carefully tune into asymmetries, in the hope of bridging them somewhere in the future.

We might thus speak of a particular translational attitude. When we say that text, story, or tune translate into body practices, images, gestures, movements, scenes, we use 'translation' in the sense of bringing one medium or site to bear upon another. We might imagine a way of shaping encounters and exchanges on stage by purposefully applying sensorial materials in ways that might be detached from their common, day-to-day usage. A piece of fabric can be endlessly interpreted on stage: a living being, a breeze, a splash of blood, or an indication of nightfall. When we as audience members view that piece of fabric on stage, we observe it with fresh attention to its material, sensorial qualities and to the ways it is used and positioned, not really detached, but bracketed as it were, from its 'original' functions in everyday life. We encounter the fabric with a heightened degree of awareness, sensing that what happens with it on stage is a process of translation. We give in to it, we imbue it with associations that seem, at first glance, to be our own, but which may take us into uncharted territories.

Obviously, such broad understandings of translation bear the danger of stubbornly remaining lofty metaphors and empty abstractions, attractive because of drawing so many different dimensions together, and messy and elusive for the very same reasons. To understand translation in performance as catachresis, necessary misapplication, implies several things. It is to acknowledge that unlike linguistic translation, which oftentimes theoretically presumes the symmetrical comparability of languages, translation from text to stage, or from one genre, cultural practice, or historical moment to another departs from an incommensurable relation between what is the 'source' and what is the 'target' language of translation, that is, where they cannot be measured in the same way. That is, somewhat different from the banal claim of untranslatability. Translation rather implies a shuttling back and forth between asymmetrically different terrains, each of which are of course also multiple and unstable. Rather than being a process of achieving equilibrium, in the sense that translation tends to be conceptualized in machinic translation systems, where a word is translated back and forth between languages until it is no longer modified, the

246   SRUTI BALA

laborious, untiring shuttling work of translation in performance requires
attending to how 'source' and 'target' differently impact upon each other
and can become co-present without being equal.

If translation in performance is bound to asymmetry and incommensurability, then questions of an ethical-epistemological order become prominent. This is another implication of thinking translation in a catachrestic
manner. How to give account, how to bear responsibility towards that
which is translated, for the sake of which the task of translation is being
undertaken? Such questions situate the pragmatic dimension of translational practice in tandem with broader socio-political concerns. Just as any
theory of language is implicitly also a theory of subject formation (consider for instance the close ties between speech act theory and embodied conceptions of the performative), one might argue that any theory
of translation is implicitly also a theory of inter-subjectivity. Reflecting
on translation is a way of reflecting on modes of encounter across differences, on self-reflection and self-transformation as resulting from the
attempt to 'cross over' to a standpoint or time entirely different from one's
own. This makes translation into a critical concept in theatre and performance, where, perhaps more than in any other art form, there is a systemic concern with how humans relate to each other and to non-human
others. In Walter Benjamin's translator's preface to his own rendering
of Baudelaire's Tableaux *Parisiens* (1921), it is the task of the translator
(*Aufgabe* in Benjamin's sense of both 'task' as well as 'being given unto',
sur-rendering) to respect and foreground the 'translatability' of the text,
its capacity to remain open to ever new possibilities of kinship between
languages.[3] Although Benjamin's enigmatic reflections tend towards the
metaphysical, they equally acquire a political, existential dimension. In
the face of the enormous challenges of planetary co-existence, the work of
translation is one of surrendering to the traces and spaces of later recall that
are already stored or available in that which is to be translated. This is how
I relate to Spivak's reference to Freud's mnemic trace in the interview in
this volume (Chapter 10 [page 231, this volume]). The translator must learn
to not only look for ways of actively recalling the traces, but also be open
to those triggers that space out into a chain of associations that activate
mnemic traces (*Erinnerungsspuren*) that connect texts in unknown ways,
thus a kind of attempt to do justice by examining hard-wired defence

---

[3] Walter Benjamin, 'The Task of the Translator: An Introduction to the Translation of Baudelaire's
Tableaux Parisiens [1921]', in *Illuminations*, edited by Hannah Arendt, translated by Harry Zohn
(London: Pimlico, 1999), 70–82.

Afterword 247

mechanisms and habits. The terms 'translation' and 'justice' here do not quite fit, but they can nevertheless not easily be substituted by other terms, for their misapplication is a necessary part of the task of translation.

The call for justice is loudest when justice is absent or when injustice has been done. Perhaps we ask if translation can do justice, because translation has historically done so much injustice. So, it is not only the injustice that needs to be addressed, but also translation's own complicity in it. It required the work of translation to imbue the imperial project with the interpretation of being a civilizational mission. Without translational practices, it would not have been possible to turn development into teleological progress, or nature into resource, or woman into commodity, or God into an excuse. And no doubt, theatre and its institutions have played their part too in setting the stage for all these injustices to become possible. Perhaps this is one way to locate Spivak's call, following Derrida, to think theatre and performance as 'the work of death' (Chapter 10 [page 233, this volume]). To ask if translation can do justice, there must be a recognition that the work of translation is also a part and parcel of the machinery of euphemism generation or ideological repurposing. It is about doing justice with one hand and injustice with the other. Or formulated in a possibly more hopeful manner, about a collective practice of trying to be truthful and showing integrity and cutting through the crap in an era of lies.

Works Cited

Ahmad, Dohra. *Rotten English: A Literary Anthology*. New York: W. W. Norton, 2007.

Ahmady, Leeza, Iftikhar Dadi, and Reem Fadda, eds. *Tarjama/Translation: Contemporary Art from the Middle East, Central Asia, and Their Diasporas*. New York: Arte East, 2009.

Ahmed, Sara. *Strange Encounters: Embodied Others in Postcoloniality*. London: Routledge, 2000.

Alazzeh, Ala. 'Seeking Popular Participation: Nostalgia for the First Intifada in the West Bank'. *Settler Colonial Studies* 5, no. 3 (2015): 1–17.

Alexander, Alfred. *Giovanni Verga: A Great Writer and his World*. London: Grant and Cutler, 1972.

Allen, Esther and Susan Bernofsky, eds. *In Translation*. New York: Columbia University Press, 2013.

Alonge, Roberto. *Teatro e spettacolo nel secondo Ottocento*. Rome: Laterza, 1988.

Anzaldúa, Gloria. *Borderlands/La Frontera: The New Mestiza*. San Francisco: Aunt Lute, 1987.

Appadurai, Arjun. *Modernity at Large: Cultural Dimensions of Globalization*. Minneapolis: University of Minnesota Press, 1996.

Apter, Emily. *Against World Literature: On the Politics of Untranslatability*. London: Verso, 2013.

Apter, Emily. 'Armed Response: Translation as Judicial Hearing'. *e-flux* 84 (2017). www.e-flux.com/journal/84/149339/armed-response-translation-as-judicial-hearing/.

Apter, Emily. 'Translation at the Checkpoint'. *Journal of Postcolonial Writing* 50, no. 1 (2014): 56–74.

Apter, Emily. *The Translation Zone: A New Comparative Literature*. Princeton: Princeton University Press, 2006.

Apter, Emily. 'What Is Just Translation?' *Public Culture* 33, no. 1 (2021): 89–111.

Archer, William. *The Theatrical 'World' of 1893*. London: Walter Scott, 1893.

Archer, William. *The Theatrical 'World' of 1894*. With an Introduction by George Bernard Shaw, and a Synopsis of Playbills of the Year by Henry George Hibert. London: Walter Scott, Ltd, 1895.

Arendt, Hannah. 'Introduction into Politics'. In *The Promise of Politics*, edited by Jerome Kohn, 93–200. New York: Schocken Books, 2005.

Works Cited

Arrojo, Rosemary. *Fictional Translations: Rethinking Translation through Literature*. London: Routledge, 2018.

Austin, John Langshaw. *How To Do Things with Words*, 2nd ed. Cambridge: Cambridge University Press, 1975.

Bailey, Richard W. *Speaking American: A History of English in the United States*. Oxford: Oxford University Press, 2012.

Baines, Roger, Cristina Marinetti, and Manuella Perteghella. eds. *Staging and Performing Translation: Text and Theatre Practice*. Basingstoke: Palgrave Macmillan, 2011.

Baker, Mona. *Translation and Conflict: A Narrative Account*. London: Routledge, 2018.

Bakhtin, Mikhail Mikhaïlovich. *The Dialogic Imagination: Four Essays*, edited by Michael Holquist, translated by Caryl Emerson and Michael Holquist. Austin: University of Texas Press, 1981.

Bala, Sruti. 'Necessary Misapplications: The Work of Translation in Performance in an Era of Global Asymmetries'. *South African Theatre Journal* 33, no. 1 (2020): 5–13. https://doi.org/10.1080/10137548.2020.1760126.

Balasubramanian, Harshadha. 'Not Just Images: Other Ideas of Vision in Audio Description of Live Theatre'. The Art of Access, Young Vic Theatre, London, 21 October 2016. https://backdoorbroadcasting.net/2016/10/audio-description-the-art-of-access/.

Bandia, Paul F. *Translation as Reparation: Writing and Translation in Postcolonial Africa*. Manchester, UK and Kinderhook, NY: St. Jerome Publishing, 2008.

Bang, Herman. 'Menschen und Masken'. In *Eleonora Duse: Bildnisse und Worte*, edited by Bianca Segantini and Francesco von Mendelssohn, 64–75. Berlin: Kaemmerer, 1926.

Bassnett, Susan. 'Eleonora Duse'. In *Bernhardt, Terry, Duse: The Actress in her Time*, edited by John Stokes, Michael R. Booth, and Susan Bassnett, 119–170. Cambridge: Cambridge University Press, 1988.

Bassnett, Susan. *Translation Studies*. London: Routledge, 2013.

Bassnett, Susan and David Johnston. 'The Outward Turn in Translation Studies'. *The Translator* 25, no. 3 (2019): 181–188.

Bassnett, Susan and André Lefevere. *Constructing Cultures: Essays on Literary Translation*. Clevedon, UK and Philadelphia: Multilingual Matters, 1998.

Bay-Cheng, Sarah. 'Translation, Typography, and the Avant-Garde's Impossible Text'. *Theatre Journal* 59, no. 3 (2007): 467–483.

Bay-Cheng, Sarah, Jennifer Parker-Starbuck, and David Z. Saltz. eds. *Performance and Media: Taxonomies for a Changing Field*. Ann Arbor: University of Michigan Press, 2015.

Beard, Mary. *The Roman Triumph*. Cambridge, MA: Harvard University Press, 2009.

Benjamin, Walter. 'The Task of the Translator: An Introduction to the Translation of Baudelaire's Tableaux Parisiens [1921]'. In *Illuminations,* edited by Hannah Arendt, translated by Harry Zohn, 70–82. London: Pimlico, 1999.

Benjamin, Walter. 'The Translator's Task'. Translated by Steven Rendall. *TTR: traduction, terminologie, redaction* 10, no. 2 (1997): 151–165.

Works Cited

Bergen, Benjamin K. and, Ting Ting Chan Lau. 'Writing Direction Affects How People Map Space onto Time'. *Frontiers in Psychology* 3 (2012): 109. https://doi.org/10.3389/fpsyg.2012.00109.

Bergvall, Caroline. *Drift*. New York: Nightboat Books, 2014.

Bergvall, Caroline. 'DRIFT excerpt 1 2013'. Vimeo video, 2:28. November 12, 2013. https://vimeo.com/79202631.

Bergvall, Caroline. *Fig*. Cambridge: Salt Publishing, 2005.

Bergvall, Caroline. 'Hafville (submerged voice)'. Soundcloud Audio, 5:27. February 24, 2015. https://soundcloud.com/carolinebergvall/hafville.

Bergvall, Caroline. *Meddle English: New and Selected Texts*. New York: Nightboat Books, 2011.

Bermann, Sandra. 'Performing Translation'. In *A Companion to Translation Studies*, edited by Sandra Bermann and Catherine Porter, 285–297. Oxford: Wiley-Blackwell, 2014.

Bermann, Sandra and Catherine Porter. eds. *A Companion to Translation Studies*. Chichester: John Wiley and Sons, 2014.

Bermann, Sandra and Michael Wood, eds. *Nation, Language, and the Ethics of Translation*. Princeton and Oxford: Princeton University Press, 2005.

Bessière, Jean and Jean-Marc Moura, eds. *Littératures postcoloniales et francophonie*. Paris: Champion, 2001.

Bhabha, Homi. *The Location of Culture*. London: Routledge, 2006 [1994].

Bigliazzi, Sivia, Peter Kofler, and Paola Ambrosi eds. *Theatre Translation in Performance*. New York: Routledge, 2013.

Blazina, Sergio. *La mano invisibile: Poetica e procedimenti narrativi del romanzo verghiano*. Turin: Tirrenia, 1989.

Bleeker, Maaike. *Visuality in the Theatre: The Locus of Looking*. Basingstoke, UK: Palgrave Macmillan, 2011.

Boniecki, Edward. *Modemistyczny dramat ciala: Maria Komornicka*. Warszawa: Instytut Badań Literackich PAN, 1998.

Borduas, Paul-Émile, et.al. *Refus Global*. Shawinigan: Anatole Brochu, 1972 [1948].

Boroditsky, Lera. 'Does Language Shape Thought?: Mandarin and English Speakers' Conceptions of Time'. *Cognitive Psychology* 43 (2001): 1–22.

Bosworth, Joseph. *An Anglo-Saxon Dictionary Online*. Edited by Thomas Northcote Toller, Christ Sean, and Ondřej Tichy. Prague: Faculty of Arts, Charles University, 2014. https://bosworthtoller.com.

Both Sides, Now: Living Well, Leaving Well. 'About Both Sides, Now'. Accessed April 2, 2018. www.bothsidesnow.sg/about/html.

Boym, Svetlana. *The Future of Nostalgia*. New York: Basic Books, 2002.

Boym, Svetlana. 'The Future of Nostalgia'. In *The Svetlana Boym Reader*, edited by Cristina Vatulescu, et al., 217–276. New York: Bloomsbury Academic, 2018.

Brater, Enoch. 'Beckett "Thou Art Translated."' In *Theatre Translation in Performance*, edited by Silvia Bigliazzi, Peter Kofler, and Paola Ambrosi, 130–139. New York: Routledge, 2013.

Brière, Eloise A. 'Quebec and France: *La Francophonie* in A Comparative Post-colonial Frame'. In *Postcolonial Theory and Francophone Literary Studies,* edited by H. Adlai Murdoch and Anne Donadey, 151–174. Gainville: University Press of Florida, 2005.

British Library Newspaper Archive. Accessed January 2, 2018. www.britishnewspaperarchive.co.uk.

Brodie, Geraldine. *The Translator on Stage.* New York and London: Bloomsbury, 2017.

Brodie, Geraldine, and Emma Cole, eds. *Adapting Translation for the Stage.* New York and London: Routledge, 2017.

Brodkin, Karen. *How Jews Became White Folks and What That Says about Race in America.* New Jersey: Rutgers University Press, 1999.

Bussels, Stijn. *Spectacle, Rhetoric and Power: The Triumphal Entry of Prince Philip of Spain Into Antwerp.* Amsterdam: Rodopi, 2012.

Butler, Judith. *Bodies That Matter.* New York and London: Routledge, 1993.

Butler, Judith. *Excitable Speech: A Politics of the Performative.* London and New York: Routledge, 1997.

Butler, Judith. *Gender Trouble: Feminism and the Subversion of Identity.* London and New York: Routledge, 2015.

Butler, Judith. *Notes toward a Performative Theory of Assembly.* Cambridge: Harvard University Press, 2015.

Butler, Judith. *Parting Ways: Jewishness and the Critique of Zionism.* New York: Columbia University Press, 2012.

Capuana, Luigi. *Teatro dialettale siciliano,* 3 vols. Palermo: Alberto Reber, 1911–1912.

CargoRecordsGermany. 'The Original Last Poets – Die Nigga!!!' *YouTube video,* 3:17. February 16, 2015. www.youtube.com/watch?v=plcKB8H9jYY.

Carlson, Marvin. *The Haunted Stage: The Theatre as Memory Machine.* Ann Arbor: University of Michigan Press, 2003.

Carlson, Marvin. *The Italian Shakespearians: Performances by Ristori, Salvini, and Rossi in England and America.* Washington: The Folger Shakespeare Library, 1985.

Cassin, Barbara. *La nostalgie: Quand donc est-on chez soi?* Paris: Éditions Autrement, 2013.

Cassin, Barbara. 'Sophistics, Rhetorics, and Performance: Or, How to Really Do Things with Words'. Translated by Andrew Goffey. *Philosophy and Rhetoric* 42, no 4 (2009): 349–372.

Cassin, Barbara, ed. *Philosopher en langues: les intraduisibles en traduction.* Paris: Éditions Rue d'Ulm/Presses de l'École normale supérieure, 2014.

Castellani, Arrigo. 'Quanti erano gl'italofoni nel 1861?' *Studi linguistici italiani* 8 (1982): 3–26.

Cavallo, Amelia. 'Audio Description: Ramps on the Moon'. *Exeunt,* June 27, 2016. http://exeuntmagazine.com/features/audio-description-ramps-moon.

Ceffino, Zanobio. *Die blijde en[de] triumpha[n]te incoe[m]ste des aldermoghensten [...] Heere Kaerle van Oostenrijcke en[de] van Spaingen [...] Rooms keyser die vijfste van*

252   *Works Cited*

die[n] name [...] geschiet de[n] v. dach in april binnen Roome[n] anno xv.c.xxxvi. Antwerpen (Antwerp): Jacob van Liesvelt, 1536.

Ceffino, Zanobio. *Ein Sendbrieff, so der edel Herr Zanobio Ceffino, dem druchleuchtigen Fürsten unnd Herrn, Hertzogen zu Florentz, dem triumphlichen einzug deß aller durchleuchtigisten, großmechtigisten Römischen Keyser, Caroli des Fünfften ... ordentlich zugeschriben Mit allem fleiß auß Welsch ins Teutsch gebracht.* Straßburg: Frölich, 1536.

Ceffino, Zanobio. *La triumphante entrata di Carlo V. imperatore augusto innelalma citta de Roma : con el significato delli archi triomphali [et] delle figure antiche,* in prosa [et] versi latini. [Rome]: s.n., 1536.

Ceffino, Zanobio. *La triumphante entree de lempereur nostre sire Charles le cincquieme tousjours auguste, faicte en sa tres noble cite de Rome, avec ses significations des epitaphes triumphantz & figures auctenticques &c.* Antwerp: Johannes Steelfius, 1536.

Césaire, Aimé. *Notebook of a Return to the Native Land.* Translated by Clayton Eshleman and Annette Smith. Middletown, CT: Wesleyan University Press, 2001.

Césaire, Aimé. *A Season in the Congo.* Translated by Gayatri Chakravorty Spivak. London and New York: Seagull Books, 2010.

Cheng, C. 'Language reform'. In *Language and Linguistics in the People's Republic of China,* edited by W. Lehmann, 41–54. Austin: University of Texas Press, 1975.

Choi, Don Mee. *DMZ Colony.* Seattle: Wave Books, 2020.

Chow, Andrew R. '*Parasite*'s Best Picture Oscar Is Historic. Is This the Beginning of a New Era in Film?' *Time,* February 9, 2020. https://time.com/5779940/parasite-best-picture-oscars/.

Chow, Rey. *Not Like a Native Speaker: On Languaging as a Postcolonial Experience.* New York: Columbia University Press, 2014.

Cixous, Hélène. *Three Steps on the Ladder of Writing.* Translated by S. Cornell and S. Sellers. New York: Columbia University Press, 1993.

Clochette. 'Vive la France de Mohamed Rouabhi', February 29, 2008. http://passiondeslivres.over-blog.com/article-17196493.html. Accessed April 9, 2020.

Coates, Ta-Nehisi. *Between the World and Me.* Melbourne: Text Publishing, 2015.

Conroy, Colette. *Theatre & The Body.* Basingstoke: Palgrave, 2010.

Cooke, Dervila. 'Hybridity and Intercultural Exchange in Marco Micone's "Le figuier enchanté."' *The French Review* 84, no. 6 (2011): 1160–1172.

Cooper, Richard. 'French Royal Entries and the Antique (1515–65)'. In *Writing Royal Entries in Early Modern Europe,* edited by Marie-Claude Canova-Green, Jean Andrews, and Marie-France Wagner. Turnhout: Brepols, 2013.

Cronin, Michael. *Translation and Identity.* London: Routledge, 2006.

D'Amico, Alessandro. 'Il teatro verista e il *grande attore*'. In *Il teatro italiano dal naturalismo a Pirandello,* edited by Alessandro Tinterri, 25–46. Bologna: Il Mulino, 1990.

Davis, Kathleen. 'Time Behind the Veil: The Media, the Middle Ages, and Orientalism Now'. In *The Postcolonial Middle Ages,* edited by Jeffrey Jerome Cohen, 105–122. New York: Palgrave, 2000.

De Felice, Francesco. *Storia del teatro siciliano.* Catania: Gianotta, 1956.

Works Cited

De Francisci, Enza. 'Eleonora Duse in *Cavalleria Rusticana*: Santuzza on the London Stage'. *Italian Studies* 69, no. 1 (2014): 95–110.

De Francisci, Enza. 'Giovanni Grasso: The Other Othello in London'. In *Shakespeare, Italy, and Transnational Exchange: The Early Modern Period to the Present*, edited by Enza De Francisci and Chris Stamatakis, 195–207. New York-London: Routledge, 2017.

De Francisci, Enza. *A 'New' Woman in Verga and Pirandello: From Page to Stage*. Oxford: Legenda, 2018.

De Francisci, Enza. 'Verga and Duse: A Silent Partnership in Cavalleria rusticana and In portineria'. In *Eleonora Duse and Cenere (Ashes): Centennial Essays*, edited by Maria Pia Pagani and Paul Fryer, 41–55. Jefferson, North Carolina: McFarland and Company, Inc., 2017.

De Francisci, Enza. 'Verga and Duse: Transposing Silence in "Il Canarino Del n. 15" and *In Portineria*: A Prelude to Symbolism?' *The Italianist* 34, no. 1 (2014): 73–87.

De Grazia, Margreta, 'The Modern Divide: From Either Side'. *Journal of Medieval and Early Modern Studies* 37 (2007): 453–467.

Deleuze, Gilles, and Félix Guattari. *Capitalisme et schizophrénie 2: Mille Plateaux*. Paris: Les éditions de minuit, 1980.

Deleuze, Gilles, and Félix Guattari. *Kafka: Toward a Minor Literature*. Translated by Dana Polan. Minneapolis: The University of Minnesota Press, [1975] 1986.

Deleuze, Gilles, and Claire Parnet. *Dialogues*. Paris: Champs essais, 1996.

Delgado, Maria M., Bryce Lease and Dan Rebellato, eds. *Contemporary European Playwrights*. London: Routledge, 2020.

De Mauro, Tullio. *Storia linguistica dell'Italia unita*. Rome: Laterza, 1995.

Derrida, Jacques. 'Archive Fever: A Freudian Impression', translated by Eric Prenowitz. *Diacritics* 25, no. 2 (1995): 9–63.

Derrida, Jacques. 'Che cos'è la poesia? [1988]'. In *A Derrida Reader: Between the Blinds*, edited by Peggy Kamuf, 221–240. New York: Columbia University Press, 1991.

Derrida, Jacques. *De la grammatologie*. Paris: Éditions de Minuit, 1967.

Derrida, Jacques. 'Des Tours de Babel'. In *Difference in Translation*, edited and translated by Joseph F. Graham, 165–207. Ithaca: Cornell University Press, 1985.

Derrida, Jacques. *Of Grammatology*. Translated by Gayatri Chakravorty Spivak. Baltimore: Johns Hopkins University Press, [1976] 1997.

Derrida, Jacques. *Le monolinguisme de l'autre: ou la prothèse d'origine*. Paris: Éditions Galilée, 1996.

Derrida, Jacques. *Monolingualism of the Other; or, The Prosthesis of Origin*. Translated by Patrick Mensah. Stanford: Stanford University Press, 1998.

De Roberto, Federico. *Casa Verga e altri sagi verghiani*. Edited by Carmelo Musumarra. Florence: Le Monnier, 1964.

Diagne, Souleymane Bachir. *African Art as Philosophy: Senghor, Bergson and the Idea of Negritude*. Translated by Chike Jeffers. Calcutta: Seagull Books, [2007] 2011.

Diamond, Elin. 'Brechtian Theory/Feminist Theory'. *The Drama Review* 32, no. 1 (1988): 82–94.

254 *Works Cited*

D'Innella, Annalisa. 'The Way I See It: Living with Partial Blindness'. *The Guardian*, November 14, 2016. www.theguardian.com/lifeandstyle/2016/nov/14/the-way-i-see-it-living-with-partial-blindness-rp.

Djebar, Assia. *Ces voix qui m'assiègent: en marge de ma francophonie*. Paris: A. Michel, 1999.

Dolan, Jill. *Utopia in Performance: Finding Hope at the Theater*. Ann Arbor: University of Michigan Press, 2005.

Dove, Rita. *Selected Poems*. New Delhi: Hemkunt Press, 1993.

Drewniak, Łukasz. 'Śmierć Fredrom I Mrożkom'. *Przekrój* 10, March 9, 2012.

Dürer, Albrecht. *Maximilian's Triumphal Arch: Woodcuts*. New York and London: Dover Publications; Constable, 1972.

Eardley, A. F., R. Hutchinson, L. Fryer, M. Cock, P. Ride, and J. Neves. 'Editorial: The Protests Are Not Just anti-CAA, but Pro-Constitution'. *The Wire*, December 31, 2019. https://thewire.in/rights/india-citizenship-protests-democracy-constitution-caa.

Eardley, A. F., R. Hutchinson, L. Fryer, M. Cock, P. Ride, and J. Neves. 'Enriched Audio Description: Working towards an Inclusive Museum Experience'. In *Inclusion, Disability and Culture*, Inclusive Learning and Educational Equity, vol. 3, edited by S. Halder and L. C. Assaf, 195–207. Basel: Springer International Publishing, 2017.

Edmond, Jacob. '"Let's Do a Gertrude Stein on It": Caroline Bergvall and Iterative Poetics'. *Journal of British and Irish Innovative Poetry* 3 (2011): 37–50.

Edwards, Brent Hayes. *The Practice of Diaspora: Literature, Translation, and the Rise of Black Internationalism*. Cambridge, MA: Harvard University Press, 2003.

Emmerich, Karen. *Literary Translation and the Making of Originals*. New York and London: Bloomsbury, 2017.

Evans, David A. H., ed. *Hávamál*. London: Viking Society for Northern Research, 1986.

Fanon, Frantz. *Black Skin, White Masks*. Translated by Charles Lam Markmann. New York: Grove, 1967.

Fanon, Frantz. *Black Skin, White Masks*. Translated by Richard Philcox. New York: Grove, 2008.

Fanon, Frantz. *Les damnés de la terre*. Paris: La Découverte, 2002.

Fanon, Frantz. *Peau noire, masques blancs*. Paris: Seuil, 1952.

Fanon, Frantz. *The Wretched of the Earth*. Translated by Constance Farrington. New York: Grove, 1968.

Faulkner, William. *Intruder in the Dust*. New York: Vintage Books, 1972.

Faulkner, William. *Requiem for a Nun*. London: Vintage, 2015.

Feldman, Lada Čale and Marin Blažević. 'Translate, or Else: Marking the Glocal Troubles of Performance Research in Croatia'. In *Contesting Performance: Global Sites of Research*, edited by Jon McKenzie and Heike Roms, 168–187. Basingstoke: Palgrave Macmillan, 2009.

Works Cited

Ferguson, Charles Albert. *Socio-Linguistic Perspectives: Papers on Language in Society 1959–1994*. Edited by Thom Huebner. Oxford: Oxford University Press, 1996.

Ferguson, Margaret, Mary Jo Salter, and Jon Stallworthy, eds. *The Norton Anthology of English Literature*, 5th ed. New York: W.W. Norton and Co., 2005.

Fifth Floor. 'Prof Gayatri Chakravorty Spivak on "What is it to Translate?" Part-1'. *YouTube video*, 29:50. February 21, 2018. www.youtube.com/watch?v=NJ8TDXET5Qw

Filipiak, Izabela. *Obszary odmienności: Rzecz o Marii Komornickiej*. Gdańsk: Słowo/Obraz Terytoria, 2006.

Fleishman, Mark, and Sruti Bala. 'Translation and Performance in an Era of Global Asymmetries'. *South African Theatre Journal* 32, no. 1 (2019): 1–5.

Flusser, Vilém. *Gestures*. Translated by Nancy Ann Roth. Minneapolis: University of Minnesota Press, 2014.

Fodor, Nandor, ed. *Freud: Dictionary of Psychoanalysis*. Redditch: Read Books Limited, [1950] 2013.

Foucault, Michel. *The Archaeology of Knowledge and the Discourse on Language*. Translated by A. M. Sheridan Smith. New York: Pantheon Books, 1972.

Foucault, Michel. 'The Philosophical Scene: Foucault interviewed by Moriaki Watanabe'. Translated by Robert Bononno. In *Foucault's Theatres*, edited by Tony Fisher and Kélina Gotman, 221–238. Manchester: Manchester University Press, 2020.

Fryer, Louise. 'The Independent Audio Describer Is Dead: Long Live Audio Description!' *Journal of Audiovisual Translation*, 1(1) (2018), 170–186.

Fryer, Louise. Keynote speech, The Art of Access, Young Vic Theatre, London, October 21, 2016. https://backdoorbroadcasting.net/2016/10/audio-description-the-art-of-access/.

Fumagalli, Giuseppe. *Chi l'ha detto?* Milan: Ulrico Hoepli, 1989.

Fusero, Clemente. *Eleonora Duse*. Milan: Dall'Oglio editore, 1971.

Ganguly, Avishek. 'Border Ethics: Translation and Planetarity in Spivak'. *Intermédialités/Intermediality* 34 (2019). https://doi.org/10.7202/1070871ar.

Ganguly, Avishek. 'Five Theses on Repair in Most of the World'. In Markus Berger and Kate Irvin eds., *Repair: Sustainable Design Futures*, 15–17. London and New York: Routledge, 2022.

Ganguly, Avishek. 'Global Englishes, Rough Futures'. In *Nicoline van Harskamp, My Name Is Language*, 21–40. Berlin: Archive Books, 2020.

Gauvin, Lise. 'Entre Rupture Et Affirmation: Les Manifestes Francophones'. *Études littéraires africaines* 29 (2010): 7–14. https://doi.org/10.7202/1027490ar.

Glissant, Édouard. 'Beyond Babel'. *World Literature Today* 63, no. 4 (1989): 561–564.

Glissant, Édouard. *Caribbean Discourse: Selected Essays*. Translated by Michael Dash. Charlottesville: University Press of Virginia, 1989.

Glissant, Édouard. *Le discours antillais*. Paris: Éditions Gallimard, 1997.

Glissant, Édouard. 'L'imaginaire des langues'. In *L'imaginaire des langues: Entretiens avec Lise Gauvin (1991–2009)*, 11–34. Paris: Éditions Gallimard, 2010.

Works Cited

Glissant, Édouard. *Poetics of Relation*. Translated by Betsy Wing. Ann Arbor: University of Michigan Press, 1997.

Glover, Kaiama L. '"Blackness" in French: On Translation, Haiti, and the Matter of Race'. *L'Esprit Créateur* 59, no. 2 (Summer 2019): 25–41.

Godden, Malcolm, ed. and trans., *An Old English History of the World: An Anglo-Saxon Rewriting of Orosius*. Cambridge, MA: Harvard University Press, 2016.

Gotman, Kélina. 'On the Difficult Work of Translating Translation; or, The Monolingualism of Translation Theory. Languaging Acts in (and after) Marie NDiaye's *Les Serpents*'. *Studies in Theatre and Performance* 40, no. 2 (2020): 162–189.

Gotman, Kélina. *Essays on Theatre and Change: Towards a Poetics Of*. London: Routledge, 2018.

Gotman, Kélina. 'The "Scene of Discourse": Foucault and the Theatre of Truth (*on parrhēsía*)'. *Cultural Critique*, no. 113 (2021): 28–71.

Gotman, Kélina. '*Translatio*'. *Performance Research* 21, no. 5 (2016): 17–20.

Gould, Deborah. 'On affect and protest'. In *Political Emotions: New Agendas in Communication*, edited by Janet Staiger, Ann Svetkovich, and Ann Reynolds, 18–44. New York: Routledge, 2010.

Gramlin, David, and Aniruddha Dutta. 'Translating Transgender'. *TSQ: Transgender Studies Quarterly* 3, nos. 3–4 (November 2016): 333–356.

Grapheus, Cornelius. *De seer wonderlijcke, schoone, triumphelijcke incompst, van den hooghmogenden prince Philips, prince van Spaignen, Caroli des vijfden, keyserssone*. Inde stadt van Antwerpen, anno M.CCCCC.XLIX. Geprint Tantwerpen: Peeter Coecke van Aelst, […] by Gillis van Diest, 1550.

Grapheus, Cornelius. *La Très admirable, très magnificque & triumphante entrée de très hault et très puissant Prince Philipes, prince d'Espaigne, filz de Lempereur Charles Ve en la très renommée, florissante ville d'Anvers, anno 1549, premièrement composée et descripte en langue latine par Cornille Grapheus, greffier de ladicte ville d'Anvers, et depuis traduicte en franchois*. Anvers (Antwerp): Gillis van Diest, for Pierre Coeck d'Allost, 1550.

Grapheus, Cornelius. *Spectaculorum in Susceptione Philippi Hispan. Princ. a. 1549 Antverpia Aeditorum Mirificus Apparatus*. Gillis van Diest, for Pierre Coeck d'Allost. Antverpia (Antwerp), 1550.

Greetham, David C. *Textual Scholarship: An Introduction*. New York: Routledge, 2015.

Gregory, George. *Haushaltung der Natur*, vol. 1. Charleston: Nabu Press, 2011.

Griesel, Yvonne. 'Surtitling: Surtitles an Other Hybrid on a Hybrid Stage'. *Trans* 13 (2009): 119–127.

Guenther, Beatrice. 'Refracting Identity in "l'écriture migrante": Marco Micone's "Le Figuier Enchanté."' *The French Review* 84, no. 6 (2011): 1173–1185.

'Haiti in Translation: Dance on the Volcano by Marie Vieux-Chauvet, An Interview with Kaiama L. Glover', accessed June 2, 2022, https://networks.h-net.org/node/116721/discussions/158058/haiti-translation-dance-volcano-marie-vieux-chauvet-interview.

Works Cited

Halberstam, J. Jack. *In a Queer Time & Place: Transgender Bodies, Subcultural Lives*. New York: NYU Press, 2005.

Hall, Stuart. 'Cultural Identity and Diaspora'. In *Identity: Community, Culture, Difference*, edited by Jonathan Rutherford, 222–237. London: Lawrence and Wishart, 1990.

Harney, Stefano, and Fred Moten. *The Undercommons: Fugitive Planning and Black Study*. New York: Minor Compositions, 2013.

Haviland, Linda Caruso. 'Considering the Body as Archive'. In *The Sentient Archive: Bodies, Performance, and Memory*, edited by Bill Bissell and Linda Caruso Haviland, 1–17. Middletown: Wesleyan University Press, 2008.

Heffernan, James A. W. 'Ekphrasis and Representation'. *New Literary History* 22, no. 2 (1991): 297–316.

Hejinian, Lyn. *The Language of Inquiry*. Berkeley: University of California Press, 2000.

Helbig-Mischewski, Brigitta. 'Warum Heulen Die "Inneren Dämonen"? Metaphorik Des Existentiellen Vakuums in Maria Komornickas "Biesy."' *Zeitschrift für Slawistik* 47, no. 1 (2002): 34–49.

Herczeg, Giulio. *Lo stile indiretto libero in italiano*. Florence: G. E. Sansoni editore, 1963.

Hester, Helen. *Xenofeminism*. Cambridge and Medford: Polity, 2018.

Hirsch, Marianne. 'The Generation of Postmemory'. *Poetics Today* 29, no. 1 (2008): 103–128.

Homer. *The Illiad*. Trans. Robert Fitzgerald. London: Everyman, 1992.

Hsia, Tao-Tai. 'The Language Revolution in Communist China'. *Far Eastern Survey* 25, no. 10 (1956): 145–154.

Hurley, Erin. '*Devenir Autre*: Languages of Marco Micone's "*culture immigrée*."' *Theatre Research in Canada/Recherches théâtrales au Canada* 25, nos. 1–2 (2004): 1–23. https://journals.lib.unb.ca/index.php/TRIC/article/view/4650/5510.

Hurley, Erin. *National Performance: Representing Quebec from Expo 67 to Céline Dion*. Toronto: University of Toronto Press, 2011.

Ignatiev, Noel. *How the Irish Became White*. London: Routledge, 2009.

Jackson, Shannon. 'Theatricality's Proper Objects: Genealogies of Performance and Gender Theory'. In *Theatricality*, edited by Tracy C. Davis and Thomas Postlewait. Cambridge: Cambridge University Press, 2003.

Jakobson, Roman. 'On Linguistic Aspects of Translation'. In *Selected Writings: Word and Language*, vol. 2, 260–266. The Hague: Mouton and Co., 1971.

Jakobson, Roman. 'On Linguistic Aspects of Translation [1959]'. In *Translation Studies Reader*, edited by Lawrence Venuti, 126–131. London, New York: Routledge, 2000.

Janion, Maria. *Kobiety i duch inności*. Warszawa: Sic!, 1996.

Johnston, John. 'Translation as Simulacrum'. In *Rethinking Translation: Discourse, Subjectivity, Ideology*, edited by Lawrence Venuti, 42–56. London: Routledge, 1992.

Jones, Amelia. 'Trans-ing Performance'. *Performance Research* 21, no. 5 (2016): 1–11.

Jones, Chris. *Strange Likeness: The Use of Old English in Twentieth-Century Poetry*. Oxford: Oxford University Press, 2006.

Works Cited

Jordan, June. *Passion: New Poems, 1977–1980*. Boston: Beacon Press, 1980.

Kaplan, Paul H. D. 'Isabella d'Este and Black African Women'. In *Black Africans in Renaissance Europe*, edited by Thomas Foster Earle and K. J. P. Lowe, 125–154. Cambridge: Cambridge University Press, 2005.

Katz, Josh. *Speaking American: How Y'all, Youse, and You Guys Talk: A Visual Guide*. Boston: Houghton Mifflin Harcourt, 2016.

Keene, John, 'Translating Poetry, Translating Blackness'. 2016, accessed June 2, 2022, www.poetryfoundation.org/harriet-books/2016/04/translating-poetry-translating-blackness.

Kemp, William. 'Transformations in the Printing of Royal Entries during the Reign of François Ier: The Role of Geofroy Tory'. In *French Ceremonial Entries in the Sixteenth Century: Event, Image, Text*, edited by Hélène Visentin and Nicolas Russell. Toronto: Centre for Reformation and Renaissance Studies, 2007.

Kershaw, Baz. *Theatre Ecology*. Cambridge: Cambridge University Press, 2007.

Kesavan, Mukal. 'Power of anthems: Plurality of Languages Threatens the Coherence Majoritarians Want'. *The Telegraph India*, January 25, 2020. www.telegraphindia.com/opinion/power-of-anthems/cid/1739593.

Khatibi, Abdelkebir. 'Bilinguisme et littérature'. In *Maghreb pluriel*, 178–207. Paris: Denoël, 1983.

Khatibi, Abdelkebir. 'Lettre-préface'. In M. Gontard, *La Violence du texte: études sur la littérature marocaine de langue française*, 8. Paris: L'Harmattan, 1981.

Khatibi, Abdelkebir. *Love in Two Languages*. Translated by Richard Howard. Minneapolis: University of Minnesota Press, 1990.

Kim, Christine Sun. 'I Performed at the Superbowl. You Might Have Missed Me'. *The New York Times*, February 3, 2020. www.nytimes.com/2020/02/03/opinion/national-anthem-sign-language.html.

Kinnahan, Linda A. 'Interview with Caroline Bergvall'. *Contemporary Women's Writing* 5 (2011): 232–251.

Kipling, Gordon. *Klaeber's Beowulf: Fourth Edition*. Edited by R. D. Fulk, Robert E. Bjork, and John D. Niles. Toronto: University of Toronto Press, 2008.

Kipling, Gordon. *The Triumph of Honour: Burgundian Origins of the Elizabethan Renaissance*. Leiden: Leiden University Press, 1977.

Knepler, Henry. *The Gilded Stage. The Lives and Careers of Four Great Actresses: Rachel Félix, Adelaide Ristori, Sarah Bernhardt and Eleonora Duse*. London: Constable, 1968.

Körner, Axel. *Politics of Culture in Liberal Italy: From Unification to Fascism*. New York: Routledge, 2009.

Kosiński, Dariusz. 'After Performatics'. *Performance Research* 23, nos. 4–5 (2018): 262–265.

Kozłowska, Agata. 'Maria Komornicka. Nieistnienie'. *Bez Dogmatu* 92 (2012). http://lewica.pl/index.php?id=26900.

Kress, Gunther, and Theo van Leeuwen. *Multimodal Discourse: The Modes and Media of Contemporary Communication*. London: Arnold, 2001.

Lacan, Jacques. *Écrits: A Selection*. Translated by Bruce Fink. New York and London: W. W. Norton & Company, 2004.

Works Cited

Lalonde, Michèle, et al., eds. *Change Souverain Québec*. Paris: Collectif Change, Seghers/Laffont, 1977.

Lalonde, Michèle, et al., eds. *Défense et illustration de la langue québécoise, suivie de prose & poèmes*. Paris: Éditions Seghers/Laffont, 1979.

Lalonde, Michèle, et al., eds. 'La deffence & illustration de la langue Québecquoyse'. In *Change Souverain Québec*, edited by Michèle Lalonde, et al., 105–122. Paris: Collectif Change, Seghers/Laffont, 1977.

Lalonde, Michèle, et al., eds. 'Petit Testament'. *University of Toronto Quarterly* 50, no. 1 (1980): 66–68.

Lalonde, Michèle, et al., eds. *Speak White*. Montréal: L'Hexagone, 1974.

Lalonde, Michèle and Denis Monière. *Cause commune. Manifeste pour une internationale des petites cultures*. Montréal: L'Hexagone, 1981.

Language Acts and Worldmaking. 'Translation Acts'. Accessed May 26, 2021. https://languageacts.org/translation-acts/.

Language Acts and Worldmaking. 'Worldmaking in the Time of Covid-19'. Accessed May 19, 2021. https://languageacts.org/worldmaking-time-covid-19/.

Laronde, Michel. 'Displaced Discourses: Post(-)coloniality, Francophone Space(s), and the Literature(s) of Immigration in France'. In *Postcolonial Theory and Francophone Literary Studies*, edited by H. Adlai Murdoch and Anne Donadey, 175–92. Gainville: University Press of Florida, 2005.

Laroussi, Farid, and Christopher L. Miller, eds. 'French and Francophone: The Challenge of Expanding Horizons'. *Yale French Studies*, no. 103 (2003).

Laundry, Donna, and Gerald MacLean, eds. *The Spivak Reader*. London: Routledge, 1995.

Lee, Tong King. 'Asymmetry in Translating Heterolingualism: A Singapore Case Study'. *Perspectives: Studies in Translatology* 17 (2009): 63–75. https://doi.org/10.1080/09076760902825925.

Lees, Clare, and Gillian Overing. *The Contemporary Medieval in Practice*. London: UCL Press, 2019.

Lefeuvre, Daniel. *Pour en finir avec la repentance coloniale*. Paris: Flammarion, 2006.

Leitch, Stephanie. *Mapping Ethnography in Early Modern Germany: New Worlds in Print Culture*. New York: Palgrave Macmillian, 2010.

Lepecki, André. 'The Body as Archive: Will to Re-Enact and the Afterlives of Dances'. *Dance Research Journal* 42, no. 2 (2010): 28–48.

Lepschy, Anna Laura, and Giulio Lepschy. *The Italian Language Today*, 2nd ed. London: Routledge, 1991.

Lepschy, Giulio. *Mother Tongues and Other Reflections on the Italian Language*. Toronto: University of Toronto Press, 2002.

Levi, Cesare. *Autori drammatici italiani: Giovanni Verga, Roberto Bracco, Marco Praga, Sebatino Lopez*. Bologna: Zanichelli, 1921.

Levin, Dana. 'Get lost'. *Boston Review*, February 3, 2015. http://bostonreview.net/poetry/dana-levin-caroline-bergvall-drift-get-lost.

Liepe-Levison, Katherine. *Strip Show: Performances of Gender and Desire*. London and New York: Routledge, 2002.

Works Cited

Lindsay, Jennifer. 'Performing across the Sound Barrier'. In *Babel or Behemoth: Language Trends in Asia*, edited by Jennifer Lindsay and Tan Ying Ying, 133–159. Singapore: Asian Research Institute, 2003.

Lindsay, Jennifer. 'Performing Translation: Hardja Susilo's Translation of Javanese Wayang. Performance'. In *Between Tongues: Translation and/of/in Performance in Asia*, edited by Jennifer Lindsay, 138–169. Singapore: Singapore University Press, 2003.

Lindsay, Jennifer.,'Translation and/of/in Performance: New Connections'. In *Between Tongues: Translation and/of/in Performance in Asia*, edited by Jennifer Lindsay, 1–32. Singapore: Singapore University Press, 2003.

Lionnet, Françoise, and Shu-mei Shih. 'Introduction: Thinking through the Minor, Transnationally'. In *Minor Transnationalism*, edited by Françoise Lionnet and Shu-mei Shih, 1–23. Durham, NC: Duke University Press, 2005.

Lisowska, Katarzyna. 'Body, Spirit and Gender in Maria Komornicka's Poetry'. *The Journal of Education Culture and Society* 2, no. 1 (2011): 96–106.

Lloyd, David. 'Representation's Coup'. *Interventions* 16, no. 1 (2014): 1–29.

Locke, Alain. 'The New Negro'. In *The New Negro: Voices of Harlem*, edited by Alain Locke, with an introduction by Arnold Ramparsad, 3–16. New York: Maxwell Macmillan International, 1992.

Manning, Erin. *The Minor Gesture*. Durham: Duke University Press, 2016.

Massai, Sonia. *Shakespeare's Accents: Voicing Identity in Performance*. Cambridge: Cambridge University Press, 2020.

Massumi, Brian. *Parables for the Virtual: Movement, Affect, Sensation*. Durham: Duke University Press, 2002.

Massumi, Brian. *The Politics of Affect*. Cambridge: Polity Press, 2015.

Matchett, Sara, and Mark Fleishman. 'Editorial: Translation and Performance in an Era of Global Asymmetries, Part 2'. *South African Theatre Journal* 33, no. 1 (2020): 1–4.

McCormick, Michael. *Eternal Victory: Triumphal Rulership in Late Antiquity, Byzantium and the Early Medieval West*. Cambridge: Cambridge University Press, 1990.

McDonagh, Tom, ed. *Guy Debord and the Situationist International*. London: The MIT Press, 2002.

McGowan, Margaret M. *The Vision of Rome in Late Renaissance France*. New Haven: Yale University Press, 2000.

McKenzie, Jon. *Perform or Else: From Discipline to Performance*. London: Routledge, 2001.

McKinney, Joslin. 'Empathy and Exchange: Audience Experience of Scenography'. In *Kinesthetic Empathy in Creative and Cultural Practices*, edited by Matthew Reason and Dee Reynolds, 219–235. Chicago: The University of Chicago Press/Bristol: Intellect, 2012.

Mehrez, Samia. 'Translating Gender'. *Journal of Middle East Women's Studies* 3, no. 1 (2007): 106–127.

Menon, M. *Indifference to Difference: On Queer Universalism*. Minneapolis: University of Minnesota Press, 2015.

Mezei, Kathy. 'Bilingualism and Translation in/of Michèle Lalonde's *Speak White*'. *The Translator* 4, no. 2 (1998): 229–247.

Micone, Marco. 'Speak What'. *Cahiers de théâtre. Jeu* 50 (March 1989): 83–85.

Micone, Marco. *Speak What. Suivi d'une analyse de Lise Gauvin.* Montreal: VLB Éditeur, 2001.

Mignolo, Walter, and Freya Schiwy. 'Double Translation: Translation/ Transculturation and the Colonial Difference'. In *Translation and Ethnography: The Anthropological Challenge of Intercultural Understanding*, edited by Bernhard Streck and Tulio Maranhão, 3–30. Tucson: University of Arizona Press, 2003.

Millar, Laura. 'Touchstones: Considering the Relationship between Memory and Archives'. *Archivaria* 61 (2006): 105–126.

Mitchell, W. J. T. *Picture Theory.* Chicago and London: University of Chicago Press, 1994.

Moe, Nelson. *The View from Vesuvius: Italian Culture and the Southern Question.* Berkeley, LA: University of California Press, 2002.

Molinari, Cesare. *L'attrice divina: Eleonora Duse nel teatro italiano fra i due secoli.* Rome: Bulzoni, 1985.

Molinari, Cesare. 'Teorie della recitazione: gli attori sull'attore. Da Rossi a Zacconi'. In *Teatro dell'Italia unita. Atti dei convegni Firenze 10–11 dicembre 1977, 4–6 novembre 1978*, edited by Siro Ferrone, 75–100. Milan: il Saggiatore, 1980.

Moten, Fred. *In the Break: The Aesthetics of the Black Radical Tradition.* Minneapolis: University of Minnesota Press, 2003.

Moura, Jean-Marc. *Littératures francophones et théorie postcoloniale.* Paris: PUF Quadrige, 2013.

Muir, Bernard J., ed. *The Exeter Anthology of Old English Poetry.* Exeter: Exeter University Press, 1994.

Murdoch, H. Adlai, and Anne Donadey. 'Introduction: Productive Intersections'. In *Postcolonial Theory and Francophone Literary Studies*, edited by H. Adlai Murdoch and Anne Donadey, 1–17. Gainville: University Press of Florida, 2005.

Muren, Gwendolen. 'Review of *Drift* by Caroline Bergvall'. *Chicago Review* 59 (2015): 276–280.

Nail, Thomas. *The Figure of the Migrant.* Stanford: Stanford University Press, 2015.

Nakayasu, Sawako. *Say Translation Is Art.* Brooklyn: Ugly Duckling Presse, 2020.

Nancy, Jean-Luc. *Listening.* Translated by Charlotte Mandell. New York: Fordham University Press, 2003.

Ndiaye, Pap. *La condition noire: essai sur une minorité française.* Paris: Calmann-Lévy, 2008.

Neveux, Olivier. *Politiques du Spectateur: les enjeux du théâtre politique aujourd'hui.* Paris: La Découverte, 2013.

Nida Research Centre for Translation. 'Nida School of Translation Studies'. Accessed May 26, 2021. www.nidaschool.org/nsts-home.

Niranjana, Tejaswini. *Siting Translation: History, Post-structuralism and the Colonial Context.* Berkeley: University of California Press, 1992.

262   *Works Cited*

Noiriel, Gérard. *Histoire, théâtre et politique.* Marseille: Agone, 2009.

Novelli, N. 'Pour une nouvelle culture et une langue de la migration: entretien avec Marco Micone'. In *D'autres rêves: les écritures migrantes au Québec. Actes du séminaire international du CISQ [Centro interuniversitario di studi quebecchesi] à Venise, 15–16 octobre 1999,* edited by Anne de Vaucher Gravili, 163–182. Venice: Supervnova, 2000.

Nowak, Anita. 'Wielki sukces Anity Sokołowskiej!' *Teatr dla Was,* March 12, 2012.

Ojetti, Ugo. *Alla scoperta dei letterati.* Postface by Nicola Merola. Milan: Fratelli Dumolard editori, 1895.

Oncins, Estella. 'The Tyranny of the Tool: Surtitling Live Performances'. *Perspectives: Studies in Translation Theory and Practice* 23, no. 1 (2015): 42–61.

Orecchia, Donatella. *La Prima Duse: Nascita di un'attrice moderna (1879–1886).* Rome: Artemide, 2007.

Owens, Richard. 'Caroline Bergvall her Shorter Chaucer Tales'. *Postmedieval: A Journal of Medieval Cultural Studies* 6 (2015): 146–153.

Owens, Richard. *Oxford English Dictionary. Oxford English Dictionary.* Oxford: Oxford University Press, 2021. www.oed.com.

Paré, François. *Les littératures de l'exiguïté.* Hearst: Le Nordir, 1992.

Perloff, Marjorie. 'The Oulipo Factor: The Procedural Poetics of Christian Bök and Caroline Bergvall'. *Textual Practice* 18 (2004): 23–45.

Phelan, Peggy. *Unmarked: The Politics of Performance.* London: Routledge, 1993.

Philip, M. NourbeSe. 'Discourse on the Logic of Language'. In *She Tries Her Tongue, Her Silence Softly Breaks,* 29–33. Middletown CT: Wesleyan University Press, [1989] 2014.

Piccini, Giulio (Jarro). 'I nervi della Duse'. In *Eleonora Duse,* edited by Leonardo Vergani with the collaboration of Luigi Pizzinelli, 93–101. Milan: Aldo Martello, 1958.

Pirandello, Luigi. 'Eleonora Duse: Actress Supreme'. *The Century Magazine,* June, 1924, 244–251.

Pontiero, Giovanni. *Eleonora Duse: In Life and Art.* Frankfurt am Main, Bern, New York: Verlag Peter Lang, 1986.

Pratt, Mary Louise. 'Language and the Afterlives of Empire'. *PMLA* 130, no. 2 (2015): 348–357.

Preston, VK. 'A Dictionary in the Archives: Translating and Transcribing Silenced Histories in French and Wendat'. *Performance Research* 21.5 'On Trans/Performance' (2016): 85–88.

Rae, Paul. 'In Tongues: Translation, Embodiment, Performance'. In *Translation in Asia: Theories, Practices, Histories,* edited by Jan Van Der Putten and Ronit Ricci, 153–66. Manchester: St Jerome Publishing, 2011.

Rae, Paul. 'Wayang Studies?' In *The Rise of Performance Studies: Rethinking Richard Schechner's Broad Spectrum Approach,* edited by James Harding and Cindy Sherman, 67–84. Basingstoke: Palgrave Macmillan, 2011.

Rafael, Vicente. *Motherless Tongues: The Insurgency of Language amid Wars of Translation.* Durham, NC: Duke University Press, 2016.

Rasi, Luigi. *La Duse. Con 55 illustrazioni.* Florence: R. Bemporad & Figlio, 1901.

Works Cited

Rayner, K. 'Eye Movements in Reading and Information Processing: 20 Years of Research'. *Psychological Bulletin* 124 (1998): 372–422.

Rayner, K. 'The Thirty-Fifth Sir Frederick Bartlett Lecture: Eye Movements and Attention in Reading, Scene Perception, and Visual Search'. *Quarterly Journal of Experimental Psychology* 62 (2009): 1457–1506.

Reason, Matthew, and Dee Reynolds, eds. *Kinesthetic Empathy in Creative and Cultural Practices*. Chicago: The University of Chicago Press, 2012.

Reed, Brian. *Phenomenal Reading: Essays on Modern and Contemporary Poetics*. Tuscaloosa: University of Alabama Press, 2012.

Reichle, E. D., K. Rayner, and A. Pollatsek. 'The E-Z Reader Model of Eye-Movement Control in Reading: Comparisons to Other Models'. *Behavioral and Brain Sciences* 26 (2003): 445–476.

Rich, Adrienne. *Poetry and Commitment: An Essay*. New York: Norton, 2007.

Roach, Joseph R. *Cities of the Dead: Circum-Atlantic Performance*. New York: Columbia University Press, 1996.

Robin, Régine. *La Québécoite*. Montréal: Les Editions XYZ, 1993.

Robin, Régine. *Le Deuil de l'origine. Une langue en trop, la langue en moins*. Paris: Presses Universitaires de Vincennes, 1993.

Robinson, Fred C. *The Tomb of Beowulf and Other Essays on Old English*. London: Blackwell, 1993.

Robson, David. 'The mind-bending effects of foreign accent syndrome'. *BBC Future*, May 13, 2014. www.bbc.com/future/story/20150513-the-weird-effects-of-foreign-accent-syndrome.

Rojas, Carlos. 'Translation as Method'. *Prism 1*, 16, no. 2 (2019): 221–235.

Rouabhi, Mohamed. All Power to the People! Unpublished play, typescript.

Rouabhi, Mohamed. Vive la France. Unpublished play, typescript.

Royal National Institute of Blind People. 'Theatre Audio Description FAQs'. Last modified March 13, 2015. www.rnib.org.uk/nb-online/theatre-audio-description-faqs.

Sadie, Stanley, ed. *The New Grove Dictionary of Music and Musicians*, vol. 3. Bollioud-Mermet-Castro. London: Macmillan, 1980.

Sakai, Naoki. *Translation and Subjectivity: On Japan and Cultural Nationalism*. Minneapolis: University of Minnesota Press, 1997.

Sakai, Naoki, and Sandro Mezzadra. 'Introduction'. *Translation: A transdisciplinary journal* 4 (2014): 9–29.

Salgado, Jenny. 'Speak White au Moulin à Paroles'. https://jennysalgado.ca/videoclips/mes-articles-video/60-speak-white-au-moulin-a-paroles. Accessed 19 May, 2022.

Sampson, Fiona. 'Mind the Gap: Translation as a Form of Attention'. British Centre for Literary Translation Research Seminar, February 21, 2018.

Savci, Evren. *Queer in Translation: Sexual Politics under Neoliberal Islam*. Durham: Duke University Press, 2021.

Schaubühne Berlin & Complicité. 'Beware of Pity Live Stream', YouTube video, February 12, 2017. Accessed January 30, 2021. www.complicite.org/live-stream.php#.

Works Cited

Schechner, Richard. *Between Theatre and Anthropology*. Philadelphia: University of Pennsylvania Press, 1985.

Schino, Mirela. *Il teatro di Eleonora Duse*. Bologna: Il Mulino, 1992.

Schneider, Jane, and Peter Schneider. *Culture and Political Economy in Western Sicily*. New York: Academic Press, 1976.

Schneider, Rebecca. *Performing Remains: Art and War in Times of Theatrical Reenactment*. Abingdon: Routledge, 2011.

Scuderi, Antonio. 'Sicilian Dialect Theatre'. In *A History of Italian Theatre*, edited by Joseph Farrell and Paolo Puppa, 257–265. Cambridge: Cambridge University Press, 2006.

Sears, Dianne E. 'Défense De Parler: Language on Trial in Michèle Lalonde's "La deffence et Illustration De La Langue Québecquoyse" and "Outrage Au Tribunal."' *The French Review* 68, no. 6 (1995): 1015–1021.

Shaw, George Bernard. 'Mr William Archer's Criticism'. In *Our Theatres in the Nineties*, vol. 1, 87–99. London: Constable and Company Limited, [1932] 1954.

Sheppard, Robert. *The Meaning of Form in Contemporary Innovative Poetry*. Basingstoke: Palgrave Macmilllan, 2016.

Siebler, Kay. 'What's So Feminist about Garters and Bustiers? Neo-Burlesque as Post-Feminist Sexual Liberation'. *Journal of Gender Studies* 24, no. 5 (2015): 561–573.

Sigurþsson, Gísli, ed. *The Vinland Sagas: The Icelandic Sagas about the First Documented Voyages across the North Atlantic*. Translated by Keneva Kunz. London: Penguin, 2008.

Silver, Larry. *Marketing Maximilian: The Visual Ideology of a Holy Roman Emperor*. Princeton: Princeton University Press, 2008.

Simon, Sherry. *Cities in Translation: Intersections of Language and Memory*. Abingdon: Routledge, 2012.

Simon, Sherry. *Le Trafic des langues: tradition et culture dans la littérature québécoise*. Montréal: Éditions Boréal, 1994.

Sirach, Marie-José. 'Vive la France, et caetera'. *L'Humanité*, November 28, 2006.

Smith, Laurajane. 'The Embodied Performance of Museum Visiting'. In *The Sentient Archive: Bodies, Performance, and Memory*, edited by Bill Bissell and Linda Caruso Haviland, 126–142. Middletown: Wesleyan University Press, 2018.

Snyder, Joel. *The Visual Made Verbal: A Comprehensive Training Manual and Guide to the History and Applications of Audio Description*. Arlington, VA: American Council of the Blind, 2014.

Sofia, Gabriele. *L'arte di Giovanni Grasso e le rivoluzioni teatrali di Craig e Mejerchold*. Rome: Bulzoni, 2019.

Solheim, Jennifer. *The Performance of Listening in Postcolonial Francophone Culture*. Liverpool University Press, 2018.

Solheim, Jennifer. 'Songs, Poems and Films: A Playlist for Protest'. *Film Companion*, January 11, 2020. www.filmcompanion.in/features/bollywood-features/songs-poems-and-films-a-playlist-for-protest/.

Spivak, Gayatri Chakravorty. *An Aesthetic Education in the Era of Globalization*. Cambridge, MA: Harvard University Press, 2012.

Works Cited

Spivak, Gayatri Chakravorty. 'Can the Subaltern Speak?' In *Marxism and the Interpretation of Culture*, edited by Cary Nelson and Lawrence Grossberg, 271–313. Urbana: University of Illinois Press, 1988.

Spivak, Gayatri Chakravorty. 'More Thoughts on Cultural Translation'. transversal – eipcp multilingual webjournal, April, 2008. http://eipcp.net/transversal/0608/spivak/en.

Spivak, Gayatri Chakravorty. 'Moving Devi'. *Cultural Critique* 47 (2001): 120–163.

Spivak, Gayatri Chakravorty. *Outside in the Teaching Machine*. London and New York: Routledge, 1993.

Spivak, Gayatri Chakravorty. 'The Politics of Translation'. In *The Translation Studies Reader*, edited by Lawrence Venuti, 312–330. London: Routledge, 2012.

Spivak, Gayatri Chakravorty. 'Postcolonialism in France'. *The Romanic Review* 104 (2013), nos. 3–4: 223–242.

Spivak, Gayatri Chakravorty. 'Rethinking Comparativism'. *New Literary History* 40 (Summer 2009), no. 3: 609–626.

Spivak, Gayatri Chakravorty. 'Translation as Culture'. *Parallax* 6, no. 1 (2000): 13–24.

Spivak, Gayatri Chakravorty. 'Translator's Preface'. In Mahasweta Devi, *Imaginary Maps: Three Stories*, translated by Gayatri Chakravorty Spivak, xxiv–xxix. London and New York: Routledge, 1995.

Sponza, Lucio. 'The 1880s: A Turning Point'. In *A Century of Italian Emigration to Britain 1880–1980s: Five Essays, The Supplement to The Italianist 13*, edited by Lucio Sponza and Arturo Tosi, 10–24. Reading: University of Reading, 1993.

Spregelburd, Rafael. 'Life, Of Course'. Translated by Jean Graham-Jones. *Theatre Journal* 59, no. 3 (2007): 373–377.

Steuernagel, Marcos. 'The (Un)translatability of Performance Studies'. In *What Is/¿Qué son los estudios de/O que são os estudos da Performance Studies?*, edited by Diana Taylor and Marcos Steuernagel. Durham: Duke University Press, 2015. https://scalar.usc.edu/nehvectors/wips/the-untranslatability-of-performance-studies.

Stevenson, Seth William, Charles Roach Smith, and Frederic W. Madden. *A Dictionary of Roman Coins, Republican and Imperial*. London: George Bell and Sons, 1889. www.forumancientcoins.com/numiswiki/.

Sturtevant, William. 'The Sources for European Imagery of Native Americans'. In *New World of Wonders: European Images of the Americas, 1492–1700*, edited by Rachel Doggett, Monique Hulvey, and Julie Ainsworth. Washington, DC and Seattle: Folger Shakespeare Library and Distributed by University of Washington Press, 1992.

Sun, F., M. Morita, and L.W. Stark, 'Comparative Patterns of Reading Eye Movement in Chinese and English'. *Perception and Psychophysics* 37 (1985): 502–506.

Symons, Arthur. *Eleonora Duse*. London: Elkin Mathews, [1903] 1926.

Taylor, Christopher. 'The Multimodal Approach in Audiovisual Translation'. *Target* 28, no. 2 (2016): 222–236.

Taylor, Diana. *The Archive and the Repertoire: Performing Cultural Memory in the Americas*. Durham: Duke University Press, 2003.

Works Cited

Taylor, Diana. 'The Many Lives of Performance: The Hemispheric Institute of Performance and Politics'. In *Contesting Performance: Global Sites of Research*, edited by Jon McKenzie, Heike Roms, and C. J. W.-L. Wee, 25–36. Houndmills, Basingstoke: Palgrave Macmillan, 2010.

Taylor, Diana. 'Translating Performance'. *Profession* (2002): 44–50.

Tcherkasski, Sergei. 'Twofaced Giovanni Grasso and His Great Spectators or What Stanislavsky, Meyerhold and Strasberg Actually Stole from the Sicilian Actor'. In *The Italian Method of La Drammatica*, edited by Anna Sica, 109–132. Milan: Mimesis, 2014.

Thornbury, Emily V. *Becoming a Poet in Anglo-Saxon England*. Cambridge: Cambridge University Press, 2014.

Trifone, Pietro. *Malalingua: L'italiano scorretto da Dante a oggi*. Bologna: Il Mulino, 2007.

Tuck, Eve, and K. Wayne Yang. 'Decolonization Is Not a Metaphor'. *Decolonization: Indigeneity, Education and Society* 1, no. 1 (2012): 1–40.

Tymoczko, Maria. *Enlarging Translation, Empowering Translators*. London: Routledge, 2014.

Ungar, Steven. 'Writing in Tongues: Thoughts on the Work of Translation'. In *Comparative Literature in an Age of Globalization*, edited by Haun Saussy, 127–138. Baltimore: The Johns Hopkins University Press, 2006.

Vaish, Viniti, and Mardiana Roslan. '"Crossing" in Singapore'. *World Englishes* 30, no. 3 (2011): 317–331.

Venuti, Lawrence. *Contra Instrumentalism: A Translation Polemic*. Lincoln, Nebraska: University of Nebraska Press, 2019.

Venuti, Lawrence. *The Scandals of Translation: Towards an Ethics of Difference*. London and New York: Routledge, 1998.

Venuti, Lawrence. *Translation Changes Everything*. London and New York: Routledge, 2013.

Venuti, Lawrence. *The Translator's Invisibility: A History of Translation*, 2nd ed. London: Routledge, 2008.

Verga, Giovanni. *Cavalleria rusticana and Other Stories*. Translated by G. H. McWilliam. England: Penguin, 1999.

Verga, Giovanni. *Lettere sparse*. Edited by Giovanna Finocchiaro Chimirri. Rome: Bulzoni, 1980.

Verga, Giovanni. *Lettere al suo traduttore*. Edited by Fredi Chiapelli. Florence: Le Monnier, 1954.

Verga, Giovanni. *Tutte le novelle*, 2 vols. Milan: Mondadori, [1877] 1982.

Verga, Giovanni. *Tutto il teatro*. Milan: Mondadori, [1884] 1980.

Visentin, Hélène. 'The Material Form and the Function of Printed Accounts of Henri II's Triumphal Entries (1547–51)'. In *Writing Royal Entries in Early Modern Europe*, edited by Marie-Claude Canova-Green, Jean Andrews, and Marie-France Wagner, 1–30. Turnhout: Brepols, 2013.

Vostre, Simon, ed. *Ces presentes Heures a lusaige de Chartres: avec les miracles nostre Dame/et les figures de lapocalipse et de la Bible et des triumphes de Cesar*. Paris: Philippe Pigouchet for Simon Vostre, 1508.

Works Cited

Wang, Shaomei. 'Chinese Writing Reform: A Socio-Psycholinguistic Perspective'. In *Reading in Asian Languages: Making Sense of Written Texts in Chinese, Japanese, and Korean*, edited by Kenneth S. Goodman, Shaomei Wang, Mieko Iventosch, and Yetta M. Goodman, 45–67. Abingdon: Routledge, 2012.

Warkocki, Błażej. *Różowy język. Literatura i polityka kultury na początku wieku*. Warszawa: Wydawnictwo Krytyki Politycznej, 2013.

Waterton, C. A. 'Performing the Classification of Nature'. *The Sociological Review* 51, no. 2 (2003): 111–129.

Weaver, William. *Duse: A Biography with 53 illustrations*. London: Thames and Hudson, 1984.

Weiss, Peter. 'The Material and the Models: Notes towards a Definition of Documentary Theatre'. Translated by Heinz Bernard. *Theatre Quarterly* 1, no. 1 (1971): 41–3.

Weizman, Eyal. *Forensic Architecture: Violence at the Threshold of Detectability*. Cambridge, MA: The MIT Press, 2017.

Welch, Rhiannon Noel. *Vital Subjects: Race and Biopolitics in Italy, 1860–1920*. Liverpool: Liverpool University Press, 2016.

Werner, Maggie M. 'Seductive Rhetoric and the Communicative Art of Neo-Burlesque'. *Present Tense* 5, no. 1 (2015): 1–11.

Worthen, William B. 'The Imprint of Performance'. In *Theorizing Practice: Redefining Theatre History*, edited by W. B. Worthen and Peter Holland, 213–234. Houndmills, Basingstoke: Palgrave Macmillan, 2003.

Yong, Li Lan. 'After Translation'. *Shakespeare Survey* 62 (2009): 283–295.

Yong, Li Lan. 'Translating Performance: The Asian Shakespeare Intercultural Archive'. In *The Oxford Handbook of Shakespeare and Performance*, edited by James C. Bulman, 1–26. Oxford: Oxford University Press, 2017. https://doi.org/10.1093/oxfordhb/9780199687169.013.37.

Yong, Li Lan, Alvin Eng Hui Lim, Takiguchi Ken, Lee Chee Keng, Hyon-u Lee, Ha-young Hwang, Michiko Suematsu, and Kaori Kobayashi. Asian Shakespeare Intercultural Archive (A|S|I|A). 2nd ed. National University of Singapore, 2015. In English, Chinese, Japanese and Korean. Accessed April 5, 2018. http://a-s-i-a-web.org/en/splash.php.

Zaho, Margaret Ann. *Imago Triumphalis: The Function and Significance of Triumphal Imagery for Italian Renaissance Rulers*. Baltimore, MD: Peter Lang, 2004.

Zang, Chuanli, Simon P. Liversedge, Xuejun Bai, and Guoli Yan. 'Eye Movements during Chinese Reading'. In *The Oxford Handbook of Eye Movements*, edited by Simon P. Liversedge, Iain D. Gilchrist, and Stefan Everling, 961–978. Oxford: Oxford University Press, 2011.

Zappulla Muscarà, Sarah, and Enzo Zappulla. *Giovanni Grasso: Il più grande attore tragico del mondo*. Acireale, Catania: Cantinella, 1995.

Zappulla Muscarà, Sarah, and Enzo Zappulla. *Le donne del Teatro Siciliano da Mimì Aguglia a Ida Carrara*. Acireale: La Cantinella, 1995.

Zappulla Muscarà, Sarah, and Enzo Zappulla. *Verga da vedere: Teatro, cinema, television*. Edited by F. Caffo, S. Zappulla Muscarà, and E. Zappulla. Palermo: Regione Siciliana, 2003.

Works Cited

Zatlin, Phyllis. *Theatrical Translation and Film Adaptation: A Practitioner's View.* Clevedon, England: Multilingual Matters, 2005.

Zhou, Y. 'Language Planning of China: Accomplishments and Failures'. *Journal of Asian Pacific Communication* 11, no. 1 (2001): 9–16.

Zorach, Rebecca. *Blood, Milk, Ink, Gold: Abundance and Excess in the French Renaissance.* Chicago: University of Chicago Press, 2005.

Zweig, Stefan. Ungeduld des Herzens [Beware of Pity]. Projekt Gutenberg, 1939. Accessed April 5, 2018. www.projekt-gutenberg.org/zweig/ungeduld/chap007 .html.

Index

Academy Awards, 2–4
access, aesthetics of, 101–102
Achebe, Chinua, 128–129
Acquin, Hubert, 114–115
AD. *See* audio description
Adapting Translation for the Stage (Brodie & Cole), 9–11
affect, emotion v., 214
African diaspora, 21–22
Against World Literature (Apter), 11–12
Aguglia, Mimì, 186, 195–199
Ahmad, Dohra, 19–20
Ahmed, Sara, 57
Alexander, Alfred, 188–189
All Power to the People! (Rouabhi), 49, 51, 56–57
   Blackness in, 57–58
   France in, 58–60
   multimedia performance in, 58
   transcolonialism explored in, 60–62
Allen, Esther, 11–12
Almeida Theatre, 101–102
Ambrosi, Paola, 9–11, 15–16
American Sign Language (ASL), 2
androgyny, 139
Ang Chin Moh Foundation, 67
anglophones, 109
anon, 35, 37
Antwerp
   susception of, 182–185
   triumph of, 175–182
Appadurai, Arjun, 3
Apter, Emily, 7–9, 11–12, 17–18
   on translation zone, 18–19
Archive Fever (Derrida), 146–147
Archive of the Gestures, 201
archives
   Derrida on, 146–147, 207–208, 220–222
   embodiment of, 211–223
   Foucault on, 202–203, 220
   memory and, 221
   in *What My Body Can/t Remember*, 216–219

Arendt, Hannah, 125
Arrojo, Rosemary, 11–12
ArtsWok Collaborative, 67
A|S|I|A video interface, 78–79, 82
ASL. *See* American Sign Language
'at large' formulation, 3
audience participation, 202, 214
   in *A Fidayee Son in Moscow*, 203–206
audio description (AD), 93–95
   for *Beauty and the Beast*, 88–89
   for blind and partially sighted audience members, 88
   coinage of, 88
   critical, 99
   embodiment and, 97–98
   gaze in, 92–95
   as intersemiotic translation, 90–91
   live description in, 88–89, 91
   touch tour in, 88–89
   the visual in, 93–94
   voice in, 102–103
   written introduction in, 88–90
Austin, J. L., 2–4, 124
   on speech acts, 6–7

Bahasa Melayu, 67, 70–71
Baines, Roger, 9–11
Bakhtin, M. M., 71–72
Bala, Sruti, 21–22, 27
Balasubramanian, Harshadha, 92–93
Bandiera Rossa, 203–205
Bang, Herman, 191
Bangladesh War of Independence, 238
Barbican Centre, 83
Barua, Owa, 216, 217
Bassnett, Susan, 7–9, 192
Beard, Mary, 155
Beauty and the Beast, 87–88, 95–97, 99, 102
   AD for, 88–89
du Bellay, Joachim, 114–115
Bembo, Pietro, 189

269

270   *Index*

Benjamin, Walter, 246–247
Benna, Zyed, 50
Benveniste, Émile, 6–7, 230–234
Beowulf, 38–39
Bergen, Benjamin K., 77–78
Bergvall, Caroline, 13–14, 23–24, 31
    language use of, 45–47
    left-to-die boat used by, 40–42
    Old English used by, 34–35
    Perloff on, 35–36
Bermann, Sandra, 7–9, 11–12, 186–187
    on translation, 48–49
Bernofsky, Susan, 11–12
Beware of Pity, 66–67, 83
    streaming of, 84–85
Beyond the Pleasure Principle (Freud), 233
Bhabha, Homi, 7–9
    on colonialism, 132
Bhartiya Janata Party (BJP), 1–2
Bigliazzi, Silvia, 9–11, 15–16
bilingualism, 116–117
    Khatibi on, 130–132
    performance and, 72
    speech acts and, 118
    xenophony and, 120–133
Birzeit University, 207
BJP. *See* Bhartiya Janata Party
Black liberation, in United States, 57–58
Black Panthers, 51, 63
Black radical tradition, 6
Black Skin, White Masks (Fanon), 50–53
blackletter typefaces, 159
Blackness
    in *All Power to the People!*, 57–58
    in France, 57
    performance of, 49
    in 'Speak White,' 122–123
    translation of, 56–63
    in United States, 57
Blažević, Marin, 9–11
Blazina, Sergio, 188
Bleeker, Maaike, 82–85
blind and partially sighted audience
    members, 88
    AD services for, 88
Bodies That Matter (Butler), 98
Boito, Arrigo, 192–193
Bong Joon Ho, 2–4
Boniecki, Edward, 139
Book of Idyllic Poetry, 150
border crossing, 17–18
Boroditsky, Lera, 77–79
Boym, Svetlana, 205
Bragaglia, Marinella, 196
Brater, Enoch, 64–65

Brecht, Berthold, 161–162
Brière, Eloise A., 130–132
Brodie, Geraldine, 9–11
burlesque, 100
Butler, Judith, 98, 202–203, 224
    on gender insubordination, 148–150
    on repetition, 143
    on translation, 18–19, 137, 142–143

CAA. *See* Citizenship Amendment Act
Calvé, Emma, 186, 191–196
Capuana, Luigi, 192, 198
Cassin, Barbara, 6–7
    on language, 125
Cavalleria rusticana (Verga), 187–191, 197–199
Cavallo, Amelia, 24–25, 87–88, 92, 95, 97,
    99–101
Ceffino, Zanobio, 166, 168–175
Cells of Illegal Education, 201–202
    interactivity in, 206–209
Césaire, Aimé, 59–60, 234–235
Chang, Jenevieve, 99
Charles V (Emperor), 154–157, 164–165, 175–176
    as emperor, 165–175
Chimera, 138–139
China, language policy in, 74–76
Chomsky, Noam, 6–7
Chow, Rey, 24–25, 111–112
    on language, 130–133
    on xenophony, 128–129
Christ III, 35
Christianity, 37–40
Citizenship Amendment Act (CAA), 1–2
Civil War, American, 42–43
    re-enactment, 43
Cixous, Hélène, 65–67
Cleansed (Kane), 144–145
Clement VII (Pope), 165–166
Coates, Ta-Nehisi, 43
code-switching, 71–72, 112–113
Cohen, Leonard, 108–110
Cole, Emma, 9–11
colonialism. *See also* Postcolonial Studies
    Bhabha on, 132
    Lalonde denouncing, 116–117
    language and, 51
    Rouabhi critiquing, 51
    violence of, 116–117
Commedia dell' arte, 190
A Companion to Translation Studies
    (Bermann & Porter), 11–12
Comparative Literature, 5
    translation in, 7–9
Complicité, 64, 83
co-naissance, 121–123

Index

271

Conroy, Collette, 146–147
Contemporary European Playwrights (Delgado, Lease, & Rebellato), 9–11
Contemporary Legend Theatre, 64
Cordy, Annie, 51–53
créolité, 240–241
critical audio description, 99
Croatia, 9–11
Cronin, Michael, 7–9
crossing, 72
The Crying Game (film), 150–151
Cultural Studies, 7–9
Cunningham, Clare, 101–102
Czernecka, Aleksandra, 144–145

Damra, Hamza, 211
D'Annunzio, Gabriele, 192–193
Dante, 40–41
Davies, Joshua, 23–24
Dawson, William L., 54–55
D'Azeglio, Massimo, 198–199
De Francisci, Enza, 26–27
De Mauro, Tulio, 189
Deaf community, 2
death, 235
  of phonic, 237
  translation and, 235
Debord, Guy, 32
deferred audience, 127–128
'La Deffence et illustration de la langue quebecquoyse,' 114–115
Deleuze, Gilles, 104–105
  on multilingualism, 125–126
Delgado, Maria M., 9–11
derive, 32
Derrida, Jacques, 7–9, 24–25, 27, 111–112, 117, 121, 124, 230–231, 233–236
  on archives, 146–147, 207–208, 220–222
  on gesture, 84, 84
  on identity, 116–117
  language and ownership, 123–125
  on spacing, 232
Diagne, Souleyane Bachir, 120–121
Diamond, Elin, 146–147
'Die Nigga!' (Last Poets), 60–62
D'Innella, Annalisa, 91
Disability Studies, 98
discourse, 220
Djebar, Assia, 123–125
Dolan, Jill, 147–148
Dove, Rita, 106
Drama Box, 24–25, 64, 67
Drift (Bergvall), 13–14, 31–32, 44–45, 47
  decentered subjectivity in, 36–37
  installation of, 36–37

line drawings in, 33–34
  medieval soundings in, 37–40
  modern movements in, 40–45
  Muren on, 37
drift, etymology of, 32
Du Bois, W. E. B., 62–63
Dumas, Alexandre, 190
Duse, Eleonora, 186, 188–189, 191–196
Dutta, Aniruddha, 14–15
Dylan, Bob, 143–144

Edward VII (King), 197
Edwards, Brent, 21–22
Ehrenpforte, 160, 162
ekphrasis, 89–90
  Heffernan on, 98
embodiment. *See also* transembodiment
  AD and, 97–98
  of archives, 211–223
  memory and, 221–222
  Spivak on, 239
  surtitling as supplement to, 70–71
  translation and, 48–49, 137, 239
  in *What My Body Can/t Remember*, 216–219
emotion, affect v., 214
The Encounter, 83
ephemerality, of performance, 222–224
Essay on the Origin of Languages, 84
Étrangers à nous-mêmes (Kristeva), 124
Exeter Book, 'The Seafarer' in, 37–38
Exit, 64
  surtitling of, 67–72
Extant Theatre Company, 92
Eykel, Marie, 121–123

Faiz, Faiz Ahmed, 1–2
Faktur typeface, 158–159
Falardeau, Pierre, 121–123
Fanon, Frantz, 50–51, 62
  on racialization, 52–53
  on whiteness, 130–132
Far Eastern Survey, 74–76
Farini, Luigi Carlo, 198–199
Faulkner, William, 43–45
Feldman, Lada Čale, 9–11
feminism
  second-wave, 151–152
  transembodiment and, 151–152
Ferguson, Charles Albert, 189–190
Fictional Translations (Arrojo), 11–12
A Fidayee Son in Moscow, 201–202, 205
  audience participation in, 203–206
The Figure of the Migrant, 31–32
Filipiak, Izabela, 139–141, 151–152
First Intifada, 206–207, 209, 216

272   *Index*

Fleishman, Mark, 21–22
'flexible essentialism' of theatricality, 146–147
FLQ. *See* Front de Libération du Québec
Flusser, Vilém, 81–82
Forensic Architecture, 40–41, 45
Foucault, Michel, 127–128, 221–222
   on archives, 202–203, 220
Frąckowiak, Bartek, 25–26, 137–138, 143–148, 150, 151
France
   in *All Power to the People!*, 58–60
   Blackness in, 57
   racism in, 55–56
francophonie, 109–112, 120–121, 129
Fraser, Mat, 24–25, 87–88
freedom, 211–212
French language, 104–105, 110–114, 116–118.
   See also francophonie
   legal enshrinement of, 119–120
Freud, Sigmund, 220, 231, 233, 246–247
Front de Libération du Québec (FLQ), 114–115
Frye, Marquette, 116–117
Fryer, Louise, 92–93, 99, 101–102

Ganguly, Avishek, 18–20, 27, 229–243
Gauvin, Lise, 123–125, 126, 129–130
gaze, 102
   in AD, 92–95
   construction of, 92–95
   deconstructing, 95–102
Gazeta Warszawska, 138–139
gender
   abolitionism, 98
   Butler on gender insubordination, 148–150
   Hester on, 98
   performance of, 143, 148–150
   translation and, 14–15
German language, 84
gesture
   archiving, 212
   defining, 202–203
   Derrida on, 84, 84
   minor, 208–209, 225
   in Palestinian diaspora, 201
   translation and, 206
Gesturing Refugees, 201–202
   archives embodied in, 211–215
   creation of, 211–212
Gettysburg, 43
Giacosa, Giuseppe, 188–190
Giusti-Sinopoli, Giuseppi, 198
Glissant, Édouard, 7–9, 20–21, 104–105, 117–119, 123–125, 128
   on monolingualism, 129
the global, 1
Global English, 19–20

'Global Englishes, Rough Futures' (Ganguly), 19–20
globalization, 3, 18–19
globes, 182–184
Gogol, Nikolai, 101–102
Gomez, Isidora Dolores Ibarruri, 203
Gotman, Kélina, 2–4, 24–25
Gould, Deborah, 214
The Government Inspector (Gogol), 101–102
Graham-Jones, Jean, 7–9
Gramlin, David, 14–15
grammar, 113–114
Grapheus, Cornelius, 175–178, 185
Grasso, Giovanni, 186, 195–199
de Grazia, Magreta, 31
Greenland, 35
grid of audibility, 6
Griesel, Yvonne, on surtitling, 64–65
Grodzka, Anna, 148–150
Guattari, Félix, 104–105
Gutenberg press, 154

'Hafville (submerged voice)' (Bergvall), 37
'Hafville 2' (Bergvall), 35–36
'Hafville 5' (Bergvall), 37
'Hafville 6' (Bergvall), 37
Hajewska-Krzysztofik, Malgorzata, 144–145
Halberstram, Jack, on transgender body, 151
Hapsburgs, 154
   genealogy of, 154–155
Harney, Stefano, 225
Harrison, Olivia C., 14–15, 23–24
Haviland, Linda Caruso, 220
Haynes, Todd, 143–144
Heffernan, James, 89–90
   on ekphrasis, 98
Hegel, G. W. F., 233
Heijinian, Lyn, 36–37
Helbig-Mischewski, Brigitta, 139–140
Hemispheric Institute, 13–14
Hester, Helen, on gender, 98
Hirsch, Marianne, 137
History against the Pagans (Orosius), 35
Hokkien, 67–68, 70–71
Homobiografie (Tomasik), 140–141
Hurley, Erin, 109

identity
   Derrida on, 116–117
   language and, 116–117
   migrant bodies and, 116–117
idioms, in translation, 21–22
Illustrazione Italiana, 198–199
image, language and, 88–92
In a Queer Time & Place (Halberstram), 151

Index 273

In Translation (Allen & Bernofsky), 11–12
Inferno (Dante), 40–41
infiltration, 71
informatics, 233–234
integrated access, 101–102
interactivity, 202, 205
    in *Cells of Illegal Education*, 206–209
Interdom, 203, 203
interlingual translation, 90
internationalism, translation, performance and,
    21–27
intersemiotic translation, 90
    AD as, 90–91
intralingual translation, 90
Intruder in the Dust (Faulkner), 43–45
Italian Renaissance, 158

Jackson, Shannon, 146–147
Jakobson, Roman, on translation, 90
Janion, Maria, 138–139, 141–142
    on Komornicka, 151–152
Johnston, David, 7–9
Jones, Amelia, 2–4
Jones, Chris, 39–40
Jordan, June, 58–60, 62–63
Jordan, Neil, 150–151
Julius Caesar, 163
justice, translation doing, 244, 247

Kane, Sarah, 144–145
Kant, Immanuel, 234
Kershaw, Baz, 86
Khatibi, Abdelkebir, 7–9, 123–125
    on bilingualism, 130–132
Kim, Christine Sun, 2
Kinnahan, Linda A., 32
Klein, Melanie, 236
Knepler, Henry, 193
Kobiety i duch inności (Janion), 151–152
Kofler, Peter, 9–11, 15–16
Komornicka, Maria, 25–26, 138–139, 150
    biography of, 146, 142–146
    Janion on, 151–152
    transition to Włast, 25–26, 138, 140–142, 150–151
Komornicka. Biografia pozorna (film), 137–138,
    142–146
    title of, 143–144
    transembodiment in, 153, 146
Komornicki, Augustyn, 138–139
Köppel, Thomas, 36–37
Kosiński, Dariusz, 9–11
Kress, Gunther, 91
Kristeva, Julia, 124

Labrèque, Jean-Claude, 108–110
Lacan, Jacques, 234

Lalonde, Michèle, 24–25, 105–106, 111–112,
    114–115, 127
    colonialism denounced by, 116–117
    on performance of language, 129–130
    as poet, 116
    speech of, 117–119
Landing Cards, 212–213
language, 17–18. *See also specific topics*
    Bergvall use of, 45–47
    Cassin on, 125
    chiasma between language and translation,
        123–125
    Chinese policy on, 74–76
    Chow on, 130–132
    colonialism and, 51
    Derrida on ownership of, 123–125
    homelessness of, 124
    identity and, 116–117
    image and, 88–92
    Lalonde on performance of, 129–130
    in Montreal, 110–111
    performance of, 6–7, 66–67,
        127–132
    Philip on, 126
    plural nature of, 111–112
    power relations bound to, 116–121,
        127–128
    Robin on, 129
    Spivak on, 230–231
    as translational, 104–105, 130–132
    violence towards, 117–119
    whiteness and, 130–132
    as xenophobic, 130–132
Laronde, Michel, 111–112
the Last Poets, 58, 60–62
Lease, Bryce, 9–11, 14–15, 25–26
Lebanon, 212
Lees, Clare A., 32
van Leeuwen, Theo, 91
Lefevere, André, 7–9
left-to-die boat, 40, 45
    Bergvall use of, 40–42
Lemański, Jan, 138–139
Leo X (Pope), 165–166
Lepecki, André, 205, 223–224
Levi, Cesare, 191
Lévinas, Emmanuel, 230–231
Li Er Zai Ci, 64, 66–67, 79
Libya, 40
Lien Foundation, 67
Liepe-Levison, Katherine, 100
van Liesvelt, Jacob, 172–173
Lim, Alvin Eng Hui, 24–25
Lindsay, Jennifer, 64–65, 82
Listening (Nancy), 66–67
listening, Nancy on, 85

274   *Index*

live description, in AD, 88–89, 91
Locke, Alain, 44–45
'Log' (Bergvall), 46
Loi 101, 119–120
Loi 178, 119–120
Lupa, Kystian, 144–145
Lyric Theatre, 196

Macbeth, 64, 73–74
Malcolm X (Rouabhi), 56–57
Malìa (Capuana), 198
*Manchester Courier and Lancashire General
    Advertiser*, 198
Mandarin, 67
Manning, Erin, 208–209, 225
Mao Zedong, 74–76, 203
Margolies, Eleanor, 24–25
Marinetti, Cristina, 9–11
Martoglio, Nino, 196
Mascagni, Pietro, 186, 193–194, 198
masculinity, in 'The Seafarer,' 39–40
Masse, Jean-Pierre, 108–110
Massumi, Brian, 206, 214
Maximilian I (Emperor), 156–157,
    181–182
    funeral of, 164
    paper triumphs of, 157–165
McDermott, Phelim, 95
McKinney, Joslin, 218
Mediterranean Sea, 212
memory, 217, 218, 230–231
    archives and, 221
    embodiment and, 221–222
Menon, M., 98
Metternich (Prince), 189
Mezzadra, Sandro, 21–22
Micone, Marco, 108–110, 119–120, 127
migrant bodies, 5–6
    identity and, 116–117
Millar, Laura, 221–222
mimicry, Brière
Mingus, Charles, 56–57
minor gestures, 208–209, 225
Miron, Gaston, 114–115
Mitchell, W. J. T., 87, 93–94
Modi, Narendra, 1–2
Moins qu'un chien (Rouabhi), 56–57
Molinari, Cesare, 191
monolingualism, 130
    Glissant on, 129
Le monolinguisme de l'autre (Derrida), 116–117,
    123–125
Montfort Care, 67
Montreal, languages in, 110–111
Morita, M., 76–77

Moten, Fred, 6, 225
Motherless Tongues (Rafael), 11–12
multilingualism
    Deleuze and Parnet on, 125–126
    granularity of, 123
    'Speak White' and, 123–125
    speech acts and, 123
multimedia performance, in *all Power to the
    People!*, 58
Muren, Gwendolen, on *Drift*, 37
Musco, Angelo, 196
Muz, Julie Atlas, 24–25, 87–88

NAD. *See* National Association for the Deaf
Nadmiar życia. Maria Komornicka (film),
    144–145
Nail, Thomas, 31–32
Nalazek, Bartosz, 148–150
Nancy, Jean-Luc, 24–25, 66–67
    on listening, 85
National Association for the Deaf (NAD), 2
National Football League (NFL), 2
national languages, 5–6
National Register of Citizens (NRC), 1–2
nationalism, 25
Négritude, 120–121
Nelligan, Émile, 116–117
Newton, Huey P., 60, 62
NFL. *See* National Football League
Niranjana, Tejaswini, 7–9
Noiriel, Gérard, 55–56, 56
Norse settlements, 35
nostalgia, 205, 209
Notebook of a Return to the Native Land
    (Césaire), 59–60
Nowak, Anita, 148–150
'NOÞING,' 46
NRC. *See* National Register of Citizens
La nuit de la poésie, 107–110

Obama, Barack, 57–58
OED. *See* Oxford English Dictionary
Of Grammatology (Derrida), 233–236
Old English
    Bergvall using, 32, 34–35
    oral circulation of poems in, 38
Olson, Tillie, 240
*Ordine, Pompe, Apparati, et Ceremonie Della
    Solenne Intrata Di Carlo V*, 166–168
Orecchia, Donatella, 192
Orosius, 35
Ortelius, Abraham, 184, 185
Oslo peace process, 216
Othello (Shakespeare), 196
Oxford English Dictionary (OED), 35

Palestinian diaspora, gesture in, 201
Palestinian Occupied Territories, 216
Parasite (film), 2–4
Parnet, Claire, on multilingualism, 125–126
'Parsley' (Dove), 106
Parting Ways (Butler), 18–19
Pawelec, Dariusz, 144–145
performance
    bilingualism and, 72
    of Blackness, 49
    in comparative mode, 5–21
    defining, 9–11
    ephemerality of, 222–224
    of gender, 143, 148–150
    internationalism and, 21–27
    Lalonde on language and, 129–130
    of language, 6–7, 66–67, 127–132
    multimedia, 58
    Taylor on, 9–11
    transcolonial, 50–56
    as transformational, 16–17
    trans-ing, 14–15
    translation imbricated with, 6–7, 13–16, 23,
        48–49, 246–247
Performance Research, 2–4, 14–15
Performance Studies (Schechner), 9–11
Performance Studies, global expansion of, 9–11
Performance Studies international (PSi), 11
performance writing, 13–14
performatics, 9–11
Performing Remains (Schneider, R.), 42
Perloff, Marjorie, on Bergvall, 35–36
Perteghella, Manuella, 9–11
Pessoa, Fernando, 123–125
'Petit Testament' (Lalonde), 116
Phelan, Peggy, 222–223
phenomenology, 66–67
Phenomenology of Spirit (Hegel), 233
Philip (Prince), 184
    susception of, 175–182
Philip, M. NourbeSe, on language, 126
Pinyin, 74–76
Pirandello, Luigi, 191
'Poem About My Rights' (Jordan, J.), 58–60
Pontiero, Giovanni, 192–193
Porter, Catherine, 11–12
Postcolonial Studies, 7–9
'Postcolonialism in France' (Spivak),
    235
post-nationalism, 25
Poulin, Julien, 121–123
Pound, Ezra, 39–40
Praga, Marco, 190
printing press, 158–159
Public Enemy, 57–58

Québec separatist movement, 106–108
La Québécoite (Brière), 131–132
Quiet Revolution, 119–120

Rabah, Hassan, 212
race, translation of, 48, 62–63
racialization, Fanon on, 52–53
racism, 49
    in France, 50–51, 55–56
    Rouabhi critiquing, 51
    in United States, 50–51, 55–58
    Vive la France on, 51–53
Rae, Paul, 9–11, 68
Rafael, Vicente, 11–12
Ramallah, 216–217
Rasi, Luigi, 192
Rayner, Keith, 69–70
Rebellato, Dan, 9–11
Reed, Brian, 40–41
Refus Global movement, 117–119
rekkies, 34–35
repetition, Butler on, 143
'Report' (Bergvall), 40–41
Ristori, Adelaide, 190–191
RNIB. See Royal National Institute of Blind
    People
Roach, Joseph, 21–22, 25–26, 154–155, 163
Robin, Régine
    on language, 129–132
Rod, Édouard, 197
Rome, 154
    emperors of, 155–157
    triumphs in, 155–157
Roslan, Mardiana, 72
Rossi, Ernesto, 190–191
Rossignol, Michelle, 106–108
Rotten English, 19–20
Rouabhi, Mohamed, 49, 50
    critical responses to, 55–56
    racism and colonialism critiqued by, 51
Rousseau, Jean, 84
Royal National Institute of Blind People
    (RNIB), 92–93
Rubin, Gayle, 146–147
Ruppel, Dan J., 25–26
Rusconi, Carlo, 196

Sakai, Naoki, 21–22, 25–26, 162
Saleh, Farah, 26–27
Salgado, Jenny, 121–125
Salvini, Tommaso, 190–191
Scarano, Nicola, 188
'Scarf Dance,' 87–88, 95, 99–102
Schaubühne Berlin, 64, 83
Schechner, Richard, 9–11, 35

Index

Schino, Mirella, 191
Schneider, Jane, 199
Schneider, Peter, 199
Schneider, Rebecca, 42–43
'The Seafarer,' 31, 33–34
  in Exeter Book, 37–38
  masculinity in, 39–40
Sears, Dianne, 112–113
A Season in the Congo (Césaire), 234
Second Intifada, 216
second-wave feminism, 151–152
self-determination, 62–63
self-dramatization, 132–133
Senghor, Léopold Sédar, 120–121
Seven Years' War, 106
Shaftesbury Theatre, 197
'Shake' (Bergvall), 45–46
Shakespeare, William, 73, 78–79, 117–119,
  121–123, 196
Shaw, George Bernard, 195
Sicily, 186–187, 195–199
  Sicilian otherness, 199–200
Siebler, Kay, 100–101
Sika, Hervé, 57–58, 60
silent speech, 65–66
Simon, Sherry, 108–111
Simplified Chinese, surtitles in, 76–77
Singapore, 67, 71
Słowacki, Julius, 151–152
Smith, Kirstin, 24–25
Smith, Laurajane, 217–218
Sokołowska, Anita, 144–145, 147–148
Southern Question, 198–199
spacing, 27
  Derrida on, 232
'Speak What' (Micone), 108–110, 119–120
'Speak White' (Lalonde), 105–121
  Blackness in, 122–123
  multilingualism and, 123–125
  xenophony and, 120–133
spectatorship, 94–95
speech acts, 127–128, 132–133
  Austin on, 6–7
  bilingualism and multilingualism and, 117
  translational, 128–129
Spivak, Gayatri Chakravorty, 7–9, 18–19, 27,
  152, 229–243, 246–247
  on embodiment, 239
  on language, 230–231
  on subaltern, 238
  on theater and meaning-making, 232–233
  on translation, 6, 20–22, 229–230, 244
Stabius, Johannes, 158
Staging and Performing Translation (Baines,
  Marinetti, & Perteghella), 9–11

Stark, L. W., 76–77
streaming, of *Beware of Pity*,
  84–85
striptease, 100–101
stutterance, 68
subaltern, Spivak on, 238
subjectivity, in *Drift*, 36–37
subtitles, 2–4, 70–71
  Traditional Chinese, 74–76
'The Subversion of the Subject and the
  Dialectics of Desire' (Lacan), 234
surrogation, 21–22, 25–26
surtitling
  in digital medium, 73–82
  of *Exit*, 67–72
  Griesel on, 64–65
  multilingual, 66–67
  operators, 69–70
  in Simplified Chinese, 76–77
  streaming lines, 82–85
  as supplement to embodiment, 70–71
  as translation, 64–66, 73
Symons, Arthur, 191, 196
Szczawińska, Weronika, 25–26, 137–138, 143–148,
  151–152
Szczęśniak, Małgorzata, 144–145

Tainaner Ensemble, 24–25, 64, 73–74
Taylor, Diana, 13–14, 223
  on performance, 9–11
Telok Blangah, 67
text alignment, 78–79
Thalidomide, 95–96
theater and theatricality. *See also* performance;
  specific topics
  flexible essentialism of, 146–147
  Spivak on, 146–147
Theatre and Performance Studies, translation
  in, 7–11
Theatre Ecology (Kershaw), 86
Theatre Translation in Performance (Bigliazzi,
  Kofler, & Ambrosi), 9–11, 15–16
Theatrical Translation and Film Adaptation
  (Zatlin), 9–11
Theatrum Orbis Terrarum, 185
Theuerdank, 159–160
Thompson, Hannah, 93
Till, Emmet, 57–58
Ting Ting Chan Lau, 77–78
Tito, Josip Broz, 203
Tomasik, Krzysztof, 140–142
Tong King Lee, 71
Tory, Geoffroy, 177
touch tours, 88–89
Traditional Chinese, subtitles, 74–76

Index

277

trans-, 16–17
  trans-ing of performance, 14–15
transcolonial performance, 50–56
transcolonialism, 14–15
  in *All Power to the People!*, 60–62
transembodiment, 14–15, 137
  feminism and, 151–152
  in *Komornicka. Biografia pozorna*, 146, 153
transgender body, 14–15, 138–139
  Halberstram on, 151
'Translating Performance' (Taylor), 9–11
'Translating Transgender,' 14–15
translatio, 2–4, 111
'*Translatio*' (Gotman), 2–4
translation, 1
  Bermann on, 48–49
  of Blackness, 56–63
  Butler on, 18–19, 137, 142–143
  chiasma between language and translation, 123–125
  in Comparative Literature, 7–9
  in comparative mode, 5–21
  death and, 235
  defining, 2–4, 5–6
  embodiment and, 48–49, 137, 239
  as ethical act, 6–9, 18–19
  gender and, 14–15
  gestural, 206
  idioms in, 21–22
  interlingual, 90
  internationalism and, 21–27
  intersemiotic, 90–91
  intralingual, 90
  Jakobson on, 90
  justice done by, 244, 247
  language as, 104–105, 130–132
  performance imbricated with, 6–7, 13–16, 23, 48–49, 246–247
  power relations refused via, 117–119
  of race, 48, 62–63
  of speech acts, 128–129
  Spivak on, 6, 20–22, 229–230, 244
  surtitling as, 64–66, 73
  in Theatre and Performance Studies, 7–11
  translational attitude, 245
  as transmedial concept, 5–9
  as vector, 6–7
Translation and Subjectivity (Sakai), 162
Translation Changes Everything (Venuti), 11–12
Translation Studies, 7–9
  outward turn in, 12–13
  performative turn in, 17–18
translation zone, Apter on, 18–19
translational collaboration, 15–16
The Translator on Stage (Brodie), 9–11

transmutation, 90
transposition, schemas, 138–142
Traoré, Bouna, 50
Travelling acts, 4–5
Travelling concepts, 4–5
La triumphante entrata di Carlo V (Ceffino), 168–170, 173
Trujillo, Rafael, 106
Tymoczko, Maria, 7–9

ul Haq, Zia, 1–2
undercommons, 225
United States
  Black liberation in, 57–58
  Blackness in, 57
  racism in, 50–51, 55–58
untranslatability, 9–11

Vadeboncoeur, Pierre, 114–115
Vaish, Viniti, 72
Venuti, Lawrence, 7–9, 11–12, 92–93, 154–155
  on domesticating effect, 161–162
Verga, Giovanni, 186–188, 191, 194, 199
Via (Bergvall), 40–41
video, translated scripts displayed with, 73–82
Vinland Sagas, 35
violence, 43
  of colonialism, 116–117
  towards language, 117–119
virtuality, 239
visual sound, 24–25, 66–67
Vive la France (Rouabhi), 49, 55
  critical responses to, 55–56
  on racism, 51–53
Vocaleyes, 96
Vostre, Simon, 171–172

Waked, Fadi, 211
Warkocki, Błażej, 148–150
Warlikowski, Krzysztof, 144–145
Waterton, Clare, 88
Watts race riots, 116–117
wayang, 9–11
Wayang Studies, 9–11
Weaver, William, 192–193
Weinreich, Max, 189–190
Weiss, Peter, 50
Weisskunig, 159–160
West Bank, 201–202, 213–214, 216
What My Body Can/t Remember, 201–202
  bodily archives in, 216–219
whiteness
  Fanon on, 130–132
  language equated with, 130–132
  relational nature of, 117–119

Index

Włast, Piotr, 25–26, 150. *See also* Komornicka, Maria
  biography of, 142–146
  Komornicka transition to, 25–26, 138–142, 150–151
  literary reappraisal of, 139
  pronouns of, 138
Worthen, W. B., 16–17
wrecan, 32, 34–35
writing, complexities of digital, 81–82
written introduction, in AD, 88–90

Xenofeminism (Hester), 98

xenophony, 111–112, 130–133
  bilingualism and, 120–133
  Chow on, 128–129
  of language, 130–132
  'Speak White' and, 120–133

Yishun Health, 67
Yong Li Lan, 73
Young Vic Theatre, 96
YouTube, 64

Zatlin, Phyllis, 9–11
La zolfara (Giusti-Sinopoli), 198

Printed in the United States
by Baker & Taylor Publisher Services